A Hundred Years of
INTERNATIONAL
RELATIONS

A Hundred Years of
INTERNATIONAL
RELATIONS

F. S. Northedge

M. J. Grieve

PRAEGER PUBLISHERS

New York · Washington

Published in the United States of America in 1971
by Praeger Publishers, Inc., 111 Fourth Avenue,
New York, N.Y. 10003

Printed in Great Britain

Contents

Maps

Acknowledgments

The authors are grateful to Mrs Margaret Sinclair and Mrs E. Wilson, of the Geography Department of the London School of Economics and Political Science, for drawing the maps.

Abbreviations

ECOSOC	Economic and Social Council
EPTA	Expanded Programme of Technical Assistance (now a component of the United Nations Development Programme)
FAO	Food and Agriculture Organization of the United Nations
GATT	General Agreement on Tariffs and Trade
IBRD	International Bank for Reconstruction and Development
IDA	International Development Association
ILO	International Labour Organization
IMF	International Monetary Fund
OECD	Organization for Economic Co-operation and Development
SDR	Special Drawing Rights
UNCDF	United Nations Capital Development Fund
UNCTAD	United Nations Conference on Trade and Development
UNDP	United Nations Development Programme
UNESCO	United Nations Educational, Scientific and Cultural Organization
UNICEF	United Nations Children's Fund
UNIDO	United Nations Industrial Development Organization
WHO	World Health Organization

Preface

This book stems from a sense of the limitations of two types of writing about international relations : orthodox diplomatic history with its heavy emphasis on primary archival material, and general theory of international relations, which seems to us to be principally contemporary international affairs with a semblance of social-science analysis and a heavy ballast of incomprehensible jargon. The former tends to degenerate into a strict day-by-day diary of events divorced from the wider framework of the international political system which helps to shape the external behaviour of states. The latter appears to be too abstract, too uninformed about the historical dimensions of the subject, to throw much light on the living realities of state behaviour.

Central to our present study is the assumption that there exists, and has existed for two or three centuries, an international system of sovereign states in continuous mutual interaction; that this system is an important, though not the only, determinant of state behaviour within that system; that the system gives rise to a form of politics essentially different from the political process within the frontiers of states, though having many affiliations with it, and as worthy of scholarly study as that internal process; and that this system, while many of its basic features remain the same from generation to generation, is, like everything else, in constant process of change and evolution. This book is a study of the development of that system over the past hundred years.

In writing this book we have necessarily had to recount the story in the manner of an historical theme, and the student of international history since 1870 will find as much detail here as he requires to grasp the main thread of events. At the same time, we have tried never to lose from sight the central subject of the development of the international system since unless the record of state behaviour is placed within the framework of that development, the historical data are, in our view, meaningless.

One thing stands out above all on the broad canvas of this study and that is, amid all his sordid politics and cruel wars, the extraordinary adaptability of the human animal : his capacity to survive the most terrible ordeals of battle, the most hateful persecutions and the most pitiless domination by irresponsible political régimes, and to rebuild his life, and his political community, in conditions of general ruin and devastation. International relations at any time— and the hundred years covered by this book are certainly no exception—often appear to us in the guise of public life at its worst, its most undignified for the human animal. And yet through all this comes the persistent human drive for something better. Idealism has a way of sowing the seeds of later bitter disappointment and angry resentment with a world which pertinaciously fails to conform to the ideals. But it bestows a touch of grandeur on this violent and tempestuous tale.

F. S. NORTHEDGE

M. J. GRIEVE

JANUARY 1971

1 *The Epoch of Peace*

From the violence and stress of the twentieth century men look back nostalgically to the mid-nineteenth century as a time of peace. That indeed it was. The five great powers of the European system, Austria, Britain, France, Prussia and Russia, fought no war after the defeat of Napoleon in 1815 until the Crimean war in 1854 and in that conflict Austria and Prussia were neutral. Napoleon III's war against Austria in 1859 and the wars of German unification—in 1864 against Denmark, in 1866 against Austria and in 1870 against France—though heavy with consequences for the European balance of power, were all local wars of brief duration in which three of the five European giant powers remained neutral. Europe was brought to the brink of a more general war in 1878, as a result of the Russian invasion of European Turkey, but after the settlement at the Berlin Congress in 1878 there began for Europe about forty years of peace until the holocaust of 1914 threw all five European powers into the four-and-a-quarter year conflict. During this forty-year period four brief wars were fought among the smaller states in South-East Europe in which none of the great powers was involved.

While Europe was enjoying this unprecedented peace, the extra-European world had more than its share of war. The American civil war of 1861–65 tore that country apart in a conflict which, though brief in character, had all the ideological tensions and foreshadowed the technical aspects of twentieth-century war. The Latin American states had their own conflicts. The European colonial powers, Britain, France, Germany, Italy, Holland and Belgium, fought wars of conquest of increasing frequency in Africa and Asia. Britain fought her war against the Dutch in South Africa from 1899 to 1902. Japan, after the Meiji Restoration in 1868, compelled China to accept the humiliating peace of Shimonoseki in 1895 and defeated Russia in 1904–05 in a conflict arising out of competition between these two powers in Manchuria. And America fought Spain in 1898 and gained Cuba, the Philippines, Guam and Puerto Rico. But, at the core of the international system, peace between the five great powers held secure for about a hundred years.

That the second half of the nineteenth century was an era of peace is all the more surprising considering that the century as a whole was by no means one of stagnation : on the contrary, the pace of technological and economic change was almost unprecedented; the rate of increase of population in all the European states was unparalleled; the change from the old social order which the Congress of Vienna had sanctified in 1815 to the urban democracies which were becoming established forms in Europe at the close of the century was immense; the advent of imperialism, industrialism, democracy, social revolution was momentous in its effects. Moreover, far-reaching changes in the map of Europe were in process throughout the century : Germany was formed as a united national state by 1871 from the thirty-nine fragments of the German Bund established in 1815; Italy, too, by 1870 had created a united national state from the patchwork quilt assembly of foreign-ruled kingdoms and Austrian principalities which emerged from the Napoleonic wars; Belgium was divided from Holland, to which it had been joined by the peacemakers of 1815; above all, the ramshackle Ottoman Empire was successively deprived of its European elements, Greece in 1832, the principalities of Moldavia and Wallachia, which later formed the state of Rumania, in 1856, Bulgaria in 1898, Bosnia and Herzegovina in 1908, without the European powers being plunged into war, except in 1854, over the spoils. Change, like a hurricane, blew through the European system with immense violence at home and abroad without the house being brought down in ruins. Revolutions, intra-national and international, were achieved with the minimum of violence.

Peace was reflected in the confidence which men shared about the international system. Since 1918 the process of international diplomacy, which had come to be known disapprovingly as 'power-politics', has never ceased to be the subject of general protest and proposals for reform, ranging from the replacement of the interstate system by the rule of one dominant race, as urged by the German Nazis in the 1930s, or of one dominant class, as claimed by the Communists, to the establishment of a new world-wide Rule of Law under a League of Nations or world government. In the midnineteenth century some social theorists held that the international system was a bulwark against domestic reform, but this was not true of the period before the 1848 liberal revolutions, except that Metternich's Austria was still the core of Conservatism in the European system. Such reforms of the system as were advocated, as in the

European and American peace movements of the late nineteenth century, were modestly confined to widening the provisions for settlement of international disputes, for instance by mediation or international tribunals. Otherwise, European governments were not bombarded by popular protests to change the international system by disarmament, the creation of Leagues of Nations or the compulsory settlement of disputes. The general feeling was that, with the inevitable course of progress, war would of its own accord gradually become obsolete, along with state controls of social life. This complaisant mood changed in the twenty years preceding 1914, when the rival European alliances ranged themselves in opposition for the coming battle and the armaments race got under way. But a century ago the international system was proving itself by its own success in managing to overcome each crisis without armed conflict.

The factors responsible for the nineteenth-century peace are not to be found in the institutions then existing for the settlement of international disputes. These were rudimentary in character and, in so far as they were successful, their success reflected other forces which made peace possible. The very fact that, in the twentieth century, permanent international institutions of a highly complex character have become the order of the day reflects the stress of our times rather than gives hope that our contemporary international problems will be settled by these devices. The nineteenth century had less rule of international institutions because economic, social and political forces making for peace were then stronger.

Prominent place among the forces making for international peace in the second half of the nineteenth century must be given to the spread of modern machine industry and the effects of industrialization in almost all the European states; these tended to turn their attention inwards and fostered the illusion that no social problem is insoluble with the application of scientific techniques which were then revolutionizing all social life. The Napoleonic wars themselves gave an immense fillip to the European industrial revolution, especially in France. But the leader in the field of industrialization and urbanization was clearly Britain. In the 1830s and 1840s Britain outstripped all her European neighbours in output of coal, iron and steel and the export of manufactured goods. Britain became the banker of Europe, as Europe was, by 1900, to become the banker of the world. The industrial revolution spread through the European great powers, filling their towns with new proletarian masses, expanding their populations, increasing and diversifying the ties between them. Europe was gradually linked by a network of railways and this, together with the need to provide a substantial mass market with increased ability to purchase the products of modern industry, made nonsense of old divided states such as Germany and Italy and made sense of the great national state. The industrial and commercial revolution led to social changes in creating a middle class of essentially peacefully minded entrepreneurs, lawyers, middlemen and exporters, whose weight was thrown behind the demands for a constitutional state in 1848 and who identified themselves with the great national states of the late nineteenth century. It also helped create the urban proletariat which, after the spread of universal adult male suffrage and popular education in the 1870s and 1880s, formed the basis for the revolutionary discontent which governments had somehow to satisfy and which, as late as the decade preceding 1914, could be diverted into chauvinism and rancorous demands for colonies.

Industrialism, rapidly increasing populations and rising living standards were echoed in the change of intellectual mood from the romanticism of the 1830s and 1840s to the harder realism of the last quarter of the nineteenth century. But the flood of unbounded optimism was apparent : men felt that, so long as the industrial machine could continue to produce its marvels, there was hardly need or time for international quarrels. Industrialism also broke down barriers between the nations. The example of free trade which Britain set in her Cobden Treaty with France in 1860 seemed, for ten to fifteen years at least, to set the tone for an age emancipated from national boundaries and freed from the nightmare of war. Over this industrial system Britain presided, dominant with her fleet within a generally disarmed European system, and capable, by loosening and tightening her purse strings when occasion demanded, of bringing now this state, now that into line within the general comity of Europe.

A second factor in keeping peace in Europe was the solidarity of the European powers based on the consciousness that they were European, Christian, civilized and white, and thus enjoyed a common stock of traits and values which separated them from the rest of the world. While this common European self-consciousness rose to the surface only on occasion, it was at all times the first premise on which all European international relations were carried on. The international system was, after all, a European system; it had originated in Europe with the collapse of the European medieval order and its history was to be the expansion of Europe into the world. The European system had grown to its eighteenth-century maturity from its beginnings in the defence of Europe against Asia, represented by Turkey. Almost all writers on international relations until the French Revolutionary wars had based their claim for European unity on the idea of a common front against Turkey. Kant and Rousseau in their calls for a European federal state had established their chief claim for the uniqueness of Europe, namely its character as a multiplicity of mighty equal states, in opposition to the barbaric empires of the East. European international law, as expressed by Grotius in the mid-sixteenth century, had derived almost all its binding character from Europe's singular religion, Christianity.

The European powers which emerged from the Napoleonic wars were of roughly equal strength in that none had the capability to overthrow the rest and establish a European hegemony. This was what Napoleon I had tried to do and his failure overhung the nineteenth century like a spectre. Moreover, the European powers in the first half of the nineteenth century needed no state outside their continent as a weight in the balance which they formed between themselves. Canning, the British Foreign Secretary in 1822, spoke of calling 'The new world into existence to redress the balance of the old', but in fact the old world balanced itself quite well without the need for strength from outside, even if the Latin American colonies, which Canning was then in the act of recognizing as independent states, could have supplied it. The price of Canning's recognition was paid in the mid-nineteenth century when Britain, partly because of her interest in Latin America and partly because of pressure from settlers in Belize (British Honduras) and Nicaragua, made the Clayton-Bulwer Treaty of 19 April 1850. Under this treaty, which was highly unpopular in the United States, both states pledged themselves not to take exclusive control over the Panama Isthmus and not to colonize any part of Central America. This treaty caused considerable anti-British feeling in the United States and was abrogated in favour of America by the Hay-Pauncefote Treaty of 18 November 1901, allowing the United States to take exclusive control of the Panama Canal and to fortify it. This arrangement ran counter to British naval interest in international waterways, but it had to be allowed because of increasing British fears of Germany and Russia. British fears about these two countries meant that at the least American friendly neutrality had to be secured should conflict occur. Similarly in 1902 Britain made an alliance with Japan as a direct result of her isolation during the Boer War. This latter agreement is the first major occasion when Britain needed to call upon an extra-European power for aid in the Far East in order to leave her free to concentrate her naval forces in waters nearer home. In short, the European balance was, from 1815 until the 1880s, enough in itself to maintain equilibrium.

The two states in the European system which were not wholly European were Britain and Russia. The Vienna Treaty of 1815 finally established Britain as a world-wide imperial power and Russia, from the mid-eighteenth century until the end of the nineteenth century, was steadily extending her conquests in Asia. Two of the other three great powers, Austria and Prussia, were states of strictly continental interests until imperial adventures began to beckon to them in the 1880s. Britain and Russia, with their increasing extra-European commitments, had the strongest interest in ensuring, not merely that their three partners remained continentally oriented, but that they never moved to form a common front. By the balancing role which Britain played in European politics for the first sixty years of the century, she provided herself with freedom to attend to her overseas concerns; by suitable interventions, as in the Belgian war of independence against Holland in 1830, the Greek war of independence against Turkey in the late 1820s, the Crimean war in 1854–56 and the Russo-Turkish war in 1877–78, she saw to it that struggles in Europe would not interfere with her sea communications around the European periphery and that European international politics would be held internally balanced within the periphery. Russia, for her part, had her own varied means for keeping a united Europe at bay : her Holy Alliance of 1815 or League of the Northern Courts, which kept herself, Austria and Prussia in unison against revolutionary France; her control of Warsaw Poland, which created a common bond between herself and Prussia, later Imperial Germany, and in opposition to the pro-Polish impulses of Napoleon III of France; and her stake in the Dardanelles Straits and Constantinople, which divided her from Britain while providing her with alternating opportunities of making common cause with Prussia and Austria.

Thus, while Britain and Russia had a common interest in keeping these three European partners divided, these powers themselves had enough to occupy them within the European perimeter. France had the problem, after 1815, of re-establishing her primacy, this time in peaceful form; after 1871, she had the far greater problem of her Rhine frontier. Prussia had the problem, first, of uniting Germany, then, after 1871, of preventing Europe uniting against her. Austria, ever since 1848, was too preoccupied with the question of internal unity to have much energy for looking outside Europe. Europe was thus, until at least the 1880s, sufficient unto itself.

Moreover, outside Europe were wide open spaces in which, when the European powers looked abroad to cope with dissatisfaction they could not resolve at home, expansion could take place and glory could be sought. Tension created in the diplomatic core of Europe, as population grew and a sense of living in too confined a space mounted, could be resolved in Africa and Asia. Napoleon III, who tried to foist Maximilian of Habsburg on Mexico in 1864, thought he could do the same in Latin America until the United States re-asserted the Monroe Doctrine against him after the Civil War. But in Africa and Asia there was no rampant nationalism to resist European military power, no United Nations to create a furore against imperialist aggression. France could be invited to take Algeria when she threatened to become troublesome in Europe in 1830. Bismarck could invite her to seek solace in her imperial ambitions in 1881 by annexing Tunis, just as his successor, Bethmann-Hollweg, and Austria-Hungary, his ally, could suggest to Italy that she take Tripoli in 1911 to reinforce her interest in the Austro-German Dual Alliance of 1879 which she had joined in 1882. If the extra-European world resisted this process of alleviating tension at the centre by compensation beyond the European periphery, as Abyssinia did when she inflicted a major defeat on Italy at Adowa in 1896, the other European powers did not spring to Italy's defence because her grievance was of no great consequence to them. For Britain, however, the frustration of France, when she was forced out of the Sudan after the confrontation with Britain at Fashoda in 1898, was sufficiently important as marking the end of France's Egyptian ambitions that, six years later, when the Anglo-French Entente was formed, British endorsement was given to French predominance in Morocco in return for French recognition of British predominance in Egypt.

Moreover, the European powers at all times adopted a different and much lower standard of conduct towards the extra-European world from that which they followed in their relations *inter se*. Turkey, for example, being non-Christian, was an object of European diplomacy; the Turks had to inflict a military defeat on a European power, as they did on Greece in 1897–98 and again in 1920–21, before the Allies agreed to treat Turkey as an equal. When China blindly revolted against the 'barbarians' in the Boxer Rebellion of 1900, all the European states with interests in China, together with Japan and the United States, formed a common front in defence of the traditional right of the international system to lubricate its machinery with the resources of the non-European world.

But the European diplomatic system was bound together, not only by the threat of revolt from abroad, from Asia and Africa, but also against the fear of revolution from below. The peacemakers of 1815 had driven the demon of revolution, Napoleon, from France and built the Quadruple Alliance of November 1815 on the premise that united action was essential if Napoleonism returned to France. France herself joined this repressive system at the Congress of Aachen in 1818 and shortly afterwards Britain left it, on the traditional British plea that internal revolutions are not occasions for united great power actions unless they actually threaten the balance of power. The use of the European alliance to suppress revolution from below disappeared during the Anglo-French Entente of the 1830s, when Britain and France sided with European Liberalism against the three Eastern powers; in any case, in 1848 the liberal revolutions on the continent proved too strong for international action against them. Nevertheless, the European governments in the second half of the nineteenth century were all too conscious of the revolutionary forces below their thrones and cabinet rooms; the one thing which united them was the tacit agreement that none of them must ever act as the Sorcerer's Apprentice and provoke revolution in another state. No one knew where this process of setting on fire the house next door would stop. This is why Napoleon III was regarded with almost universal mistrust and was isolated in his supreme testing time in 1870. He constantly hankered after conferences to awaken the sleeping dogs of Europe, especially the suppressed nationalities. The obvious comment was that if dirty linen— in other words, the internal affairs of Russia and Prussia—were to be washed in public, what about that of France and every other state? The celebrated reply of Lord John Russell on behalf of Britain, to Napoleon III's call for a second Congress of Vienna to deal with the Polish uprising in 1863, speaks the language of the time :

H.M. Ministers would feel more apprehensive than confident at the idea of a Congress of Sovereigns and Ministers, ranging over the map of Europe and exciting ambitions which they might find difficult to satisfy or to quiet.

A time was to come in the international system when its dominant members, so far from standing shoulder to shoulder in defence of the internal *status quo* in their several countries, would energetically seek to stir up revolution abroad in the interest of weakening their rivals. But in the nineteenth century the system acted as a conservative compact against the devils in the basement.

Finally, two of the dominant issues of the nineteenth century, the unification of Germany and the unification of Italy, concentrated the attention of their peoples on internal problems until the 1890s and although both of these acts of unification were achieved through war, for a variety of reasons no general war resulted. The unification of Germany and Italy was to all intents predetermined after the French Revolution had communicated to Europe the thirst for national unity, and after the Napoleonic wars had shown the military weakness of small units of social organization; the only question was under what auspices and on the basis of what kind of political principles these two states were to be united. So far from European public and governmental opinion being opposed to German and Italian unity, both causes had powerful allies among the European courts and cabinets. Italian unification enjoyed the wavering but convinced support of Napoleon III, whose alliance with Cavour, Prime Minister of Piedmont, secured the addition of Lombardy to the new Italy in 1860; British sympathy for Italian nationalism made possible Garibaldi's expedition which added Naples and Sicily to the new Italy in the 1860s; without Bismarck's connivance Italy's attack on Austrian Venetia in 1866, when Austria was engaged with Prussia, would not have been feasible. When Rome finally became the Italian capital in 1870, after the withdrawal of the French garrison during the Franco-Prussian war, Italy had not 'made herself', as Cavour had claimed in the 1850s, but had attained its unity with the good will of all the active European powers. Austria was too occupied with its struggle with Prussia for hegemony in Germany to prevent Italian unity; Russia, who had some cause to suspect the revolutionary nationalism of the Risorgimento, was too distant, and also too weakened after the Crimean war to offer any serious resistance.

It is strange, in retrospect, that the unification of Germany, secured by Bismarck on the basis of Prussian hegemony and austerely conservative political principles, should have aroused so little alarm in Europe considering not merely the later history of the Reich but also earlier Prussian militarism. But governments have to deal with problems of the day; the problems of the next century cannot seriously concern them. It is a matter of history that German unity, for all its momentous consequences for the European equilibrium, stirred little or no opposition among the other European powers who might have combined to resist it. Austria, the competitor with Prussia for leadership of the 1815 German Bund, was weakened by the 1848 revolution which destroyed her as the conservative core of the European system created by the Vienna Congress in 1815. She lagged behind Prussia in 1866 chiefly because she had not applied the lessons of railway transport to the mobilization and conveyance to the battlefields of her armies. She was at all times involved with Russia in commitments in the Balkans from which Prussia was happily free. Russia for her part had no incentive to oppose German unification; so long as Bismarck respected Russia's interests in Poland and looked as if he might hold Austria in check in the Balkans, Alexander II of Russia sided with the conservative Prussians who had refused in 1848 to unite Germany on the basis of liberal principles.

In the West, France had, by every test, a stake in preventing the consolidation of central Europe under the control of Berlin; but Napoleon III believed, until it was too late, that he could win compensations from Bismarck in Belgium, Luxembourg, southern Germany and Italy, as a price for acquiescing in German unity. Above all, Britain, the later naval antagonist of united Germany, regarded Prussia as a useful counterbalance to an unpredictable and troublesome Second Empire in France. Britain was for a time ineffectually engaged in commitments to Denmark immediately prior to the joint Austro-German attack on that country over the Schleswig-Holstein question in 1864; but the main objectives of Bismarck's unification policies in Germany commanded the support of the ruling middle class of Britain. Prussia in 1871 seemed by no means a prospective world power capable of challenging Britain at sea; and Bismarck appeared to be a pillar of respectability and industrial progress, promising to control the meddlesomeness of France. To all these factors working in favour of German unity must be added the astute diplomacy of Bismarck himself : his power to moderate fear abroad, his capacity to exploit another state's dissatisfaction or cupidity, his promise of a stable order of moderate conservatism.

By 1871 Germany and Italy had been united without the European equilibrium being upset. Moreover, for all but thirty years the transformation of the international system resulting from this unification had in the public eye no apparently serious consequences

Europe in 1871

for the equilibrium. This is abundantly obvious in the case of Italy. Lacking the raw materials for modern heavy industry, hampered by a large and rapidly growing population, Italy was destined for colonial adventures in the Mediterranean and Africa. She hitched her star to the Austro-German Dual Alliance in 1882, which was confirmed in 1887, but the dependence of Italian national security, as indeed her colonial policy, on Britain's naval support meant that her diplomatic scope was always limited. So long as Italian membership of the Triple Alliance was consistent with such agreements as she reached with Britain in 1887 to maintain the *status quo* in the Mediterranean, she was forced to side with the highest bidder for her favours. But if a time came when Britain was ranged on France's side against Germany, as happened in 1914, Italy was bound to abstain from European alignments until the Allies could offer her satisfaction, chiefly at the expense of Austria-Hungary, to induce her to throw in her lot with them. This was to happen when Italy signed the Treaty of London with Britain, France and Russia in May 1915.

Germany, with her developing industrial power, based on the coal reserves of the Ruhr and Silesia, with her numerous and highly skilled population and with her military and inventive genius and central position in Europe, was a wholly different proposition. Yet in the twenty years between his defeat of France in 1871 and his dismissal by William II in 1890, Bismarck was a force for order in Europe. While seeking to destroy France's power to form alliances against Germany, Bismarck pursued no vindictive course towards the French. He encouraged their colonial ambitions and, apart from the war scare in 1875, sought to give no cause for forcing a renewal of the war against France. It was partly with the object, futile as it proved, of restraining Austria-Hungary in the Balkans that he formed the Dual Alliance with that state in 1879. Towards Russia his policy was courteous and dedicated to respectful friendship, as indicated by his Reinsurance Treaty with Russia in 1887. Bismarck also had on his hands serious internal troubles, such as the struggle with the Socialists and Catholics, which helped to close the doors against adventuresome external politics. The more Germany could remain untrammelled by colonial commitments (the brief excursion of Germany into colonialism in 1884 was largely imposed on the Chancellor), the more she could give an appearance of moderation and stability, the more her central geographical position could be a source of strength and diplomatic influence.

Once the powers of Europe began to fear Germany, however, her central position was an irritant and danger, all the more so as her industrial raw materials which were the basis of her military power were sited on her periphery in East and West. But even after the initiation of the 'New Course' in Germany when Caprivi, with the assistance of Holstein at the Wilhelmstrasse, took over from Bismarck, the course of German policy was far from being set towards the destruction of the European equilibrium. Germany severed her bonds with Russia and prepared for a strategy in which the main offensive strength would be thrown against the Tsar, while the Reichswehr remained on the defensive against France in the

West; but this policy was predicated on the assumption that Russia was still the *enfant terrible* of French liberals and British imperialists. Some German statesmen continued, from 1898 until the early years of the twentieth century, to believe that a conservative alliance could be reached with Britain which might maintain the European equilibrium. War fanatics like Friedrich Bernhardi might write of the glories and necessity of war but until the twentieth century opened the cautious maxims of Bismarck continued to exercise their spell in Berlin.

Peace in Europe in the second half of the nineteenth century then was based on political and economic forces, which, together with their resulting mental attitudes, gave no strong reasons for general war. The mechanisms for maintaining international relations reflected this combination of forces, rather than created it. Nevertheless, certain instruments of equilibrium existed. Foremost among them was the balance of power, taken for granted before 1914, vilified after 1918, rehabilitated in public esteem after 1945, and subjected to Teutonic analysis by American political scientists more recently. The balance of power has been variously defined as the current distribution of power within the international system, the policy of forming coalitions against preponderant states, a tendency towards equilibrium between the great powers, and many other things. For present purposes it is sufficient to say that wherever there exists a number of formally independent states with no common superior to impose its will upon them, all have a tendency to fear the predominance of any single one of them and will tend to form alignments so as to prevent the emergence of the single hegemonial state. The security and independence of any one member of the system are dependent upon its being alive to the emergence of a dominant state in the system and its taking steps to inhibit what Queen Anne called 'the growth of exorbitant power'. The statesmen of Europe in the 1860s and 1870s had had experience of the pretensions of a single state, France, to dominate the system. The peace treaties of 1815 were based upon a compact to prevent a recurrence of that attempt, and throughout the nineteenth century the fear of hegemonial dominance as aspired to by Napoleon I exercised the minds of Ministers and diplomats, which was one reason why his nephew, Napoleon III, was regarded with almost universal suspicion.

The balance of power was sometimes thought to operate as a self-acting mechanism, and this mental image (like that of the Gold

Standard) no doubt suited an age newly impressed with the marvels of machine industry; it also chimed in with the conception of the 'hidden hand' which was supposed to be at work constantly correcting disequilibriums in other aspects than the economics of a *laissez-faire* era. But this was only an appearance. The fact was that the logic of the international system, with its decentralized parts, imposed balance of power considerations; all of which was so obvious that ministers and diplomats did not need constantly to remind themselves of its principles. Moreover, the objective state of the international system of the day made the balance of power a relatively easy system to operate and aroused none of the kind of difficulties which prompt men to ask whether it is the correct or moral policy to apply.

It is sometimes said that an effective balance of power system requires a rough parity of strength among the members of the system. While it would be statistically incorrect to claim this of the nineteenth-century system, it is true to say that no one of the five or six great powers in 1871 was head and shoulders above the rest in the elements of economic and military strength. In addition, an illusion of parity was created by the mere fact that no general wars had been fought since the beginning of the century and, as the first year of the 1914–18 war showed, no one fully understood the effects of machine industry on the distribution of military strength in the international system. Germany showed her superiority to Austria in war in 1866 but no one assumed from this that she could overthrow France. When she did overthrow France in 1871, Europe, including perhaps Prussia, was amazed; certainly no inference was drawn that Prussia was a match for Russia, or of France and Russia together. Had it been assumed that, if war broke out, Germany could dominate the system and the United States would have to be drawn in to redress the balance, alliances against Germany would have been speedily formed; the fact that they were not indicates that there was no fear of potential German hegemony.

The two states which in the 1840s and 1850s could be regarded as standing above the others in physical strength were Britain, by reason of her naval and economic leadership, and Russia, by reason of her manpower and geographical inaccessibility. But these states had little interest in seeking to dominate Europe. British policy after 1815, certainly after Castlereagh's suicide in 1822, sought disentanglement from European commitments and thereafter profited from the disunity of Europe rather than its unity under British leadership. Britain's overseas commitments alone, to say nothing of the emotional past of her people, demanded insulation from Europe. The policy of the free hand and timely intervention to correct the equilibrium on the Continent was practised by London, with diminishing success, until the end of the century. As for Russia, her economic backwardness and Asian interests weakened her in Europe; Russia's vast and empty spaces required an industrial revolution, a settlement of peasant problems such as malnutrition and literacy, before she could be brought to bear with all her potential force into European politics. Whatever the statistical parity, or lack of it, among the European powers, then, the semblance of parity meant that, until the early years of the twentieth century, and perhaps not even then, no European great power sought to challenge the balance of power system.

To conclude, the main arguments with which this chapter is concerned are : *first* that early industrialization, aided by powerful extra-European factors such as imperialism, gave Europe a longer period of peace than occurred in earlier history, and, *second*, that the balance of power in the nineteenth century up to the formation of permanent alliances was an equally powerful factor in creating peace. But the long-term effects of industrialization, far from being conducive to peace, were the reverse, for once the lessons of industrialization were applied to war by the military and aristocratic élites of Central Europe, then the hounds of war were unleashed to an extent never seen before. Similarly, since a balance of power among five or six states presupposed no permanent alliances or alignments because the states had to feel free to switch their alliance from one state to another as national interest and the distribution of power in the system as a whole prescribed, once the era of permanent alliances began with Bismarck's secret Austro-German Dual Alliance of 1879 a rigidity was introduced into the international system which tilted the balance of power towards war rather than peace.

REFERENCES

Albrecht-Carrié, R., *A Diplomatic History of Europe Since the Congress of Vienna*, London, Methuen, and New York, Harper, 1958.

Beales, A. C. F., *The History of Peace. A Short Account of the Organised Movements for International Peace*, London, Bell, 1931.

Gulick, E. V., *Europe's Classical Balance of Power*, Ithaca, N.Y., Cornell U.P., 1955.

Holbraad, C., *The Concert of Europe*, London, Longmans, 1970.

Medlicott, W. N., *Bismarck, Gladstone and the Concert of Europe*, London, Athlone Press, and Westport, Conn., Greenwood, 1956.

Mowat, R. B., *The Concert of Europe*, London, Macmillan, 1930.

The New Cambridge Modern History, Vol. XI, *Material Progress and World-Wide Problems, 1870-1898*, Cambridge, C.U.P., 1962, Introduction.

Pribram, A. F., *England and the International Policy of the European Great Powers, 1871–1914*, Oxford, Clarendon Press, and New York, Barnes and Noble, 1931.

Schenk, H. G., *The Aftermath of the Napoleonic Wars. The Concert of Europe— an Experiment*, London, Kegan Paul, and New York, Fertig, 1947.

Taylor, A. J. P., *The Struggle for Mastery in Europe, 1848–1918*, Oxford, Clarendon Press, and Fair Lawn, New Jersey, 1954.

Woolf, L. S., *International Government*, London, Allen and Unwin, 1916.

2 *Growth of the European Powers*

By the 1870s many European states had wealth derived from trade and industrialization the like of which they had never known before. Governments were faced by the problem of deciding how to use the new power conferred by this wealth. Should the decision be left to the individual citizen or should the decision-making powers of government be increased? If *laissez-faire* was to be the answer of the politicians the problems brought by the new wealth still forced themselves irresistibly before governments. On the other hand, if the state centralized too much power and the flow of too much of its citizens' wealth through taxation, the traditional basis of relationship between the individual, citizen and the state would be undermined. Each country had to make its own decision and this was weighted by the effect of particular political structures, geography and resources.

The new wealth opened up a variety of possibilities: it could enhance the powers of conspicuous consumption of social élites, it could be spread—through evolution or revolution—in the form of wider social improvement or it could flow into the traditional channels of government decision-making which, day-to-day affairs apart, largely concerned military and naval matters. The dangers of a combination of this time-honoured, restricted field of governmental decision-making and the new wealth accruing from industry and trade led nineteenth-century men of ideas to champion Free Trade. Under this system, attractive to the taste of the time because it would be on the whole self-regulating, economic relations would operate in such a way as to improve and widen the morality of international politics. But Free Trade amongst developed economies required, relatively quickly, a degree of supranational control which late nineteenth-century states could hardly envisage, let alone encourage. There were also practical economic problems which checked Free Trade, and in addition its ideas of a socio-economic brotherhood of man came up against existing political élites, often connected with military hierarchies, which got in the way of the conscious choice for peace which many political theorists anticipated.

A state which has a well-established political structure and a mature economy, whether industrial or pre-industrial, is faced with the problem of how to use its surplus social and financial resources. In a traditional society with a relatively old élite the excess can be siphoned off in higher levels of consumption as happened in the ancient empires of China and Rome. Alternatively, the existence of external tension which provides the basic justification for the continued existence of the separate state may be invoked so that war or aggression can focus outwards the surplus energy or violence within the state, thus improving the level of internal cohesion. Finally, the excess product within the mature state may be employed for social development but in practice most states have found it extremely difficult to use this method.

States, like individuals, on the whole do not like the responsibility of making major decisions. Often the choice of using the excess product for war was made but was not considered to be a conscious choice. States have argued that 'the choice was forced upon us' and historians in their turn buttressed this view by writing not infrequently that 'then war came', not that it was deliberately chosen. The theme of states and historians, the latter often employed by or acting for the former, has been the same : the international system is a pattern of states which set up insuperable tensions which must be released periodically by war. In this way, war has often been the answer to a state's need to make political and socio-economic decisions. Apart from this function of war as a *displaced* or *transferred activity*, the difficulty of using excess energy within a state for social improvement lay in the probable political disruption if it was so used. Hence for centuries governmental decision-making remained restricted and it was easy for the new wealth of the late nineteenth century to run along the channel of least resistance, i.e. in the direction of preparedness for war and war itself. So a combination of social tenacity on the part of élites and institutional inertia, including that of the Church, made the use of wealth for social change a relative latecomer on the historical scene. Late nineteenth-century militarism was a fiery brew : the new wealth giving ever more powerful weapons went hand-in-hand with aggression released as the developing nation states jostled together for status and territory. Britain was among a number of European states which could direct new-found energy outwards in the form of imperialism but for land-based states such as Prussia the release of tension was demanded within Europe itself; as Bismarck once said, Europe was his Africa.

Bismarck was faced relatively quickly with the problem of deciding how his creation, modern Germany, should use her new industrial wealth. Politically, modern Germany had only existed since 1871 but the economic basis of modern Germany dated back to the 1820s and 1830s when the German states (excluding Austria) set up their economic common market or customs union. It was Prussia's early start through the Zollverein in getting rid of trade impediments internally and among the German states which by the 1870s gave her the economic and political headstart which other states, such as Bavaria and once-dominant Austria, never managed to overcome. The resentment of the other German states when Prussia bid to be *primus inter pares* was shown when they fought against her in 1866. But by then Prussia was too strong for them, and the strands of German political power along with the new German railway network came together in the Prussian capital of Berlin.

The establishment of modern Germany is frequently explained in terms of Bismarck's 'blood and iron' policy or the ruthless use of war. No doubt the military caste which surrounded the Prussian throne may have viewed the three wars which preceded the creation of Germany in this way, and their dominant influence encouraged German writers and philosophers to glorify war as a purification rite necessary for the growth and continuance of the state. Treitschke wrote in this vein around 1874 : 'The grandeur of war lies in the utter annihilation of puny man in the great conception of the State, and it brings out the full magnificence of the sacrifice of fellow-countrymen for one another. In war the chaff is winnowed from the wheat.' Nietzsche also, in 1822, welcomed 'all signs that a more manly, a warlike age is now starting, an age which will honour valour again'.[1]

But war was a more prosaic and calculated business matter to Bismarck who had a number of particular aims when he used it. He expected territorial gains to give modern Germany a militarily viable frontier and it was a useful bonus when these gains brought in economic resources. He also expected the wars he allowed to be chosen and conducted in such a way that Germany would be given if not permanent at least semi-permanent immunity from *revanche* by the defeated powers. This was particularly so in relation to the

[1] Cited by Hans Kohn (ed.), *The Modern World*, New York, 1964, pp. 110, 164.

Franco-Prussian war of 1870–71 which Bismarck seems to have assumed would have granted this immunity for ten or fifteen years and it was France's rapid regrowth which in part encouraged the war scares of the mid-1870s. Also, following the economic thought of his day, Bismarck expected a defeated state such as France to pay a heavy penalty clause or war indemnity. Such a payment usefully symbolized defeat but it was also then believed that net removal of capital or movable assets would weaken the economy of the defeated state. In practice, however, the economic effect was to stimulate France into a quick recovery while the German economy itself suffered a degree of inflation. It had been assumed that France would pay off the indemnity of five billion francs (approximately 200 million pounds) by 1875 but it was paid off by 1873, freeing the French from having to endure any longer the German army of occupation in northern France.

During the 1840s to the early 1870s Free Trade had spread rapidly among the European states and had been the basis of prosperity in states such as Britain and Germany but while Free Trade appealed strongly to countries in the early stages of industrialization it could not, for most countries which lacked Britain's imperial markets, maintain this appeal once industrialization was steadily under way. France and Germany initially welcomed Free Trade because it made it easier to import goods such as British machinery for setting up factories or lines for railways. But once the factories were established they were in direct competition with British industry and steps were soon taken to protect them. On the continent there was a strong reaction against economic *laissez-faire,* including Free Trade, and this sharpened the growing sense of nationalism. Businessmen who ten years earlier had praised the cutting down of trade barriers, and listened more or less willingly to British talk of the brotherhood of man to be achieved through trade, now argued that the new industries of Germany, France, Italy and Austria-Hungary must be protected against the more advanced industrial states such as Britain and Belgium. This continental tendency was intensified by what was happening in North America, for the USA was taking the lead in the high era of Protectionism which was to reach the high level of 57% on average duty under the Dingley Tariff of 1897.

There had been indications of a return to Protectionism in France by 1871 but it was not until 1881 that French tariff restrictions were extended to cover all manufactured imports. Germany re-imposed a protective tariff in 1879. Early in the 1870s Germany had experienced boom conditions particularly in heavy industry and railway development. Speculation had also been encouraged by the successful war against France and the indemnity gained. But capitalism in the nineteenth century was marked by cyclical periods of growth and recession and by the later 1870s the boom in Germany had ended leaving both industry and agriculture suffering a depression. In order to promote new business confidence which would give him political leeway, Bismarck led Germany back to Protectionism in 1879. Under the tariff of July 1879 duties on industrial imports returned to the 10–15% levels prevailing up to 1868, while agricultural imports now carried 5–7% duties.

These agricultural duties were insufficiently high to protect German farmers against imports from Russia and America but Bismarck appears to have realized that industry was the horse to back. His conclusion, with its social implication of relatively moderately priced food for German industrial workers, and its political implication of the possibilities of a widened social basis of support for Bismarck's modern Germany, was a sound one.

Germany's military adventures had brought economic advantage. In 1864 the gain of Schleswig-Holstein gave Germany ports suitable for naval and industrial expansion such as Kiel, Altona, and Flensburg; it also meant that the Kiel Canal could be constructed during the mid-1880s to 1895 to link the Baltic and the North Sea. The economic gains from France in 1871 were equally important: Alsace was one of the leading textile-producing regions while Lorraine brought to Germany the largest iron ore deposits in western Europe along with a complex of iron works and heavy engineering plants. In 1872 the iron ore production of Lorraine stood at 634,000 tons but by 1882 it had risen to 1,859,000 tons. German coal output was also growing rapidly and by 1871 Germany was the second leading coal producer with a total of $37\frac{1}{2}$ million tons as compared with the French total of 16 million tons. Coal and iron were the backbone industries of modern Germany after 1870 particularly in the Ruhr, Saar and Upper Silesia.

Industrialization was also revolutionizing war technology. As early as 1859 Germany was one of the leading arms producers with work mainly centred upon the Krupps combine. In 1861 this firm employed about 2,000 workers but by 1864 the number had increased to some 6,000. Industrialization was disciplining workers in a neo-military way the world over and reinforcing the passivity which was to lead to so many deaths in the First World War. This tendency was enhanced in modern Germany where trade unions were frowned upon and where Bismarck used state social welfare[2] to prevent a workers' political party developing. Bismarck's wars themselves also stimulated mechanization of warfare for it was in the Franco-Prussian war that the first machine gun was used. While Krupps held the field in Germany similar work was going on in Britain at Vickers Armstrong's and at the Creusot works in France. Industrialization brought with it the dubious benefit that plants could be turned over to arms production relatively easily in the event of war.

Nationalistic competition further increased the drive towards quicker and better production of arms, and was an extremely strong factor in promoting change. This effect showed particularly clearly in the naval race. In 1905 the launching of the Dreadnought battleship which carried new heavier guns made earlier battleships obsolete (see below, p. 31).

Accompanying this swift rush of technological change on the Continent were changes in population which also vitally affected the attitudes of states towards their ranking in peacetime and their potential power in war. German industry had, as mentioned earlier, many advantages over France in terms of resources. Banking was also much more closely associated with the development of industry. But population growth was now giving Germany yet another advantage. In the early 1870s Germany had a population of about 40 million, France 36 million and Britain 32 million. By 1910 Germany had a population of 64 million, France only 39 million while Britain had reached 45 million. Thus Germany had a much more powerful peacetime labour force than France and greater military potential in the event of war. Germany like France but unlike Britain had a national service system. During this period of conscription young men were schooled in the importance of their national interests. One British diplomat in the 1890s noted the effect of national service in Germany and how it increased nationalism. He also noted that while the young Germans were taught that France was their old enemy they also learned that Britain might be a new one.

---

[2] Bismarck's ideas on the subject were much influenced by schemes he saw in operation at Krupps.

II

Growing population, immense industrial power and an increasingly sophisticated war technology marked the new Europe of the 1870s. The question was how and where these new powers would be used once people became accustomed to industrialization and were able to concentrate on other issues. And even by the late 1870s nations were beginning to wonder how to test their new strengths.

Rough parities of power had been established on the Continent and the eyes of Europe, for the moment, were trained outwards. Potential gains might be made in the vast empires of Russia, Austria-Hungary or Turkey. But Russia lay far away, gripped by ice and snow for many months of the year, and Napoleon's retreat from Moscow was well remembered. The Austro-Hungarian Empire was ripe for plucking but it was dangerous for Germany to allow or encourage covetous states such as Italy to move in that direction. Should the Austro-Hungarian Empire be slashed away, then German Austria would be a separate unit with a good claim to be incorporated in Bismarck's Germany perhaps to the detriment of its Prussian core. Separatism within Austria-Hungary could trigger off trouble in the so recently united modern Germany. Moreover, Austria-Hungary was Germany's first line of defence against Russia.

This left the Ottoman Empire as the main focus of Europe's gaze, and Turkey received the label of 'the sick man of Europe'. But Turkey's sickness had endured for centuries and as the Europeans were later to be taught repeatedly, she had a surprising capacity for recovery. Each power had its segment of Turkey marked off for possession once the occasion offered. In Egypt, Britain and France were engaged in a battle for control, occasionally conducted with weapons, but more often through money and diplomacy. Britain had also obtained Cyprus under a convention of 1878 as the price of warding off a Russian attack on Asiatic Turkey, and had the right to station troops there.

This convenient position for Britain, should any race for Turkey commence, was confirmed by the Congress of Berlin in 1878 when Bismarck and the other European powers forced Russia to give up her own plans for gains after the Russian victory over Turkey in 1877–78. The Russian plans for the partial partition of European Turkey had been indicated in the Treaty of San Stefano of 3 March 1878. But during the late spring and early summer of that year negotiations went on between the interested powers to see that

Russia paid due tribute to the prevailing theory of the balance of power. When the Congress met in Berlin, thus marking the rise in the importance of Germany, the work of scaling down the Russian plans had gone a long way. Three main pre-negotiation settlements had been made : the Anglo-Russian exchange of notes of 30–31 May, the secret Anglo-Turkish Convention of 4 June and the Anglo-Austrian agreement of 6 June. Under the first arrangement Russia was to keep Bessarabia, Batum and Kars but had to give up Erzeroum, while under the third settlement Britain agreed to accept an Austrian occupation of Bosnia and Herzegovina should Russia take Kars and Batum. Under the second agreement, Britain, as mentioned earlier, received Cyprus but this gain lost much of its strategic importance after Britain occupied Egypt militarily following her defeat of Egypt in 1882.

The main agreement, the Treaty of Berlin, was signed on the final day of the Congress, 13 July 1878. Rumania received with dissatisfaction part of Bessarabia instead of the Dobrudja and 'big' Bulgaria was dismantled in an illogical way. There were now to be two Bulgarias : the main section was to remain tributary to Turkey although autonomous while the smaller section, Eastern Bulgaria, was to be renamed Eastern Rumelia and to remain subject to Turkey but was to be allowed a Christian government and a degree of political freedom. Rumania, Serbia, and Montenegro were also trimmed down and lost the territorial gains made under the San Stefano agreement. European commissions were to draw up the detailed frontier settlements, and the rest of the treaty remained unaltered.

The major participants in the Congress of Berlin returned home to assure their domestic audiences that the Treaty of Berlin brought them all individual gains. In the case of Britain, for instance, Lord Beaconsfield claimed he had achieved 'peace with honour' while Salisbury optimistically believed that British influence and authority would increase with the Sultan. Most writers on Germany and Bismarck treat the Congress of Berlin as a high triumph for the state and the man.

But was the Congress of Berlin such a success for the pattern of international relations? It neither satisfied Slav nationalism nor helped the Austro-Hungarian Empire nor that of Turkey. In the interests of spreading compromise thin it doled out Balkan and Turkish territory piecemeal. Apart from the Congress of Berlin's failure in relation to the increasingly important issue of self-determination, no reasonable provisions were made for carrying out reform in the Ottoman Empire. The European states such as Britain which became guarantors for the security of Christians living in the Turkish Empire were, in fact, unlikely to protect them. These unfortunate people who were already regarded with suspicion by the Turks were now even more hostages to fortune since they could be seen as potential traitors who might aid European Christians in partitioning Turkey. Neither Russia nor Austria, the major powers most concerned with the Balkans, was satisfied, and in their dissatisfaction lay the seeds of much future conflict.

The Congress of Berlin produced a treaty typical of nineteenth-century diplomacy and the conduct of international relations in its attempt to ignore the growing force of nationalism. It also usefully illustrates another characteristic of diplomatic technique, i.e. use of the buffer state. This technique was a valid one if the state chosen as a buffer had a serious claim to independence. But this was not the case as far as Eastern Bulgaria renamed Rumelia was concerned. Rumelia lay across the path of Russian potential access to the Aegean Sea but since it was such a fragile non-state Britain felt little security. Hence when in 1885 the Bulgarians defeated the Serbs and so obtained a united Bulgaria, Britain acquiesced in the tearing up of this part of the Treaty of Berlin. The Russians on the other hand, who had championed the Big Bulgaria of 1878, were now opposed to it since they had found that Bulgarian nationalism was developing too strongly for them to control. Bulgaria provided a barrier to Russian advances towards the Aegean in spite of and not because of the Congress of Berlin.

Greece, like Bulgaria, was dissatisfied with the Berlin settlement. She had received part of Thessaly under the demarcation process by May 1881 but was to fight Turkey in 1885 and 1897–98 in an attempt to get what she considered her due share of territory.

The Congress of Berlin had averted major war in the short term but its long-term results were particularly dangerous for Germany and Britain. Bismarck in his role as 'honest broker' had produced a settlement which did not satisfy Slav nationalism nor Austria nor Russia. It could be argued that nationalism was the time-bomb of the Balkans and that Bismarck had done all that was possible, given the great power conventions of nineteenth-century diplomacy, in postponing the time when that bomb would explode. But if Bismarck is to be classed as a great diplomat something more must be expected of him than a settlement which ignores powerful changes undercutting the basis of conventional nineteenth-century international relations. In the creation of modern Germany itself he had recognized and used the growing force of nationalism so it is clearly insufficient to argue that he failed to understand the problem nationalism posed. More probably, Bismarck intended the Berlin settlement to leave Austria and Russia dissatisfied and so force them to look towards Germany as the arbiter of their Balkan destiny. Yet such a polarization could not be maintained indefinitely and Bismarck must have realized that repeated frustration would cause mounting tension only too likely to explode into war. It is hardly surprising that Bismarck's self-confessed nightmare was of coalitions : to Germany's west lay revanchist France, to the east stood expansionist Russia, while restless Austria lay to the south.

III

Bismarck's diplomacy gave Germany national stability at the price of international instability and this was true both before and after 1871 and on both the eastern and western frontiers. But he revelled in tension and his diplomacy after 1871 was characterized by a nervous flexibility which contrasts oddly with his earlier powerful and decisive strokes which established modern Germany.

He had played the 'honest broker' role at the Congress of Berlin but the price to be paid later was a heavy one and quickly demanded. In July 1878 the Treaty of Berlin was signed and little over a year later, on 7 October 1879, Germany entered into a secret defensive alliance with Austria. Germany was to give Austria military aid if Russia attacked Austria, so 1 versus 1 was to produce 2 versus 1. But Austria was only to give Germany military aid if Russia and one additional power (i.e. France) attacked Germany, giving a formula of 2 versus 1 producing 2 versus 2. Clearly, the crux of the agreement was Germany's military promise to Austria and that country's security was underwritten in the event of trouble with Russia. But what would Bismarck have done if this trouble had come in his time of office? He must have worried about this for as early as 18 June 1881 he drew Russia into a collective defence pact with Austria.

This agreement or secret *Dreikaiserbund* of 1881 contained much verbiage designed to act as a smokescreen covering the real German aim of keeping control over both Austria and Russia. In some respects it resembles the non-aggression pacts so popular in the period between the two world wars and now again in the late 1960s and early 1970s *détente* between East and West. The *Dreikaiserbund* exemplifies another characteristic of nineteenth-century international relations in that it is a diplomatic agreement concerned more with avoiding doing things than carrying out action; this type of agreement is common except where fundamental collective war pacts are concerned. Under the agreement, the three powers were to harmonize their foreign policies and to act from a stance of benevolent neutrality towards each other whilst also co-operating against Socialism. The fact of the existence of the *Dreikaiserbund* was important as linking Russia and Austria but its terms were not significant. These three major states each with different short- and long-term policies could not harmonize their foreign policy. Benevolent neutrality also meant very little. At home Bismarck was dealing efficiently with restraining Socialism by his own state socialism, through welfare plans such as those of 1881–84 and 1889, but Austria and Russia dealt with it more clumsily, identifying Socialism with subversion and trying to blunderbuss it through the secret police. What could these states do together to keep down Socialism? Little or nothing beyond exchanging dangerous expatriate socialists.

The military clauses of the 1881 *Dreikaiserbund* concerned action itself and attempts to pre-empt ways in which crises should be tackled. The three states were to consult on changes in the Turkish *status quo* and this was designed to hold back Austria and Russia from stealing a march on one another. Similarly, they reaffirmed that the Turkish Straits should be closed to war vessels. The crux of the military section of the understanding was that Germany, Austria and Russia would be neutral if war occurred between any one of them and one other power except if this other power should be Turkey. The general effect of this part of the agreement was to cause a moratorium on Austro-Russian action against the Turkish Empire unless Britain fired the starting gun for partition by sending war vessels through the Straits to coerce Turkey or Russia as she had done in 1878.

The *Dreikaiserbund* suited Bismarck because for the moment it focussed potential Austrian or Russian hostility away from Germany and from each other, and made Britain the power to centre their suspicions upon. It also linked Germany to Britain in the sense that both of these powers now, on the whole, wanted to maintain and not to disrupt the European *status quo*. The sequel to this common interest was the Mediterranean Agreements made in the 1880s between Britain, Italy and Austria, but not directly with Germany. But the success of Bismarck's strategy for maintenance of the *status quo* depended on Austrian and Russian inactivity and these countries were like two coach horses which looked good together but pulled apart if the coach started to move. Events in the Balkans would not stand still : Russia and Austria were alienated by the Balkan crisis of 1885–86 when, as mentioned earlier, Serbia and Bulgaria tore up their parts of the Treaty of Berlin. In 1887 the *Dreikaiserbund* itself lapsed as tension over the Balkans continued between Austria and Russia.

Bismarck then tried to run the two recalcitrant horses separately. He made a new treaty with Russia, the secret Reinsurance Treaty of 18 June 1887, while still keeping his main alliance with Austria. Under this treaty, Germany and Russia were to be neutral in war except if Germany attacked France or Russia attacked Austria-Hungary. The tripartite game between Germany, Austria and Russia thus becomes quadrilateral with the introduction of France as a technical makeweight. This important alteration, giving added stability to the play of international relations in Europe, also reveals the small number of major players then on the international scene. For it was this paucity of states as actors rather than any developed Russo-French relationship which at this stage brought France into the diplomatic game. The inclusion of France within the effects of the Reinsurance Treaty illustrates the inevitability of the later Franco-Russian Alliance.

Writers sometimes make much of the conflict between the alliances and agreements made by Bismarck, but although these discrepancies provide interesting individual detail, overall they lack positive importance. Their value is important but negative since they merely reflect the much more important fact, and the one which should engage our attention, that Bismarck's Germany had no stable diplomatic basis for her existence. Modern Germany had come hastily into existence through war and, in terms of geography, she was one of the most vulnerable states in Europe. The effects of this vulnerability are seen in later German history : a stress on military preparedness and first-strike capability, an over-emphasis on internal political cohesion leading to a neurotic preoccupation with politico-economic scapegoats such as the Jews and the Communists, and a diplomatic mesh of agreements which was often as comprehensive as it was inconsistent. Both Bismarck and Hitler appreciated the fact that German peacetime diplomacy could not be consistent but this tended to be forgotten or not fully understood by William II and Chancellors such as Caprivi who followed Bismarck. Many later German leaders wanted logical ranges of alliances and tried to blind themselves to the fact that if they dropped Russia and allowed her free diplomatic play she would turn to France as an ally. In view of the German fears of encirclement, their probable response to the Russian link with France would be to threaten to give Austria her head in the Balkans but, as time was to show, this was a threat to Germany as much as to Russia. As we have seen, Bismarck in 1878 only postponed the explosion of the Balkan time-bomb, he did not defuse it. He could not do so in case he destroyed his own modern Germany in the process. The vulnerability of modern Germany has remained a constant problem. The issue was shelved in the late 1940s by the Cold War and only now, in the late 1960s and early 1970s, is the issue of Germany's two-edged vulnerability and power being approached in the current East-West *détente*.

IV

Germany could have secured a firm diplomatic basis for her existence as a modern unified state by maintaining a good understanding with Britain. Britain was an island power with naval strength while Germany, until comparatively late in the nineteenth century, was essentially a land power with military attributes. In this sense the two powers were complementary. Again, Britain was an imperial power while Germany was on the whole little concerned with colonies and had small need of them, although recent research indicates that Bismarck may have been more interested in empire abroad than was earlier believed. The two countries were also linked historically by what Joseph Chamberlain flamboyantly called the natural Anglo-Saxon alliance. Many families in Britain, particularly those connected with trade and finance, had German relations. Queen Victoria herself was the Kaiser's grandmother. With all these ties of past co-operation, relationship, and the links between the British and German thrones, very few nineteenth-century writers would have believed that Britain and Germany would be lined up against each other should major war develop.

Why then, with all these reasons for keeping together in international politics, did Britain and Germany drift apart? Family relationships can mean tension as well as understanding and there is no doubt that William II as the leader of a strong modern Germany resented family homilies from his grandmother, or from his uncle, later King Edward VII. Since the days when Queen Victoria's daughter, Victoria, had married into the German royal family, there had been a sense of strain because of the more rigid German court traditions and the contrast between Britain with its constitutional monarchy and growing democracy and Germany where although a parliament existed the crown still ruled and did not merely reign.

Another factor in the drifting apart of Germany and Britain was growing trade rivalry. Britain was a trade competitor of other states such as the USA and there were occasions when Anglo-American tension ran high at the end of the nineteenth century. But in terms of communications the USA was still comparatively far away from Britain and had a large internal market whereas Germany was hitting British trade with the continent in a far more obvious way. Germany was the gainer from the fact that Britain had been the earlier workshop of the world. Now, later on in the industrial revolution it was Germany which was moving ahead in the newer technologies such as chemicals and electricity. A complex of British feeling towards Germany was building up composed of resentment at Germany's success in the newer industries and envy because Britain was no longer undisputed master of world industry and trade. A modern parallel would be the British sourness towards the postwar German 'economic miracle'.

In a different way the rapid changes caused by technology were also contributing to a deterioration in the Anglo-German relationship. In earlier years tension between the two countries worked itself off harmlessly because no easy means of expression existed. This stability, caused by the fact that one state was a major land power and the other a leading sea power, was in the 1890s being rapidly destroyed. Britain was so identified with the concept that its strength, and even its very existence, lay in being the major naval power, that fears and resentment were bound to come once Germany began to develop a navy. But if this had occurred before the nineteenth century, it would have come more slowly and Britain would have had time to accustom itself to the change. As it was the change occurred within about ten years.

By the end of the nineteenth century, Germany was an extremely wealthy country and anxious to establish itself in the international pecking order by acquiring the necessary status symbols such as a powerful navy. Salisbury, Britain's Prime Minister at the end of the nineteenth and beginning of the twentieth centuries, had been born in 1830 yet he had a strong interest in science. But even this interest was insufficient to make him grasp how quickly technology could provide Germany with an efficient navy. He tended to think that although Germany might have the machines she would lack the trained personnel to operate them, and worried about the possibility of intermarriage between the Dutch and German royal families since this would give Germany at a stroke the sailors she needed. But naval technology leaped ahead so rapidly between 1895 and 1905 that these fears were soon out of date. The decisive change came in 1905 when, as mentioned earlier, the Dreadnought battleship made strengths in earlier battle fleets unimportant. By 1914 Britain had 19 Dreadnoughts at sea and 13 on the stocks while Germany had 13 at sea and 7 in various stages of readiness. But the figures of 19/13 and 13/7 give Britain an appearance of security which is misleading. The new battleship was so expensive and such a large target that naval strategy concentrated on avoiding rather than encouraging action in war. This passivity meant that Britain's relative lead in battleships was lost; it also meant that action in war was strongly identified with the military level as the First World War was to demonstrate.

Britain and Germany were also drifting apart because once Germany showed interest in colonial gains, Britain was unable to do a deal with her since Germany lacked suitable material to exchange. Paradoxically, it was easier for Britain to make agreements to reduce tension with her traditional enemy, France, than with her traditional German friend, simply because France possessed colonial material in plenty to rearrange in more logical patterns, particularly futures in Morocco and Egypt as the 1904 Entente demonstrated.

Earlier in the nineteenth century, it had seemed as though Britain and Germany might draw together as stabilizing powers intent on restraining Italy and Austria. But the very fact that the contact was to be through other powers emphasizes the lack of direct links binding Britain and Germany together.

Britain favoured Italian independence and unification and was inclined to help Italy to establish itself as a new state. Modern Italy by the 1870s turned outwards to colonial expansion and dreamed of reviving the glories of the Roman Empire in the Mediterranean and Africa. Britain was willing to exploit these grandiose schemes so long as Italy was not too demanding. Rapidly, however, the

British realized that the Italians wanted a great deal. Colonialism for Italy was not a mere decoration of foreign policy but it was seriously sought after to relieve population pressure in the northern towns of Italy and to ease the poverty amongst the workers living on the land in the south. Italy planned to settle any colonial territory gained with time-expired soldiers as in Eritrea. But the Italians tended to take risks and overreach themselves. At Adowa in March 1896 they were decisively beaten by Menelek of Ethiopia. As a result of such episodes Britain became disenchanted with Italy, and this mood was enhanced by Italian dabblings in the Byzantine intricacies of the Eastern Mediterranean.

German disenchantment with Italy nearly rivalled that of Britain. It was common knowledge that the new Italian army was a broken reed. Hence Germany, although allied with Italy since 1882 along with Austria in the Triple Alliance, never knew whether Italy would capitalize on her military weakness by making a political settlement with France in order to achieve significant colonial gains. The Italian weakness led the Germans to hope that Britain would underwrite Italy's colonial adventures particularly in the Red Sea area.

Bismarck similarly hoped that Britain would look after Austrian (as well as Italian) interests in relation to a possible partition of the Turkish Empire, while also hoping that the *status quo* would be maintained as long as possible. But why should Britain do all this for Germany? It was, to a certain extent, in the British interest to control Austria and Italy since by appearing to aid these states she could manipulate them. This policy went hand in hand with Britain's attempt to prevent Turkey from sliding further into the Russian grip, although in fact it was Germany rather than Russia whose influence was increasing in Turkey. Even so, the Mediterranean Agreements remain a puzzling factor in Salisbury's foreign policy unless it is remembered that he expected Germany to support Britain in Egypt against France. The Germans believed that they paid this price by not fully exploiting Egypt which was the British Achilles' heel but Salisbury and many of the senior men in the British Foreign Office were alienated, perhaps excessively, by the fact that the Germans tended to present a bill for a *quid pro quo* during or after each phase of Anglo-French tension over Egypt or the Sudan. As mentioned, it can be argued that the British bitterness over Germany's *chantage,* to use Salisbury's term, was out of proportion considering the poor gains which Germany made from these threats. But we must not ignore the fact that until 1898–99

France was still taking action to affect the Egyptian question by moves in Ethiopia and the Sudan.

The first Mediterranean agreement was recorded by an exchange of notes between Britain and Italy on 12 February 1887. The two powers were to consult on maintenance of the *status quo* in the Mediterranean, the Aegean and the Black Sea. A few months later Austria was drawn into this partnership when a second exchange of notes took place on 12 December 1887 between these three powers. Under this agreement Turkey was to be prevented from giving up any of her rights in the Balkans or Near East. The second agreement was designed partly to check Russia, and in so far as this aim was concerned, the agreement conflicted with Bismarck's other obligations to pursue a pro-Russian policy. But as has been stressed earlier, inconsistency in diplomatic agreements was not merely the hallmark of Bismarck's work but its necessity. Apart from being intended to check Russia the agreements were also designed to hold back France. The agreements were both secret although some knowledge of their existence leaked out. Salisbury's attitude towards the agreements was cautious and his insistence on their being kept secret negated their influence on French and Russian policy.

The most important aspect of the Mediterranean Agreements is not so much practical but the way they illustrate how Bismarck wanted to link Britain with the Triple Alliance, and how British naval power was the essential link binding Austria and Italy together. These agreements, the only formal link between Britain and the Triple Alliance, exemplify Germany's difficulty in drawing closer to Britain since the necessary diplomatic material was lacking. The agreements had a relatively short life, for Rosebery, who became British Foreign Secretary in 1892, allowed them to lapse. When Salisbury returned to power in the mid-1890s the possibility of reviving the agreements was considered. But whether because Salisbury put the Austrians off because he did not appear keen on the renewal or because the Austrians wanted a free hand in the event of a partition of the Turkish Empire, the talks came to nothing.

v

To conclude, the practice of international relations was undergoing considerable modification in the nineteenth century. This alteration stemmed from the growth of a number of powerful nation states within Europe itself based on industrial and population changes. Whereas in the eighteenth and early nineteenth centuries Europe had been composed of many small units, held together on what remained essentially a feudal basis, now in the nineteenth century the strong force of nationalism, at once disrupting and unifying, was making itself felt. The actual conduct of international relations remained in the hands of a relatively small élite and depended largely on the character and will of individuals such as Bismarck of Germany or Salisbury of Britain. But the people were making themselves felt as in the case when the Bulgarians tore up the Treaty of Berlin in order to achieve their independence. In the following chapters we will see how the people further influenced international relations through their attachment, encouraged by the developing popular press and certain new demagogic politicians, to another form of nationalism, i.e. imperialism.

The development of a number of roughly comparable nation states within Europe had a variety of results in international relations. It initially intensified the view that diplomacy was in essence a matter of maintaining the balance of power, and this balance went right down the scale from armies and navies to economic power and the size of populations. International relations were thus by the first decade of the twentieth century a unifying factor in the modern state tending to draw all aspects of a nation's life together in preparedness for war. As the new states jostled one another first for power, possessions and precedence in Europe itself, and then abroad in areas such as Africa, tension grew. Two main developments then occurred. Firstly, the danger of war or some flare-up almost led to neo-institutionalization of the conference or congress system. We saw this at work in the Congress of Berlin when Russia was forced by general European pressure to disgorge the excessive gains which, according to the balance of power theory, she had taken by the Treaty of San Stefano. Secondly, the increasing tension also led to the dangerous polarization of alliances and by the end of the nineteenth century had divided Europe into two camps, one containing Germany, Austria and Italy, and the other France and Russia. As mentioned in the first chapter, the balance of power worked well enough so long as it was not too rigid, so long as states could switch their alliances in accord with changes in the power of individual states. But once this flexibility was gone with the creation of the Triple Alliance in 1882 and the Dual Alliance in 1893–94 the system of international relations based on the balance of power tended to favour war rather than peace.

International relations were moving into the phase which has continued up to the present and is marked by division of the nation states into two main power blocs, although now a bloc of non-aligned states also exists. Military alliances were no longer temporary coalitions forming and re-forming during war but had, by the end of the nineteenth century, become semi-permanent features of peacetime. There was a tension between the informal and now almost institutionalized conference system, which when major crises occurred righted the balance of power, and these semi-permanent alliances. In future, if conferences occurred it would not be the case of many powers combining to make one or two powers act in accordance with the balance of power but power blocs would meet face to face. Whichever bloc lost at the conference would suffer humiliation and resentment. International relations were ceasing to have a natural self-righting balance and were about to enter a phase of crisis. This phase affected the development of imperialism to which we now turn.

REFERENCES

Albrecht-Carrié, R., *A Diplomatic History of Europe since the Congress of Vienna*, London, Methuen, and New York, Harper, 1958.

Ashworth, W., *A Short History of the International Economy 1850–1950*, London, Longmans, 1959, and New York, Humanities, 2nd Ed., 1926.

Condliffe, J. B., *The Commerce of Nations*, New York, Norton, 1950.

Feis, H., *Europe, the World's Banker*, New York, Keller, 1961.

Hearder, H., *Europe in the Nineteenth Century, 1830–1880*, London, Longmans, and New York, Holt, Rineart and Winston, 1966.

Hinsley, F. H., *Power and the Pursuit of Peace*, Cambridge and New York, C.U.P., 1963.

Joll, J., ed., *Britain and Europe. Pitt to Churchill, 1793–1940*, London, Kaye, and New York, Barnes and Noble, 1950. 2nd Ed., 1961.

Manchester, W., *The Arms of Krupp, 1587–1968*, London, Joseph, and Boston, Little, Brown and Company, 1968.

Medlicott, W. N., *The Congress of Berlin and After*, London, Cass, 1963.

Ramn, A., *Germany 1789–1919. A Polilical History* London, Methuen, and New York, Barnes and Noble, 1967.

3 *Early Imperialism*

I

Imperialism is a human phenomenon almost as old as recorded history. Present views are mainly dominated either by classical Roman imperialism or by the dynamic period which occurred towards the end of the nineteenth century and is usually called 'New Imperialism'. The ancient Roman imperialism which lasted for many centuries is currently, rightly or wrongly, generally thought of as military and it is assumed that this era was less harmful both because it provided ways for the conquered to rise and because of its skill in disseminating conventions—such as law and order— which have been foundations of the modern Western world. In any case by the mid-nineteenth century the evils of Roman imperialism were ancient wrongs dignified and enhanced in the histories, legends and poetry of the classics. The advantages of classical imperialism were kept fresh through innumerable Western traditions and through clerics who plundered the classics to grace their sermons. Ancient imperialism and that of the late nineteenth century are linked through the careers of young men like Alfred Milner who spent formative years at Oxford University.

Why should ancient imperialism have been considered the foundation of a good education in the nineteenth century? Today, we would be inclined to ask, wrongly, what relevance did classics have to the nineteenth century. But until comparatively late in the century this was not the question which was asked. Partly, no doubt, the answer lies in the fact that then learning was largely the classics; there was also the appeal of law and order on a large scale. Many intellectuals, Fabians as well as right-wingers, liked the idea of large, efficiently governed, multi-national units in which power and force would be both used and controlled. Here technology interplayed with international relations. Large industrial units were developing in countries like the United States of America. They were being hailed as efficient productive units and beneficial to citizens in reducing prices. Similar political benefits were expected to accrue from imperialism such as good government based on central manipulation of resources. But in practice this theory tended to break down and native populations were exploited by having their interests subordinated to those of the ruling country.

This exploitation, on the whole, did not initially occur as part of a systematic policy but followed inevitably from the fact that the Western world was economically and technologically so far advanced compared with the regions conquered in Africa, the Pacific and on the fringes of Asia. Admittedly, the end product was the same, but unless we remember that this phenomenon derived from an economic rather than a political basis we will misunderstand the way in which many imperialists prided themselves on not interfering with the religion and culture of the areas which they ruled. Their attitude will be dismissed as hypocrisy and this would be, in many cases, wrong.

The imperialists were also proud of their achievements in introducing good government and democratic standards of honesty into their territories. Their reforms were often laudable but they failed to recognize that ideas of public responsibility were an organic part of a state's development towards democracy. An eighteenth-century Englishman, political pensioner of one of the early Georges, would have been quite at home in mid-nineteenth-century Egypt, manœuvring himself about in a tide of intrigue and corruption. The English abroad tended to condemn natives as though they were doomed to remain forever at a lower stage of political development. This classification of the temporal as the finite was convenient to the imperialists, but was it conscious? Probably not; perhaps just as Americans today like to forget the amount of violence which went into the making of the United States, so nineteenth-century imperialists wanted to forget that their own standards of public accountability were not even a century old.

At this point it is worth stressing that although there is an image of the nineteenth century as a static, staid period, this is inaccurate. It was, as the instance cited above indicates, a time of rapid and violent change. No doubt consciousness, however suppressed, of the weakness of the case for social imperialism, i.e. the dominance of one national group over another less advanced in written culture and technology, played a part in the way in which the increasing and successful middle classes quickly appropriated to themselves a neo-scientific gloss for imperialism from Darwin's *Origin of Species* (1859). The sentiments were not new, but Darwin's material was used to give racialism an apparent respectability. Science, therefore, seemed to endorse the earlier idea of Christians as a chosen people, and appears to have reinforced missionary religion at a time when other factors were reducing the appeal of religion at home.

The classics cast a lustre over the hard realities of imperialism : the slaughter, the lust for power, and acquisitiveness; they endowed it with a romantic melancholy, a loneliness, a sense of missions carried out on the rim of the known world which undoubtedly appealed to many imperialists. Even Cromer, the British Agent and Consul-General in Egypt, who had a poor education, felt it his duty to acquire a knowledge of the classics. But while he struggled with glosses on original texts which enabled him to use a Greek quotation here and there in his writings, he considered that it was unnecessary for him to learn Arabic, the language of the people whom he ruled. Although British administrators tended to act as though they believed that imperialism would go on forever, contradictorily, they also enjoyed the idea that if Tyre, Nineveh and Rome could disappear and leave few traces so also could Victorian imperialism. This melancholy relish for a doomed Empire was catered for in Rudyard Kipling's poetry. Ironically, in view of this strain in his verse, he is often described as the poet of imperialism, as though this meant that he approved of all that occurred under its name. But this is not the case, for he not only stressed the impermanence of imperialism[1] but reprobated the unchristian pride and boasting which too often accompanied it.[2] Along with all the usual attributes of imperialism—strategy, duty, religion, trade and finance—we must add this sense of doomed missions carried out in alien lands.

This attitude reflected the contemporary sense that modern imperialism, the by-product of industrialization, international trade and a more powerful military technology, was self-destructive. When imperialism occurred in the early days of history it was often military in form long after the initial conquest occurred, and the policing of a vast empire such as that of Rome was carried out by employing on one frontier soldiers taken from tribes conquered on another frontier. In this way the empire renewed itself over and over again. But when nineteenth-century imperialism took place Europe was at a high point of growth and confidence. The result was that the earlier method of keeping power by drawing on con-

[1] See, for instance, verse 3 of 'White Man's Burden', in *The Modern World*, ed. Hans Kohn, New York, 1964, p. 126.
[2] See 'Recessional' in the same work, pp. 127-8.

quered peoples was never seriously considered by most imperial nations although sometimes the rough edges were smoothed over by *assimilation* theories as in the cases of Portugal and France. But these experiments cannot be considered convincing in view of what occurred in Algeria and what still occurs in Angola. In addition the new imperialism relied so heavily on military technology—guns, railways, telegraph wires—that conquered races felt they had been conquered not, as the westerners asserted, by superior races but by improved technology. Menelek of Ethiopia demonstrated this in 1896 when better military equipment obtained from France enabled him decisively to defeat the Italian would-be conquerors. The same lesson was administered in 1904–05 to Russia by Japan, in this case using British war material. At a different level the self-destructive tendencies of modern imperialism occurred in civilian life. It can be said that for the European states it created a race of administrators while for the less-developed world it produced, particularly in India, a race of ill-paid, underfed clerks. No doubt they were also underworked since labour was plentiful and it was in this social strata at once promoted and checked that the colonial revolt spread.

II

Modern and economic imperialism are generally equated with each other partly because they both occurred in the context of an expanding industrial Europe and partly through the vigour of Communist writing on the subject. But the term economic imperialism must be carefully defined. Many non-Communist writers seem to feel it is sufficient to disprove the theory of economic imperialism by showing that Lenin was wrong in the way he associated finance capitalism with the high period of imperialism.[3] But George Paish[4] had demonstrated that this theory was wrong before Lenin put pen to paper to write *Imperialism* (1917). It must be remembered that this work by Lenin was originally intended to be an indictment of Russian Tsarist policy in areas such as Poland, Finland and Courland. But the Bolshevik revolution occurred more quickly than Lenin had anticipated and so, as it turned out, his book did not

[3] See, for instance, C. E. Carrington, 'Frontiers in Africa', *International Affairs*, October 1960, Vol. 36, No. 4, pp. 431–2.
[4] See 'Great Britain's Capital Investment in Other Lands', *Journal of the Royal Statistical Society*, Vol. LXXII, September 1909, pp. 465–80; also 'Great Britain's Capital Investment in Individual Colonial and Foreign Countries', *J.R.S.S.*, Vol. LXXIV, New Series, January, 1911, pp. 167–87.

have to pass through the Tsarist censorship net which had been his motive for stressing tropical or semi-tropical imperialism instead of the Russian variety.[5] What Lenin did was to fit his own reasoning on Russian imperialism to the facts on colonies supplied by Hobson in his book *Imperialism* (1902). Poland, of course, was an extremely wealthy agrarian country and profitable for Russia. Earlier communists, notably Marx and Engels, both stressed that colonialism although profitable to the ruling sector of the British population was not nationally profitable because of the high costs of imperial defence.[6] As mentioned below, the British Treasury shared this view.

But the case for or against the existence of economic imperialism does not stand or fall merely because Lenin wrongly linked the stages of imperialism and the export of capital. The fundamental argument for it is that through expanding international trade in the nineteenth century the developed economies of the western sector[7] established a relationship of exploitation with less-developed countries. In economic terms this nexus meant that the less-developed sector must remain perpetually at a lower stage of industrialization than the western world or must remain a producer of primary products which the developed sector would use. The profits for the developed sector would consequently always remain higher than those for the less-developed sector. Over a period of time political and social rationalizations would develop to reinforce the effects of this economic patterning. No fault can be found with this case for economic imperialism, and the persistence of the same economic imbalance after decolonization strengthens the argument. But to argue that this is why imperialism occurred is not the same as saying the statesmen saw it in these terms and therefore undertook formal imperialism. Rather they took part in it with reluctance and often realized that the profits would be low because of the type of areas taken and the high cost of providing military protection and administration for them. But, increasingly, their elbows were jogged by the new vigorous middle classes who were now not merely

[5] V. I. Lenin, *Imperialism, The Highest Stage of Capitalism*, Moscow, 1947, Russian preface, p. 10.
[6] See Marx's essay 'British Incomes in India' (1857) in K. Marx and F. Engels, *On Colonialism*, Moscow, 1962, p. 161.
[7] It is sometimes argued that this case is wrong because countries like Russia (with poor, underdeveloped economies) were also imperialist. But as Lenin knew Russian imperialism was essentially both Continental and traditional. Ethiopia was unimportant in this context.

expressing their views through the press but were also breaking through into the ranks of government. Moreover, the importance of European competitiveness should not be overlooked.

It was mentioned earlier that late nineteenth-century imperialism was socially self-destructive, but there was also a powerful economic influence which made it unlikely that British imperialism in particular would last indefinitely. In the case of Britain, the empire was consistently starved of funds for development. According to Lenin, colonial profits were so attractive that large banks would equip and send out whole expeditions of engineers, agricultural experts, and mineral prospectors. Here he was thinking of the high degree of vertical integration present in the American and German economies, and particularly of the close links between banking and industry in Germany.[8] But this was so different from the situation prevailing in many imperial areas such as Egypt that if administrators like Cromer ever read Lenin's *Imperialism,* they must have found it remarkably inaccurate. Similarly, when Joseph Chamberlain, British Colonial Secretary (1895–1903), became engrossed in imperialism and wanted development grants he met with serious opposition. The British Treasury, harassed by the upwards spiral of defence costs,[9] simply (like Marx and Engels) totalled up the costs of imperial maintenance, and by setting this figure against Chamberlain's demands were able to dismiss his cases. Apart from this, the more sceptical minds of the property-owning Cecil family also operated a cost/benefit analysis against Chamberlain. Just as the classical economists equated the state with the individual and opposed Keynes' theory of deficit finance in the 1920s and 1930s, so Salisbury and Balfour in the late 1890s equated the state with a private landlord and argued that it would be wrong to spend money on areas within the British Empire unless the tenure was to be a lengthy one as in the case of Crown Colonies.[10] A landlord, so the argument ran, does not spend money on an estate if it is not his in perpetuity. This attitude indicates considerable uncertainty about the future of empire.

[8] E. J. Passant, *A Short History of Germany 1815–1945,* Cambridge University Press, 1962, pp. 110–12. But even with this closer link and exploitation of railway and mining concessions in areas such as China, imperialism in the German case was not particularly profitable, see A. Ramm, *Germany 1879–1919,* London, 1967, pp. 395–6.

[9] E. J. Hobsbawm, *Industry and Empire. An Economic History of Britain since 1750,* London, 1968, p. 202.

[10] R. Robinson and J. Gallagher, *Africa and the Victorians,* London, 1961, pp. 397–400; Salisbury Papers, Christ Church, Oxford.

In addition to the *vis inertiae* of the Treasury and the Cecil family, private industrialists and financiers saw no reason why they should sacrifice 4–5% profits obtainable, say, in the USA, for the $2-2\frac{1}{2}$% available in areas such as Egypt.[11] Much capital had flowed to Egypt in the 1860s and 1870s in the period of high risk when the country was under Khedivial rule and before the British and French assumption of financial control after the mid-1870s. In this period interest rates were extremely high, averaging about 16–17%. But once the political *status quo* was certain under Anglo-French and later British control from 1882, rates of interest fell rapidly. Since European capital did not tend to flow to the areas of national empire in large amounts there was no drive towards industrial take-off.[12] Instead imperialism stimulated production of primary goods such as cotton and did not encourage more intensive industrial growth which alone could have pushed up revenue sufficiently to make serious improvements in the native standard of living. Politically, the restriction on the increase of native income levels enabled the imperialist nations to maintain their domination. As a result, through lack of education, the anti-imperialist propaganda of the late nineteenth century and early twentieth century was crude but it was not ineffective. It created the subsoil which the ideas of more intelligent and powerful leaders like Gandhi later fertilized.

III

Improvements in native standards of living did occur particularly from the Europeans' insistence on high standards of public health in order to check diseases like cholera to which they themselves were susceptible. Once disease ceased culling population so heavily, high fertility rates soon led to rapid rises in population especially in Egypt and India. This factor also made long-term western supremacy unlikely since the increase of population combined with low and near-static levels of native income meant that the problem of poverty and its attendant stresses such as malnutrition, famine and disease became more and more overpowering. Although initially there was some improvement in native standards of living through

[11] See M. J. Grieve, unpublished B.Litt. thesis, Bodleian Library, Oxford, 'The Egyptian Policy of Lord Salisbury, 1895–99'.
[12] For further evidence on the British case, see W. K. Hancock, 'Agenda for the Study of British Imperial Economy, 1850–1950', *Journal of Economic History*, Vol. XIII, No. 3, 1953, pp. 257–8; on the French case, see W. L. Langer, 'A Critique of Imperialism', *Foreign Affairs*, New York, Vol. 14, no. 1, October 1935, p. 104.

western suzerainty the long-term trend was one of accelerating deterioration visible especially in centres of high population density like Calcutta.

The basic weakness of western imperialism was that it pushed the subject peoples towards a degree of economic and social improvement and then, in effect, said : 'Thus far and no further'. In fact it created economic and political disequilibria which it could not solve and for this reason decolonization in the late 1950s and 1960s is not so much a cause for western self-congratulation, but an admission of defeat, occurring as it has done rapidly, often ill-managed and not because of liberal thinking so much as because of problems which could no longer either be shelved or successfully handled.

If more money had been available for the economic and social development of the Empire in the late 1890s and early 1900s then Chamberlain's farsighted scheme for making it into an efficient economic community might have succeeded. But since British manufacturers and financiers were making good enough profits by dealing with the developed world they could not see why they should bother to pay out money to improve less-developed areas. As mentioned earlier, the high phase of nineteenth-century imperialism coincided with a time when defence costs were rising, partly because of a degree of inflation, but also because of hardening alliance tensions. Colonial statesmen, then as now, were not over-anxious to help Britain to bear the burden of imperial defence. Apart from this shortage of money, caused by rising costs and unwillingness to increase income tax,[13] there was the fundamental problem of doing more for subjects in imperial possessions than European nations did for their own working classes. Taking Britain, only in the exceptional case of Ireland—held to be the cornerstone of the Empire,[14] loss of which might cause collapse of the whole imperial edifice— did Britain do more for a colonial area (for instance, in land reform) than for her own country.

British Liberals, Fabians and Socialists also had a strong incentive to hasten the process of imperial self-destruction. So long as the Empire existed it tended to act as a check on reforms in Britain itself, for it created a playback of artificially maintained élite, obsolete ideas into British society. Cromer, for instance, went out to

[13] Asquith still talked of getting rid of income tax at the end of the nineteenth century.
[14] Partly, as Richard Koebner shows, because after the loss of the American colonies, Britain and Ireland constituted the 'Empire', see *Empire*, Cambridge University Press, 1961, pp. 247–8.

Egypt as a Liberal; he returned a Conservative and a fierce opponent of reforms, including those on female suffrage. And even more than creating this anachronistic feedback, imperialism led to avoidance of radical reform in Britain for about two decades at the end of the nineteenth and the beginning of the twentieth centuries. It was all too easy to divert the attention of the new industrial proletariat into the adventure and financial gamble of imperialism, and many young men also went from the land into the army in search of wider horizons, secure pay and the certainty of a pension if they survived their period of service. The same sort of deprivation encouraged labourers to volunteer for the army between 1914–16 before conscription was introduced.

In novels produced for the working-class market at the end of the nineteenth century, and for at least a decade after, the male equivalent of the heroine's making good by marrying the handsome young squire was the young British adventurer who went off to war or to the colonies to make his fortune. Cecil Rhodes himself epitomized this sort of success and left £6 million. Buchan's *Thirty-Nine Steps* also exploits this material as did Rider Haggard in an earlier period. Similarly, imperialism to politicians like Chamberlain was to be both bread and circuses for the close-packed industrial masses whose political importance grew after electoral concessions were made following Palmerston's death in 1865.[15] One million town labourers got the vote in 1867, further additions were made in 1885 and in 1918 all men over 21 (and women over 30) were enfranchised. Similar reforms gave the vote to the agricultural labourer, for example the Third Reform Act of 1884 which enfranchised two million.

It appears that at a time when conditions were on the whole improving for the British masses, as wages increased in real terms owing to cheap food imports from countries like USA, the danger that the working class would use their new health and energy to demand radical social and political reform was damped down by diverting their attention to the Empire. Imperial possessions allowed the European working class to feel superior to conquered and more primitive (although equally exploited) natives. Some of the more extreme left-wing workers did stress that imperialism was inimical

---

[15] The working class had political importance before the Reform Acts but it was of a different kind. Skilled upper-class leaders like Palmerston, who managed the workers through getting their support in foreign policy, drew much of their power from this aid.

to all workers since they, whatever their colour or creed, were exploited by capitalism. But the majority of the working class went nationalist and accepted Chamberlain's propaganda that imperialism was increasing their standard of living. Such early sociological comment as exists supports this diversion of working-class attention away from radical domestic reform to imperialism. Cecil Rhodes, for instance, believed that by 1895 the British class structure had absorbed as much radical reform as it could. He concluded that only by colonial expansion would Britain avoid civil war. Lenin noted this comment with interest.[16]

Rhodes' view gains credence if we look at the violent and uncontrolled way in which even Liberals in Britain responded to imperialism at the end of the nineteenth century. Men like Rosebery, Liberal Prime Minister from 1894–95, and later leader of the Liberal Opposition, made speeches intoxicated by ideas of force and supremacy. These Liberal speeches went further than those of the Conservative Imperialists, and certainly outran the reasoned pessimism of the Prime Minister, Salisbury. This paradoxical situation resulted from the fact that the modern Liberal Party was based on the dynamism of middle-class industrialists, and this manufacturing interest was well aware of the importance of cheap raw materials. In a sense empire, for this sector of the Liberal Party, was made acceptable by regarding it as part of the Free Trade system. In addition, the older reforming Whig interest which formed the other sector of the Liberal Party had been interested in reforms to produce good government rather than radical reform of society. Some members of the Liberal Party, like Bright and Morley, could not bring themselves to accept imperialism; others like Chamberlain himself turned away from radical reform to imperial reform. No doubt many of the Liberal imperialists felt twinges of conscience in turning away from radical domestic reform and hence tended to surpass the Conservatives in imperialistic vehemence; the Conservatives being without this stress were able to contemplate the Empire more dispassionately. We know that politicians respond as much to crowd passions as they create them. It appears that the industrial masses of the late nineteenth century, packed in decaying squalid tenements or oppressive workshops and factories, vented their frustration in the vicarious violence of imperialism.

[16] *Imperialism*, p. 96.

Late nineteenth-century imperialism is often called 'new', and one of the questions which must be considered is whether this epithet has any real meaning. One of the reasons why imperialism received this description was accidental. Many histories towards the end of the century referred in their titles and texts to the 'New Europe', the Europe of industrial revolution and modern nationalism. When Europe engaged in imperialism, this was christened 'new imperialism'. New in this sense stresses the extent to which late nineteenth-century imperialism was the product of modern technological Europe. The intensification of nineteenth-century industry called for raw products from all over the world, and as more countries industrialized, the competition for raw materials passed from the old, informal controls of trade and finance into the new phase of formal possession. Imperialism was still imperialism and only the method had altered under the stress of European competition.[17] Modern technology when applied to war gave late nineteenth-century imperialism another of its distinguishing features, swift ease of conquest. Railways, for example, could be used as Kitchener used them in the Sudan Reconquest, 1895–99, to take the danger out of much of desert warfare. The technical disparity in weapons of the modern type and those of pre-industrial warfare was vast. The ratio of native casualties to imperialist ones illustrated this discrepancy over and over again. At the Battle of Omdurman, for instance, on 2 September 1898 while British and Egyptian killed (and wounded) totalled 386, by contrast on the native, Dervish, side 11,000 were killed and 16,000 wounded; probably a sizeable number of the latter died afterwards.[18]

This ease of slaughtering other human beings gave the imperialists a sense of superiority which they did not care to analyse too closely. Sometimes their uneasiness was got rid of by making a joke of it and calling the natives various names, comparing them to animals rather than humans. This practice was not so very different from the way in which Nazi fascists later classed Jews and Slavs as 'Untermenschen'. The brutalizing effects of these episodes of slaughter, the so-called 'sporting wars', cannot be exaggerated; it goes some way towards illuminating the military and political mentality

[17] The accidental aspect was often overlooked, and as a result 'new' was equated with 'different'. It was then argued that nineteenth-century imperialism lacked continuity.

[18] Lord Cromer, *Modern Egypt*, London, 1911, one vol. edition, p. 541.

which tolerated the even greater European slaughter which followed only sixteen years later.

Imperial conquest had always rested on superior military power. But apart from the high degree of military superiority this period of imperialism was also distinguished by ease in retaining power after the initial conquest. Modern technology gave Europeans not merely swift means of conquest but also provided wireless transmission, telegraphs, telephones and more easily serviced coal and oil-fired vessels to replace the old wood-burning types. The improvement of communications between home governments and diplomats or colonial administrators meant that important decisions could be taken more quickly and at the centre of political power. The individual importance of Foreign Office or Colonial Office representatives declined sharply, although this alteration was masked in the years before the First World War, partly because imperial representatives still kept up style and protocol to impress those governed, and partly because there were a number of administrators like Lord Curzon, Viceroy of India (1898–1905), whose detailed knowledge far outranked that of their departments at home.

One of the major aspects of interest of new imperialism is the attempt to understand why informal imperialism altered to formal imperialism. European competition not merely for markets (often illusory) or raw materials but also for status to affect their ranking as European great powers clearly had a great deal to do with the change. But it seems probable that another major factor was the impact of modern communications on government in the sense that central government could now not only reach speedy decisions but could also enforce them with despatch. In the earlier years when communications were slow and infrequent and at times hazardous central governments were forced to delegate political and economic power usually to trading associations—such as the East India Company—but sometimes also to missionaries. In addition, since the development of railways and steamboats, apart from sea-going gunboats, facilitated retention of colonies, it was not now vital to colonize imperial possessions. This tendency was also encouraged by the unhealthy nature of many of the new colonies. It was sufficient to set up a number of consular posts and to provide relatively small garrison forces; if an emergency occurred, the home authorities were alerted and sent military or naval reinforcements. This factor —the absence of a need to colonize—meant that in many cases the central governments did not become involved in disputes with white-settler communities which wanted more political freedom. Political power in many of the areas of new imperialism remained concentrated in the hands of central governments. These two influences, the central governments' ability to reach and enforce speedy decisions and the absence or small size of settler communities, both encouraged formal imperialism instead of the earlier informal control. The shift from informal to formal imperialism is, in this sense, an aspect of the increasing power of the state in the late nineteenth century.

But in what other sense was new imperialism different from that of earlier years? It is difficult to argue that it was new in the sense that it represented, as used to be argued, an important swing back to imperialism after the swing away from it following the loss of the American colonies. As argued above, imperialism had always gone on throughout the nineteenth century and only the shift in key from informal to formal is important. Writers who have argued that there was a break in the chain tended to attach great importance to the date when, as they considered, late nineteenth-century imperialism began. Some authors consequently dated the new imperialism from the time of the Berlin Conference when Bismarck in 1884–85 took a hand in outlining a code of imperialism. But if this date is singled out, earlier and vital steps like Disraeli's purchase of 40% of the Suez Canal Shares in 1875 for about £4 million are passed over.[19] Or if 1875 is taken as the starting date, then this choice ignores the fact that between 1815 and the 1870s Britain worked away quietly in the colonial field stabilizing earlier gains. To mention only one case, in 1871 Britain purchased the Dutch forts on the Gold Coast (Ghana) and so united the whole coast under British control.[20]

The striking fact about the new imperialism at the end of the century was that it received—through the development of the cheap modern press[21]—much more publicity, for this was the time when

[19] More accurately 7/16ths of the shares. The voting powers of these Khedivial shares were limited and so Britain did not gain a controlling interest in the largely French-owned Suez Canal Company. In addition, the profits had already been mortgaged up to 1895 and it was not until then that Britain received an income from the shares. Their importance was political and commercial, i.e. they allowed the British government grounds to manœuvre for better representation on the management board of the Suez Canal Company.

[20] Britain had purchased the Danish forts on the Gold Coast in 1850. For further examples, see J. Gallagher and R. Robinson, 'The imperialism of Free Trade', *Economic History Review*, 2nd Series, Vol. IV, No. 1, 1953, pp. 2–3.

[21] The career of Lord Northcliffe (1865–1922) illustrates the growth of the popular press: in 1888 he founded *Answers*, in 1896 the *Daily Mail* followed by the *Daily Mirror* in 1903. Earlier, in 1894, he had taken over the *Evening News*.

the Education Acts of 1870 and 1891 were beginning to break down illiteracy. The Empire was news and made papers sell. In this way the British public became involved and knew of national events. When popular commanders who had won imperial victories returned to Britain in the 1890s they received adulation. Citizens flocked down to Dover to meet Kitchener on his return, and sang 'For he's a jolly good fellow' when his presence was noted at the theatre. But although there was by the 1880s and 1890s a strong degree of popular support for imperialism, it would be wrong to consider that the people had initiated imperialism. Clearly, the initiating work had been done earlier, in the 1870s, when the importance of colonies for the European balance of power began to be realized.

Earlier in the nineteenth century, formal imperialism was looked on unfavourably as a result both of Adam Smith's championing of Free Trade and the expensive wars attending the breakaway of the American Colonies. But this argument for an official and economist's dislike of colonization may not have influenced the public, and so the reaction against imperialism should not be overstressed. In 1849 the Radical M.P., J. A. Roebuck, commented :

> The people of this country have never acquiesced in the opinion that our colonies are useless; and they look with disfavour upon any scheme of policy which contemplates the separation of the mother country from the colonies. For this opinion, the people have been seldom able to render any adequate reason.[22]

Roebuck's argument, however, should perhaps be taken with a pinch of salt : he was one of the rising industrial middle class, an ironmaster, and the sort of man who wanted imperialism in order to provide cheap food for his workers and to keep down the prices of exports by using cheap raw materials.

v

The significant watershed for British views on imperialism occurred in Disraeli's closing years, and he, with his gift for political showmanship, did much to create public support for the new trend. In his earlier period, Disraeli took the conventional view of the colonies. In 1852 he dismissed 'these wretched colonies' as 'mill-

[22] Cited by A. G. L. Shaw, *Modern World History*, Melbourne, 1960, Vol. II, p. 1.

stones round our necks'; later, in 1867, he queried the value of these 'colonial deadweights'. Yet a few years later, in 1874, he came to power on a policy based on helping the first Empire colonies such as Canada, he instituted the title of Empress of India for Queen Victoria in 1877, and in 1875 had purchased the Suez Canal shares and sent the Prince of Wales to tour India. He pursued a forward colonial policy, and it was checks to this policy in Afghanistan and South Africa which partly led to his defeat in 1880.

The alteration in Disraeli's views on imperialism did not come from a deepening of his views on colonies as such, but rather from the realization that economic and diplomatic factors connected with Europe now made empire a significant exercise. No doubt, too, the element of mystery—which regions still far off and relatively unknown in those days held—also exercised a spell over him.

On the economic side of the balance sheet, it was becoming evident by the mid-1870s that although Free Trade had conquered Britain it was not going to conquer the world. Both on the Continent and in America Protectionism was growing (see above, Chapter 2, pp. 20–1). The success of Free Trade in Britain in the 1840s and 1850s under Peel and Gladstone in defeating mercantilism had encouraged a lack of interest in colonies. Yet politicians did not hasten to rid Britain of the supposed colonial encumbrances, and indeed, when forced to consider the colonies, ministers soon became interested in them.[23] In the 1870s, tariff barriers abroad were making it more difficult and more expensive for British goods to compete, and the emphasis was now on competition, for the former 'easy sell' of Britain's early days as 'workshop of the world' was gone. A permanent supply of cheap primary products from the colonies seemed a logical answer to the problem of keeping down the costs of British exports. It was not so much that Disraeli's colonial views *per se* altered but rather that growing Protectionism abroad modified his attitude towards Free Trade. He did not discard earlier well-based arguments on colonies as such, but now came fresh to the study of imperialism. This fact makes his enthusiasm understandable, for in age he had discovered a new, bright and exciting political toy.

The second factor which altered Disraeli's attitude towards colonies was equally Europe-oriented, and concerned balance of

---

[23] See, for example, Lord John Russell's comment on becoming Colonial Secretary in 1839, cited by Sir Llewellyn Woodward, *The Age of Reform 1815–1870*, Oxford University Press, 1962, p. 367.

power politics which were just beginning to become world politics again after the long lull since 1815. Britain was accustomed to keeping Europe open to her trade by giving judicious help to powers whenever it seemed that a hegemonial dictatorship might develop. But after the Franco-Prussian War of 1870–71, when Disraeli looked at the Continent, he saw the increase of peacetime and wartime strength in both France and Germany deriving from the industrial revolution and their large standing armies. The small British professional army could not compete with this sort of military power, for the commercial, peace-loving bias of the British, while it would tolerate naval expenditure, was unlikely to respond favourably to demands to build up the army unless an emergency had already occurred. Under Disraeli, therefore, the New World begins to be called in to redress the balance of the Old World, to use the famous but misleading phrase coined by Canning in 1822 (see above, Chapter 1, p. 5). Acting upon this strategy Disraeli sent Indian Army reinforcements to Malta in April 1878 to help coerce Russia into revising the Treaty of San Stefano (see above, Chapter 2, pp. 23–4). Once British power in the Near and Middle East increased, the value of troops hardened to service in a hot climate such as India went up. As Lansdowne, Minister for War (1895–1900), said later, when the Sudan was being reconquered, such British troops performed far better than those taken from a British city slum.

Disraeli's view that Britain must retain world power by increasing her Empire and strengthening the ties with white settler colonies like Canada was shared by a number of eminent publicists. One of these men was Sir Charles Dilke whose book *Greater Britain* was published in 1870. Another was Sir John Seeley, Professor of Modern History at Cambridge University (1869–94). To Seeley the dominant features of the nineteenth century were the rise of great men in association with nationalism. He had studied Napoleon's career, and his book *Ecce Homo* (1865) showed a balance of emphasis on the importance of great men and more long-term determinist factors. As Seeley saw it, Prussia was rising to major importance as the power-core of modern Germany. But if world history was looked at on a larger scale, he believed that the USA and Russia would dominate world politics in view of their economic and military potential. He argued that if Britain wanted to retain world influence, she must build up her empire so that her population and economic strength would match up to those of America and Russia.

Seeley published these views in *The Expansion of England* (1883) which became a widely read book.

VI

In this way the early stages of new imperialism began in the 1870s among the European states : for Britain, the impetus was the need to prevent the continental states from taking formal possession of colonial territory and establishing there the same high tariff pattern which might exclude Britain from former trading areas; for the continental states the argument was reversed. As they saw it, Protectionism at home and in their colonies was a defence against Britain's early start in industrialization.

It will always be difficult to disentangle the economic and political strands which created the early pattern for formal imperialism. European statesmen of this period were far more accustomed to thinking and talking in terms of political advantage rather than in the relatively new economic terms. For this reason it is easy to find that nearly all the statesmen associated with imperial gains had doubts about imperialism and often committed their countries to a course of aggrandizement with reluctance, amusement about hyperbolic terms such as 'civilization' and very little clear idea of what was to be gained. But one and all, they felt that new and powerful changes were taking place and that they could not allow their states to be pushed aside in the collective frenzy for colonies which took place from the 1870s onwards.

Late nineteenth-century imperialism meant that a system of international relations which had originated in Europe was now being spread outwards to draw into its grasp the rest of the world. Since the areas which were seized contained either relatively primitive peoples or peoples whose ancient culture had relapsed into primitiveness, the exercise of imperialism brutalized the European system of international relations by arousing easy assumptions of racial superiority. This brutalization affected the conduct of international relations within Europe itself and damaged conventions of diplomacy which, rather than use of force, had been developing. In the next chapter we will look at this sort of change as later imperialism develops.

REFERENCES

Cromer, Lord, *Modern Egypt*, London, Macmillan, and New York, Fertig, 1911.

Hobsbawm, E. J., *Industry and Empire. An Economic History of Britain since 1750*, London, Weidenfeld and Nicolson, 1968.

Koebner, R., *Empire*, Cambridge and New York, C.U.P., 1961.

Kohn, H., ed., *The Modern World: 1848 to the Present*, New York and London, Macmillan, 1964.

Lenin, V. I., *Imperialism, the Highest Stage of Capitalism*, Moscow, Foreign Languages Publishing House, 1962.

Marx, K. and Engels, F., *On Colonialism*, Moscow, Foreign Languages Publishing House, 1962.

Morrell, W. P., *British Colonial Policy in the Mid-Victorian Age*, London and Fair Lawn, New Jersey, O.U.P., 1970.

Passant, E. J., *A Short History of Germany 1815–1945*, Cambridge and New York, C.U.P., 1962.

Robinson, R. and Gallagher, J., *Africa and the Victorians*, London, Macmillan, and New York, Doubleday, 1961.

Woodward, E. L., *The Age of Reform, 1815–1870*, Oxford and Fair Lawn, New Jersey, Clarendon Press, 2nd Ed., 1962.

4 *Later Imperialism*

Initially new imperialism was connected more with European nationalism and nascent Protectionism than with any well-based assessment of the value of tropical and semi-tropical areas. In proof of this argument, we need only look at the poor returns gained from much of Africa in this period with the exception of Rhodesia. Most of the early British trading companies staggered along, narrowly avoiding bankruptcy, and had to be bought out by the state. The Royal Niger Company which had been chartered in 1886 to administer a trading concession around the Lower Niger river found that its revenue from palm oil was not sufficient both to provide profits and to build the necessary roads, bridges and railways. This company surrendered its charter to Britain in 1889.

The continental states pursued a different colonial policy from Britain. Not infrequently areas were first explored by soldiers or sometimes even administrators on long leave. The state then took over and tended to spend heavily on communications and set up administrative systems centralized with those in operation at home. This policy resulted, particularly in the case of Germany, in colonies top-heavy with civil servants and soldiers and increasingly strangled by bureaucratic red tape, which generally provided little profit, if any, once the running costs were deducted from revenue. The motivation for colonial involvement amongst the continental states varied a good deal, but almost invariably a tinge of envy existed towards Britain. The new states of Europe which had come late to nationhood were anxious to possess all the physical characteristics of their new status and tended to look towards older states like Britain to see what was desirable. It appeared that Britain was strong because she had an empire and so the new nations were emulative. Italy, as mentioned earlier, hoped to relieve high unemployment and to revive the glories of *mare nostrum* and the Roman Empire. For Jules Ferry, French Prime Minister in the 1880s, colonial development was in part a continuation of the earlier French overseas empire, and in part required in order to relieve French domestic tension over the German defeat of 1870–71. He wanted to divert his people away from dangerous brooding on the loss of Alsace-Lorraine and use up their energy in North and West Africa. Unfortunately, the similarity between French mortification over the loss of Alsace-Lorraine and chagrin at the fact that the British had displaced the French from obtaining control of Egypt meant that French anger with Germany mainly flowed into a new channel of anger with Britain. Thus, although French colonization went on elsewhere in Africa, it was Egypt which disastrously became the French pole star, and the frustrations which could not be relieved over one grievance were transferred to the other. This transference of feeling accounts for the extreme emotionalism and lack of reality of much of the French policy on Egypt after 1882. Belgian colonialism was different in that it was based on Leopold II's ambitions as sovereign and his main aim was to get money from the rubber industry in the Congo.

German imperialism was a much more complicated matter. Bismarck tried to avoid colonial involvement as long as possible since he knew that Germany might run into trouble with Britain or France or possibly both. So far as these two states were concerned he followed a policy of 'Divide and Rule' and tried to set them at each other's throats—with varying degrees of success—particularly over Egypt. Bismarck considered that colonies were a luxury which Germany with her Empire in Europe could not and need not afford. He also believed that to expect an extra-European empire as well as one in Europe might mean the risk of losing all by trying to grasp too much. As he used to remark : *'Qui trop embrasse mal étreint.'*[1]

But by the mid-1880s Bismarck's attitude towards German colonization was changing. Possibly he was a little bored with the success of his European diplomacy which meant that there could be little change in Europe. Perhaps, too, he wanted to channel off German industrial potential by expenditure on a skein of widely scattered and unprofitable colonies. While the reasons for his more relaxed control on German demands for colonies remain obscure, the pressures put upon him were clear enough. Politically Bismarck relied for support on the Conservatives and the National Liberals, but his state socialism had antagonized influential businessmen as well as landed gentry. To placate these groups, he allowed Dr. Peters in

[1] Count Bernstorff, *Memoirs*, London, 1936, p. 3.

c

1884 to take up a large area at Zanzibar, declared Angra Pequena (Orange River) a protectorate, and permitted Dr. Nachtigall to make treaties with West African chiefs as well as annexing Northern New Guinea. Later, under strong urgings from pressure groups such as the German Colonial League[2] and the German Colonization Company[3] and from individual businessmen such as the Godeffroys (Samoan Islands traders), the Woermanns (Cameroons traders), the Luderitzs (Angra Pequena) and the Hansings (Zanzibar), Bismarck allowed measures to be taken to improve and stabilize German colonization.

Bismarck's statements on German imperialism made it clear that he had no grandiose ideas about it : the aim was to increase and protect trade and to try to check the loss of population (to areas such as the USA) caused by the pockets of depression in the German economy in the 1870s and 1880s. But it remains doubtful how seriously he took these views, for not only was it soon apparent that the cost of German colonies was high and that, on the whole, they brought little gain, but also—even if Bismarck forgot these facts, which was unlikely—he was constantly reminded of them by criticism. The Social Democrats and the Radicals kept hammering away at the facts that the colonies taken were not good for settlement and brought poor economic gains. Bismarck's imperialism, particularly in the way he allowed it to occur over such a wide area, may have been intended by him as counters for later exchanges, but was more probably aimed at giving Germany a colonial foothold which would allow Bismarck to intervene if serious colonial trouble between other European states threatened to bring repercussions which might destroy the diplomatic checks and balances he had set up in Europe. This inherently contradictory system in Europe—as argued earlier —only existed on the assumption that the great powers remained inactive (see above, Chapter 2, pp. 27–8).

II

It is frequently implied that imperialism allowed for the harmless working-off of tensions generated among the nation states in Europe. This is a convenient but inaccurate theory, for war threatened on a number of occasions over colonial issues. Colonization did

---

[2] Founded in 1882 and by 1885 had 10,000 members.
[3] Founded in 1887 and later amalgamated with the German Colonial League to form the German Colonial Company.

not provide a successful substitute area for settlement of major European rivalries such as that between France and Germany,[4] although, as mentioned earlier, gains abroad did help for a time to lessen tension or to lubricate the working of what remained an essentially European system of international relations. But imperialism brought new problems and even as early as 1884 Bismarck was concerned about the possibility of a European backlash from abroad and consequently tried to take some of the heat out of colonizing. He convened a conference on imperialism in Africa and fifteen nations sent representatives. The Berlin West Africa Conference lasted from November 1884 to February 1885 and those present drew up a set of rules for the colonial game. The slave trade in Africa was to be outlawed. This worthy but inadequate resolution related to visible evidence of slave trading for export and not to the traditional use of slaves or neo-slaves in Africa (and Arab states), a problem which still exists today. The Conference also recognized the Belgian Congo State and gave it the name of Congo Free State, with access to the sea. All states were to have freedom of navigation for commerce on the Congo and Niger rivers.[5] It was agreed that states must establish effective control over their 'spheres of influence' before annexation took place. This provision was made in an attempt to check the near-farcical but explosive practice of rival Europeans following each other on circuits to persuade chiefs to sign treaties.

Many of these treaties were signed[6] but their legality was doubtful since the tribal leaders in most cases were unaware of their far-reaching implications. This disregard of the normal European criteria for legal documents—that those signing should realize the implications—is one more piece of evidence of the way in which customary European standards were ignored during imperialism. But the chief basis of imperialism in so far as the relationship between the European powers and the natives was concerned was conquest or so-called effective occupation; it was mainly in relation to inter-European disputes that the treaties had importance. Finally, the West Africa Conference stated that boundaries should be de-

[4] Even in the case of Franco-British rivalry over Egypt, powerful additional factors—such as the growth of the German navy—were needed to produce the 1904 Entente.

[5] When the Europeans wished to send troops on this route, they dressed them in civilian clothes and sent them upriver in small groups.

[6] On the treaty-signing race, see S. C. Easton, *The Rise and Fall of Western Colonialism*, New York, 1964, p. 89.

limited for the Congo Free State and the British and French West African territories. Thus, by this and similar arrangements, the European boundary system was imposed on Africa and lines were drawn often on inadequate maps with the result that tribes were split up and grazing and water rights ignored. In the decolonization phase even more serious political difficulties—such as so-called 'civil wars'—have occurred because of these arbitrary boundaries.

Looked at from a European point, however, the provisions of the Berlin West Africa Conference were admirable but the difficulty was to apply them in the colonial chaos then existing. The conference had been convened because of the dangers of European distrust: Portugal was annoyed because she had 'discovered' the Congo years before, but now Leopold II was opening it up to trade, and France was also showing an unwelcome interest; Britain and France were both involved in West Africa while Germany was now revealing ambitions in East Africa and the Cameroons, and had already in 1883 established the South West Africa colony. In the event, the West African area led to a number of serious disputes between the European powers and in particular to the Anglo-French war scare of 1898. From February to March of that year, war seemed to threaten, but Salisbury (with the knowledge that the autumn of 1898 would see the Anglo-French Nile crisis explode) was determined not to allow distractions in West Africa or China to weaken Britain in the Sudan or Egypt. After much diplomatic haggling a compromise settlement was made in June 1898.

The West African crisis had hardly been smoothed over when the even more tense Upper Nile dispute occurred. Technically, this crisis concerned only the Sudan and took place when British and French lines of conquest and exploration intersected but the French had cherished hopes that they could use it to force a resistant Britain to negotiate about the future of Egypt. However the French failed to persuade Menelek of Ethiopia to link his fate decisivly with them and the British threat of a naval attack in the Mediterranean led to a French climb-down. Hopes lingered that some Russian pressure might be applied, possibly by a threat concerning India but although the Russians had made such feints in earlier years they did not do so now.[7] By 1899 when it was clear that Russia (allied

[7] They lacked the necessary railway communication to carry out an effective Indian attack. Later, Delcassé, the French Foreign Minister, insisted on part of the French loans going towards this work but the improvement in Anglo-French relations rendered it superfluous. The railway concerned was the Orenburg-Tashkent line completed in 1904 which linked Moscow and the Afghan border.

with France since December 1893)[8] would not, or rather could not, do anything to help, the French accepted on 21 March an agreement with Britain which shut them out of the Nile Basin but left them free to control a vast area of 'light soil' (Salisbury's term for sand) running from Darfur on the east to Lake Chad in the west. The ultimate outcome of the Fashoda crisis, and of this agreement, was the Anglo-French Entente of 1904 but in the years immediately following 1899 relations between Britain and France remained poor.

III

By the end of the nineteenth century new imperialism had almost run its course in Africa. By then the balance sheet showed that Britain had obtained the lion's share of territory and this included much of the better land on the east of the continent. In 1884 Cecil Rhodes encouraged Britain to declare Bechuanaland a protectorate and in the following year Southern Bechuanaland was made into a Crown Colony. From 1889–93 Rhodes' British South Africa Company developed Matabeleland and this became part of Rhodesia. The Sudan itself became an Anglo-Egyptian Condominium in 1899 with Britain as the senior partner and in this way Britain made good the loss of the Egyptian Sudan which had followed the British occupation of Egypt in 1882. Uganda was declared a protectorate in 1894 and with Kenya became the British East Africa Protectorate in 1895 and moved to full Crown Colony status in 1920. Nyasaland had become a protectorate earlier, in 1891, and Zanzibar the year before. Somaliland acquired protectorate status in 1884. On the west coast of Africa, Ghana or the Gold Coast was annexed by the British as a territory in 1901 after a turbulent struggle with the Ashanti tribe. British West Africa or Nigeria was taken over by the British government in 1889 and the 'indirect rule' system based on combined use of tribal power and District Officers was established by Lord Lugard. In 1906 Lagos and Southern Nigeria were united and later, in 1914, North and South Nigeria were joined together. By 1899, apart from areas taken by France, Germany and Leopold II of Belgium, and territory held by Britain's traditional ally,

---

[8] From 1891 France and Russia had shared an informal agreement to consult if war threatened. During December 1893 and January 1894 the powers drew up a military convention (continued in 1899) for co-operation if trouble threatened from the Triple Alliance. In 1912 the Alliance was strengthened by the addition of a naval convention.

Portugal, most of the African map had been painted British red. But South Africa remained tantalizingly apart and desire to absorb this region led to the Boer War of 1899–1902.

By 1900 Britain had fifty colonies, using the word in the general and non-technical sense, France came second with thirty-three and Germany third—with the most scattered and least profitable empire —having thirteen. The British share of colonies covered 11½ million square miles, the French had approximately 3¾ million square miles while the Germans held over 1 million square miles. France had about a third as much territory as Britain, and Germany about a third as much as France. The areas which Britain held were the most highly populated : over 345 million natives; the French regions held just under 56½ million and the German areas had nearly 14¾ million. These figures are problematic, but they do illustrate the way in which population was rising rapidly as Western insistence on a high standard of public health, primarily in their own interests, cut mortality rates. To the French this accretion of population was welcome. Many of the French military élite were at heart revanchist and expected one day to be allowed to avenge the Franco-Prussian War of 1870–71 and to wrest back Alsace-Lorraine from Germany. The idea of using colonial troops to balance up France's own population of 39 million (1910) with Germany's of just under 64 million was welcomed.

IV

As the nineteenth century ended the question was where the compass needle of nationalistic competition would settle. Would it turn towards China, where Marx and Engels had expected it to settle in the 1880s, or to Africa? Or would it swing back towards Europe? In China the Manchu system was decaying but it might be expected to put up stronger resistance to the European incursion than had been provided by the indigenous population of Africa. This area was also far from the Central European heartland and consequently, unlike Africa, was not so easily seen as a field for the extension of European politics. Britain had taken part in the conquest of Africa to a great extent because of the importance of the Cape route, and later the Suez Canal route, to India. But Britain had no Egypt in China and was markedly reluctant to abandon the policy adumbrated by Lord Clarendon in 1870 that British interests in China were primarily commercial (on China, see below, Chapter 7). By the early twentieth century countries were also becoming aware of the relatively high cost of formal imperialism and they wanted mining and railway concessions, entrepôts and naval docks, but did not so keenly want large-scale territorial annexation in China. The states which had gained least from the conquest of Africa—Germany, Russia and Italy—were those which (apart from Japan) were most interested in the possible division of China.

Europe and China were the alternative fields for nationalistic competition at the end of the nineteenth century. It was clear to writers and diplomats that if the compass needle of competition did swing back to Europe, then conflict would be destructive to a degree never before witnessed, partly because of heavy armaments and the wide spread of alliances, but also because the European states had become accustomed to a freedom of action in Africa which had never existed in Europe. A feeling of uncertainty existed in diplomatic circles. With the ending of the struggle for areas in Africa, some of the tensions which had helped to influence the patterns of European diplomacy for about thirty years had worked themselves out. The most important of these cases was the technical ending of the Anglo-French struggle for Egypt after the Sudan failed to prove the French key to Egypt in 1898. But other new tensions had developed particularly concerning modern Germany. William II considered that although Germany should now rank with the main powers in Europe yet her extra-European influence and status did not match up to her European position. Germany had picked up a handful of colonies in Africa and the Pacific but these were not commensurate with her European grading.

v

When the German sovereign asked himself why this discrepancy existed he found various answers: one was that Germany had entered the colonial race late because Bismarck took little interest in gains outside Europe. But even this argument could be considered exaggerated since Bismarck had exercised less restraint over colonial ambitions by the mid-1880s, and William II looked for the answer elsewhere. He found convincing explanations of Germany's relatively poor colonial gains in the weakness of the German navy, and the over-indulgence of her diplomacy towards Britain. In the second instance, one notable example was the way in which Germany in 1890 abandoned her claims to Witu, Uganda, Nyasaland and Zanzibar in return for Heligoland. Admittedly, Heligoland was important as a naval base, but had too much been given for it? German speculations along these lines led to a growing view that while Britain almost invariably received German diplomatic complaisance, she did little to deserve it and tended to ignore any informal German aid when agreements were made.

William II's policy from the mid-1890s was directed at remedying these two weaknesses. But he failed to calculate seriously enough how Britain would react to the growth of a powerful German navy just across the North Sea and to repeated German diplomatic pinpricks. The pinpricks without the navy would have been irritating to the British but it was the combination of an apparent German tendency to threaten and the increasing power of doing serious naval harm which began to alarm the British Foreign Office. When William II started this policy, Britain and France were still at loggerheads over the future of Egypt and there was a possibility that this antagonism might even lead to war between them. To the German ruler, who had grown up in the period when Anglo-French enmity caused by colonial competition was the norm and so equally seemed Anglo-German friendship, radical change in these British relationships seemed possible in theory but not in practice. But he overestimated the degrees of enmity and friendship and while he believed he was playing a game to modify diplomatic relationships, in fact he helped to destroy some of these relationships and to create other new ones.

The diplomatic revolution which occurred between 1899 and 1904 was sudden. Britain and France moved from a danger of war over Egypt in 1898–99 to a general colonial settlement and entente in 1904. William II had considerable knowledge of the workings of diplomacy and of the state of feeling in Britain and France, but the speed of the change outran his expectations. And it is clear that the change also outran national emotion in Britain and France, as the quick revival of British sympathy for Germany and lack of understanding of French difficulties showed immediately after the First World War. The 1904 revolution in Anglo-French relations was mechanical rather than one of matched thought and emotion and this brought considerable problems in the inter-war period as well as helping to pave the way to the Second World War. William II's miscalculations about Britain and France on his western front were matched by similar misunderstandings about Russia. He tended to believe that the strength of the Franco-Russian Alliance was less than it was in reality because he could easily spin about the opinions of his cousin, Nicholas II.

VI

By 1900 uncertainty was the keynote of European diplomacy. To some observers, it seemed as though Britain and France might go to war with each other once the Paris Exhibition of that year was over. To William II, it seemed politic to encourage increasingly expensive naval programmes, partly in order to solve the practical problem of Germany's tremendous economic power and partly for security. To the British, who since Trafalgar had always used naval power as the gauge of their strength, it appeared equally necessary to begin to improve their naval position by clarifying and defining responsibilities and the means of executing them. In this way, events were set in train for the Anglo-Japanese Alliance of 1902 and the Anglo-French Entente of 1904. Success in imperialism had for about thirty years disguised from the British that the rise of modern Germany had destroyed Britain's balancing role in European diplomacy. Britain was now, unwillingly, sliding back into active diplomatic play and the consequences of this change were to be of world-wide importance. The problem was that the long peace on the European continent had derived, apart from concentration on industrialization and imperialism, from the relative balance of French and German power. It had also rested on British acceptance of a certain reduction in French power and prestige and the understanding that after 1870–71 Germany was a sated power. But now, as Germany seemed about to upset this system, pressures grew on Britain to side with France. This re-alignment was dangerous since France was already allied with Russia, and inevitably German fears of encirclement revived swiftly. The Triple Alliance of Germany, Austria and Italy was stronger on paper than in reality. The Austro-Hungarian Empire was split by nationalist divisions, and Italy was veering towards France which seemed more likely to satisfy her colonial ambitions than Germany. From 1900 onwards all, therefore, depended very much on what Germany would choose to do, and particularly on the degree of freedom of action which she would accord to her Austrian ally in the Balkans.

This potential danger existed at a time when the system of compromise diplomacy associated with the Concert of Europe had become static in part because of the damaging effect which imperial-

ism had on Europe. It is often argued and with economic accuracy
that Western imperialism caused long-term impoverishment of
colonial areas. But it is equally true that imperialism was of major
disservice to Europe itself, not merely because it used abroad scarce
resources which would have been better employed at home in industry[9] and social development but also because for about thirty years
Europeans concealed from themselves the dangers which nationalism and industrialization operating hand-in-hand brought to the
practice of international relations. Earlier in the nineteenth century,
the Congress System followed by the Concert of Europe had some
success in ameliorating the rougher edges of nationalistic competition. But by the end of the nineteenth century when tension was
flowing back into Europe itself, as Salisbury saw it, the nation states
had a choice between carrying on along potential collision courses
or of subordinating their ambitions and giving up a portion of their
authority to the Concert of Europe. By 1897, however, British
experience of international co-operation, as seen at work in the
Egyptian Public Debt Commission (i.e. *Caisse de la Dette Publique*), and in relation to the disorders of the Ottoman Empire, led
Salisbury to conclude that 'the Concert of Europe has conclusively
shown that it can never be trusted with even the slenderest portion
of Executive Authority'.[10]

Had European attention not been focussed on overrunning
Africa, the tensions in Europe, and the reasons for those tensions,
might have been analysed and some system of control or adjustment
through the Concert of Europe might have developed. As it was,
statesmen merely lamented the dangers of war and acceded to popular demands for more and more armaments. By 1900, too, the arrogance with which the European powers carried out their imperial
duties was being translated back to the European scene, and in
battles between national presses bullying slogans lost nothing of
their virulence. Every nation blamed some other nation. The
apotheosis of this name-calling came after the First World War,
when instead of admitting that the system was rotten, the victor
nations chose to label Germany as the nation with the greatest
responsibility for the war.

[9] Hobsbawm, *Industry and Empire*, 125, 202; A. R. Hall (ed.), *Export of Capital from
Britain 1870–1914*, London 1968; D. H. Aldcroft, *The Development of British Industry
and Foreign Competition 1875–1914*, London 1968; A. L. Levine, *Industrial Retardation
in Britain 1880–1914*, London, 1968.
[10] Salisbury to Sir Philip Currie (British Ambassador in Turkey), 19 October 1897,
Salisbury Papers, vol. 138, Christ Church, Oxford.

Study of international relations demonstrates that history flows in tides. There are periods of inflow when there is a growth of tension and when inter-state co-operation takes the form of alliances or arrangements for war. In the time of ebb, after sharp crises or war itself, change and relaxation follows, and the inter-state agreements concern maintenance of peace settlements or, as in more recent periods, intensive attempts at social and economic co-operation in order to check factors—such as poverty and industrial depression—which provide breeding grounds for aggression and war. Late nineteenth-century imperialism is one aspect of the inflow of tension building up to a climacteric and release by territorial conquest largely in Africa. But it is wrong to separate land annexation in Africa from that which occurred slightly earlier in Europe when Germany defeated France, for both of these developments were part of the same phase of territorial annexation and aggression. Had Africa not existed, or had modern technology not related it so closely to Europe, probably there would have been intensified struggle on the European continent. Fear and collective hysteria play a large part in international politics and it seems that once a strong channel of aggression is carved out, other tensions tend to find expression along the same channel. The cumulative factor in late nineteenth-century imperialism must not be overlooked. From 1870 to 1914 there was a build-up of tension between the nation states in part due to the sense that national boundaries and national alliances were hardening. As populations grew and industrialization developed, the old system of change by war became more and more difficult; there seems also to have been a sense of constriction and a desire to find new areas where change could express itself more easily. Imperialism was only one aspect of European aggressiveness at the end of the nineteenth century. Imperialism did not, of course, end abruptly with that century but continued to exist as a strand of nation-state aggression, but it was never again displayed so clearly until the period of Japanese expansionism prior to and during the Second World War.[11]

Late nineteenth-century imperialism was a complex phenomenon born of technology, new military strength and desire for change; it often represented a field of action for influences which were begin-

[11] By contrast, the 'imperialism' which in documents of the 1920s is often held to account for the outbreak of the First World War was a much more mixed phenomenon, an omnibus term of abuse and dissatisfaction used as comprehensively as the 'imperialism' of the 1960s.

ning to find expression within Europe itself more difficult, factors such as religion, conquest, class domination. Not infrequently statesmen of this period, accustomed to war as an accepted means of change, yet equating the increase of industrialization with growth of European civilization, would express the view that it would not be right for such nations to war together. War must be banished to the periphery of the European state system and conducted against those not civilized by industrialization. As for the motivation of imperialism, this depends on the strata of society under analysis and on the professions of those concerned. To statesmen in charge of national policy, imperialism was primarily a medium where European tensions found a vent but, necessarily, as time passed and involvement grew, this basic attitude was overlaid by new complications. There were some politicians who never shared this European preoccupation to the same extent, men such as Chamberlain, but they were the exception, or at least the exception at the governing level. For the Europe-oriented statesmen, strategy was the main consideration in relation to imperialism, i.e. European rivals must not be allowed to gain a march outside Europe because ultimately this might redound on the European stage.

This approach, inevitable in national leaders of the period brought up and educated at a time when Europe led the world, meant that although individual administrators in the colonies might have considerable status, yet their views in a crisis were subordinated to European considerations.[12] As a result of this attitude, combined with the class structure of the period, native populations were subjected to an off-hand paternalism usually thought out in relation to European rather than extra-European populations. The African or Asian was considered to be an imperfect version of man, one who might at some far-off time in the future be allowed to rule his own people.

If evidence on imperialism is sought from economic writers or the early politico-sociologists like Lenin, then the economic motive tends to be uppermost and the gains of imperialism are overstressed. Some politicians like Chamberlain no doubt exaggerated the economic motive in order to appeal to the powerful and politically rising ranks of industrialists who would welcome cheap supplies of raw

[12] Cromer, for example, at the height of the Fashoda crisis would have been willing to allow the French a foothold in the Bahr-el-Ghazal in return for French financial concessions concerning Egyptian revenue. But this idea never received serious consideration by members of the British Cabinet except the Chancellor of the Exchequer, Sir Michael Hicks Beach.

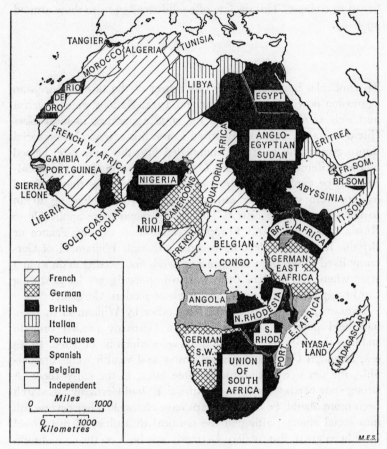

The Partition of Africa, 1914

materials. If we turn to historians of the time, we find that they saw
imperialism very much in the terms of the upper middle class from
which they mostly came. For these writers, money was a dirty word,
a subject one did not discuss. They saw empire in larger and more
grandiose terms : it was the individual and national response of the
superior western races to their responsibility for those races which
God had chosen to endow less richly. Similarly, but even more selectively, Christians believed that it was their mission to carry the one
religious truth to the heathen. Confidence is the factor which unites
all these views. Imperialism was a gigantic Western confidence
trick. Once Europeans became less confident, the whole system

began to collapse. This decline of confidence begins to show around 1906–07.

VII

To conclude, imperialism was one aspect of the tide of European aggression flowing between 1870 and 1914. Nations were powerful and rich as never before, and the state apparatus, in most cases élite-dominated, was not organized to use this new wealth on social improvement and so it was channelled into the arms race, helped by the vociferous popular press. One writer has argued that imperialism can be explained in terms of social atavism, i.e. that national leaders were still acting out warrior-type roles belonging to an earlier structure of society.[13] This theory seems more applicable to Russia and the Central European states than to, say, France or Britain. But it is misleading because although William II of Germany liked to posture with sword in hand, and needed to do so in a state where the military caste was so important, yet his posturing can be explained in terms of the needs of modern Germany.

Bismarck, who was dismissed from office by William II in 1890, had held power in the period when Germany needed time to stabilize the gains made by the three wars which he initiated. In his era, although German industrial power and wealth were considerable, the decisive breakthrough came later, in the early 1890s. A strong state needs some form of expression; had Germany's monarch been more liberal, he could perhaps have channelled her new wealth into social change, although the political difficulties of this would have been great. But modern Germany was built on the core of military Prussia and her institutions were geared to war and not peace. When William II looked for new lines of development, he chose naval power and imperialism, no doubt partly because Bismarck had frowned on these choices.[14] Similarly, for other Western leaders at this time, there were reasons why they felt they must go along with the imperial tide although often with considerable scepticism, as in the case of Salisbury. The aggression in Western European society at the end of the nineteenth century was not so much due to

---

[13] Joseph A. Schumpeter, *Imperialism and Social Classes*, London, 1951.
[14] The tension between Bismarck and William II, contrary to what is sometimes stated, had already showed itself before the death of Emperor Frederick. When the emperor was dying it was being said at court, 'Then we might have to bury two Emperors within no long space of time!' F. Curtius (ed.), *Memoirs of Prince Chlodwig of Hohenlohe Schillingsfuerst*, London, 1906, II, p. 381.

excess panache in its élite leaders but to the fact that governmental institutions were slow to develop to accommodate the new wealth and power conferred by industrialization and the rapid expansion of world trade and finance. Similarly, the international system failed to keep pace with this growth in power amongst the nation states.

The search for a common denominator in late nineteenth-century imperialism seems, therefore, a wild goose chase. The different strata of society had their own reasons for emotional and intellectual involvement in imperialism, and, strategy apart, individual leaders exhibit different patterns of reason in relation to it. The unifying factors in imperialism were general European confidence inspired by economic growth and the intensification of the ordinary competitiveness of European nation states by transference to the extra-European area where the normal checks and balances on aggression did not exist. It was easy to use economic window-dressing to try to interest both businessmen and the working class in imperialism. But the economic and financial gain from much of the territory taken at the end of the nineteenth century was low compared both with the expectations and the gains made from exporting goods and capital to the developed world sector. We must also remember that the technological gap between Europe and say, Africa, was immense and the consequent ease of conquest meant that a little motive went a long way; or, to put it differently, we should not forget Max Weber's comment that it is military rather than economic organization which makes history.

REFERENCES

Beloff, M., *Imperial Sunset*, Vol. I, *Britain's Liberal Empire, 1897–1921*, London, Methuen, and New York, Knopf, 1970.

Bernsdorff, Count, *Memoirs*, London, Heinemann, 1936.

Easton, S. C., *The Rise and Fall of Western Colonialism*, London, Pall Mall, and New York, Praeger, 1964.

Grenville, J. A. S., *Lord Salisbury and Foreign Policy*, London, Athlone Press, and Fair Lawn, New Jersey, O.U.P., 1964.

Judd, D., *The Victorian Empire 1837–1901*, London, Weidenfeld and Nicolson, and New York, Praeger, 1970.

Langer, W. K., *The Diplomacy of Imperialism 1890–1902*, New York, Knopf, 1956.

Lowe, C. J., *Salisbury and the Mediterranean 1885–1896*, London, Routledge and Kegan Paul, and Toronto, University of Toronto Press, 1965.

Porter, B., *Critics of Empire*, London, Macmillan, and New York, St Martin's, 1968.

Priestley, H. I., *France Overseas*, New York, American Historical Association, and London, Cass, 1938

Schumpeter, J. A., *Imperialism and Social Classes*, Oxford, Blackwell, and New York, Kelley, 1951.

5 *The Approach to the First World War*

I

In the last two chapters we have seen how the European great powers were becoming stronger through the profits of commerce, shipping and finance. They also had increasing power over their subjects; and citizens, affected by the neo-military discipline of industry, came to accept controls on their behaviour and on their purses which a generation or so earlier would have been unthinkable. In most countries the press aided the state in leading citizens along the paths which the state indicated. This was not simply because some countries, like Germany and Russia, had semi-official newspapers, but because even in countries like Britain most newspapers—and especially the new popular ones such as the *Daily Mail* —supported capitalism and were an important aspect of it. The influence of the press then was greater than it is now when people have more education and greater means of comparing information given in newspapers with that presented by other media such as television. This period before the First World War was still a time when people tended to believe that what they read in their newspapers must be true. And the bright new dailies, packed with information and also hints of how to make slender budgets go further, which had tended to stir up imperialism in the 1890s, now concentrated in the early twentieth century on material showing trade rivalry and tensions between the great powers. These sort of newspapers had found that nationalism was a winner; they did not forget this lesson of the imperialist outburst, but just turned it to different ends. It is evident that many workers responded easily to the nationalist drum, for the press did not create nationalism. But the press rendered this aspect of society obvious and probably magnified it; the press made nationalism volatile and a subject of news. Just as today the Balance of Payments figures focus attention and concern, so did nationalism at the end of the last century. Any editor who could report on a clash between the major states could sell his papers. And the tension was such that even minor embroilments—

such as the Dogger Bank Incident in 1904—between nationals of different states might spark off trouble.

Nationalism at the end of the nineteenth century was a product of the striving of states to be strong and to make their influence felt in world affairs. It created a vicious circle in that it urged the state to encourage research to obtain the best and latest weapons of war, weapons which, if used, would tear down the fabric of international trade and finance which had been created in the years of peace. Statesmen were well aware of the dangers which use of the new weapons would bring. But then—as now—they tended to argue, as Salisbury did, that their use was unthinkable, so there was a thought vacuum between the military technologist who concentrated on how to obtain maximum kill and destructive results in war and the civilian sector which did not like to contemplate the holocaust which could ensue. But since none of the major powers wished to give up the right to wage war should they consider that the vital interests of their states required this, little was done to prevent the danger that any minor crisis might set the army machines into action. Even the Hague Conferences of 1899 and 1907[1] were more concerned with refining war rather than seriously encouraging disarmament.

Apart from these difficulties in the way of checking the danger of war, the legacy of *laissez-faire* in nineteenth-century thought also impeded action. One of the most striking aspects of nineteenth-century history was the tremendous economic change associated with industrialization. A web of international trade held the nation states together in mutual interdependence. It was believed that both self-interest and the importance of industrialists and financiers—who it was assumed would lose and not, as happened often, gain more money in war than in peace—would restrain the sections of society which might want war. This is the favourite nineteenth-century device of automatic adjustment again at work. But writers such as Henry Noel Brailsford, author of *The War of Steel and Gold* (1914), underestimated the effect of nationalism on industrialists and financiers and did not allow sufficiently for the fact that although these individuals might be very wealthy they often did not have political importance commensurate with their wealth. Nor did such thinkers allow sufficiently for the inbuilt nature of war in modern society based as it was on competing nation states, and

[1] The Conferences originated from a proposal made by Tsar Nicholas II in 1898 when Russian finances necessitated a reduction of pace in the arms competition.

their heavy emphasis on the wrongs of individual armaments makers[2] in making profits from death indicates this superficial approach to the problem of war. Another argument, connected with nineteenth-century prosperity and the middle-class society which arose with it, was that war could not occur between major civilized states. This view was heard towards the end of the century when countries like Britain and France were being urged to turn their military capabilities against natives and not against each other. But this argument tended to be used selectively as, for instance, when Hanotaux, the French Foreign Minister, was trying to avoid war with Britain over the Sudan.

II

But areas for imperialist activity were now in short supply. By 1900 most spare territory in Africa had been seized upon. The major powers then turned their gaze towards China and considered the tempting profits which might come from its conquest. However, Britain and America were not keen to see China split up into high-tariff regions under control of powers like Germany and France and they used their influence to check a scramble for China (see below, Chapter 7). Also, it had been clear since the episode after the Sino-Japanese War of 1894–95 when Germany, France and Russia interfered to check Japanese aggrandizement that Japan was preparing for war with Russia over areas such as Korea. This did not occur until 1904–05 when Japan soundly defeated Russia. But by this date the major European powers were too concentrated on difficulties within their own area to take advantage of Chinese weakness, and it was Japan which in the inter-war period gained control of much Chinese territory. Instead of a partition of China, France took most of the southern areas later known as French Indo-China, Korea passed to Japan in 1905 and was formally annexed in 1910 and Russia negotiated annexatory treaties now (1971) in dispute with Communist China. But the other major states did not make vast territorial gains and contented themselves with taking ports such as the British Wei-hai-Wei and trade concessions. In 1911 the Kuomintang revolution took place and Dr. Sun Yat-sen came to power and began to try to reform China; on his death in 1925 Chiang Kai Shek obtained control.

[2] Now, in the early 1970s, the inbuilt aspect of war is clear as states have succeeded individuals in arms making and selling.

The failure to precipitate a scramble for China was particularly disappointing to William II of Germany. As early as 1894 he had told the Russian Tsar, Nicholas II, that he would like Germany to have a Chinese port in a region where it would not annoy Russia. Later on the German navy carried out surveys of the Chinese coast and when two German missionaries were murdered, William II used their deaths as justification for sending naval forces to take Kiaochow in November 1897. Germany set up a naval base at Tsingtao as well as obtaining a ninety-nine-year concession over a vast area of about two hundred square miles. This concession included mining and railway rights and led to the extension of German power in the Shantung province and the construction of a railway from Tsingtao on the Yellow Sea to Tsinan on the Hwang (Yellow) River. But by the late 1890s it was proving difficult to persuade German banks to subscribe capital for German colonies and so little profit either in terms of returns on capital or export of goods seems to have accrued to Germany from her territory in North China. But, as stressed earlier, economic gains or their possibility provided good window-dressing. William II's motives however were more concerned with demonstrating that Germany was a world power and gains in China symbolized this status. But the German position was relatively weak and in 1914 Japan overran the area and took Kiaochow which she held until 1922.[3]

As a result of the seizures of ports and the gain of concessions by Germany, Britain, Russia and France, Chinese xenophobia developed (see below, Chapter 7). The ageing Empress Dowager Empress Tzu Hsi decided to use this feeling and encouraged 'The Society of Harmonious Fists' or 'Boxers' in their attacks on foreign missionaries, traders and diplomats. The German Minister, Baron von Ketteler, was murdered by an Imperial bannerman. His fate had been sealed earlier when he allowed German troops to fire on Tung Fu-hsiang's Moslem cavalry.[4] The legations were put under siege, but on 14 August a force with units from six nations lifted the siege. A disgraceful looting of Peking then occurred, followed later by an equally disgraceful but more selective plunder of Chinese Imperial treasures by the great powers.[5] Strong punitive measures were taken by the Europeans against the Boxers and the resentment they aroused encourage Sun Yat-sen's nationalist republican movement.

[3] Japan retook Kiaochow in 1938 and held it until 1945.
[4] Peter Fleming, *The Siege at Peking*, London, 1960, pp. 84–94.
[5] Fleming, *The Siege at Peking*, p. 217.

But even after this furore died down China remained largely intact and was still nominally independent, but although not torn apart by a European scramble for territory such as Africa had seen, her future history for many years was to be dismal. The power of the central government, weakened by superstition and protocol and struggles for leadership, steadily declined. War lords took over throughout China, and the law and order given by the Manchu dynasty became a thing of the past. Isolation and poverty stamped the Chinese in this period and these two features, combined with traditional intellectual arrogance, led Communism to be adopted in an extreme form.

III

The failure of the Boxer Rising to sound the tocsin for a European scramble for China coincides with the time when European eyes were turning again to their own continent. Precisely why this change should have occurred around 1900 is difficult to explain, although how it happened is clear enough. But it is important to remember that imperialism continued well on into the twentieth century and that no hard and distinct line can be drawn. One of the major factors was that imperialism as it occurred at this time contained a large element of nationalistic competition between the major European powers. If the competition for an area was strong enough, new patterns of strategical thought came into play. In the case of Africa, this happened both internally and concerning the maritime coast, particularly in the Mediterranean and at its three entrance points of the Gibraltar Straits, the Black Sea and the Suez Canal. But similar intense competition did not occur over China. Africa and the Mediterranean area had an immense appeal to the European mind, steeped as it was in knowledge of Greek and Roman imperialism. But China had been on the world's edge of these classical cultures. And, at the beginning of the twentieth century, China's distance from the European heartland still tended to check the full effects of attempts to draw her into the extra-European network of politics.

The force of British imperialism was also beginning to decline,[6]

[6] Although British (and other) imperialism flared up again before, during and after the First World War, since that war provided the possibility of gains in areas such as the former Ottoman Empire territory in the Near and Middle East. The discovery of oil initiated a fresh wave of economic and financial imperialism in this area.

and since Britain had been such an important pathfinder for the other European states, we must not underestimate the significance of her new critical path. The rule for many years had been that where Britain went, it would be economically profitable and strategically necessary to follow. And now the needle of Britain's compass was quivering round to the home area. She had taken more imperial territory than any other country but now she needed time to absorb the implications, economic, social and political. However this time for thought never came. After the Boer War, overt interest in empire declined. Then rapidly came the build-up towards the First World War followed by the Depression of the 1920s and 1930s, followed in its turn by the Second World War and the shifting off of colonial responsibilities grown too heavy which we over-dignify by the name of decolonization.

By 1900 empire was no longer a bright new idea. It had become part of the Establishment and as such was up for attack. The willingness to attack was connected with economic and social changes in Britain. The rise of the trade unions and the initial foundation of the Labour Party as the 'Labour Representation Committee' in 1900 gave a new political importance to the working class.

The Boer War was a considerable shock to British confidence. It showed up the obsolescence of military tactics and materials, as well as revealing bitter feuds amongst the army chiefs. After a struggle whicn was often intense Britain managed to win the war by the spring of 1902. But the war had considerably dented the British image of successful competence. This was particularly so in relation to Germany. The Germans had argued earlier that prosperity had weakened the 'English fibre', but, as Lloyd George noted, the defeat of British forces during the war encouraged continental and German belief that Britain was now degenerate.[7] If he was correct, this view may partly account for German willingness to try to push Britain in the years before 1914, perhaps in order to see just how much she would take. But apart from encouraging German belief in British degeneracy, the Boer War, like the 'sporting' colonial wars, foreshadowed what was to come when military logic was applied to civilian populations. This war led Kitchener to check civilian support for Boer guerillas by setting up the first modern concentration camps. To the British the Boer War taught the lesson of vulnerability. This came partly through fears of continental combination against Britain while she was bogged down in South Africa and

[7] *War Memoirs of David Lloyd George*, London, 1938, 1, p. 19

partly through the realization that although Britain had a vast peacetime spread in terms of territory, naval power and military links, yet she lacked efficient defensiveness if her empire was challenged.

For Britain, one result of the Boer War was a process of reform throughout the Army, Navy and Foreign Office. In the Army reforms were carried out by men such as Broderick and Haldane. The latter, for example, created the General Staff in 1906 and organized the nucleus of the British Expeditionary Force which was to interpose such an effective spoke to check the implementation of the Schlieffen Plan in 1914. The Boer War also taught the British that they must overhaul their imperial rule and must begin to make some concessions to the peoples whose lands they ruled. This process began in South Africa itself when the Orange Free State and Transvaal were granted self-government in 1906–07. In 1909 the Union of South Africa was created from these two states plus Natal and Cape Province. By the constitutional arrangements then made, Britain accepted a built-in situation of inferiority for the coloured peoples, since in the former Boer states only the whites with property had the right to vote whereas in Cape Province all persons with the required property qualifications could vote. The tension between the one attitude to the natives and the other was to prove a source of much future trouble. But in other colonies where the dominant pressure was from the coloured population itself, Britain made similar concessions to their élite. This occurred notably in India.

As early as 1892 some Indian notables were nominated as members of the Legislative Council and were also appointed to similar councils in the provinces. But, as in the Egyptian Chamber of Notables, these nominees could only ask questions and criticize; in short, they lacked power. In 1909 the Morley-Minto reforms gave India another step forward. By the Indian Councils Act the legislative councils were to become essentially elective and Indians were to be nominated to sit on the Executive Council in India and the Secretary of State for India's Council in London. These reforms are sometimes treated as though they were a step on the way to self-government, but this is misleading. Certainly the reforms gave more Indians practice in government, but they gave little or no training in political power for, as members of the councils objected, not infrequently the elected members would defeat a proposal emanating from the Viceroy only to find that the nominated members remained in the council and that the defeated proposal was implemented.[8] Indeed, it might well be argued that the Minto-Morley Reforms, combined with the need to promise political concessions during the strains of the First World War, were the major irritants encouraging Indian resistance to British political control.

IV

But while the decline in British confidence caused by the lessons of the Boer War began to produce a chain reaction of varied imperial concessions, the tide of danger in European international relations was rising and British attention was focussing on Europe itself and the possible sources of war. Misuse of a quotation by Salisbury sometimes leads to the term 'splendid isolation' being used as a shorthand phrase to cover British diplomacy prior to 1902 when the Anglo-Japanese alliance was made. Britain never could have safeguarded her wideflung interests, nor her vital need to keep Europe open to her trade, by anything resembling splendid isolation. But there is a distinction between British diplomacy before and after 1902. Up to 1902 Britain, largely because her power was on the whole unchallenged, occupied a fulcrum position in international relations. She was a central magnet and around her clustered patterns of alliances composed of other sovereign states. The British balancing position, existing because there was tension between the two other major European states, Germany and France, required that Britain stand aloof from their alliances.

This was the policy which Britain followed. It did not mean that arrangements for co-operation were not made when required, although it did mean that almost without exception these arrangements were for once and for all action. There were exceptions such as the British links with the Triple Alliance through the Mediterranean Agreements made to deal with the long-continued and potentially explosive question of partitioning the Ottoman Empire. But even the Mediterranean Agreements were amorphous, and the more their implications and operation are studied, the more nebulous they become. Again, it may be argued that even Salisbury sometimes made arrangements which involved future co-operation and tied up Britain for an indefinite period. The Anglo-German Portuguese agreement of 30 August 1898 laid down that in return for

[8] Minutes of International Advisory Committee, Labour Party Archives, Transport House, London.

Germany renouncing interest in Delagoa Bay, Britain would allow Germany to take up part of any loan to Portugal with the Portuguese colonies as collateral. If it had become operative this agreement would have involved Britain in co-operation with Germany to divide up the empire of Portugal which by tradition was a British friend.

But Britain did not want more colonies nor did she want Germany, which had tended to encourage the Boers, to develop near South Africa. Why then should Salisbury, one of the most skilled diplomats of his time, have made such an unlikely agreement? It has been argued that he was buying time before the Boer War[9] but it is also important to note that he demonstrated to his Cabinet, particularly Chamberlain, that over-activity in diplomacy is a fault. He also demonstrated that Britain lacked material to make a colonial agreement sufficiently important for German policy to be materially affected. Irony is a major vein in Salisbury and no doubt privately he enjoyed following every letter of the new forceful diplomacy advocated by Chamberlain and yet at the same time making a complete mockery of it. No loan was made by Britain and so the agreement never became operative. So much for Britain's arrangements for indefinite co-operation in the years before 1902.

The advantage of the type of diplomacy practised by Salisbury was that it laid stress on the fact that problems needed time to mature before solutions could be found through peaceful bargaining. In addition, although Salisbury's diplomacy was based on a firm awareness of British vital interests, he did not believe in having fixed lists of these interests. These two attitudes meant that he was well aware of the dangers of over-activity in diplomacy. But the new diplomacy of the late 1890s and early twentieth century as practised by men such as William II of Germany or Chamberlain consisted essentially of diplomatic shopping lists headed 'We want'. This new diplomacy was affected by the prevalent business ethic, not the older *compromise* formula of international relations which underlay agreements such as the Treaty of Berlin, but the *compensation* theory. On this formula each nation had a list of interests, and better relations between states could be achieved by a compensatory exchange which would give a more logical or easily worked state periphery.

Chamberlain had tried to obtain better relations with Germany

[9] A. J. P. Taylor, *The Struggle for Mastery in Europe, 1848–1918*, Oxford University Press, 1960, p. 379.

in this way in the late 1890s but had failed.[10] His failure had high-lighted the fact that if this was the chosen way to better Anglo-German relations, the material for such an improvement was lacking. On the other hand, although at this time British diplomats were too preoccupied with preventing France from raising the Egyptian question through invading the Sudan to consider this, if the compensation theory of diplomacy was applied to Anglo-French interests, there was an abundance of material for a colonial exchange.

Two other aspects of compensation diplomacy should be noted : *one,* that while agreements for exchanges could be reached to improve interstate relations public opinion might—as in the Anglo-French case—be slow to respond; *two,* compensation diplomacy only alleviated late nineteenth- and early twentieth-century inter-state tensions momentarily, since the peripheral material for exchange was quickly exhausted and the very stress on the reason-ableness of this method of improving international relations added to the existing tension when no future avenues for agreement could be seen. This alteration from the traditional compromise diplomacy of the nineteenth century to the compensation method of the close of that century and beginning of the next one sprang partly from a tidying-up of twenty years or so of imperialism, but was linked with the older alliances, between Germany, Austria and Italy on the one hand and Russia and France on the other, and pointed towards the ententes which were to link Britain decisively with the latter camp. To these alliances and ententes we must now turn.

v

In 1902 Britain took the first decisive step away from her traditional policy of avoiding involvement in alliances. It was in this year that Britain made a naval alliance with Japan (see below, Chapter 7) in order to prevent a Russo-Japanese *rapprochement* on China. Lansdowne was not so much looking forward to co-operation with Japan in the Far East, for this involved difficulties with Australia and New Zealand as Sir Edward Grey emphasized in his memoirs,[11] as hoping to avoid 'dangers of commitment . . . by careful diplomacy

[10] J. A. S. Grenville, *Lord Salisbury and Foreign Policy,* University of London, 1964, Ch. VII *passim,* 279 ff, 314–18; A. Ramm, *Germany 1789–1919,* p. 400; A. J. P. Taylor, *The Struggle for Mastery in Europe,* pp. 390, 396.
[11] Viscount Grey of Fallodon, *Twenty-Five Years 1892–1916,* London, 1928, III, pp. 32–4.

and precise drafting'.[12] Lansdowne, like Chamberlain, believed that British diplomacy must enter a new era marked by alliances, and did not accept the older British attitude taken by Salisbury that Britain's balancing position between the major continental alliances meant that her diplomacy should lack emphatic links through alliances. Apart from needing the Japanese alliance to block Russia in the Far East, the British Cabinet also knew that only with Japan's aid could the British naval position in eastern waters be buttressed. An added incentive to make the alliance was the fear which existed concerning Britain's weakness in relation to a potentially hostile combination of the major continental powers which at times had seemed to threaten during the Boer War of 1899–1902. Hence the Japanese alliance might allow Britain to relax her efforts in the Far East in order to make her fleets nearer home stronger.[13]

The Anglo-Japanese naval alliance was concluded on 30 January 1902.[14] It was to last in the first instance for five years; it was then regularly renewed until 1921. It was a remarkable occurrence in modern international relations. On the one hand, it symbolized Britain's inability to muster naval force against her rivals in Europe and the Far East at the same time; thirty years later this was to become brutally clear when Britain was forced humiliatingly to conciliate Japan, now a decidedly hostile power, in order to face the growing Axis menace in Europe. On the other hand, the alliance marks the first occasion when one of the great European powers, or rather the *primus inter pares* of European diplomacy, was obliged to make friends with a non-European, an Asian, country in order to be able to cope with a rival, Russia, within the European international system. In all preceding international relations the European great powers vied with one another from the basis of their own strength and that of their overseas dependencies, if they had any; or they stood together, as during the Boxer rebellion in China in 1900, in defence of their common supremacy over the extra-European world. Now a member of the inner circle of European great powers was calling on an Asian state to join the international system in order to redress an imbalance of power at the core of that system.

[12] George Monger, *The End of Isolation . . . British Foreign Policy 1900–1907*, London, 1963, p. 47.
[13] *Ibid.*, pp. 49–50.
[14] *Ibid.*, p. 62.

The alliance laid down that Britain and Japan both had political and economic interests in China while accepting that Japan had a special interest in Korea. In technical terms, the independence and territorial integrity of China and Korea were recognised; these were soothing words for the layman but implied for the initiated dominant Japanese interests in Korea and joint resistance, at least diplomatically, to further European encroachments to the disadvantage of the two signatories in China. The 'open door' for foreign trade in both China and Korea was guaranteed. The key clause in the treaty, however, was that which committed either party to neutrality if the other was attacked by a third state and to rendering it assistance if it was attacked by more than one such state. In concrete terms this meant that if a Russo-Japanese war broke out Britain would stand aside but if France aided Russia then Britain must come to the aid of Japan. Curiously enough, Lansdowne does not seem to have realized the dangers which the alliance involved of bringing Britain into a war which concerned Japan; this may have been because he assumed that Britain's link with Japan would be sufficient to discourage any Russian move in force to change the *status quo* in the Far East now that she was confronted by the novel backing of a European great power for an Asiatic state, or that he assumed France would stand aside.

Lansdowne's blindness on this matter indicates he valued the passive rather than the active values of the Anglo-Japanese naval alliance. But, if Lansdowne failed to appreciate the dangers of the agreement, they were certainly understood by Balfour.[15] As time passed and the implications of the alliance were more fully grasped, the British realized that they must cultivate better relations with France. If France could be persuaded to improve relations with Britain then the dangers of France taking Russia's part in a quarrel with Japan over Korea would be lessened. Lansdowne's task became to improve Anglo-French feeling and throughout 1903–04 he negotiated for a general colonial settlement. These negotiations which began in August 1903 were also necessitated because Lansdowne had already tried and failed to get either an alliance with Germany or an adjustment with Russia. France was the last diplomatic stone to be turned. This must be borne in mind since it shows that although the Anglo-French Entente of 1904 became an instrument for co-operation against Germany, it was not initially designed to have this effect.

[15] Monger, *The End of Isolation*, p. 58.

The Anglo-French Entente of 1904 was not made without considerable difficulties as the painful process of matching up compensation claims took place. But by the spring of 1904 Britain and France were both concerned about the possibility of trouble in the Balkans and this spurred them on to settle. The agreement was signed on 8 April 1904 and ended the main colonial disputes between Britain and France concerning Madagascar, Siam, West Africa, the New Hebrides and the vexed question of fishing rights off Newfoundland. Cromer had always been anxious to win a free financial hand for Britain in Egypt and to achieve political independence by casting off the dead hand of the Public Debt Commission or international *Caisse de la Dette Publique*. But this involved final acceptance by France that Britain was supreme in Egypt and so was a most delicate matter touching French national pride. The problem was that no equivalent compensation seemed available for France, but at a late stage in the negotiations, Delcassé, the French Foreign Minister, who was anxious to get France out of the dangerous position of being on poor terms with Germany in Europe and Britain in Africa, suggested that Britain and France should exchange promises of mutual aid concerning the futures of Egypt and Morocco. The British accepted this balance although earlier they had held back from making arrangements about Morocco partly to stave off the day of partition and partly because Germany which had a third share in economic developments in Morocco would expect territorial recognition of her stake.[16] A secret article recorded the Anglo-French promises of diplomatic support concerning Egypt and Morocco, and Lansdowne misleadingly told the Germans in August 1904 that 'Britain could not be pledged by the new article to dispose of the rights of third powers'.[17] Perhaps Lansdowne, with his liking for 'precise drafting', really believed that Britain had not in effect decided that France should be supreme in Morocco in the future, just as Britain was to be dominant in Egypt. But crises over Morocco in 1905 and 1911 were to find Britain co-operating with France against Germany.

[16] The German attitude on Morocco prior to 1904 vacillated. In the late 1890s the Germans showed interest in Morocco's future, but later they declared it did not interest them.

[17] France further improved her future in Morocco by concluding an agreement with Spain in October 1904.

VI

Germany is treated in many books as the diplomatic troublemaker of Europe from the 1890s to 1914 and it is worth looking afresh at this assumption. The European diplomatic system was based on competition up to and including war if necessary; it was also, by the late 1890s, based on the idea that interstate relations should be improved by compensatory exchanges of territory or promises of aid. The weakness of European international relations in the early twentieth century was that the traditional nineteenth-century view that any diplomatic agreement concluded should be in rough harmony with the interests of all major powers was tending to be ignored. In the early nineteenth century the European powers had been taught by the Napoleonic wars to achieve a degree of harmonization of interests when diplomatic agreements were made. It was not merely a philosophical point for debate that each state had a certain importance in European international relations, and therefore had a certain title from its relative ranking to consideration when agreements were made. Napoleon's rise to power and his victories had taught the European states that they must respect each other and must be wary of any state seizing undue power through territorial gains. When this danger seemed to threaten, as for instance when Russia tried to become successor to the power of the Ottomans in Turkey in 1878 through the Treaty of San Stefano, the European powers concerted action and held conferences which forced the offending state to recognize and respect other powers' interests.

The problem created by German dynamism in the late 1890s and early twentieth century was that material—territory—for the dispersion of this energy was lacking. In this respect, the problem posed in European relations at this time was comparable to that created by the Napoleonic state at the beginning of the nineteenth century. Modern Germany, like Napoleonic France, could only express its power by trying to reassemble European territory in new patterns. Germany, it is true, did make intermittent efforts to obtain an outlet through colonization but part of the explanation of her failure to succeed in this territorial media appears to lie in the fact that she did not—because of her fluctuating attitude—manage to convince other states of the reality of her colonial ambitions. Even when Germany pressed a colonial case, there tended to be a degree of ambiguity and disengagement which puzzled and misled other colonizing states. Statesmen were never quite sure just what Germany would do, and on occasions became highly indignant because she showed aggressive interest in territory which they had been led to believe concerned her not at all. But in any case most of the useful colonial territory, China apart, was gone by the time Germany showed interest.

When the other major European states, including Britain, were at a similar stage of historical growth as Germany, there was sufficient territory to absorb their energy : Austria-Hungary and Ottoman Turkey had occupied themselves with the Balkans and the Near East, Prussia had turned eastwards, Russia had ample scope in the Far East and in Central Asia while Britain, like France, had sent her ships out over the high seas and taken her empire. No such development lay open for modern Germany. In colonial matters she could push and try to blackmail states like Britain in order to make them disgorge some of their gains but, and here lay the danger for the European state system of the nineteenth century, the easiest way for Germany to express her economic and military power was by trying to tear apart the thin ligaments of order which held Central Europe together, to attack Poland or even Russia or to turn west against a France already depleted by the losses of the war of 1870–71. If modern Germany had been a liberal democracy, the problem she posed in international relations in the early twentieth century might not have existed. There would have been controls through argument and discussion which would have alleviated the dangers of war, but modern Germany above all was an efficient bureaucratic and military machine created by Bismarck. He had been able to manipulate it—although even he towards the end of his period of power had had serious difficulties—but his successors were not his equal in will or intellect. The machine dominated the men and it was geared towards war sooner or later.

From 1871 onwards modern Germany had been the key to European history. If she had wanted stability in Europe, this could have been achieved by some understanding with Britain but, as we have seen, on a number of occasions the Germans resisted British attempts at *rapprochement*. At its best, an understanding with Britain could only have given Germany colonial gains at the expense of France; it could not have given Germany the freedom of action in Europe which she was *never* able to bring herself to abandon, although it could have given her security. Yet, even allowing for this background, it is clear that to single Germany out as the

international troublemaker of the early twentieth century is misleading.

This can be illustrated by looking at the two Moroccan crises.
The first occurred in March 1905 and arose out of a complex of
German motives, political, military and economic. Germany had
claimed that she welcomed the Anglo-French Entente of 1904,
although all her earlier diplomacy from 1882 onwards had relied on
the assumption that friction over Egypt would keep Britain and
France apart not only in Africa but also in Europe. Politically, it
was important for Germany to assess the weight of the Entente and
to see just how far Anglo-French co-operation would stretch. Germany had economic and financial interests in Morocco and had a
good case for being considered in any future partition of the country—yet she was ignored. But perhaps the most important catalyst
in provoking Germany into action lay in the fact that during 1904–
05 Japan was engaged in war with Russia and, to the initial surprise of European complacency about Asiatics,[18] gained victory
after victory. By 1905 not only was Russia a beaten power militarily
but the defeats and the privations of war had created a revolutionary situation at home; in short, Russia was in no position to aid
France should Germany choose this moment to strike against her.
The idea of a further strike at France had never ceased to exercise
the minds not only of German military men but also of her politicians. How seriously they took the idea is difficult to assess, but
whenever there seemed an opening for attack, someone would be
sure to canvass the possibility.

This mixture of political, military and economic motives led Germany to put pressure on France in 1905 over Morocco. The Kaiser
visited Tangier on 31 March 1905 and announced that Germany
would aid the Moroccans. The French government was seriously
alarmed and tried to appease the Germans by engineering the fall
of their Foreign Minister, Delcassé, and attempting a *rapprochement* with Germany. It is possible that further concessions might
have been forthcoming, but the Germans made a serious tactical
error. They pressed for an international conference without ensuring, as Bismarck had done in 1878, that the members would back
German wishes. By the time the conference was held at Algeçiras in
January to April 1906 the nations were not so much concerned
about the future of Morocco but about the German war scare

[18] Maurice Paléologue, *Un Grand Tournant de la Politique Mondiale (1904–1906)*,
Paris, 1934, 10 February 1904, p. 22.

against France.[19] The outcome was that Britain, backed by the United States, supported France and only Austria-Hungary stood by Germany. Yet Germany had had a good case for being considered in relation to Morocco but unfortunately the Germans did not know when to stop.

Germany had set out to disrupt the Anglo-French relationship by using the Moroccan issue as a test case but instead she cemented the co-operation between the two powers. A similar effect resulted from the second Moroccan crisis which developed over Agadir in 1911. The Germans, again with good cause, considered that the growth of French power in Morocco was likely to infringe upon their rights. The gunboat *Panther* was despatched to Agadir, a little harbour on Morocco's Atlantic seaboard, but this show of German force frightened the British because it implied that the Germans might develop Agadir which lay too close to Gibraltar for comfort. Again, the French were more conciliatory than the British and more willing to recognize that Germany had a claim to compensation. Early in November 1911, a Franco-German agreement was made by which Germany recognized the French position in Morocco in return for compensation in the shape of territory in the French Congo. Both of the Moroccan crises increased Anglo-French technical co-operation : the first episode led to joint military talks on policy should war occur with Germany, and the second crisis caused similar joint naval discussions. It is true that the conjectural nature of Anglo-French co-operation was emphasized, but by the early twentieth century, war for states had become a ponderous business, and the likelihood was that plans made beforehand would structure future military conflicts.

The crises also stimulated Germany military planning. The Schlieffen Plan which dominated German tactics in the First World War was finalized in December 1905. We can see that the tidying-up of colonial material through the *compensation* technique which went on between 1899 and 1914 was not only important *per se,* but also increasingly represented much deeper European attempts to manœuvre support with an eye to the potential continental conflict which seemed to threaten each year, either through some scare about Germany and France or over the Balkans. This tidying-up process also went on in the Near East and in Central Asia. Some historians stress that such negotiations, as for instance between Britain and Germany over the Baghdad Railway, were going on

[19] Fallodon, *Twenty-Five Years 1892–1916*, I, pp. 140–1.

D

right up to the eve of the First World War, as though this meant the outbreak of war was an accident, or as though there existed an underlying current of international relations flowing in favour of peace. But it is difficult to accept this view. Certainly, as one historian has commented, 'No war is inevitable until it breaks out',[20] and the old *simpliste* view of a number of steps leading inevitably to the First World War in the form in which it occurred needed rebutting. But there were factors in international relations in the early twentieth century which tipped the scales in favour of war, not any particular war, but some form of aggression arising from the mixture of fear and acceptance of war which prevailed then.

It was this fear which had initiated the chain reaction of compensation diplomacy which characterized the period before 1914. It was evident to the Germans, even though they were by no means convinced that Britain would stand by France if major war occurred, that Britain, France and Russia had strengthened their diplomatic and general position by successful compensation diplomacy. This grouping of powers had become known as the 'Triple Entente' although there were few direct links between all three except some financial ones. On 31 August 1907, Britain and Russia had made an entente based on an acceptance of regions of influence in Persia and the supremacy of British interests in Afghanistan, and both powers accepted that they should not intrigue in Tibet. The Russians also considered that the entente, although it did not say so, meant that Britain would no longer bar Russian dominance at the Straits provided this was accepted by the other states. Yet the fluctuating nature of European diplomacy in this period is well illustrated by the fact that Russia, which had strong economic links with Germany, might well have made some agreement with that power instead of with Britain. But the balance towards Britain resulted from the Russian desire—springing from the high cost of industrialization and the arms race—to float loans on the London Stock Exchange.

VII

In retrospect it hardly seems surprising that Germany should have decided to unleash Austria in the Balkans and so trigger off the First World War. The German state was powerful and important, but it did not receive the diplomatic consideration commensurate with its

[20] A. J. P. Taylor, *The Struggle for Mastery in Europe*, p. 518.

status in the early twentieth century. This situation was partly accidental in that the forces in German political life favouring colonial
development were relatively slow—although not as slow as once
claimed[21]—in asserting themselves over the well-known views of
Bismarck. It is true that colonies seem a somewhat artificial growth
for Germany if we consider her position in Central Europe, her three
land frontiers and her military tradition. These factors also account
for the vagaries of German colonial policy. But the serious aspect of
this relative lack of colonial gains made by Germany was that, when
in the early twentieth century states became especially conscious of
the dangers of war and began to try to lessen interstate tension
through colonial compensation agreements, Germany remained
isolated and outside these moves, partly because she lacked colonial
material[22] and partly because her unsubtle diplomacy, even when
she had a good case as over Morocco, tended to range important
states against her. But German diplomacy, after Bismarck had gone,
was in the hands of much weaker men; it became an unstable combination of threat, duplicity and vacillation. On the eve of the outbreak of the First World War, although Germany had pressed
Austria to war with Serbia before the other states could interfere,
yet at the same time there were contra-indications. William II
wanted only a partial attack on Serbia and favoured the 'Halt in
Belgrade' plan and even the German Chancellor, Bethmann-
Hollweg, showed interest—when, however, it was too late—in stop-
ping major war.

In the relatively slow run-up to the First World War[23] and the
consequent mobilizations, declarations of war and summoning of
fleets, it is clear that there was no copybook application of the terms
of the formal alliances. The alliances were merely the ridges which
showed the fear and tension of the major states in 1914 and all the
powers, in one degree or another, seemed afflicted by the view that
if they did not act now it might be worse for them later on. War,
or Armageddon as it was often called, came on 28 July 1914 when
Austria declared war on Serbia. Trying to look ahead, and with the

---

[21] Hartmut Pogge von Strandmann, 'Domestic Origins of Germany's Colonial
Expansion under Bismarck', *Past and Present*, No. 42, February 1969.
[22] Colonel House, President Wilson's informal peace envoy, was well aware of the
importance of the colonial factor in Germany's position, and discussed with the
Germans the possibility of developments in China and Latin America; see *The
Intimate Papers of Colonel House*, Boston, 1926, I, pp. 239–40.
[23] There was a month between the assassination of Archduke Franz Ferdinand and
Austria's declaration of war on Serbia.

failure which generally attends prophecies in international relations, Colonel House commented :

> The saddest feature of the situation to me is that there is no good outcome to look forward to. If the Allies win, it means largely the domination of Russia on the Continent of Europe; if Germany wins, it means the unspeakable tyranny of militarism for generations to come.[24]

REFERENCES

Albertini, L., *The Origins of the War of 1914*, 3 vols., London and Fair Lawn, New Jersey, O.U.P., 1952–57.

Andrew, C., *Théophile Delcassé and the Making of the Entente Cordiale*, London, Macmillan, and New York, St Martin's, 1968.

Fay, S. B., *The Origins of the World War*, 2 vols., New York, Macmillan, 1930.

Fleming, D. F., *Origins and Legacies of World War One*, New York, Doubleday, and London, Allen and Unwin, 1968.

George, David Lloyd, *War Memoirs of David Lloyd George*, 2 vols., London, Odhams, 1938.

Viscount Grey of Fallodon, *Twenty-Five Years 1892–1916*, 3 vols., London, Hodder and Stoughton, 1928; first published 1925.

Monger, G., *The End of Isolation—British Foreign Policy, 1900–1907*, London, Nelson, 1963.

Paléologue, M., *Un Grand Tournant de la Politique Mondiale, 1904–1906*, Paris, Plon, 1934.

Rolo, P. J. V., *The Entente Cordiale. The Origins and Negotiations of the Anglo-French Agreements of April 8th, 1904*, London, Macmillan, and New York, St Martin's, 1969.

Schmitt, B. E., *The Coming of the War 1914*, 2 vols., New York, Scribner's, 1930.

Siebert, B. von, *Entente Diplomacy and the World*, London, Allen and Unwin, 1924.

Stolper, G., *German Economy, 1870–1940*, London, Allen and Unwin, and New York, Harcourt Brace, 1940.

[24] *The Intimate Papers of Colonel House*, I, p. 285.

6 *The Morrow of Armageddon*

I

The nineteenth century ended in effect, not in December 1899, but in August 1914. Before the First World War, the European international system had worked with intermittent crises which had provoked jingoistic outbursts in the states concerned, but for the most part neither the mass of ordinary people nor even the ruling few were much concerned with foreign affairs. The war closed the door for ever on that world of an automatically functioning international system and general unconcern with politics between nations. In so doing, it inaugurated the twentieth century, with its total war, its obscuring of the dividing lines between war and peace and domestic and foreign affairs, its ideological crusades and mass appeal of leaders and foreign policy, its propaganda, subversion and political warfare, its recruitment behind foreign policy of world public opinion, as opposed to the quiet negotiation of professional diplomats in secret chancelleries, its conception of international affairs as the struggle for improvement of the common man's condition, as opposed to the classic conception of them as the daily ordering of a coherent society, its giant international organizations and search for the integration of sovereign states. Above all, the First World War began the destruction of the primacy of Europe in the international system and its empires overseas which the Second World War completed.

The European War of 1914–18 was a total war in the sense that, to ensure victory, the belligerents were finally compelled to mobilize totally their resources, their manpower, manufacturing and extractive industries, their farming, shipping, transport and communications systems. The states which failed to do so, like Tsarist Russia, went down in defeat and revolution. Millions of men were drafted into the armies, millions of men and women were moved, or moved themselves, from peacetime occupations or no occupation at all, into the war industries. The governments were suddenly forced to do what all their principles and experience had taught them could not or should not be done, to take over the direction of industry, farming, labour. For all practical purposes by the end of the war in November 1918 all the belligerents which had survived the ordeal were socialized states in which hardly any major economic decision could be made without the government's consent. This experience bequeathed to social critics in all countries the idea that national economic planning which had served the cause of war in 1914–18 could equally well serve the cause of peace. Moreover, the fact that economic weapons, such as blockade, the seizure of the enemy's financial assets abroad, the systematic destruction of his foreign trade and shipping, had been used alongside military weapons during the war meant that after the war these weapons were still available for use, whether by the new League of Nations against an aggressor or by one state against another in the ordinary course of international affairs.

The origins of socialist and fascist planning and of economic warfare as part of the normal techniques of foreign policy are thus to be found in the First World War. But the sheer scale of the warfare itself had its impact on the international system. It bred, for instance, at least in the Anglo-Saxon world, an intense desire to avoid any similar catastrophe in future by abolishing the most conspicuous aspect of the conflict to the ordinary eye : the sheer weight and numbers of armaments. These armaments, or rather the industrial and technological capacity to manufacture them, had quietly accumulated during the long years of peace preceding 1914 and then were consumed at a rate undreamt of by minds reared in the nineteenth century, and this fostered the illusion that the shortest way to the avoidance of conflict on the pattern of 1914–18 was to scrap by international agreement the whole diabolical apparatus of arms and arms-producing industries. Hence the vast efforts devoted almost throughout the inter-war period to the task of trying to secure world-wide agreement on the limitation and reduction of armaments.

The scale of mechanized destruction in 1914–18 also had far-reaching effects on the techniques of diplomacy and on preparations for any future war in the period between 1918 and 1939. In the first place, it forced diplomats and politicians to the conclusion that, if there was to be another war, their own countries must not at any cost be the ones to take the first shock of Armageddon; wisdom would surely lie in waiting until late in the day before launching one's resources into any future armed conflict. Thus

British Ministers in the mid-1930s vaguely hoped that Fascism and Communism might destroy each other without the democracies being involved; American opinion determined never again to be sucked into a European bloodbath through financial deals, as had seemed to be the case in the First World War; and Stalin, when he signed the Nazi-Soviet Pact in August 1939, congratulated himself on escaping being drawn into 'pulling British and French chestnuts out of the fire', as he called it. In the second place, the attrition warfare on the Western Front between 1914 and 1918 stimulated those who experienced it to try new methods of warfare, of which the Nazi brand of *Blitzkrieg* became the most notorious. *Bitzkrieg* was essentially not total, but psychological, warfare. It was an attempt, which proved highly successful against France in June 1940, to avoid the bloodletting of total war by terrifying the opponent into thinking that unless he submitted he *would* have to face total warfare on the 1914–18 model, but with mass bombing from the air added as an extra horror.

The extraordinary thing about the military struggle in the First World War was how the ordinary fighting man could survive the privations, misery, hideous wounds and continuous prospect of ugly death for so many years on end, if he was not released by becoming one of the countless casualties. One explanation is that the length and intensity of the conflict was wholly unexpected, except by a few professional soldiers like Lord Kitchener. At first, it was cheerfully assumed that the men would be home 'before the leaves of autumn fell', and then, when the full horrors became known, that anything so dreadful must end soon. But the more likely explanation lies in the stability and optimism of the ordinary man's vision of the world as he marched to battle in August 1914. Life was hard for the industrial worker or farm labourer in all countries, but there was a sense that this was either part of the order of nature or perhaps the retribution for human sins. In any case, it was relieved by occasional holidays, family celebrations or bouts of drunkenness. Scott Fitzgerald has written of this psychological climate of the war generation as follows :

This West-front business couldn't be done again, not for a long time. The young men think they would do it again but they couldn't. They could fight the first Marne again, but not this. This took religion and years of plenty and tremendous sureties and the exact relation between the classes—you had to have a whole-souled sentimental equipment going back further than you could remember. All my lovely safe world blew itself up with a great gust of high explosive love.[1]

With the destruction of this religiously tinged acceptance of the existing social order in the tragic battles of 1914–18, new beliefs were needed to fill the vacuum. The most important for its later effect on international relations was revolutionary Communism, with which Lenin and his associates inspired the Russian masses when their age-old belief in the sanctity of the Tsarist social and political order collapsed in the great military defeats of 1916 and 1917. But in all the belligerents it became necessary, as the struggle went on, to reconcile armies and peoples in the rear to the conflict by holding out hopes of a better future, and at the same time by ascribing to the enemy purposes and policies which had to be totally destroyed before the bases of a new world order could be created.

It was in this way that President Wilson became the new messiah for Allied peoples, and for many in the Central Powers as well, just as Lenin became messiah for the ordinary Russian worker and peasant. It is no coincidence that the international vocabularies of Wilson and Lenin were in many respects almost identical, even though one was the head of the world's greatest capitalist state and the other the prophet of anti-capitalism. Both denounced imperialism, power politics and war to line the pockets of a few; both upheld the ideals of struggle for the benefit of the common man, national self-determination, peace without annexations and indemnities. The latter were the slogans which converted a classical European war begun by governments for reasons of prestige and gain, and without consulting their peoples, into a People's War for Right and Justice, an ideological campaign directed towards making life better for the common man. The war socialized and democratized foreign policy, as an ideal if not always as a reality, and as such it was to remain until the present.

But if foreign policy was to be democratized a new type of national leader and new methods of mediating his ideas, or more often emotions, to the new mass electorate were needed. The old aristocratic or middle-class politician, like Salisbury, Asquith or Sir Edward Grey, must give way to a Lloyd George or Ramsay Mac-Donald, the Emperor with his court, generals and archbishops to the demagogue in cloth cap or belted raincoat, like Lenin or Hitler.

[1] Quoted in Alistair Horne, *The Price of Glory*, London, 1962, p. xii.

This meant, too, that the language of politics must change, from the parliamentary or diplomatic to the forensic or demagogic; it must be simpler, more repetitive and emotional, the language, in other words, of propaganda. And propaganda was indeed to become the new instrument for consolidating national unity and winning support on the widest possible international scale for national policies. Propaganda in international relations may be said to have its origins in the deadlock on the Western Front after the first battle of the Marne which halted the great German sweep of August 1914 to encircle Paris, the emasculated Schlieffen Plan. As the casualty-lists rose and the prospect of a final military breakthrough faded, governments were compelled to organize the minds and feelings of their peoples for the long, hard road that lay ahead, and at the same time to appeal for the support of still uncommitted nations which might tip the balance.

The collapse of Russia in 1917 and of Germany a year later bred in both these countries the notion that propaganda can achieve anything, that, in the words of Hitler's *Mein Kampf*, 'clever and persistent propaganda can make Heaven look like Hell and Hell like Heaven'. As men looked back on the unspeakable horrors of 1914–18, many of them dreamed that by 'winning the war of words' they could ensure victory in any future international conflict without actually shedding blood. Diplomacy has often been compared to chess. With the advent of organized propaganda as part of the normal equipment for the conduct of foreign policy, it began to resemble chess in a new sense, namely that, as in chess, the object of the exercise becomes not so much the capture of the king, but the placing of him in a position in which he cannot defend himself, and this by undermining the foundations of the domestic and foreign support on which his defence depends.

The war, too, had its effect on the practice of diplomacy in another sense. We have remarked earlier how the conflict, by exacting unparalleled sacrifices from the ordinary man, compared with which the secret treaties concluded between the belligerents on both sides seemed shabby and mean, made some kind of popular support for future diplomatic agreements essential. This in itself necessitated the total subordination of the professional diplomat to the popularly elected head of government. But, in addition, the need to co-ordinate momentous military and political decisions between heads of government, especially on the Allied side, during the war habituated the world to the idea of diplomacy by 'summit' confer-

ences of leading Ministers, to which the postwar newspapers gave
the greatest publicity. Besides, the tangle of unresolved or half-
resolved problems left in their train by the war and the peace
treaties of 1919 seemed to require the organization of large-scale
ministerial conferences as a method of dealing with them, and the
institutionalization of this in the Council of the League of Nations,
which the peace settlements created, facilitated the process. Distances between one country's capital and another's, too, had been
shortened by wartime improvements in transport, which made
ministerial journeys to foreign conference sites easier, and Foreign
Offices, though undeservedly, had fallen out of favour as responsible
for the abhorred secret treaties from which the war was widely felt
to have sprung. Bilateral diplomacy remained the standard method
of conducting international relations after the war and was largely
unaffected by President Wilson's principle, the first of his Fourteen
Points of January 1918, of 'open covenants openly arrived at'. But
multilateral 'summit' diplomacy came to rival it as a close second,
especially in the early 1920s.

These are all, or almost all, visible changes in the system of international relations effected by the war. But the invisible changes in
morale, mood and thought produced by the conflict were equally
important and perhaps of even greater immediate, if not long-term,
consequence. The war was, to state it moderately, an unprecedented
emotional shock for those who experienced it, and, as often happens
after a great traumatic event, reactions to it were ambivalent.
Horror and revulsion predominated, especially among the victors,
and more especially in the Anglo-Saxon world. The foreign policies
in the inter-war years of Britain and the United States, and only to
a slightly lesser extent, France, cannot be understood except against
the sombre backcloth of the First World War. The congeries of
myths which grew up in these countries about the war and its
politics testify to this. There was the myth of the 'Carthaginian
Peace', which Lord Keynes first disseminated in his *Economic Consequences of the Peace* (1919) and which the Germans later did
their best to foster as their strongest sentimental weapon, the legend
that Germany had been brutally treated at the peace settlement in
1919 by Allied Parliaments made up of 'hard-faced men who looked
as if they had done well out of the war', in Stanley Baldwin's tren-
chant phrase. There was the idea, too, that 'war settles nothing',
that the war had been caused by capitalist imperialism, by international finance, the private manufacturers of armaments, the General

Staffs or the Jews. All these ideas, held tenaciously on the political Left as well as the Right in the Entente states after the war, tinged the attitudes of these countries towards international politics in the twenty years before the next bloodletting and affected their actions in those politics.

The war left in many soldiers, more especially in Germany and Italy, but also on the political Left and Right in Britain, France and Belgium, a sentimental, bitter-sweet nostalgia for the comradeship of the trenches when life was supposedly simpler and, if not heroic, at least more manly and honourable than the cut-throat competition and pervasive ruthlessness of peacetime industrial and commercial society. These attitudes strengthened the anti-capitalism of working-class ex-soldiers in Western Europe and laid the basis for the revival of militarism in Germany and Italy. The fact that Germany had lost the war and that Italy, although she came out on the winning side, considered herself cheated of the gains promised when she joined the Entente powers in 1915, did not reflect, in the militarists' view, the inadequacy of war as a means of achieving national justice. On the contrary, it underlines the need for leaders like Hitler who professed to know the feelings and interests of the ex-service man. In short, the 1914–18 war nourished, at one and the same time, the soldierly spirit inspiring the fire-hot nationalism in the revisionist states from which the Second World War sprang, and the dread of renewed war from which unwillingness on the part of the democracies to resist that nationalism by force also sprang.

II

Three great European empires were strained and finally collapsed during or near the end of the First World War, and with them fell, too, the conservative social order in Europe which they represented, and the paramountcy of Europe in world politics. These empires were the Russian, Austro-Hungarian and German. The signal for the collapse of the old Russian empire of the Romanovs was the abdication of Tsar Nicholas II after the bread riots in Petrograd and other Russian cities in March 1917, but it was not until the seizure of power by the Bolsheviks in November that the withdrawal of Russia from its western fringe in Europe began. By the Treaty of Brest-Litovsk concluded with Germany on 3 March 1918, Russia lost most of the Ukraine, where a German-supported puppet government was installed. Finland declared its independence in December 1917 and the Baltic republics of Estonia, Latvia and Lithuania between February and November 1918. When the Brest-Litovsk treaty lost its validity as a consequence of Germany's military defeat on the Western Front in 1918, and the Ukraine came once more under Russian control, her new Bolshevik rulers found themselves in conflict with the reconstituted Poland, whose access to the sea by a corridor separating East Prussia from the rest of Germany and whose western frontiers with Germany were established by the Paris peace conference in 1919. The Russo-Polish war wavered to and fro until the Poles received substantial military assistance from France and a promise of further help from the British Prime Minister, Lloyd George, and a new Russo-Polish frontier was established by the treaty of Riga in March 1921. This settlement was highly prejudicial to Russia since it incorporated nearly three million Ukrainians and White Russians in the new Polish state. It was even far less favourable to Russia than the so-called 'Curzon' line which the British delegation had proposed as a suitable ethnigraphic frontier between Poland and Russia at the Paris peace conference in 1919.

The Bolsheviks were compelled to accept this settlement of their frontiers in the west, though only parts of it, namely those concerned with the independence of Finland and the Baltic states, were in accordance with the principle of national self-determination to which the Bolsheviks professed to adhere. The Russians also lost Bessarabia to Rumania, Sub-Carpathian Ruthenia to the new state of Czechoslovakia, and all their gains, including the annexation of Constantinople and the Straits leading from the Mediterranean into the Black Sea, which had been assigned to Nicholas II by a secret inter-Allied agreement of February 1915. Although the Bolsheviks tended later to write off these losses as being in accordance with the 'no annexations, no indemnities' proposals in the terms for peace which they promulgated as soon as they came to power in November 1917, there is no evidence that they did so willingly. Under the stress of civil war, internal controversies on foreign policy within the Bolshevik party itself and the economic stresses of the period of war, they hardly had an option. The Liberal government under Prince Lvov which assumed office after the March revolution gave no sign of wanting to renounce the territorial promises made to Russia by the secret treaties. Alexander Kerensky, who became Prime Minister in July 1917, was almost equally lacking in enthu-

The Peace Settlement, 1919–23

siasm for this form of national self-denial; and when the Supreme Allied War Council called on the anti-Bolshevik leader they were backing, Admiral Kolchak, after the Leninist seizure of power and the outbreak of civil war, to repudiate the secret treaties in return for Allied support, he calmly replied that that would be for a future freely elected Constituent Assembly in Russia to decide. Even Lenin was far from heedless about Russia's territorial integrity; he told Trotsky, the first Soviet Foreign Commissar, during the negotiations at Brest-Litovsk that he was willing to continue fighting the Germans if Trotsky could provide an army. But since neither Trotsky nor anyone else could oblige by doing so, it was essential, he said, to sign a peace to prevent the Germans penetrating further into Russian territory even if it meant paying a very high price to attain it.

Thus Russia entered the years of peace after 1918, or rather 1921, with a grievance against the east European *status quo* resulting from the peace settlement, certainly against Poland and Rumania and to a lesser degree against Czechoslovakia. But that Soviet Russia was a dissatisfied state in eastern Europe was overlooked by most people, except, of course, by the Poles and Rumanians. The political Left in western Europe considered Russia to be far too advanced a country to be concerned with anything so base and old-fashioned as the recovery of lost territory; that was a characteristic of 'revanchist' states like Germany. The Right, on the other hand, considered that Russia was too weak and inefficient ('Communism rots the soul' was how Winston Churchill put it) to make good her claims even if she wanted to; in any case, Communist propaganda, the Right thought, was a far more serious danger to the West than any territorial irredentism the Russians might harbour. In Britain, too, Russia's alleged designs on British interests in Central Asia, especially in Afghanistan and India, attracted more attention than her attitudes towards eastern Europe; they played an important part in the British decision to break off diplomatic relations with Russia in 1927. As for Russia's Far Eastern interests, these were not diminished in the same way by the First World War, though Russia's collapse in that war confirmed her losses to Japan in the Russo-Japanese war of 1904–05, namely the southern half of Sakhalin and her lease of the naval base in Port Arthur, Manchuria, known to all sailors in the Tsarist and Soviet fleets as 'sacred Russian soil'. As soon as Russia had revived economically from war and revolution and took her place once again in the inner circle of great powers, it required no foresight to see that she would begin to press her dissatisfactions in Europe and the Far East. In the meanwhile, however, her best policy lay in pursuing a quiet life in order to dispel all risk of the capitalist West, possibly in collusion with Japan, encircling and crushing the socialist motherland. The Soviet government remained pathologically afraid of such an encirclement throughout the 1920s.

There are, however, two other aspects of the fall of the Romanov empire in the First World War which need attention. The first is that the German defeat of Russia in 1917 and Russia's surrender thereafter to Germany of the great agricultural resources of the Ukraine suggested to many German politicians after the war that, if ever they had to fight another war, they could best do so by meeting their food and raw material needs from Russia, whether with or without Russia's agreement, and so defeat the maritime blockade which the British and French fleets imposed in 1914–18. The German victories in Russia in 1916 and 1917 may thus be said to have planted the seed of the great ideology of a *Lebensraum* in the East in the German mind which never ceased to intrigue it afterwards, and which the Western democracies did nothing to discourage.

The second aspect of Russia's position in 1918 was that it was much more vulnerable than it had been in Tsarist times, not only because of the loss of territory by the peace settlement on her western borders and the German aspiration to do again in the future what they had done at Brest-Litovsk in March 1918, but because her danger had been much increased in the Far East. Japan, as an ally, though not an active one, of the Entente powers, had naturally profited from the war. She acquired by the peace settlement Germany's former possessions in Shantung, though she was forced to disgorge these at the Washington conference in 1922, and Germany's island territories in the Pacific north of the equator, though these were, formally at least, entrusted to her as League of Nations mandates. Moreover, Japan had contracted an alliance with Britain in 1902 which was renewed in 1911. This meant that Japan could rely on Britain's understanding and sympathy if she was ever involved in hostilities with Russia, as she was when the Allied Supreme War Council egged her on to attack Russia's Far Eastern provinces in March 1918. It also meant that if the alliance with Britain were to be wound up, as it was at the Washington conference in 1922, Japan could be sure to get a good price from agreeing to relieve Britain of what had become an embarrassing commitment, and that price might well include British diplomatic support for a Japanese attack on Russia.

After all, Britain and Japan were in the same capitalist boat which Soviet Communism made no concealment of its intention to sink if it got the chance. Thus, as imperialist aspirations and policies grew in Japan throughout the inter-war period, Russia's leaders could never ignore this threat to her eastern flank (for the post-war situation in the Far East see the following chapter). Her natural interest lay in playing the international game as softly and quietly as possible in order to avert all danger of having to fight a full-scale war on two widely separated fronts.

Russia's old antagonist in the Balkans, the Austro-Hungarian empire, based on the *Ausgleich* of Austria and Hungary of 1867, also collapsed in 1918, leaving south-eastern Europe as a weak corridor into which Germany could and did expand when she revived in the 1930s. Towards the end of the First World War it had been an aim of British policy to try to keep the Habsburg empire in being after the war as a counterweight to Germany, but this conflicted with the ideals of national self-determination which had now become inscribed in Allied war aims, and the centrifugal forces within that empire itself. The Austro-Hungarian collapse made possible the formation of Czechoslovakia, with its patchwork quilt of nationalities and its Achilles heel in the form of three million German-speaking people in the fringe of Sudeten uplands half-encircling the Bohemian plateau and facing post-war Germany in the west; the triune state of Serbia-Croatia-Slovenia which became Yugoslavia; and the enlargement of Rumania with the acquisition of Transylvania from Hungary. Austria itself was reduced by the peace treaty of Trianon in 1919 to a weak core of six million German-speaking people, too small to be called even a pale shadow of the former vast dominions of the Habsburgs, in an economically unviable country from which all the old agricultural hinterland had been shorn away.

The consequence in terms of the stability of the European international system was weakness and a mass of tensions. Most of the states of south-eastern Europe lacked the basic framework for an industrial state. They depended on the export of a limited range of primary raw materials, notably timber, grain, tobacco and oil, which experienced during the 1920s a long-term decline in world prices, partly as a consequence of the invention of substitutes for, or economies in the use of, raw material after the war, partly through the fall in purchasing power of the industrial nations in the economic depression which swept Europe after a short-lived boom following the 1918 armistice. South-eastern Europe, consisting as it did of a group of economically and militarily weak states, was destined to become the prey of any power which seized control of Central Europe, and no one was better fitted for that role than Germany. But these economic weaknesses of the area were as nothing compared with the political rivalries and tensions.

The new Austria was far too involved in its own economic plight and political faction fighting to have much time or energy to spare for irredentism, except in relation to the Austrian Tirol which was handed to Italy, in accordance with wartime engagements, in 1919. But partly for that very reason there was always political capital to be made in Hungary by any party which undertook to recover the legendary territories of the Holy Crown of St. Stephen, and, in particular, to achieve the retrocession of Transylvania from Rumania. Ranged against Austria and Hungary were the countries forming the Little Entente, Czechoslovakia, Poland and Yugoslavia, with their obsessive, unrealistic dread of a restoration of the Habsburg monarchy over its old dominions. Of the three, Czechoslovakia had least to fear from designs on its territories by other powers, at least in the 1920s, though the ragged argument with Poland continued over the disposition of the district of Teschen. But Poland faced on either side temporarily recessive great powers which she did nothing to conciliate until 1934, when President Pilsudski made his non-aggression agreement with Nazi Germany. It was all but inevitable that when these two giants, Russia and Germany, revived they would reclaim territory lost to Poland which made the formation of that state possible in the first place. To the south, Yugoslavia faced a disillusioned Italy whose expected gains on the Dalmatian coast by the Treaty of London of April 1915, when she joined the Entente in the war, had been frustrated by the creation of the triune state. On the other side of the Balkans, Rumania had profited from her costly war effort as part of the Allied coalition by the acquisition of Bessarabia from Russia, Northern Bukowina from Bulgaria and Transylvania from Hungary. Here again the message was clear, namely that any great power which wished to fish in the muddy waters of the Balkans would find many territorial grievances there which it could champion.

The First World War, at least in its concluding stages, had ostensibly been fought by the Allies to establish the principle of national self-determination, though in the event, as Lloyd George testified, a leading consideration of the four peace-makers in Paris in 1919 was to 'free from the clutches' of the successor states which they had created territory to which they were not entitled.[2] This identification of the cause of national self-determination with that of the Allies meant that the ultimate Allied victory resulted in a belt of weak states in Eastern Europe, from Finland in the north to Rumania in the south. Towards these states the leading Allied powers, Britain and France, had contrary attitudes. The French by means of bilateral military treaties sought to make Eastern Europe a flank of the security system which they began to build against a German revival almost as soon as the ink on the peace treaties was dry. France mistrusted the security offered by the new League of Nations because it lacked the international force to implement its decisions which the French had pleaded for at the peace conference. She had seen her demand for a separation of the west bank of the Rhine from Germany and a permanent occupation of the Rhineland turned down during the peace talks in preference to an Anglo-American guarantee to France against future aggression which fell to the ground as soon as the United States failed to ratify the treaties. She was implacably hostile towards, and suspicious of, Germany. British politicians, on the other hand, Conservative and Labour alike, considered that France, Britain's hereditary enemy, was the most likely troublemaker in Europe because of her innate fear of Germany. It was Germany, not France, whom they came to think of as having been hardly done by at the peace conference. They suspected France's east European allies either as French client states or as incorrigible meddlers in great power affairs which they did not understand. Even before the treaty was signed they entertained an unabashed sympathy for Germany's territorial losses to Poland through the peace settlement. This fact is indispensable to an understanding of British attitudes towards German revisionism in Eastern Europe in the 1930s.

We thus come to Germany as the third, but militarily by far the strongest, European empire to collapse, creating the vacuum, or at least part of it, out of which the new eastern Europe was formed. The German empire of William II, who abdicated in November 1918 to give way to the ill-fated Weimar Republic, ruled unimportant possessions in Africa, namely the Cameroons and Togoland in west Africa, Tanganyika in east Africa, and south-west

[2] David Lloyd George, *The Truth about the Peace Treaties*, London, 1938, Vol.I, p. 91.

Africa. These territories fell into British Empire hands and became British (and, in the case of south-west Africa, South African) mandates under the League of Nations. Germany's colony in Central Africa, Ruanda-Urundi, became a Belgian mandate. Germany's possessions in Shantung and her island territories in the Pacific north of the equator came under Japanese administration as mandates as a reward for Japan's siding with the Allies in the war; her island possessions in the Pacific south of the equator fell into British Empire hands as 'C' mandates under the League. But these overseas territories had never made any important contribution to the German economy in peacetime and were only of value so long as Germany was a considerable naval power. They had been acquired in the 1880s as the trappings and outward insignia of great power status. Once lost, Germany made no serious effort to regain them.

Germany's territorial losses in Europe, however, were far more serious. In the west, the retrocession of the provinces of Alsace and Lorraine to France, from whom they had been seized after the Franco-Prussian war in 1870, was the least grievous blow. The loss of the Saar, which came under League of Nations control for fifteen years after the Treaty of Versailles was ratified, after which there was to be a referendum to decide its future, was more humiliating, and the fact that the west bank of the Rhine, the Rhine bridgeheads and a zone fifty kilometres wide on the east bank of the river were to be permanently demilitarized, with an Allied army of occupation quartered there for a maximum of fifteen years, more humiliating still. But the most intolerable territorial loss for Germany under the peace treaties was the severing of Prussia, the nursery of the German army, into two parts so as to give Poland a corridor to the sea—'the next war will begin in Danzig', prophesied Lloyd George in 1919—and the handing over to Poland of the coal-rich districts of Silesia.

To these provisions of what young Germans were taught as they grew up to loathe as the '*Diktat* of Versailles' were added the demilitarization of the German army and its deprivation of the major weapons of war. The proud legions of the Hohenzollerns gave way to a volunteer force of 100,000 men to whom tanks, aircraft and guns above a certain calibre were denied. The High Seas Fleet, with which Germany had challenged Britain in the years before 1914, was towed into the harbour of Scapa Flow, where its officers scuttled it in the summer of 1919, the British holding up their hands in what may have been feigned surprise and shock. To all intents Germany was denuded of the instruments of war which had been its pride and terror. But the German soil had never been ravaged in battle during the four years and a half of the war; the German army had marched home, defeated but intact. Though the Germans in their hour of humiliation forgot it, they had held at bay the greatest coalition of nations the world had ever seen for fifty-one months with no considerable help from their allies. Russia they had totally defeated, France they had brought to her knees and the flower of Britain's manhood had fallen as before a scythe in face of the German army.

The German situation, at home and in foreign affairs, looked bleak in 1918, so bleak as to make the German High Command eager to shuffle off the odium of leading the country in defeat to the democratic politicians of the Weimar Republic. A year later, by the Versailles Treaty, Germany had shouldered legal responsibility for the war and thereby assumed liability, not defined in money terms until the inter-Allied Reparation Commission created by the treaty issued its report in May 1921, for all the loss and damage inflicted on their enemies by the war. But their country's international position was far stronger than the Germans believed. On the eastern side, they had it in their hands, if they could swallow their revulsion against Communism, to make common cause with Soviet Russia, at that time another pariah nation which had somewhat similar irredentist claims against the successor states of eastern Europe, especially Poland, as Germany herself. In the West stood victorious France, but a France divided from her wartime ally, Britain, by differences over Germany and the enforcement of the Versailles Treaty against Germany.

Germany was to agree at the Locarno conference in October 1925 to respect her new western frontier and the demilitarization of the Rhineland imposed in Paris in 1919. This agreement was hailed in Britain as marking the true dividing line between the years of war and the years of peace, as the British Foreign Secretary, Sir Austen Chamberlain, who signed the Locarno accords for Britain, called it. It signalled, or seemed to signal, the voluntary acceptance by Germany of the only territorial agreement concerning Germany signed at Paris which British opinion with one voice held to be just. But it went unnoticed at the time that by giving France and Germany a British and Italian guarantee against 'flagrant' aggression by the other, the Locarno agreements effectively debarred France from entering Western Germany in the event of any future German attack on France's east European allies. By signing the Locarno accords Germany thus pleased Britain, and in doing so widened the rift between Britain and France, while at the same time freeing her hands for the revision of her east European frontiers when she was strong enough to do so. But before this Germany had made common cause with Bolshevik Russia at Rapallo in 1922, at one stroke bringing home to the Western powers who had defeated her that she now had an option in foreign policy, and laying the basis, to be brought to completion in the Nazi-Soviet Pact of August 1939, for co-operation with the other great revisionist power in eastern Europe. These facts went far to make Germany, the object of Allied diplomacy in 1919, the arbiter of Europe in the twenty years' breathing space which followed.

There was, however, a fourth empire which collapsed in 1918, predominantly a non-European one, though it remained with a foothold in Europe, an empire which many Europeans had done their best before 1914 to expel 'bag and baggage', as Gladstone put it in the 1880s, from Europe. By a curious turn of events Turkey, which in the form of the Ottoman Empire had been a protégé of Britain in the nineteenth century, became its enemy during the First World War, and then, after the long-delayed peace settlement at Lausanne in 1923, its friend again. Although the Ottoman Empire had been the subject of many secret inter-Allied agreements during the war which first, in 1915, handed over Constantinople and the Straits to Russia and then, in 1916, by the Sykes-Picot agreement divided the Arab portions of the empire between Britain and France, the revolution in Turkey led by Kemal Pasha in 1920 preserved the Anatolian core as the nationalist base of the revived Turkey and succeeded in keeping Constantinople and the Straits under Turkish sovereignty. The Arab territories were shorn away, to become League of Nations 'A' mandates, under French control in the case of Syria and Lebanon, under British control in the case of Iraq and Transjordan, and Biblical Palestine, the poisoned chalice, was shaped into a British mandate intended, according to the Balfour Declaration of 2 November 1917, to be a National Home for the Jewish people.

But two circumstances kept the new Turkey in friendly relations with the Western powers, despite the annexationist Treaty of Sèvres which the Allies had imposed on the Sultan in August 1920 and which the Kemalist revolution rendered null and void, and despite Britain and Turkey being brought to the brink of war in September 1922 when Kemalist and British occupation forces confronted each

other at Chanak, on the coast of the Straits. One was the necessity
for Britain as a maritime power, or rather the greatest of the existing maritime powers, to make friends with Turkey as the guardian
of the Straits. The other was the common interests of Britain and
Turkey, which Lord Curzon developed during the peace negotiations at Lausanne in 1922, as against Bolshevik Russia, which at
that time was sedulously cultivating Turkey in opposition to the
capitalist Entente. The Lausanne Treaty was the final peace settlement to be made by the Allies with their wartime opponents, and
perhaps for that very reason was the most enduring, except that in
1936 the Lausanne convention of the Straits was peacefully revised
and the Montreux treaty, with full British approval, was negotiated; this gave Turkey the right, denied to her at Lausanne, to
militarize the Straits.

The Turkish settlement, and especially the retention by Turkey
of her foothold in Europe, testified to the strength of anxieties about
India in the making of British policy. During the long discussions
in the British Cabinet about Turkey and the Near East in 1920 and
1921, the Foreign Secretary, Curzon, pressed, with Admiralty support, for the expulsion of the Turks from Europe, though it was
never quite clear who, in that case, would be sovereign of the Straits.
The war had, however, excited the strongest nationalist feelings in
India, as it did in the rest of Asia, and the British made a concession
to these feelings in the Montagu-Chelmsford reforms of 1919. It
was Edward Montagu who, as Secretary of State for India, persuaded the Cabinet that the post-war aftermath was no time for
adding fuel to the discontents of Muslim India by expelling the
Turks from Europe.

The Turkish settlement is also interesting in that it was a Near
Eastern counterpart to the concurrent Anglo-French tensions over
the settlement in Europe. First, Britain, or rather British officers and
officials on the spot, irritated the French by seeming to intrigue
against them with the Arabs in Syria and Lebanon and by installing
the Arab leader, Prince Feisal, as ruler of the British mandate, Iraq,
after the French had expelled him from Syria. Then France dis-
gusted the British by coming to terms with Kemal Ataturk in the
Franklin-Bouillon agreement of October 1921, thus breaking what
Britain had hoped would remain a united Allied front until a
definite peace settlement with Turkey was reached.

III

The coalition which joined forces against the Central Powers in August 1914, consisting of Belgium, Britain, France, Japan, Russia and Serbia, to which Italy, formerly an ally of the Central Powers, was added in April 1915, had been transformed by the end of the war owing to Russia's retirement from the conflict in 1917 and the United States' entry into the war on the Allied side in April of that year. Germany's defeat in the autumn of 1918 was not due in the first instance to America's weight being thrown into the scale against her, but the Germans had to calculate, when they considered suing for peace, that if the war continued the United States could carry on fighting longer than any other belligerent. At meetings of the Supreme War Council of the Allies in October and November 1918 which reviewed Germany's correspondence with President Wilson, to whom she had applied for peace on the basis of the Fourteen Points, General Pershing, the commander of American forces in Europe, was the sole Allied military leader who anticipated having to fight, if need be, until 1920 and 1921.[3] But, although the European struggle had to be resolved by America's entry into the war and her ability to continue fighting when all the rest had stopped, the United States withdrew from the European balance of power as soon as the peace treaties were signed by refusing to ratify them. Henceforward she took no part in enforcing the peace or the treaties.

This left Britain, France and Italy, states which could not overthrow Germany unaided during the war, as the major guardians of the peace settlement. Italy had no interest in enforcing the peace because, apart from acquiring the South Tirol and the Trieste peninsula from Austria by the treaty of Saint Germain, she regarded herself as having been cheated of the promises made to her of compensations in Dalmatia, Anatolia and Africa when she adhered to the Entente by the Treaty of London of April 1915. These feelings played an important part in the support which Italian public opinion gave to the ex-Socialist Benito Mussolini, who seized power in Rome in October 1922 and revived the romantic programme of re-creating the ancient Roman Empire in the Mediterranean. Britain and France, the remaining two of the trio, were an ill-matched pair for maintaining the peace even had they been able to do so. Most British people regarded the French as still harbouring Napoleonic

[3] See H. R. Rudin, *Armistice, 1918*, Yale, 1944, pp. 183–4.

ambitions to dominate Europe, as needlessly vicious towards Germany, as likely to plunge the world back into war again through their policy of great armaments and military pacts designed to tie Germany up in fetters. In any case, Britain had far too many domestic worries on her hands—Ireland, India, nationalism rampant even in the white dominions of the Empire, unemployment, industrial unrest and the spectre of Communism unleashed by the new forces at work in Soviet Russia—to have much time for Europe. She wanted pacification; an end to great land armies and talk of war; peace and quiet. The French, on the other hand, regarded Britain as unrealistic about Germany, ignorant about security questions, uninterested in Europe and insufferably hypocritical in denouncing French imperialism while hanging on to her own empire and even intriguing to expand it at France's expense.

The peace settlement which these two, with the United States, had made and were now expected to enforce alone—and Britain doubted if it could be enforced—had no support from Russia. On the contrary, the Bolsheviks denounced the settlement, as did most on the Left in Britain, as a capitalist peace intended either to keep Russia imprisoned within a *cordon sanitaire* or to provide a framework within which capitalist Europe could plot and plan aggression against the socialist homeland. While the peace settlement in the West was reasonably secure, at least after the Locarno treaties in 1925, the belt of states in eastern Europe, for the defence of which Soviet assistance was essential, was a most unlikely proposition. This structure never had the wholehearted support of Britain, who in any case had had no real interests in eastern Europe since the eighteenth century; nor of Italy, who sought rather to divert Germany in that direction to take her mind off an *Anschluss* with Austria; nor, of course, of Germany or Russia. The east European states were riddled with minority problems and with resentments and counter-resentments against each other. They had been brought into existence, or brought themselves into existence, under United States patronage, and now the United States had quitted the stage. How, in these circumstances, could any German government which hoped to remain popular with its own people avoid committing itself to the revision of the east European settlement? The Allies had demanded a democratic Germany in 1918 on the ground that it would be more law-abiding than a régime like the Kaiser's. They then gave Germany a peace settlement, which, though perhaps not unjust in itself, German democracy must perforce attack if it was to survive. If it did not attack the peace settlement, there were more sinister forces waiting in the wings in Germany which would do it for them.

But these were not the issues which the world was most interested in on the morrow of the Great War. The questions which held their attention concerned putting the guilty on trial, exacting reparations from the defeated, settling the tangled problems of inter-Allied war debts, resettlement and rehabilitation after the great conflict. Somehow the world returned to work and there was an illusory golden age of prosperity in Europe, mainly based on the inflow of American capital and loans, until the world economy blew up, or ground to a halt, in the great depression of 1929–33. But before we come to that we must consider another area of the international system from which most European eyes also tended to be averted : the Far East.

REFERENCES

Baker, R. S., *Woodrow Wilson and World Settlement*, 3 vols., London, Heinemann, 1922.

George, David Lloyd, *The Truth abouth the Peace Treaties*, 2 vols., London, Gollancz, 1938.

Howard, F. W., *The Partition of Turkey*, Norman, University of Oklahoma Press, 1931.

The Journal of Contemporary History, Vol. 3, No. 4, '1918–19: From War to Peace', London, Weidenfeld and Nicolson, and New York, Harper, October, 1968.

Macartney, C. A., *Hungary and her Successors: the Treaty of Trianon and its Consequences, 1919–1937*, London, Royal Institute of International Affairs, 1937.

Mantoux, E., *The Carthaginian Peace*, London, O.U.P., and Pittsburgh, University of Pittsburgh Press, 1946.

Marston, F. S., *The Peace Conference of 1919*, London, O.U.P., 1944.

Mayer, A. J., *Politics and Diplomacy of Peacemaking: Containment and Counterrevolulion at Versailles, 1918–1919*, London, Weidenfeld and Nicolson, and New York, Random House, 1968.

The New Cambridge Modern History, Vol. XII, *The Shifting Balance of World Forces, 1898–1945*, Cambridge, C.U.P., 1968, Chapter 8.

Nicolson, H., *Peacemaking, 1919*, London, Constable, and New York, Grosset and Dunlap, 1933.

Ullman, R. H., *Anglo-Soviet Relations, 1917–1921*, Princeton, N.J., Princeton U.P., 1961, continuing.

7 War and Politics in the Far East

By 1870 the European international system was fully mature. It was characterized by the legal equality of its member-states, by sovereignty, in the sense of the legal supremacy of the state's organs within its own territory, by a rough equality of strength between its five or six great powers and by a shifting complex of alliances and alignments between those powers such that no one of them could dominate the rest. There were continuous contacts between member-states and rules of law formally based on sovereign equality to regulate those relations. In the rest of the world, however, the pattern of intercourse between dissimilar peoples had from time immemorial followed different principles. Where conditions were favourable, tribes and settlements were yoked together by a single focus of imperial power which recognized no equal, relations between one imperial conglomerate and another being governed by naked military force where contact was not rendered impossible by distance or the roughness of the intervening terrain. Such an imperial focus had governed China through a succession of dynasties interrupted by periods of warring states from almost a thousand years before the birth of Christ until the impact of the West in the nineteenth century. In Chinese thinking, the Emperor, the Son of Heaven, had no equal and all must bow before him. This claim to supremacy over all other peoples was not based on race, religion or military superiority, but on the quality of Chinese civilization. The claim was only modified in practice when the Chinese came into contact in contiguous areas either with Buddhists, whose religious ideas they respected and even assimilated, or with peoples they could not overcome in war.

The first contacts through trade between Chinese and Europeans were marked by haughty disdain on the part of the Chinese and their refusal to allow Europeans to do business in China except on the basis of their total prostration before the Emperor. Since Europeans themselves entered Asian countries a hundred years ago with a strong sense of their own superiority and their divine mission to rule the lesser breeds without the law, all the elements of violent conflict were present from the outset. The first official British missions to the Chinese imperial court, those of Lord Macartney in 1792 and of Lord Amherst in 1816, failed to reconcile the Chinese demand for the acceptance of the Emperor's supremacy with the British demand for the recognition of Europeans at least as equals. Then, following the Opium War of 1839–42, Britain made the first inroad into Chinese sovereignty by securing in the Treaty of Nanking in 1842 the cession of Hong Kong island, the opening of four more ports besides the existing open port of Canton to European trade, the appointment of British consuls in the southern ports with the right to deal directly with the provincial authorities and the fixing of the Chinese tariff at five per cent ad valorem. By a supplementary Anglo-Chinese agreement in 1843 most-favoured-nation treatment was accorded to Britain, by which it obtained any trading concessions China should grant to other countries. Moreover, by the same agreement China granted Britain extra-territorial jurisdiction by which British subjects in China could only be tried by courts under British control.

The next step came in 1858, after an Anglo-French war against the Chinese in 1856–60, when by the Treaty of Tientsin China was compelled to accept a permanent British diplomatic mission in Peking. This was the first time that the Chinese agreed to the essentially European principle of permanent diplomatic representation by which a portion of a country's territory is regarded as being under the sovereignty of another state. It was a principle wholly at variance with the Chinese conception of the complete supremacy of the Emperor, not only in his own territory, but over all other peoples. At the same time the maritime customs of China were placed under the control of an Anglo-French inspectorate as a result of the Anglo-French war. The expedient had been tried on a temporary basis at Shanghai in 1854. It was to remain a dominant restriction on Chinese sovereignty for almost a century.

China was thus forced into the European international system during a period when the peoples of that system were largely ignorant of the long history of Chinese government and civilization and most ruthless in their exploitation of non-European countries for purposes of trade. The fact that this enforced entrance into the international system was achieved in circumstances intensely humiliating to the Chinese has affected their attitude towards international relations ever since.

Where Britain led other countries followed. By 1870 the European great powers had established diplomatic relations with the Imperial regime in China and created their settlements in China's ports where their own armed forces kept the peace and their own courts administered the law. Shanghai, for example, was divided into three parts, an international settlement under British and United States control, a French settlement and the rest, Greater Shanghai, under Chinese government; the former two areas were wholly under foreign rule, their municipal affairs being decided by foreign rate-payers until limited Chinese representation was conceded in 1926. China's foreign trade was almost entirely in European hands and was managed to the benefit of Europeans. The Chinese, while still despising Europeans, were compelled to respect their material power, their troops and navies and their ruthless spirit. By a strange irony an ancient country which based its claim to rule over others on its civilization, had had its independence sapped and undermined by Europeans who came to shower on the benighted heathen the blessings of trade and Christianity. Meanwhile, its peripheral territories were being brought under European rule. By a treaty signed in 1860 the Manchu Emperors had no option but to sign away to the Russian Tsar vast areas lying between Manchuria and Lake Baikal as well as the Amur River province with its port of Vladivostok, though this was frozen for four months of the year. Thus, as Imperial China exposed itself practically defenceless to the dynamic force of the West, Russia, rebuffed in Europe by the Crimean War at the end of which the Peace of Paris in 1856 denied her the use of the Black Sea for her warships, became a Pacific power. While this was happening in the north, China was losing some of her old tributary states in the south. The French fastened their grip on Cochin China in the 1860s and by 1885 had control of the better part of Annam. In 1882 the British annexed Burma.

There was a striking contrast between the ways in which China and the neighbouring country of Japan reacted to the impact of the West. China had an ancient system of ordered power, ruled by an almighty Emperor and administered in practice by a vast civil service recruited by competitive examination in which the candidate was required to reveal a detailed knowledge of the Chinese classics. This complex and stable system, rooted in the Chinese sense of superiority over all other peoples in the world, had been rocked by the reformist T'ai P'ing rebellion for fourteen years between 1850 and 1864, the first great internal stirring against the impact of the West. But it was still too stable to collapse at once under the West's intrusion and too inflexible, too self-assured, too much governed by scholars, had too plentiful a labour supply to feel the need to mechanize, to adapt itself to the new world of technology which the West brought with it. The result was a slow, and then accelerating decline, marked by the inability of the ruling classes to accommodate themselves to change, and by blind outbreaks against Europeans, their ideas and instruments of conquest.

Japan, on the other hand, though it had remained in a similar seclusion since medieval times, with foreign trade confined to the port of Nagasaki and limited to the Chinese and the Dutch, was ruled, centrally and locally, by a semi-feudal military class; its soldiers almost at once saw the folly of resistance when the American 'Black Ships' under Commodore Perry sailed into Uraga Bay in February 1853. On Perry's second visit in 1854 two Japanese ports were opened to foreign trade and consular representation was conceded. Four months after that voyage Admiral Stirling, for Britain, secured a similar treaty, by parading his four warships in Nagasaki Bay. This demonstration of force against Japan was brief in time, not the long-drawn-out agony of China. When in the summer of 1865 the ships of four nations, Britain, France, Holland and the United States, sailed into Osaka Bay to demand the ratification of the treaties with foreign powers which the Japanese authorities had signed, it was the last occasion on which the Western powers had to use force against Japanese xenophobia. Within a few years of the appearance of Perry, the Japanese had bowed to the necessity of foreign trade and permanent diplomatic missions. Moreover, in 1868 the old Shogunate, the system of military dictatorship established at Yedo which had ruled the country for more than a thousand years, was abolished and the Imperial government was restored under the Emperor Meiji, a boy of fifteen at the time of the restoration. Japan embarked upon an industrial revolution, revised the constitution and began to make herself look like a European state. An inherent adaptability in the Japanese national character played some part in this response to the impact of the West. But another important reason is that the Japanese never had the indigenous political structure or culture which characterized the Chinese; they had lived a simple, feudal, isolated life until Commodore Perry came, with no pretended title to the world's homage. They had less to lose than the Chinese from modernization. Above all, their soldier-rulers were better able to understand the meaning of Western military force than China's philosopher kings.

Hence, while the Chinese resentfully smouldered under spreading European control, the Japanese began their industrialization which was to make them in the mid-twentieth century the solitary industrial nation in the Far East, gave themselves a constitution in 1889 which was closely modelled on the German example and eagerly cultivated relations with the European powers. In becoming Europeanized, the Japanese learned the lessons of European diplomacy, especially the dangers of power vacuums in areas adjacent to their own territory and the need to fill such vacuums with her own forces if they were not to be occupied by hostile agents. The European powers were advantaged by the decline of Imperial China; it provided an unresisting prey on whose flesh they could feed. At the same time, in their capacity as traders they had no wish to see the Imperial régime disintegrate into utter chaos and hence were free with loans to prop up the rickety structure. For Japan, on the other hand, the situation was different. Having narrowly escaped the fate of China herself, she had no wish to see that country so weakened as to be completely replaced by European powers established on the Chinese mainland in all their military strength. The most likely aspirant to succeed China's waning power was Russia. Following the well-known Russian tendency to swing backwards and forwards between expansion in Europe and expansion in Asia when her path forwards was blocked in one or the other, the Tsarist government reacted to the setback to the Berlin conference in 1878 and the formation of the Dual Alliance between Germany and Austria-Hungary in 1879, which for the time being checked Russia's progress in the Balkans, by seeking compensations in the Far East. In 1891, when Russia began actively to build her military alliance with France, construction of the trans-Siberian railway was started, the first fruits of the movement of French capital into Russia, and by this means Tsarist forces were later transported from Europe to Russia's Far Eastern port of Vladivostok.[1] At the same time Russia embarked upon the economic penetration of Manchuria.

These developments could not but stir the deepest alarm in Japan. With Russia, backed by another European power with Far Eastern interests, France, stepping into China's shoes, Japan's situation began to look parlous indeed. The immediate need was to

---

[1] It was finally completed in 1917 but by 1904 most of the work was finished.

establish a sphere of interest in neighbouring Korea which projected like a shield between the Japanese islands and the Chinese mainland. In this promontory Japanese armies, engaged for the first time in modern war against the forces of an opposing state, overwhelmed the Chinese in 1894 and the resulting Treaty of Shimonoseki in 1895 established Japan as a Far Eastern power to be reckoned with. In the familiar fashion of the European international system, Japan had made good her claim for recognition in that system by overthrowing another comparable state.

Japan's gains by the Treaty of Shimonoseki, though she was immediately compelled to disgorge some of them, were immense and laid the basis for Japan's imperial career which reached its climax during the Second World War. Besides being forced to pay an indemnity, now a well-established form of penalty for failure in the international system, China was compelled to hand over Formosa and the Pescadores to Japan, to cede to her the strategically vital Liaotung peninsula with its great naval base at Port Arthur which controls the Yellow Sea, to open more of her ports to foreign trade and to recognize the independence of Korea, another phrase in the European diplomatic vocabulary for an area becoming a client state of another great power. In successive agreements with China and Russia in the following decade, Japan's grip on Korea tightened and was gradually accepted as a reality until that country was finally annexed in 1910.

The Treaty of Shimonoseki was almost as bitter a blow to Russia as it was to China, and it is not surprising that in the years immediately after its signature those two countries moved closer together. The immediate task for Russia, however, was to organize an international front against Japan of a similar kind to that which had been organized against herself by Britain before the Berlin conference of 1878. By now Russia could count on her alliance with France for this purpose, and William II's Germany had no wish to see these two powers acting alone on the Far East to revise the Treaty of Shimonoseki. Germany, too, had every interest in diverting Russia's ambitions from the Balkans to the Far East, provided Germany was there to see that Russia did not expand too much. The result was the formation of the *Dreibund* between these three powers which confronted Japan with the demand to return the Liaotung peninsula to China. Neither Britain nor the United States would side with Japan and she had therefore to bow to the inevitable.

But the picture was radically changed by Russia's subsequent behaviour. Working in close co-operation with France, the Russian Finance Minister, Count Witte, made arrangements with China for the financing of railway construction in that country and the first fruit of this was reaped in June 1896 when, by the Li-Lobanov secret agreement, Russia secured permission to construct the Chinese Eastern Railway (CER) across the great Manchurian salient to Vladivostok, thus shortening the journey to that port as the terminus of the trans-Siberian line by almost 600 miles. By Article VI of the agreement Russia was granted the right of administration over the land necessary for the construction, operation and protection of the railway, an early indication of the close association of politics and business in the Far East. In return China received, besides a pledge of Russian assistance against aggression, the option to purchase the Chinese Eastern Railway in 36 years' time, that is, in 1932, or to acquire it freely in 1976. Then, in 1898, Nicholas II crowned this success by securing a 25-year lease of the Liaotung peninsula with the right to build a branch line, to be called the South Manchuria Railway (SMR), from Port Arthur to the Chinese Eastern Railway at Changchun on the same terms as the agreement of 1896. This arrangement was concluded on the advice of the Tsar's War Minister, General Kuropatkin, and contrary to that of Count Witte. Witte considered that such a move, coming so soon after the action of the *Dreibund* in forcing Japan to return the Liaotung peninsula to China, would have alarming effects on the existing policies and alignments of the powers in the Far East. This prophecy proved correct.

Russia's expansion into Manchuria served as a signal to the other European states to take what they could in China while the going was good. The presiding authority in Peking, the Empress Dowager, Tzu Hsi, could not but comply with whatever demands were made. Russia's ally, France, concentrated her depredations in south China, Germany seized the naval base of Kiaochow and other properties in Shantung, facing the Liaotung peninsula and sacred to the Chinese as the birthplace of Confucius. Britain in 1898 retorted by securing a lease of the naval base of Wei-hai-Wei. The ensuing prospect of the imminent dissolution of China made its impact both on the United States and on Japan. The American Secretary of State, John Hay, circulated his famous identical notes to the powers in 1899 insisting on the principle of the 'Open Door' in the commercial exploitation of China. In so far as this move was levelled against the creation in

China of exclusive spheres of interest from which the trade of other countries would be prohibited, it chimed in with the British viewpoint, and the Hay notes are in fact generally credited with having been inspired by Britain. But the 'Open Door' notes also reflected the entrance of the United States into the Far Eastern sector of the international system as a force to be reckoned with.

It was now a generation since the American Republic had been torn into two by the civil war and the almost equally savage period of 'reconstruction', as it was euphemistically called, which followed. During that generation the open spaces to the west in the North American continent had been filled in. There was no more moving frontier at home, no new opportunity for pioneering enterprise between the Atlantic and the Pacific, except towards Mexico, and that did not offer the richest rewards. Politicians, poets, religious leaders were so dazzled with American success in subjugating and civilising a continent, building in it a society immeasurably superior, or so it seemed, to the Europe they or their fathers or grandfathers had left, that it required no great feat of the imagination to conceive America as having been divinely inspired to civilize mankind, especially its less fortunate members in Central America and the Far East.[2] As it happened, America could play an anti-imperialist role in the Far East, true to its traditions, by helping defend China against being sliced up into exclusive spheres of interest by the European powers, while benefiting from the trade which the European powers had forced on China. As missionaries and teachers in China they could derive satisfaction from converting the heathen to the one true faith while thanking God that they were not as the Europeans were.

But it was primarily the combination of the need for export markets and strategic considerations which involved the United States in the now complex diplomatic situation in the Far East. In 1898 America won an easy victory over Spain and in doing so acquired the Philippines and liberated Cuba from European rule. This at once implicated the United States in the naval balance of power in the Pacific; since the United States, with its long western coastline, was now in every sense a Pacific power, that involvement could never afterwards be renounced. America, too, like the European great powers, had now begun to dream of dominating the oceans with her giant ships and had her own prophet, Admiral

---

[2] See Richard Hofstadter, *Social Darwinism in American Thought, 1860–1915*, Philadelphia, 1945.

Mahan, to tell her why and how to do so. These imperial and naval pretensions might have been submerged beneath the anti-colonial sentiments which were second nature to all Americans. But at least two circumstances combined to prevent this happening. One was the realization, at least among the informed, that the Monroe Doctrine of 1823, by which the United States aspired to keep the Americas free from European colonization, was dependent upon an understanding with Britain, whose fleet in effect kept the Pacific and Atlantic oceans free from forces hostile to the United States. But in the 1890s Britain was hard put to it to muster the naval strength to set against her two main rivals at sea, Russia and France, with the later addition of Germany as a third naval contender, to say nothing of contributing to America's security. If the Monroe Doctrine was to be a reality, America would have to back it by her own naval power and that in itself might have the effect of discouraging Britain still further from helping America with her naval problems. Secondly, like Europeans, Americans were impressed or rather mesmerized, by the prospects of the Far East as a market for their exports. When Congressmen lobbied President McKinley to annex the Philippines in 1898, many of them were thinking of the innumerable yellow bodies American textile manufacturing firms could clothe. Only later was it realised that those bodies might not have the financial wherewithal necessary to fulfil this plan.

But in addition, Russia's gains at the expense of China in 1896–98, the impetus which this gave to the other European powers to stake their claims on the moribund China, and the unity which these powers showed against the futile but understandable Chinese backlash in the Boxer rebellion of 1900, alerted Americans to the growing danger of being pushed out of east Asia by the Europeans. Only a minority of Americans really wanted their flag actually to fly on Asian soil, but they would rather have this than be shut out of Chinese markets and reduced to a nonentity in the naval balance of power in the Pacific. The effect of these developments on Japan, however, was far more serious. Unless the Japanese grappled with the problem of Russia's mounting strength in China, their turn to be served up to the Russian bear would inevitably come.

Japan sought to deal with this situation in two ways, firstly, by trying to secure from Russia a formal recognition of Japanese interests in east Asia and then, when this failed, by embarking on the ambitious programme of toppling Russia as a dominant military force in the region. As for the first of these efforts, in the same

year that Russia secured from China the lease of the Liaotung peninsula, namely 1898, Japan obtained from Russia through the Nishi-
Rosen agreement a recognition of her own rights in Korea. But the
Tsar's Ministers saw no reason why they should be too scrupulous
towards an upstart Asian country and when Count Ito went to St.
Petersburg two years later and attempted to effect an exchange of
Russian freedom of action in Manchuria for Japanese freedom of
action in Korea, the Russians agreed informally but resisted all proposals to write the deal in treaty form. In the result Britain, now
experiencing the effects of isolation, which showed conspicuously
when she was cold-shouldered by all the other great powers during
the Boer War, made the Anglo-Japanese naval alliance of 1902
which has been discussed earlier (see above, Chapter 5, pp. 80–2).
As we have seen, Britain, the *primus inter pares* of the European
system of international relations, was forced through realization of
her naval weakness to ally with Japan in order to check Russia in
the Far East. This alliance of the first power of Europe with an
Asiatic state subtly altered the status of both. It called attention to
the relative downgrading of Britain and the evident upgrading of
Japan. It symbolized Japan's entry into the select European club of
great powers for this was the first important treaty which she had
signed on a basis of equality with a European power.

It is hard to know whether without the alliance with Britain
Japan would have been so foolhardy as to provoke Russia so much
into the war of 1904–05. Russia, after all, had enjoyed an acknowledged status in the European international system since at least
the time of Peter the Great. She had overthrown Napoleon and was
in consequence, although herself part Asiatic, one of the four pillars
of the European international order created by the Congress of
Vienna in 1815. Militarily Japan was an unknown quality, apart
from the evidence of her fighting capacity shown by her victory over
China which had been no great military force when defeated in
1895. Japan's assets in the war with Russia which broke out in
February 1904 were, however, considerable. Her army had been
thoroughly reorganized and her navy developed with British advice
and finance from the Chinese war indemnity of 1894. She was also
fighting both on land in Manchuria and in the Yellow Sea close to
her home islands, and the supply of her forces was relatively easy.
Russian troops, on the other hand, had to be supplied by the one-
track Trans-Siberian railway, and after her Far Eastern fleet had
been bottled up in Port Arthur by Admiral Togo, her Baltic fleet

had to sail half way round the world to the Pacific, where it was promptly worsted by the Japanese in the battle of the Tsushima Strait. Above all, whereas Russian soldiers and sailors were fighting for rights in a far-away country which seemed of greater benefit to rich capitalists than to poor Russian peasants and workers, Japanese fighting men regarded themselves as battling for a sacred cause, their own brand of nationalism, and this feeling was enhanced by their fear and hatred of the Russian imperialist who would undoubtedly do to Japan, if he got the chance, what he had already done to China.

Japan's victory over Russia in 1905 rang around the world. It astonished the military experts and while some people, as in Britain, admired the Asian David who had vanquished an intensely disliked European Goliath, there were many, especially in the United States, who now bitterly faced the reality that here in Japan was a new, unknown force to be reckoned with in the Far East. But Japan's victory also stirred the hearts and bolstered the self-confidence of millions of Asians living under foreign rule. Like Japan's victory over the British at Singapore in February 1942, her triumph in 1905 showed that European power, which had seemed to Asians so irresistible, could be overthrown if Asians had the nationalistic pride and cohesion, and the modernization, to equip themselves for that task; in short, the end of Western power in the Far East, if not in other parts of the non-European world, too, was forecast in the battle of Tsushima Strait. But of more immediate concern was the effect on the balance of power in the Far East, partly to be measured by the gains Japan made under the peace treaty signed with Russia at Portsmouth, New Hampshire, in May 1905, where President Theodore Roosevelt for the first time exhibited the United States as a new venue for world diplomacy. First, Russia at long last acknowledged Japan's paramountcy in Korea and did so formally. She also transferred to Japan her lease of the Liaotung peninsula and the southern branch of the Chinese Eastern Railway from Port Arthur to Changchun; the southern half of the island of Sakhalin, lying to the north of the Japanese home islands, also went to Japan. Both countries agreed to withdraw from Manchuria which was then declared an 'Open Door' zone.

In the years following the Treaty of Portsmouth, Japan consolidated her gains, with Russia, smarting from defeat in war and an internal revolt sparked off by that defeat, now acting as her auxiliary. In secret agreements between these two countries in 1907 and

1909, which the Russian Bolsheviks revealed to the world after they seized power in November 1917, they united their efforts against any attempt on the part of the United States or China to shake the hold the two of them had now acquired over the railway system of Manchuria. In 1906 the South Manchuria Railway was incorporated with a capital of 200 million yen. Japan transferred all her railway holdings in Manchuria to the company in return for half its shares and the right to appoint its president, vice-president and directors. The company became to all intents a branch of the Japanese government.

Thus, by the time the European war of 1914–18 broke out, while the European powers maintained on the whole the network of concessions, extra-territorial rights, control of customs, leases of railway lines, ports and harbours they had wrested from the Manchu emperors in the second half of the nineteenth century, Japan was definitely within reach of dominating the Far East. Her people, industrious, intensely patriotic and almost entirely unrebellious, could be counted on to endure any sacrifice on behalf of the national cause. Her industrial, political and military leaders, energetic, flexible, dedicated men, were extraordinarily gifted with skill in seizing opportunities presented to them by circumstances. They had brought Japan in fact, if not always in the opinion of Europeans, almost to the summit of the international ladder by their military victories over first China and then Russia. They had established a stranglehold over the strategically vital Manchurian railway system with a right to protect it with their own armed forces. They had brought Korea, Formosa, Southern Sakhalin, and the Pescadores within an empire they had created in not much more than a score of years. For the time being at least, Russia was an acquiescent co-operator. China, where the Manchu dynasty fell in ruins in 1911, was weak and divided with President Yuan Shi Kai in Peking formally holding the allegiance of a group of provincial war lords, a ripe candidate when the time came either to become a Japanese protectorate or the very junior partner in a Sino-Japanese condominium. Above all, Japan had entered into alliance on terms of equality and reciprocity with the old *doyen* of the international system, Britain, and her diplomats were accorded all, or almost all, the respect due to the envoys of a great power in the world's capitals. Only the United States cast suspicious eyes in Japan's direction and so long as Britain, France, Germany and Russia remained reasonably well-disposed, that did not count for much.

II

But it was the First World War that was Japan's great opportunity. The European powers, who had spent fifty years bringing China to the point of dismemberment in their Battle of Concessions, could hardly tear themselves to pieces in four and a quarter years of savage fighting without leaving Japan with a clear field for expansion in China. Russia, Japan's most formidable rival in Manchuria, totally collapsed in revolution in 1917, and Japan was well placed to become a leading member of the inter-allied expedition which invaded Siberia through Vladivostok in March 1918. The Japanese Government did not succeed in their efforts to plant an anti-Bolshevik buffer state in eastern Siberia and their participation in the interventionist movement in Russia had the drawback of intensifying United States suspicions of their designs. Japanese forces, however, did not retire from Vladivostok until 1922 and three years later the Japanese government were able to wrest concessions from Russia in northern Sakhalin. For the time being at least the Japanese had nothing to fear from a Soviet Russia struggling for sheer survival and pathologically afraid of attack from a combination of capitalist powers in the West. Moreover, the war saw the total eclipse of Germany as a Far Eastern power, and the gains she had made in the Battle of Concessions, notably the properties in Shantung, including the naval base of Kiaochow, and her island possessions in the Pacific north of the equator, fell to Japan. At the Paris peace conference in 1919, these gains from Germany were confirmed to Japan on condition that the Shantung properties were later returned to China (which raised the question why they were not at once handed back to China without passing through Japan's hands at all) and provided the island territories in the Pacific became 'C' mandates of Japan under League of Nations supervision. The Chinese delegation at the peace conference were so indignant at this settlement that they returned home without having signed the peace treaty.

The fact that Britain, Japan's ally, was a leading victor in the war on the Allied side also served Japan's interests. The British Government had not been keen at first on Japan's entering the war against Germany, telling Tokyo that they expected no more assistance from Japan than they had given that country during its war with Russia in 1904. However, when the Allied military situation became critical in 1917, Japanese help was welcome, but the

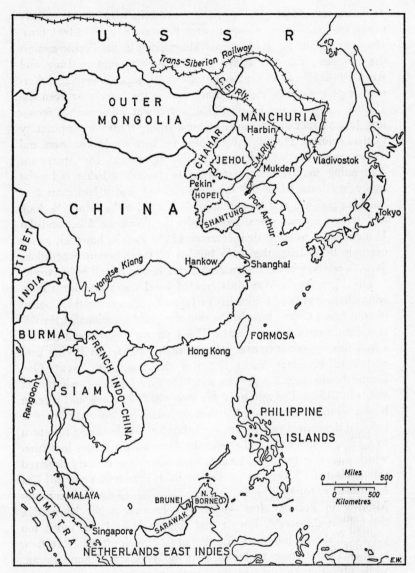

The Far East, 1919–39

Japanese refused to give it in the form Britain expected, namely troops for the Western Front, though these were supplied by China. Hence in return for Japanese naval activities in the Pacific against the Germans, the four Allied powers, Britain, France, Italy and Russia, formally agreed, as stated above, to Japan's acquiring Germany's possessions in the Far East, and in the same year even the United States, by the Lansing-Ishii agreement, consented to recognize Japan's special interests in China arising from her propinquity to that country. Dispute later sprang up between Washington and Tokyo as to the interpretation of this agreement, the Americans contending that it merely referred to Japan's existing rights by treaty in China, while the Japanese claimed that it had more far-reaching political and economic implications for the future. So long as Japanese assistance was required by the European Allies and the United States to serve their interests in the Pacific, however, as for example by bearing the main burden of the Siberian expedition, Japan's position in the international system was bound to be strong.

The First World War thus created ideal conditions for Right-wing chauvinists and militarists in Japan to press home their policy of converting China, now in the mid-stream of a nationalist revolution, into a virtual protectorate. The Japanese Government quickly seized this opportunity and in 1915 their Minister in Peking presented to President Yuan Shi Kai the notorious Twenty-One Demands which, in five groups, sought to give Japan a predominant status in China. The sole *quid pro quo* which China would receive if she submitted to this relegation of herself to the position of a colonial dependency of Japan was a Japanese undertaking to return to China at the end of the war the German properties in China which Japanese troops had seized soon after their country declared war against the Kaiser on 23 August 1914. President Yuan Shi Kai emitted a cry for help by 'leaking' the Demands to the United States Minister in Peking, after which they became public knowledge throughout the world. But at that time the world was much too preoccupied with the war in Europe to pay much attention. In fact, a United States note to Japan, sent by Secretary of State Bryan, while objecting to some of the Demands as infringements of the 'Open Door' policy, recognized once more that Japan's territorial contiguity to the mainland created certain special relations between herself, China and Manchuria.

When eventually a Sino-Japanese treaty was signed in May 1915, following a Japanese ultimatum to the Yuan Shi Kai regime, it marked a beginning of the process of embodying the Twenty-One Demands in legal form. The leases to Japan of the Liaotung peninsula and railways in southern Manchuria were extended to ninety-nine years. Japanese subjects were given the right to lease, though not to own, land in southern Manchuria and to exploit certain mines in that country. Japan was authorized to appoint advisers to the government in Peking and agreed in return for all these concessions to secure Chinese consent to any future arrangements about Shantung. Later, in 1916, Japan obtained further mining and railway concessions in Manchuria by making loans to corrupt Chinese politicians and military leaders.

Hence, at the time of the peace settlements in 1919, the Japanese could regard themselves at or near the apex of their power in the Far East. Their major European rivals were for the moment either defeated or, if victorious in the war, licking their wounds. One of the latter, Britain, appeared to have no objection to the Japanese implementing their will in China; two of Britain's partners in the British Empire, Australia and New Zealand, positively preferred that Japanese imperialist energies should be spent in China rather than turned in their own direction. China herself had hardly any power with which to resist Japanese designs, and China's chief protector, the United States, was for the time being deeply involved in helping to make the European peace settlement and then in deciding whether to take a share in enforcing it. Moreover, for all practical purposes Japan had established a stranglehold over the railway system and economy of Manchuria. It seemed that it would be only a matter of time before that whole vast country fell under her control.

But there for the present Japan's advance was halted, and attention was then turned to the question of how the new power of the United States was to be fitted into the Far Eastern sector of the international system. The American administration of President Harding (1920–24) remained deeply suspicious of Japan. Besides the question of Japan's intentions towards America's traditional protégé in the Far East, China, there was the bad blood stirred up between the two countries over Japanese immigration into the United States. In 1907 Japan and the United States had entered into the so-called Gentleman's Agreement by which the Japanese Government pledged themselves to limit the migration of their people into the west coast of the United States. The Americans charged the Japanese with bad faith in carrying out this agreement, and American suspicions were further aroused by Japanese efforts at the Paris peace conference in 1919, which President Wilson with some assistance from the British succeeded in blocking, to incorporate into the new League of Nations Covenant a clause prohibiting discrimination on grounds of race. Eventually, in 1924, the United States finally slammed the door on Japanese immigration by passing an act which excluded the Japanese from settling in its territory.

The United States would have no difficulty in dealing with Japan alone over the immigration issue. But so long as Japan had her alliance with Britain, whose navy was supreme in the Pacific before the First World War, Americans had something to fear. Could a situation arise in which the United States was engaged in naval hostilities with Japan during a conflict arising out of the immigration issue and with British naval strength thrown on to the Japanese side of the scales? It seems scarcely conceivable today. But at that time there was no love lost between the two Atlantic democracies. Outside government circles, Britain had warmed to the personal magnetism and idealism of President Wilson, but then America had repudiated Wilson and retired from the implementation of the peace settlement, leaving Britain to wrangle alone with France in Europe and the Near East, with Italy in south east Europe. American Congressmen were perpetually inflaming Irish opinion, or so it seemed from London, while Britain wrestled with the Irish Home Rule question which finally ended in the partition of Ireland in 1922. Above all, America, by her great Navy Law of 1916, was claiming parity at sea with Britain, a claim which Britain had never conceded to any country and which she at length conceded only with extreme reluctance to America in 1921. If America continued with her naval rearmament, it would put paid to all the British hopes for a disarmed world in which government spending could be reduced and a beginning made at last on recovery from the economic depression of the years immediately following the war. On the American side, on the other hand, there was a deep emotional revulsion against the war, into which the United States had allegedly been dragged by British imperialist machinations and by American financiers who had waxed fat on loans to the Entente powers. With unshakable ideas like these on both sides of the Atlantic, it was not at all inconceivable in American eyes that Britain might join hands with Japan in making trouble for the United States in the Pacific.

The Harding administration therefore dedicated itself to two

tasks : the destruction of the Anglo-Japanese alliance and a programme of naval disarmament which would at one and the same
time sanctify American naval parity with Britain and clip Japan's
wings, or rather her ships. The alliance had been modified at its
latest revision in 1921 so as to rule out British assistance to Japan
against any country with which Britain had a general arbitration
agreement, and she had such an agreement with the United States,
though it had never been ratified. British and Dominion opinion
was divided about continuance of the alliance. On the one hand,
to drop it meant running the risk of alienating Japan and arousing
suspicion of racial discrimination which no responsible leaders of a
multiracial empire could afford to incur. Besides, as Australian and
New Zealand statesmen at the Imperial Conference in London in
1921 argued, a friendly Japan would be less likely to look covetously
towards their own territories in Australasia. On the other hand,
there were to be counted in the reckoning the prospective gains from
a naval disarmament treaty which might halt American naval
building, and which it seemed could be had from agreeing to
drop the alliance. There was also the Canadian argument, which
was the one eventually to prevail, that the United States, besides
having common interests with Canada in resisting Asian immigration, was too important a country for the British Empire to quarrel
with.

And so, at the Washington conference on naval disarmament and
the Far East in 1921–22, the Anglo-Japanese alliance was replaced,
not, as some British politicians had hoped, by a three-cornered
arrangement to include the United States, but by a weak four-
power treaty (Britain, France, Japan and the United States) to
respect the *status quo* in the Pacific. Alongside this, a five-power
naval disarmament treaty was agreed, based on the principle of a
ten-year holiday in the building of capital ships and the scrapping
of such ships as were then building so as to produce a ratio in these
vessels of 5 : 5 : 3 : 1.75 : 1.75 for Britain, the United States, Japan,
France and Italy respectively. No agreement could be reached on
the limitation of cruiser strength nor, as the British devoutly wished,
on the abolition of the submarine. Coupled with the naval disarmament treaty was an arrangement for the demilitarization of naval
bases in the Pacific with the exception of the Japanese home islands,
Hong Kong, Hawaii and Singapore. The effect of this, as the world
was to realize ten years later, was to confer on Japan a virtual
immunity against being attacked from the sea should she ever again

be engaged in hostilities in mainland China. As one Japanese diplomat is reported to have said to a British delegate at Washington, 'at least you gave the alliance a splendid funeral'. The Washington agreements were rounded off with a nine-power pledge, written in the most general terms and with no indication as to how it was going to be implemented, to respect the territorial integrity and political independence of China. At the same time, and largely as a result of British and American pressure, Japan at length agreed to retrocede to China the former German properties in Shantung which the Kaiser had lost to Japan in the First World War.

The Washington conference thus marked a realignment of forces in the Far East. A new coolness developed in Anglo-Japanese relations while many British politicians regretted the ending of an alliance which had served Britain well in the past and might have been serviceable again in the future as a means for bringing influence to bear on Japanese foreign policy. The United States, moreover, was committed for the first time by an international agreement, though in the most general terms, to uphold the *status quo* in the Far East and now stood on a par with Britain in giant naval warships there. But nothing definite had been provided against the possibility of a future threat to the *status quo* and although Britain and the United States now enjoyed by right of treaty as well as in practice an overwhelming superiority over Japan at sea, they would have to act together, and of that there was little likelihood, if they were to restrain that country in future. Each alone could hardly maintain a naval superiority over Japan in the waters adjacent to north China and surrounding the Japanese islands over the immensely long supply lines now rendered necessary by the demilitarization of naval bases in the Pacific by the Washington treaties. For the present, however, there appeared to be little heart in Japan for further expansionist adventures. A succession of Liberal governments under Baron Shidehara were committing that country to peaceful commercial victories rather than to conquests by the sword. The military were encountering the emotional revulsion against the soldier class which swept the world immediately after the armistice of 1918. And in the year after the signature of the Washington treaties Japan was rocked by the worst earthquake in her history. It took years to recover from this national disaster.

III

Meanwnhile in China the nationalist revolution smouldered on. In Peking, the conservative regime of Yuan Shi Kai presided over a loose agglomeration of semi-independent war lords who governed the territories where their writ ran rather in the manner of feudal barons. Only in the south of the country was the real meaning of the revolution being worked out. There, in Canton especially, with all that city's exposure to world-wide movements of opinion, the break-away Kuomintang party was being organized by the erratic genius of Dr. Sun Yat-sen. His political philosophy belongs to the internal history of China with which we are only obliquely concerned here. It is enough to say that the essence of his ideas, as summed up in his famous *San Min Chu I*, or three principles of the revolution, Nationalism, Democracy and the People's Livelihood, were sufficiently vague and all-embracing to attract a wide variety of followers, from bourgeois liberals to communists. But they reflected the kind of will for a modernized, democratic, united state which other Asian leaders, notably Kemal Ataturk in Anatolia, were striving to implant in their country as the means to freedom from foreign, and especially Western, control. In effect, what men like Sun Yat-sen and Kemal were trying to do was to equip their countries for participation in an international system they had been forced into as inferiors; but that participation must now be on a basis of equality. What Europe had seen in the revolutions of 1848, China was now striving towards as the Kuomintang under Sun Yat-sen conceived it. But the difference was that the scattered fragments of China had first to be brought together in one piece and the terrible grip of the West finally shaken off.

The question was where the military force was to be found to forge national unity. China was not lacking in manpower and her industrial workers, such as they were, were highly skilled. But China's armies had not won any considerable battle in recent times, and the distances over which those armies had to march in the absence of an adequate railway system were vast. It was at this point that Russia made her re-entry, though it was to be a short-lived one, into Chinese national life. After the failure of the long-awaited communist revolution in Europe in the troubled aftermath of the Great War, the Leninists turned their attention to the destruction of the main bastions of Western capitalist strength in Asia. The issue was whether this was best to be done by encouraging local communist formations to enter into non-doctrinaire 'popular fronts' with bourgeois nationalist movements like those of Kemal Ataturk in Turkey and Sun Yat-sen in China; or whether to press on at once with converting the Asian nationalist movements into proletarian communist revolutions on the model of the Russian revolution of 1917. Lenin, before his death in 1924, had formed a liaison with Sun Yat-sen based on the renunciation of all Tsarist policies in relation to China, the training in Moscow of such nationalist Chinese leaders as Chiang Kai Shek, who assumed the leadership of the Kuomintang after Sun Yat-sen's death in 1925, and the despatch to China of a Soviet mission led by Michael Borodin and Marshal Galen to teach the Chinese Nationalists the strategy and tactics of struggle against Western imperialism and to found military schools, like the Whampoa military academy, in which Chiang Kai Shek was to train the military arm of the Kuomintang.

The fundamental ideological issue of Russia's attitude towards the Chinese revolution remained, however, unresolved and was to prove a key question in the dispute between Stalin and Trotsky for control of the Soviet communist party after Lenin's death. That this famous quarrel was won by Stalin with his doctrine of Socialism in One Country and that Trotsky was forced into exile and his associates purged was due in part to Stalin's greater skill in organizing individual leading members of the party on his own side. But it was also influenced by developments in Sino-Soviet relations. Chiang Kai Shek was bitterly hostile to the Chinese communists, as he remained until his eventual exile with what remained of Kuomintang forces to Formosa in 1949 after Mao Tse-tung's victory in the civil war. Accordingly Kuomintang forces turned on the Chinese communists in 1925, inflicting on them a decimating massacre in their own home base, Canton. The effect of this was to strengthen the position of Trotsky in Moscow since he had argued that peaceful co-operation between communists and bourgeois political parties was impossible, and new orders were sent to the Borodin mission in China to switch from a policy of working with the Kuomintang to one of overt communization of the Chinese nationalist movement. Chiang Kai Shek at once severed all links with the communists and began their systematic persecution. The Borodin mission had to be recalled and Stalin was able to argue that Trotsky's policy of fomenting permanent revolution would only have the effect of surrounding Russia with enemies. And Russia could not afford to make more enemies since Germany, which had joined with Russia in a compact of pariah nations by signing the treaty of Rapallo with the Soviets in April 1922, had now ended its quarrel with the Western powers, Britain and France, by the Locarno treaties of 1925.

Having dealt with the communists, the Kuomintang was now ready for the great northern expedition which began in 1926 and two years later had succeeded in bringing the whole of China as far as the Great Wall under Nationalist control with the device of a reforming nationalism inscribed on its banners. By 1928 only Manchuria lay outside the Kuomintang's administration; there the Japanese demonstrated their power to shape events by planting a bomb on the railway line on which the ruler of Manchuria, Marshal Chiang Hsueh-liang, was travelling in flight from Peking after the Kuomintang army had taken the capital. The Marshal lost his life and by this means the Japanese hoped to secure a more acquiescent Manchurian ruler in the person of his son, the 'Young Marshal', as he was called, Chang Tso Lin. But Chang proved himself to be by no means a puppet of the Japanese. Meanwhile, in the two years taken by the Kuomintang's northern expedition, the full force of the Chinese anti-foreignism which it aroused fell on the thickly scattered foreign concessions in its path, especially the British settlements and businesses in the Yangtse valley. It was as though China, which had been for so many years the helpless prey of the foreign soldier and business man, was at last rising up to demand equality and revenge.

The reply from Britain was a far-sighted circular to the interested powers despatched by the Conservative Foreign Secretary, Sir Austen Chamberlain, in December 1926. This proposed that, instead of opposing the Chinese nationalist revolution, the powers should come to terms with it by making a start on negotiating away the special privileges they had wrested from China and restoring full sovereignty to that country. This move was not uninfluenced by the desire to exploit the widening rift between the Kuomintang and Soviet Russia; 1926 was, after all, the year of the General Strike in Britain and in the following year the British Government actually broke off diplomatic relations with Russia. But a more important reason for the circular was Chamberlain's recognition that as a united and prosperous country China might be more profitable as a trading partner than the unpredictable chaos which it had been since the fall of the Manchu dynasty in 1911. However that may be, these British proposals received a dusty answer from the other powers; they felt that here was another example of Britain's habit of sacrificing other countries' interests in order to save her own vastly greater possessions. The discussion which the British Government, later followed by the United States, then began with the Kuomintang authorities on the liquidation of the unequal treaties made very slow progress. Not until 1944, when China had for three years been locked in a partnership with Britain, Russia and the United States in the war against the Axis powers, were the final restrictions on her sovereignty removed.

Because of the difficulties Britain experienced in ensuring international support for her new policy towards the Chinese Nationalists, some sympathy was felt in British governmental circles towards Japan, who began to sustain the brunt of the Chinese attack on foreign rights when Japanese concessions in Shantung came within the reach of the northern expedition in 1928. Japan now seemed to many in Britain to be fighting for the same cause of international legal rights which Britain had fought for in the Yangtse basin two years earlier. This factor was to play an important part in the British Government's attitude towards the Japanese conquest of Manchuria which began with an explosion on the South Manchuria Railway, the lease of which Japan owned and which her troops protected, on the night of 18 September 1931.

Internal and external reasons combined in the making of the Manchurian adventure, which marked Japan's entrance upon the second stage of her empire-building after the interregnum of quietness following the Washington conference. Firstly, the military, who since the restoration of 1868 had played a dominant role in Japanese politics as the constitution could not be worked without serving officers in the Cabinet, had never lived easily under the quietism of the Shidehara era. Working hand-in-glove with countless secret societies which never shrank from the murder of insufficiently chauvinistic politicians, the army was able to argue that Japan could only exist as things were so long as the Western world was prosperous. With the collapse of the American stock market in October 1929 followed by severe financial crisis and protracted economic depression all over the world, Japanese exports, especially of raw silk, were cut radically. With an empire of its own (possessing rich mineral resources) in Manchuria, Korea and north China, Japan, the militarists argued, would be free from the booms and slumps of the Western economic system. But if such a self-contained economic bloc were to be built, it would have to be soon. The Kuomintang had now mastered almost all China except for Manchuria;

for the first time for at least a century national unity was within China's grasp. These arguments for decisive action by Japan in Manchuria were applauded to the echo by young officers in the Japanese Kwantung Army on the Manchurian plains; they saw no future for themselves on the bankrupt farms they had left behind at home and longed to carve out an empire for themselves which they could call their own.

The seizure of Manchuria, which was followed by the Japanese creation there of a puppet state, called Manchukuo, which the last Emperor of China, Pu Yi, was installed to govern, met with surprisingly little resistance from the other powers and from the League of Nations, which now faced its greatest challenge. Russia, as we have seen, had joined with France and Germany in 1898 to deprive Japan of the Liaotung peninsula which she had seized from China. But now Russia was in no military position to oppose Japan with force in far-away Manchuria. Germany had ceased altogether to be a Far Eastern power; so to all intents had France, except that she retained her colonies in Indo-China. In Britain, many Conservative politicians and business men had a sneaking sympathy for Japan, who seemed to be carrying the flag for foreign business and legal rights in turbulent and lawless China, a friend moreover, or former friend, of Bolshevik Russia. Besides, as the British Foreign Secretary, Sir John Simon, tirelessly argued, this was by no means a straightforward case of one country invading another, as the League Covenant envisaged; it was an instance of an external power defending its legitimate rights in a country in which no central government control existed. Above all, the Manchurian crisis occurred just as Britain was going off the Gold Standard and coping with the mutiny of naval ratings at Invergordon provoked by pay cuts which the government had imposed as a remedy for the economic crisis; the crisis, too, had destroyed the Labour Government in Britain and ushered into office a National Government to deal with the country's financial plight. As for the United States, without whose co-operation Britain could not hope to use naval force against Japan even had she been willing, domestic public opinion would certainly not permit the Hoover administration to join with Britain in any hostilities in East Asia. The most Secretary of State Stimson could do was to issue notes declaring that America could not recognize changes forcibly brought about in defiance of the Nine-Power treaty respecting China which had been signed in Washington in 1922. The British Government noted this with a certain wry satisfaction; apart from sending a naval force when the Japanese attacked Shanghai in February 1932, they sat through the crisis with arms folded.

Thus, by the opening of the 1930s, the Far Eastern sector of the world international system had developed as an autonomous and separate theatre. That development was coincident with the rise and fall of European powers in east Asia and the Pacific; it also symbolized the contraction of Europe until it could do little but manage its own affairs, and not even those without external help. Both China and Japan had been opened to world trade and diplomatic relations by the European powers, which then propelled these two countries by force into the international system. The responses of both countries to the impact of the West were dissimilar from each other, but in both instances the ultimate form these responses took was the transformation of the two countries into united, modernized, national states with the kind of armed forces which experience had shown was necessary for defence against external powers. This transformation was remarkably rapid in Japan's case; in China it was much slower and was far from being complete even when Japan struck again with her full force against China in July 1937.

The modernization of Japan and China was the other side of the medal of the decline of the European powers in the Far East which the First World War immensely accelerated but did not initiate. Apart from Britain, with her now threatened imperial position, only two external powers, the United States and Russia, remained as countries still deeply involved in the affairs of East Asia, the United States because of her perennial and natural concern with the balance of power in the Pacific, Russia because of her long land frontier with China. But, for the present, Japan was the unchallenged master of the Far East. With the acquisition of Jehol in northern China in 1932 and the formation of the puppet Hopei-Chahar Political Council in 1933, Japanese forces looked down on China as though poised for its conquest.

REFERENCES

Craigie, R. L., *Behind the Japanese Mask*, London, Hutchinson, 1946.

Galbraith, J. K., 'The Imperial Conference of 1921 and the Washington Conference', *Canadian Historical Review*, 1948.

Grew, J. C., *Ten Years in Japan*, New York, Simon and Schuster, 1944.

Hsü, I. C. Y., *China's Entrance into the Family of Nations: the Diplomatic Phase, 1858–1880*, Cambridge, Mass., Harvard U.P., 1960.

Hudson, G. F., *The Far East in World Politics*, London, O.U.P., 2nd Ed., 1939.

Jones, F. C., *Japan's New Order in East Asia*, London, O.U.P., 1954.

Peffer, N., *The Far East. A Modern History*, Ann Arbor, Michigan U.P., 1958.

Pratt, J. T., *War and Politics in China*, London, Cape, 1943.

Utley, F., *Japan's Feet of Clay*, London, Faber, 1936.

Willoughby, W. W., *The Sino-Japanese Controversy and the League of Nations*, Baltimore, Johns Hopkins Press, 1935.

8 *The League of Nations*

One of the most dramatic consequences of the First World War and the peace conference which followed it was the formation of the League of Nations, known in French, perhaps more accurately, as *la Société des Nations*. The League consisted throughout its life of most of the fifty-odd states of the inter-war international system; it was the first permanent international organization for general purposes to embrace the whole international community, though participation in its work by the great powers was intermittent. Britain and France remained members from its formal birth in 1920 until its formal death in 1946. Japan and Italy, allies of Britain and France in the First World War, were also members with permanent seats on the League Council from 1920 until Japan withdrew in 1933 and Italy in 1937. Germany, the leading Central power opposed to the Entente during the war, was kept out of the League until the partial Franco-German reconciliation which followed the Locarno treaties in 1925. Germany then entered the League as a permanent member of the League Council in 1926 and withdrew in 1933, following Hitler's accession to power and the failure of the world disarmament conference which opened in February 1932.

Soviet Russia was also a pariah state in Western eyes and in any case regarded the League as a 'band of robber nations' bent upon the destruction of the world's first communist state. Her attitude changed, however, with the remilitarization of Germany under the Nazis, and she joined the League in 1934, only to be expelled, the only member-state to suffer this experience, when her forces invaded Finland in 1939. Finally, the United States, whose President in 1919, Woodrow Wilson, was the chief influence in attaching the League's constitution, the Covenant, to the peace treaties as the first twenty-six articles of each of them, refused to ratify the treaties and hence never became a League member. Although American governments co-operated to a limited extent with the League in its peace-enforcement efforts in the 1930s, America's absence from an institution she had so helped to shape was a serious blow to its prospects and an important reason for its failure.

The League of Nations was an umbrella organization under which many different forms of international co-operation were carried on; co-operation, for instance, in the fields of economics, finance, communications and transport, for improving the world's medical services, for suppressing the traffic in drugs and white slavery, for increasing intellectual relations between the different countries and improving the rights of and facilities available to intellectual workers. The League also inherited many responsibilities, some of them full of the seeds of international conflict, from the 1919 peace treaties, such as supervision of the administration of the German port of Danzig on the shores of the Baltic, which was included in the territory of the new Poland in order to give that country an outlet to the sea. Under the League, too, was placed the Saar territory, inhabited mainly by Germans, with provision for a plebiscite to determine the wishes of the population in 1935; and also the supervision of the colonial dependencies of Germany in Africa and the Pacific and the Arab portions of the old Ottoman Empire as territories mandated to certain Allied powers. This system was a half-way house between outright Allied annexation of the former colonies, which the more idealistic climate of the times seemed to rule out, and their internationalization, which was considered too novel and impractical. The mandatory power was formally answerable for its administration of the territories to a Permanent Mandates Commission of the League, but the extent to which this provided for effective international control of the territories varied; the Japanese, for instance, treated their former German mandated territories in the Pacific as though they were to all intents part of their own country. Nevertheless, the mandates system marked a striking step towards the principle of the international accountability for dependent territories and to that extent anticipated the trusteeship system of the United Nations and the extensive control of all non-self-governing territories envisaged in Chapter XI of the UN Charter. It is in fact no exaggeration to see in the League mandates system the distant beginnings of international organizations as one of the leading forces behind that post-1945 revolution in international affairs known as decolonization.

The League was also closely associated with the International Labour Organization, also founded in 1919, which survives today. The aim of this body, which was based on the unusual threefold representation of governments, employers and workers, was to improve the conditions of labour of all kinds in all countries by the adoption of conventions and recommendations for the attainment of higher labour standards throughout the world, on the principle that there could be no peace between nations except on the basis of social justice for all. Closely associated with the League, too, was the Permanent Court of International Justice (PCIJ) formed in 1921, which was situated at The Hague and consisted of nine highly qualified judges with authority to determine legal disputes between League member-states and to give advisory opinions on legal questions when asked to do so either by the League Council or the Assembly. Members of the League were automatically adherents to the Court's Statute. Other states were entitled to adhere and the United States did so in the 1930s while still remaining outside the League.

But in spite of these multifarious activities, for which the League was most grudgingly provided with funds by its member-states, the principal aim of the Geneva organization was the maintenance of peace and the avoidance of the kind of catastrophe the world had experienced in 1914–18; and it is on its work in this sphere that its value has been and will continue to be mainly judged. The League did not prevent the outbreak of a second world war in 1939; indeed after the fiasco of economic sanctions against Mussolini's attempts to conquer Ethiopia in 1935–36, the League was for all practical purposes dead. Nevertheless, by 1939 the League idea, if not the League itself, had become a permanent feature of the international landscape and there was no question among the victorious Allies in the Second World War that a further attempt should be made to preserve peace through a general international organization. This second attempt, the United Nations Organization, is certainly better endowed with resources and legal authority than the old League, but it is founded upon much the same general lines and has borrowed many features and principles from its predecessor, despite the protests of many statesmen present at the San Francisco conference to draw up the UN Charter in May–June 1945 that they were beginning on an essentially clean sheet.

II

The idea of a general association of nations to curb threats to the peace gathered force on both belligerent sides in the closing stages of the First World War when the costs of that terrible conflict seemed hardly bearable unless some new machinery for averting future conflict was firmly established as soon as the war ended. Moreover, the liberal revolution in Russia in March 1917 with its pleas for 'no annexations and no indemnities' seemed to send a new shaft of light through the old gloomy places of power politics. When the Bolsheviks seized power in Russia in November 1917 they aimed at the overthrow of the whole international system, lock, stock and barrel; according to Lenin and his colleagues, there would be no more war simply because in the classless society of the future the 'contradictions' of capitalism which allegedly caused wars would be swept away. Viscount Cecil, an outstanding British and perhaps the only leading Conservative supporter of the League, tells the story in his memoirs that after talking to workmen at the end of the First World War, he came to the conclusion that only by the creation of machinery to make impossible a second international bloodbath would the working man's allegiance to the capitalist system be restored.[1] A second important extra-European influence making for the foundation of the League was that of the American President, Woodrow Wilson, whose visit to Europe in January 1919 to attend the peace conference was regarded by many millions of war-weary people as the coming of the Messiah. Wilson carried with him all the traditional American mistrust of the 'power politics' of Europe which the ordinary soldier had grown to loathe as the result of his wartime experience. The President refused to recognize the secret agreements drawn up among the European allies for distributing between themselves their gains from the war. He claimed to substitute for the old principles of diplomacy—national interest, the balance of power and secret negotiations—the new and, in those days, exhilarating ideals of the international interest and the organization of a world-wide 'community of power' to stand firm against aggression.

There is reason to doubt whether President Wilson had ever worked out in his own mind what a 'community of power' actually meant or how it would work. Quite possibly he was trying to educate the American public, which instinctively recoiled against the whole notion of the balance of power, in the necessity to partici-pate in the European balance of power, in the strict interests of their own security, though under a different name. However that may be, Wilson's own temperament, unbending, touchy and self-righteous,

[1] *All the Way*, London, 1949, p. 159.

robbed him of the subtlety required to sell the revolutionary idea
of the League to his own people; his unwillingness to associate
leaders of the Republican party with his journey to Paris was
merely one of the more blatant examples of this. Moreover, it is
wrong to regard Wilson as the sole or even chief author of the
League Covenant, though it was he who insisted upon its being an
integral part of all the peace treaties, perhaps unwisely, and he
acted as chairman of the conference commission to draw up that
document. Wilson's chief contribution to the League, Article 10,
which committed League members to respect and defend against
external aggression the territorial integrity and political independence of all members of the League, proved to be one of the most
controversial items on the commission's agenda, Britain and the
then Dominions being most critical of this attempt to ossify the
status quo. It was also the first League Article to be whittled down
by interpretative resolutions of the League Assembly in the early
1920s.

The centrepiece of the Covenant, however, dealing with the submission of international disputes to political and juridical means of
settlement (Articles 12 to 14) and with economic and military sanctions to be used against states which resorted to war without complying with the obligation to settle disputes peacefully (Article 16),
was essentially a British invention. It was embodied in the so-called
Phillimore Report, the work of a committee appointed by the
British Government in 1918, which the government did not, however, explicitly endorse. The importance of the Phillimore committee's emphasis upon the peaceful settlement of disputes as the
touchstone of a state's title to membership of the international
system, failure to comply with which would involve sanctions being
imposed by the rest of the international community, was that it
reflected the way in which the world war had broken out in August
1914.

As the war progressed with increasing devastation and bloodshed, which far outran the expectations of all the governments
involved, it was felt in Britain that had there been provision for
inquiry and delay in the Austro-Serbian dispute, had these states
been bound not to resort to war until several months had passed,
and had the rest of the international community been obliged to
ostracize whichever of them failed to comply with the 'rules of the
game', the world would not have been catapulted into war.

But it is easy to see, from the hindsight of today, that any state which wished to resort to force could have its way by exploiting the very means chosen by the framers of the Covenant to avoid the errors of 1914. It could do so by achieving a speedy *fait accompli* while the rest of the League was inquiring into the facts of the situation. And indeed precisely this was done when in 1931–32 Japanese forces quickly established their control over Manchuria, nominally a province of China. The incident produced an excellent case study of international conflict by the League's Lytton Commission but no readiness on the part of any League member-state to try to reverse Japan's *fait accompli*. We shall see later, in discussing the formation of the United Nations Organization in 1945, how that body's method of preserving the peace reflected the manner in which the world war broke out in 1939. Just as generals are often charged with fighting the previous war, so peacemakers often make it their chief object, to their own cost, to avoid the mistakes of the previous peace.

Before examining further the circumstances of the birth of the League of Nations, however, it is worth recalling what an international organization is and how far the League represented an advance upon the machinery for international co-operation as it had existed in 1914. Supporters of the League cause—and one must remember that in the inter-war years, as contrasted with the post-1945 period, support for an international agency to keep the peace *was* a cause which had to be fought for in the teeth of bitter opposition, not only in the dictatorships but in the democracies as well—used to argue that the League represented an essentially new method of conducting international relations, namely by international co-operation in the solving of common tasks rather than by international conflict and rivalry. But this is hardly the truth. International relations had always been carried on by each state seeking to secure as much co-operation in the achievement of its aims as it could. Wars occurred, not because states refused to co-operate with each other, but because they could not secure co-operation on terms acceptable to themselves. What the League did was to provide a (hopefully) permanent forum, situated in Geneva, in which member-states could institutionalize their co-operation in many different fields, from the economic and social to the task of keeping the peace; a permanent secretariat to prepare international meetings in these different fields and to implement agreed resolutions of the various League organs; and a set of rules, central to which was the axiom that no state should in future resort to war except after complying with the obligation in the Covenant to use every peaceful means to settle the dispute first.

But the rules for the conduct of international affairs and the settlement of international disputes laid down in the Covenant were definitely rules of international law, with all the weaknesses of that legal system, especially in regard to enforcement. The League Covenant was little more in effect than a contract between independent sovereign states to do and to refrain from doing certain things; the sovereignty of its member-states was most carefully safeguarded —both the League Council, a kind of executive committee, and the Assembly, consisting of representatives of all member-states, had to be unanimous when arriving at a decision, and hence no state could be bound by any resolution of a League organ without its consent. The League of Nations was decidedly not a super-power above the separate states, nor was it a supranational organization with authority to make decisions binding on member-states or their citizens. On the contrary, it represented what the historian H. A. L. Fisher once called 'the maximum of international co-operation which its member-states desired at any one time.' It is true that attempts were made, by the Draft Treaty of Mutual Assistance in 1923 and the Geneva Protocol in 1925, to strengthen the Covenant by making recourse to its procedures for resolving international disputes compulsory and by filling the famous 'gap' in the Covenant by which a member-state could theoretically resort to war if the League organs to which its disputes with other states were submitted failed to reach agreement on their report. But these proposals did not command general support, notably that of Britain, who feared involvement in efforts to enforce the 1919 peace treaties, many features of which British opinion regarded as unsatisfactory.

It is true, too, that there prevailed at the League headquarters, especially in the relatively peaceful years of the 1920s, what League supporters called 'the spirit of Geneva', which served to lubricate the process of international conciliation. Nevertheless, in the final resort, governments could not but consult their national interest as they and their people conceived it, and it required a spirit of enterprise amounting almost to recklessness to abandon the traditional expedients of national security, armaments, alliances, secret diplomacy and so on, in favour of the novel, untried and—in the presence of so many ancient conflicts of interest and outlook between the nations—speculative methods of the League. If the framers of the Covenant in 1919 had been able to work on a clean sheet and assume the absence of national sovereignty, they would almost certainly have produced a different and more effective machinery. But their task was the very different one of erecting as many obstacles as they could against the drift to war, always bearing in mind that the nations, especially the great powers, remained free to determine for themselves in the last resort where their interests lay.

In considering the framework of the new world organization, the League Commission of the 1919 Peace Conference found that many elements of the structure they were creating already existed in the international system; the problem was that of bringing them together into a coherent whole and giving the resulting arrangements a permanent legal form. In the first place, there was the old Concert of Europe, a very informal institution by which the great powers in the nineteenth century met together from time to time to discuss problems or situations which threatened to disturb the general peace. There was also the Supreme War Council of the allied and associated powers, Britain, France, Italy, Japan and the United States, which had been created, in the teeth of nationalistic resistance, in December 1917 to co-ordinate the wartime military strategies and foreign policies of those states. From this dual basis sprang the League Council, to consist of the principal victorious powers, together with some smaller states which had contributed to the Allied war effort and on behalf of which, as against the alleged great power chauvinism of their wartime enemies, the Allies were supposed to have fought. The League Council, unlike the Security Council of the United Nations, had conjoint powers with the Assembly rather than the primary responsibility for the maintenance of peace; but it had a duty which reflected the essentially legalistic character of the Covenant, as compared with the UN Charter, namely that of reporting on disputes which member-states were bound to submit to the Council under the Covenant's Article 12, if they did not submit them to arbitration or adjudication. Inevitably, in the absence of the United States, and with the somewhat ambiguous support of the Soviet Union after her entry into the League in 1934 and the defection of Germany, Italy and Japan in the 1930s, the League Council came to be dominated by Britain and France, both of whom equally inevitably came to realize that they could not cope with major threats to the peace through the League machinery alone.

Secondly, there was the considerable provision for the arbitration of international disputes which had existed in 1914 and could easily be revived after the war. During the nineteenth century, more and more countries reached agreement on treaties for the arbitration of their mutual disputes and to this complex of treaties was added, as though a crown, the Permanent Court of Arbitration created by the Hague Peace Conference in 1907. The PCA was hardly a permanent court; it consisted merely of a panel of arbitrators from which states which agreed to settle their disputes by arbitration could select third parties to help resolve their differences on the basis of respect for international law. All this machinery of arbitration was brought together in Article 12 of the League Covenant as additional means, besides the Council, by which member-states could resolve their differences rather than resort to war. But many felt, after the League itself was born, that the world should go further than this and create a permanent court of judges to determine legal issues between states. This was done in 1921 when the Permanent Court of International Justice (PCIJ), the forerunner of the present International Court of Justice (ICJ), was formed with its seat at The Hague. This was indeed a court, consisting of judges elected jointly by the League Council and Assembly. Thus adjudication, which differs only from arbitration in that states choose their own arbitrators whereas the PCIJ (and the same applies to the ICJ) was an established court with, at any given time, a fixed membership, was added to the means listed in Article 12 of the Covenant for the peaceful settlement of disputes.

There was hardly any doubt, however, both when the Court was founded in 1921 and when it was reconstituted in 1945, that recourse to it by states must be voluntary, thus again respecting the sacred principle of national sovereignty. An attempt was made by the abortive Geneva Protocol of 1925 to make the Court's jurisdiction compulsory in all international legal disputes, but this was not acceptable to all League members. The sole compromise which could be effected with national sovereignty was Article 36 (2) of the Court's Statute; this enabled League member-states to issue a declaration accepting the Court's compulsory jurisdiction but only with respect to other states which had done the same and with reservations, if the state accepting this so-called 'Optional Clause' desired them, which sometimes nullified the whole point of the declaration. In 1932, the peak year, some thirty states had accepted the Optional Clause, and it is significant that although the majority of participating states at the San Francisco conference in 1945, which drew up the UN Charter, favoured compulsory jurisdiction in principle, only about the same number of states as in 1932 have accepted the Optional Clause, even though the number of states in the world has more than doubled in the intervening years.

Thirdly, among the existing machinery for international co-operation when the League was founded, the nineteenth century had seen the signature of a number of international treaties for respecting the neutrality of certain states, notably Switzerland in 1815, Belgium in 1839 and Luxembourg in 1867. President Wilson had himself negotiated a number of similar treaties with Latin American states after his accession to the White House in 1912; this made him, as we have already stated, an energetic advocate of the exchange of mutual guarantees of respect for the political independence and territorial integrity of states, which was embodied in Article 10 of the League Covenant.

Fourthly, the nineteenth century had seen, too, the proliferation of international bureaux and agencies established by inter-governmental treaties and often having an annual general conference of member-states, permanent offices and a secretariat, for the carrying on of what we today would call functional co-operation, that is, co-operation between states to settle certain problems of a technical character and with an international bearing, the most famous being the Universal Postal Union (UPU), founded in 1874, by which states agreed to bear the cost of distributing letters and parcels from other countries within their own territories and set against this the proceeds from the sale of stamps on mail sent abroad by their own nationals.

In addition, there had grown up by 1919 a vast complex of international agreements, some bilateral, some multilateral, to respect or guarantee the rights of persons or businesses throughout the territories of the signatory states—for example, the international copyright convention of 1870. It was proposed to bring all these independent technical agencies and inter-governmental agreements under the common umbrella of the League by Article 23 of the Covenant.

But, besides this work of consolidation and co-ordination, the sub-committees of the League itself, dealing with such matters as international co-operation in health, economics, finance, transport and communications, the work of the world's academic and intellectual communities, represented a distinct contribution by the League organization itself to the world's machinery for functional co-operation between nations. The First World War had demonstrated that many new devices contrived during that struggle for associating nations together in a common effort, as for instance the control and economic use of Allied shipping resources, the Allies' purchase of raw materials for their own war effort and denial of them to the enemy, or for the exchange of information on the design of new weapons, means of transport, communication and so on, had their uses in a peace which would have to be built by joint international effort if it was ever to be built at all.[2] These wartime arrangements, therefore, together with the previously mentioned existing means of international co-operation, needed to be brought together as one of the many strands from which the League Covenant was eventually woven.[3]

Thus the League of Nations Commission in 1919 had much of its work done for it before it began its deliberations. Partly for this reason, partly because of the early adoption by the Commission of the Anglo-American, or Hurst-Miller, draft of the future Covenant, partly because of the drive provided by the Commission's chairman, President Wilson, the work was completed more speedily than that of any other major agency of the peace conference. Nevertheless, important differences did develop between the chief powers on the shaping of the Covenant and these were to play vital roles in the League's later history. As usually happens at great acts of multi-lateral international legislation such as the peace conference of 1919, no state is wholly satisfied with the resulting product and nor-mally spends its best efforts, during the life of that joint product, in trying to amend it along the lines on which it would have preferred it to be shaped originally.

First, there was the strain between Britain and the United States, the latter being supported in this by France, which took the form of a conflict between Wilson's insistence on the exchange of general guarantees of member-states' political independence and territorial integrity, which later became Article 10, and the British objection that this was to crystallize too much the territorial *status quo*. The British also argued that it made too little allowance for economic, population and other changes and committed Britain, as one of the foremost powers of the day, to defend the *status quo,* all at a time when the British people were at the beginning of a mood of sustained distaste for continental commitments.

[2]See Sir J. A. (later Lord) Salter, *Allied Shipping Control*, Oxford, 1921.
[3]See Sir A. Zimmern, *The League of Nations and the Rule of Law*, London, 1935, Part I.

The British preferred, as we have noted earlier, the exchange of obligations to submit disputes to peaceful inquiry and settlement, an undertaking not to fight until these procedures had been complied with and had clearly failed to resolve the dispute, and a commitment by all member-states to apply sanctions against states which violated these undertakings. These principles were embodied in Articles 12 to 16 of the Covenant. But the British emphasis was not really upon sanctions and enforcement but upon bringing international disputes into the light of day for rational examination, pacification and reconciliation between nations, and on the use of League machinery to remove mistakes made when the peace treaties were drawn up in the bitter aftermath of history's most terrible war, and the smoothing away of difficulties as and when they arose. In particular, the British delegation refused to accept Wilson's insistence upon guarantees of the territorial *status quo* unless this was coupled with provision for its modification as circumstances changed and the world developed. The British had their way, but their demand for a provision for peaceful change to be incorporated into Article 10 was not accepted; instead, it became embodied in a separate article (19), which provided that the Assembly might 'recommend to member-states the reconsideration of treaties which have become inapplicable and the continuance of conditions which might endanger the peace of the world'. Thus the provision of peaceful change lost much of its force by being separated from Article 10; it remained to all intents a dead letter throughout most of the history of the League.

France, being a territorial beneficiary from the peace treaties, was naturally on Wilson's side in the matter of territorial guarantees. But she sharply dissented both from Britain and the United States concerning the enforcement measures contemplated in the emerging Covenant. The French at all times mistrusted the guarantees against Germany's military revival which were being constructed in the peace treaties and, unlike Britain, who wanted to use the new League as a means for mitigating the harshness of the treaties, wished to see it used for enforcing the treaties up to the hilt. Hence they campaigned in season and out of season for an international force for ensuring that the guarantees in the Covenant would be implemented and, when they failed to secure this in 1919, tried to do so by throwing their strength behind proposals in the 1920s, such as the Geneva Protocol, for 'putting teeth' into the Covenant.

This French proposal for an international force to maintain the peace was rejected both by the United States and by Britain; by the United States because President Wilson believed that world opinion of itself would be sufficient to deter aggression once the facts of a particular international dispute had been made clear by the League —hence the American conception of the League presupposed the existence of a liberal democracy in all member-states—and by Britain partly for the same reason, and partly because she wished to keep her armed forces, which meant in effect the navy, to defend her massive empire. The French therefore fell back on the proposal for an international general staff to advise the League Council on the military sanctions to be enforced against Covenant-breakers. But this, too, was rejected. All that the French did obtain was Article 9 of the Covenant, which created a commission to advise the Council on military questions generally, but, curiously enough, this was not to apply to the Council's responsibility under Article 16 for recommending measures of armed force against aggression.

There were two other important conflicts of view in the League Commission of the 1919 peace conference and in plenary sessions of the conference itself. The first was the dispute between the great powers on one side, and the smaller states on the other, concerning the representation of member-states on the Council. Some of the former, notably Britain, wished to limit the Council to the great powers alone on the lines of the old Concert of Europe, and all of them resisted the efforts of the smaller states to enlarge the Council. Eventually, it was agreed that five powers should sit on the Council —Britain, France, Italy, Japan and the United States—as permanent members and four smaller states, elected by rotation by the Assembly, as non-permanent members. The second conflict was between the conference as a whole, led by Britain, France and the United States, against Italy and Japan respectively. The Italians, being highly dependent for their industry on the import of raw materials, sought a specific reference in the Covenant to the necessity for equality of opportunity in international trade relations and of access to raw materials, while the Japanese desired a clause in the text or the preamble of the Covenant upholding the principle of non-discrimination on grounds of race; the latter provision, had it been adopted, would have given, or could be interpreted by an international law court as giving, the Japanese the right of unrestricted immigration into Australia and the United States and hence was strongly opposed by both countries. Neither Italy's nor Japan's views prevailed on these issues and accordingly both countries had from the outset grounds of complaint against the League which in later years took on enormously swollen dimensions.

Thus, as in all international negotiation, none of the states which created the League was wholly satisfied with what it had done, and the attitude of each state towards the League in the inter-war period was powerfully influenced by this dissatisfaction. These conflicting pressures to revise the Covenant in the manner desired by each dissatisfied state was complicated by the fact that the world conditions in which the League began its operations in 1920 differed both from the conditions in which the Covenant was drafted and from those in which it was expected to operate. The most important of these changed conditions was that the United States never became a League member since the American Senate, though only by a small majority, failed to ratify the peace treaties, as it was bound by the national constitution to do so, when it debated them in March 1920. Obviously, as will be seen later, that was a tragic, if not fatal, handicap to the League's efforts to preserve the international order which the United States had played no small part in establishing at the end of the First World War. But another and less noticed effect of the American retirement from the world political scene was on the already mentioned differences between Britain and France concerning League sanctions against aggression.

The French tended to draw the conclusion that, with the absence of the United States, a much more automatic system against backsliders was necessary; hence their determined but unsuccessful efforts during the 1920s to 'put teeth into the Covenant'. Britain, on the other hand, considered that a stronger Covenant would be less likely than a weaker one to induce the Americans to change their minds about League membership; she also feared that, with the United States absent, the greater the onus that would fall upon herself for the enforcement of Covenant obligations, and in the 1920s British public opinion was chiefly bent on reducing commitments which might involve the use of force, not enlarging them. Thus, America's non-membership of the League not only removed that country's contribution to the maintenance of peace; it also deepened the divisions between the two Entente powers, Britain and France on whom the burden now chiefly lay, as to the best way in which they could bear it.

Before considering the actual historical experience encountered by the League, it is worth examining further the Covenant as it emerged from the 1919 peace conference. How in theory was it supposed to work? As already stated, we are concerned here, not so much with the non-political work of the League, the economic and social co-operation and so on, which were designed in the course of time to produce a peace-biassed world, but with the limited field of the maintenance of peace and security.

First, there was the heavy emphasis on disarmament, deriving from the Anglo-Saxon belief, about which the French were always sceptical, that arms and arms races were a primary cause of wars. Article 8 of the League Covenant laid it down as basic doctrine that peace required the reduction of national armaments 'to the lowest point consistent with national safety and the enforcement by common action of international obligations'. The League Council was charged with the task of formulating plans for arms reductions for the consideration of each member-state, taking into account its geographical situation and other such relevant circumstances. After reduction to this level, arms were not to be increased except with the Council's consent.

Article 8 was linked, as the Germans were quick to point out, with Part V of the Versailles Treaty which a German delegation signed on 28 June 1919 and which contained the military, naval and aerial disarmament to be imposed on Germany. This section began with the famous words over which there was to be so much later controversy : 'in order to render possible the initiation of a general limitation of the armaments of all nations, Germany undertakes strictly to observe the military, naval and air clauses which follow'. Did this constitute a legal obligation on the Allies to disarm if Germany complied with the stated conditions, as Germany and some of the more guilt-ridden sectors of British opinion contended? Or did it merely mean, as the French said, that they should make a serious effort to try to see if they could reach agreement on general disarmament? The question was never resolved, but it played an important role in the failure of the world disarmament conference which finally met, in fulfilment of Article 8 of the League Covenant, in February 1932. Moreover, Article 8 had the effect of drawing to the League's support advocates of disarmament, whether unilateral or multilateral, who were emotionally averse to the traditional principle of deterring aggression by organizing superior force against it, while it tended to repel those who still believed in this principle. The result was that when the world disarmament conference finally petered out in 1934 and Germany, Italy and Japan, all revisionist countries, were governed by extreme nationalist regimes which seemed to understand no language but that of force, it was hard to secure co-operation within the League between disarmament advocates and balance-of-power advocates on the basis of a policy of armed strength through the League against aggression.

Then came Article 10, President Wilson's principal contribution to the Covenant, by which League member-states 'undertook to respect and preserve as against external aggression the territorial integrity and political independence of all members of the League'. We have seen how this was modified, though ineffectually, by the British-inspired Article 19 providing for the peaceful revision of the *status quo* from time to time. But the fact that the British people, almost to a man, dissented from many of the territorial settlements of 1919, especially those relating to Germany's eastern borders, seriously weakened the force of Article 10. Besides, British reluctance to endorse every detail of the 1919 peace settlement was echoed in even stronger form in the self-governing Dominions of the Commonwealth—Australia, New Zealand, Canada and South Africa—so that it was from Canada that proposals came in 1921 for 'interpreting' Article 10 so as to rob it of much of its rigidity, and these proposals were adopted by the Second League Assembly. Moreover, in response to French pressures in the early 1920s to commit Britain more firmly to the *status quo* as established in 1919, the British Conservative government at length consented, by the Locarno agreements signed on 16 October 1925, to join with Italy in guaranteeing the Belgian-German and Franco-German frontiers west of the Rhine, the Versailles provision that Germany should never put troops or war equipment into the west bank of the Rhine being thus reaffirmed. This was one of the 'special arrangements to meet special needs' which Austen Chamberlain called for in the League Assembly in March 1925 in preference to the general guarantees envisaged in the abortive Geneva Protocol. But, significantly, the Locarno agreements, the first of the 'special arrangements' Chamberlain was referring to, were also the last to which Britain agreed to be a party. The effect of this, though unnoticed at the time, was to put revisionist states on notice that Britain so far from regarding herself as bound to the strict observance of

Article 10 of the League Covenant, would consider each and every challenge to the *status quo* severely on its merits and in the light of the unique circumstances of the time.

Thirdly in the Covenant came procedures for the peaceful settlement of international disputes. By Articles 12, 13 and 15, member-states pledged themselves, if a dispute arose between them which was 'likely to lead to a rupture', to refer it either to arbitration or judicial settlement (after the creation of the Permanent Court of International Justice at The Hague in 1921) in the case of legal disputes, or to inquiry by the League Council in the case of disputes of a more political nature. In no case would they go to war until three months had elapsed after the report on the dispute by the arbitral organ or the Court or the Council, and in no case would they resort to war against any member-state which accepted the arbitral or judicial award, or the Council's report, assuming that the latter was unanimously agreed to, not counting the votes of the disputing states themselves. This was the celebrated 'cooling off' period.

It amounted to a partial renunciation of war, but war remained legal provided it was waged after the prescribed delay of three months, or if it was waged against a state not complying with a court's award or the Council's report, or if it was waged in circumstances in which the arbitral or judicial body had been unable to issue an award or judgment or in which the Council had failed to agree on a unanimous report. It was because war still remained legal in such circumstances within the League system that attempts were made in the 1920s, first unsuccessfully by the Draft Treaty of Mutual Assistance of 1923–34 and the Geneva Protocol in 1925, and then successfully by the Kellogg-Briand Pact of 1928, which was signed by almost all members of the existing international system and which illegalized all war except that of a defensive character. Though the Kellogg-Briand Pact, having no machinery of enforcement, did virtually nothing to prevent the collapse of international order in the subsequent years, ending in the outbreak of world war for the second time in September 1939, it was deemed relevant enough at the Nuremberg Trials of Major War Criminals in 1945 to be considered one of the laws of peace which Axis leaders were charged with having broken.

The League system, however, to resume our analysis of its Covenant, did have a sanctions machinery. Under Article 16 it was laid down as each member-state's duty, automatically and without waiting for instructions from any League organ, to apply economic and financial sanctions against any state which had resorted to war without complying with the procedures for the pacific settlement of disputes described in the previous paragraph. Such a state was deemed to have 'committed an act of war' against all other League member-states, and these were obliged to sever all trade and financial relations and all personal intercourse with the offending state. This was to be the first stage—the virtual ostracizing of the Covenant-breaking state from membership of the international community. In the second stage, the Council was to *recommend* (that is, its communication was permissive rather than mandatory) to governments what effective military, naval and air forces members of the League should severally contribute to the armed strength to be used to protect the League Covenant. Finally, League members were to support one another in the financial and economic measures applied under this Article in order to minimize the loss and inconvenience they all suffered, though in varying degree, in the application of sanctions under Article 16. They were also obliged to support one another against measures of retaliation taken against any of them by a Covenant-breaking state which became the object of the sanctions process.

And then, perhaps most important of all, came the 'hue and cry' principle of Article 11 : 'any war or threat of war, whether immediately affecting any of the members of the League or not' was declared to be 'a matter of concern to the whole League' and the League was to take 'any action that may be deemed to be wise and effectual to safeguard the peace of nations'. It was also declared in this Article to be the 'friendly right of each member of the League to bring to the attention of the Assembly or of the Council any circumstances whatever affecting international relations which threaten to disturb international peace or the good understanding between nations upon which peace depends'. Here was indeed the true heart of the League idea, the revolutionary notion that in the twentieth century peace is indivisible; *that war anywhere could spread everywhere*; and that all states were involved in the defence of peace and could no longer detach themselves from the struggle to maintain the peace, by rational discussion or by force, through policies of neutrality or isolation.

IV

To describe now the actual historical experience encountered by the League is in effect to survey the whole course of international affairs from the League's official birth in January 1920 until its formal demise in 1946, although for all practical purposes it died eleven years earlier, in 1935, with the failure of League sanctions against Italy during that country's invasion of Ethiopia. The most we can do in this volume is to recall the major international disputes in which the League was involved and examine the kind of role played by it—if we can call an association of independent nation-states an 'it' and not a 'they'.

For this purpose it is useful to divide the inter-war period into two halves significantly divided by the world economic crisis of 1929–33. This crisis was heralded by the New York stock market collapse of October 1929 and the long-term decline in primary commodity prices which was continuous throughout the 1920s and reached rock bottom in 1931; the crisis was also symbolized by the world-wide financial storm of 1931 which destroyed the international gold standard and the system of uncontrolled international trade on which the League's economic philosophy was based and which its conferences, committees and study groups were and always had been trying to restore and consolidate. The period 1919 to 1929 is again usually divided for purposes of international history into two halves: 1919 to 1925, the period of post-war unsettlement symbolized by the French occupation of the Ruhr industrial region in 1923 as a reprisal against an alleged German failure to pay reparations as required under the Versailles Treaty, and by the Dawes Plan of 1924 which helped to set Europe on its feet again with the assistance of American investment capital; and 1925 to 1929, the so-called 'period of fulfilment', when Europe's greatest diplomatic problem, the tension between France and Germany, appeared to be settled at Locarno in 1925 when Germany, under Foreign Minister Gustav Stresemann's influence, willingly accepted her western frontier and the demilitarization of the west bank of the Rhine, conditions which had been 'imposed' at Versailles in 1919, in return for a British and Italian pledge of assistance against flagrant aggression by France.

But after 1931, all industrial countries were faced with problems of mass unemployment and shrinking foreign trade which tended to impose on them a mentality of *sauve qui peut* entirely inimical to the idea of international co-operation for the common good through the League of Nations. The economic slump, with the sharp social and class tensions it created or exacerbated, destroyed liberal political regimes in many countries and ushered into power in several leading states right-wing militaristic and chauvinistic governments which adopted rearmament policies as a means to full employment and foreign expansion as a method of diverting attention from the internal difficulties they were experiencing. Thus the 1931–33 economic crisis brought Adolf Hitler to power in Germany, with his contempt for the League as a means for keeping the Reich shackled under the hated Versailles *Diktat*, and a programme for the destruction of the small states created in 1919 on Germany's eastern flank, since they were considered obstacles to the 'living-space' or *Lebensraum* which the Nazies dreamed of acquiring in Russia. The crisis dethroned, too, the liberal regime in Japan in the 1920s, of which Baron Shidehara was the most outstanding political exponent, and made the army, with its ambition of expansion on the Asian mainland, the chief force in the state and the maker and breaker of governments; by the Japanese constitution of 1888, Ministers for the Armed Forces must be serving officers and hence, by withholding their collaboration, the Japanese military could virtually bring civilian government to a standstill. The world economic crisis also effected centralizing changes in the Fascist Grand Council of Italy, established after Mussolini's march on Rome of 1922, and, from being a pillar of order in the 1920s as far as the diplomatic scene is concerned, drove him into his wild dream of making the Mediterranean the Roman lake it had been two thousand years before.

Therefore, in the period of comparative international repose which lasted from 1920 until 1929, the League was not faced by any direct challenge from a great power—the Anglo-French quarrel about Germany was carried on in other bodies such as the Reparations Commission—and certainly not from any combination of great powers. But it is notable that, even so, of the four major international disputes other than the German question during this period, the two in which great powers were involved were not settled by the League and only in the two other instances, which were quarrels between minor states, was League intervention effective. As for the first two disputes, one occurred when Poland was at war with Soviet Russia in 1920 and a Polish detachment led by Zeligowski seized the city of Vilna from the newly created Baltic republic of Lithuania, formerly a part of the Tsarist Empire. The case was taken up by the League and the Council at first tried to organize a plebiscite to determine the wishes of the people in the disputed locality; but later it washed its hands of the whole affair. There can be little doubt that one of the main reasons for this was the fact that Poland was sheltered by its ally, France, the greatest military power in Europe at that time, one of the pillars of the League of Nations and a permanent member of its Council.

The second of the two instances of disputes in the 1920s involving great powers occurred in 1923 when the Italians shelled the Greek island of Corfu in retaliation for the killing of certain Italian officers engaged in demarcating the frontier between Greece and Albania. Greece was persuaded to allow this dispute to be settled, not by the League, but by the Conference of Ambassadors of the Allied Powers, which inflicted heavy damages on the Athens government and awarded Greece no compensation for the Italian bombardment of Corfu. It is conceivable that the League would have acted more vigorously and more equitably had not a great power, Italy, a permanent member of the League Council like France in the Vilna affair, been involved.

However, in the other two disputes, both in the Balkans, in which lesser powers were involved, the League was able to effect a settlement through its own machinery. These were the Albanian-Yugoslav frontier incident of 1921 and the Greco-Bulgarian dispute of 1925. These were both disputes between minor states with no significant assistance being given to either side by any great power. It is, however, to be remembered on the other side of the coin that the mere existence of the League, and the possibility that it might go into action against aggression, probably acted to deter states from acts of force which the world never heard of because they never occurred.

In the 1930s, however, the League, or rather the duumvirate of Britain and France, its leading members, was faced by challenges, not from minor countries, but from the greatest military powers of the day, and in circumstances in which to reply to the challenge in kind involved a definite risk of war, the very evil which the League was founded to avert. This meant that, as from about 1931, much of the pacifist sentiment, or simple hatred of war, which had helped to launch the League at its beginning, now began to work against it once it became evident that defending the Covenant meant more, not fewer, arms in the hands of defenders of the *status quo,* and perhaps more involvement of more states in more wars, wherever they occurred. The two major challenges to the League system in this period were, first, the Japanese attack on Manchuria, theoretically a province of China, in September 1931 and, second, the Italian invasion of Ethiopia in October 1935.

The Manchurian crisis in 1931 sprang from the action of the Japanese authorities in using an explosion on the South Manchuria Railway which Japan leased and policed, and which ran from Mukden to Port Arthur, as a pretext for bringing the whole country under their control as a puppet state called Manchukuo. China appealed to the League in Geneva under Article 11 of the Covenant and a commission of investigation was sent out to the Far East by the League under the chairmanship of Lord Lytton. The Lytton report, produced after long delay by the commission, was not wholly condemnatory of Japan, but there was no doubt that its intention was to indicate that the Manchurian affair was a breach of Covenant obligations. No action was taken on the report, however, apart from a weak League resolution refusing, like the United States Secretary of State, Mr. Henry L. Stimson, to recognize a situation which had been brought about illegally. The main reason for this was that Britain, the League member-state which alone had the naval strength necessary to force the Japanese out of Manchuria, was not only struggling with an economic crisis which put an end to the second Labour government and brought to power a coalition government dominated by the Conservatives, but was quite unwilling to take action at such a distance from the home base, on an issue in which the right was not all on one side and the wrong on the other, except on the basis of co-operation with the United States, whose naval strength was recognized as equal to Britain's at the Washington conference in 1922. And signs in Washington of that co-operation were there none.

It was the Italian invasion of Ethiopia, however, in 1935–36 which sealed the fate of the League as an agency for the preservation of peace. In this instance, Italy was actually condemned as an aggressor under Article 16 by the League, and a sanctions system for embargoing the sale of arms and strategic materials to Italy was instituted in which fifty-two League member-states participated. But the blockade was never complete, many loopholes existed and that vital raw material of modern war, oil, was never included in the embargo. Nor was any naval or military action contemplated by the League or even the closure of the Suez Canal to Italian shipping. So far from sanctions being forcefully applied under the leadership of the great powers, the French, assisted by the British, made clear to the Italian government that they would be willing to compensate Italy, in the time-honoured manner, by portions of Ethiopian territory if the Fascist authorities called off the war. The most notorious of these proposals was the Hoare-Laval plan, agreed to in Paris by Sir Samuel Hoare, the British Foreign Secretary, and Pierre Laval, the French Premier and Foreign Minister. The plan was immediately repudiated by the British government when its contents became known to the press, which published it, but this did not affect the half-heartedness with which sanctions were operated. In July 1936 they were lifted and the world saw the shameful spectacle of the Ethiopian Emperor, Haile Selassie, being denied a hearing in the League Assembly because his country had now been absorbed into the Italian domain and no longer existed as an independent state.

After the Ethiopian fiasco faith in the League of Nations virtually expired. There was no serious suggestion that the Czechoslovak crisis of 1938 and the Polish crisis of 1939, which were the immediate preludes to the Second World War, should be submitted to the League for judgment. This was not only because the great power pressing for change in these two international crises, Nazi Germany, had left the League with the failure of the world disarmament conference in 1934. It also happened because the small states of Europe, realizing that the League could not protect them when the enemy's forces were at their gates, hastened to make what arrangements they could in the hope of diverting the aggressor's appetite; and the then major League powers, Britain and France, believed that in the last resort they must make their own decisions about coming to terms with the dictator states without relying on much help from the League. The idea of collective security seemed to have been but a dream from which men now awakened to the old world of bilateral diplomacy and power politics.

v

Why did the League fail? The word 'failure' naturally needs to be used with caution and compassion. It is relative to expectations; if a woman hopes to marry a multi-millionaire and only succeeds in winning a millionaire, she can hardly be described as a failure. If the League is judged by the test of whether it failed to prevent the Second World War, only twenty years after the tragic catastrophe of the 1914–18 war, it was, of course, definitely a failure. But did it lessen the likelihood of war? Did it prevent wars which otherwise might have taken place? The mere fact that the League existed, that unprovoked aggression could not be embarked upon without some, and often immense, publicity being given to it at Geneva, may have had some deterrent effect. The League was an important part of the international environment from 1920 until 1939 and states could not but be aware that in defying the League they were under a compulsion to answer for what they were doing. This did not prevent states from doing wrong, human nature and the international system being what they are; but possibly they did less wrong than if it had never existed. Nevertheless, people do demand a more exacting test of success or failure in an international agency dedicated to the maintenance of peace, namely the ultimate prevention of war. Why did the League fail in this part of its task?

There are many theories. Some speak of the exceptional difficulties of the times; just as peace made the nineteenth-century Concert of Europe work, rather than the other way round, so the instability of the international system as a whole during the League period caused it to fail. The League was a tender plant; it had to survive in an arctic blizzard and with very many of those who actually worked in it, as politicians or diplomats, sceptical as to whether it would survive even in the most clement of times. The First World War had left behind it a mass of seething resentments—grievances in the defeated, disillusionment among the victors. The war had also alienated many millions against the existing international order, as well as the social order in their own countries. Accordingly, they either supported dictators whose entire programme was focussed on the overthrow of the existing order, or lacked the conviction to defend it. Moreover, as we have seen, the economic upheavals of the period advantaged imperialistic states and disadvantaged peace-loving states. In those years, breaking the Covenant was good business economically, if not perhaps in the long run, certainly in the short. Rearmament, for example in Germany's case, was about the only expedient known to the liberal economy of the day for recovering from mass unemployment, and, once arms are acquired, there is the strongest temptation to use them, if only as a threat. The League Covenant, on the other hand, called upon member-states already hard hit by trade depression to make their situation worse by cutting their exports to the aggressors; and it happened that the latter were about the only states in the early 1930s with a strong demand for foreign goods. The Covenant, in other words, presupposed an effectively functioning liberal world economy. This was never achieved, except perhaps for a brief period in the late 1920s. The political logic of the League, in other words, was directly contrary to the economic logic of the times.

Another theory is the 'Guilty Men' idea, that is, the notion that the democratic statesmen of the day, especially in Britain and France, never believed in the League system, never placed their trust in it; and indeed that they sought to sabotage it whenever they could. They did this either because they themselves had no confidence in the revolutionary collective security principles of the League, or because they were prisoners of a weak and unrealistic public opinion at home, to which those statesmen were fundamentally incapable of giving a lead. This was the view of such League supporters in Britain as Viscount Cecil, Gilbert Murray, Philip Noel-Baker and above all Winston Churchill; and there is some truth in it. It is doubtful whether democratic statesmen of the inter-wars period, like Stanley Baldwin, Samuel Hoare, Neville Chamberlain in Britain or Bonnet, Laval or Daladier in France, ever regarded the League as much more than claptrap of the hustings to which public deference had to be paid while traditional diplomatic processes still went on in private. The British Conservative leader, L. S. Amery, true to this style of thinking, once likened the League to the legend of the Emperor's New Clothes; everyone had to pretend to see something in it, no one was honest enough to say that it was an optical illusion.

On the other hand, even had these Anglo-French statesmen had every confidence in the League, the organization would have turned out to be not what had been intended, for reasons beyond their control. Instead of the clear-cut preponderance of League powers against aggression, as had been anticipated in 1919, the United States never joined.

The Soviet Union did not join until 1934, by which time a thick pall of mutual mistrust had intervened between Moscow and the democratic states. Finally, Italy and Japan, once among the creators of the League, were bitterly dissatisfied with the *status quo* and were swept along by a fever of romantic, swashbuckling nationalism into attempts to change it by force, which, at first at least, were strikingly successful. In the 1930s, therefore, it was Britain and France against Germany, Japan and Italy. True, as

Winston Churchill urged in the late 1930s, the two democracies might more vigorously have organized a coalition of smaller states against the dictators. But would it have had that secure preponderance against them in the absence of which there was a distinct risk of the very war the League was founded to prevent? It seems unlikely; in any case, no one could be sure.

Finally, we must question the feasibility of the collective security principle embodied in the League Covenant, though not under that name. The theory was that all member-states should combine to ostracize an aggressor whoever he might be. We may thus call collective security the theory of the *indeterminate* aggressor, as distinct from collective defence systems, such as NATO today, which presuppose a *determinate* aggressor, though he may not be mentioned by name in the treaty. However, in the ordinary course of international affairs certain states come together on the basis of common interests and often ranged in opposition to other states which have conflicting interests. This pattern of solidarity and enmity in the international system is constantly changing, but the universal rule that 'the enemy of my enemy is my friend' generally obtains. But what happens if a League member-state has to join with other member-states, with which it may be on unfriendly terms, in imposing sanctions on a state with which it happens to be on friendly terms?

Nor is this a hypothetical possibility. It occurred in 1935–36, when Britain and France were required by their League obligations to treat Italy as an aggressor when they, especially France, had every interest in treating that country as a friend and supporter against the reviving power of another state, Germany. It is significant that Winston Churchill, otherwise so ardent an advocate of the League, temporarily absented himself from British political life during the Italo-Ethiopian crisis since he had no wish to make public his reluctance to see Italy alienated; 'go as far with France as she will go', he wrote to the British Foreign Secretary, Sir Samuel Hoare, 'but no further'. It was Germany, which reoccupied the Rhineland with scarcely a murmur of protest from the League in March 1936, that was in Churchill's eyes the real danger to peace. The aggressor marked out by the League collective security system could, and on this famous occasion did, turn out to be a potential friend against the more dangerous aggressor which threatened the peace by methods the League system was not designed to prevent.

REFERENCES

Brierly, J. L., *The Covenant and the Charter*, Cambridge, C.U.P., 1947.

Cecil, Viscount, *A Great Experiment*, London, Cape, 1941.

Larus, J., ed., *From Collective Security to Preventive Diplomacy*, New York and London, Wiley, 1965, Chapters 1, 2, 3, 4 and 7.

Manning, C. A. W., 'The Failure of the League of Nations', *Agenda*, Vol. I, No. 1, January 1942.

Miller, D. H., *The Drafting of the Covenant*, 2 vols., New York and London, Putnam, 1928.

The New Cambridge Modern History, Vol. XII, *The Shifting Balance of World Forces, 1898–1945*, Cambridge, C.U.P., 1968, Chapter 9.

Niemeyer, G., 'The Balance Sheet of the League Experiment', *International Organization*, November 1952.

Noel-Baker, P. J., *The Geneva Protocol*, London, P. S. King, 1925.

The Royal Institute of International Affairs, *International Sanctions*, London, O.U.P., 1938.

Walters, F. P., *A History of the League of Nations*, 2 vols., London and Fair Lawn, New Jersey, O.U.P., 1952.

Zimmern, A. E., *The League of Nations and the Rule of Law, 1918–1935*, London, Macmillan, 2nd Ed., 1939.

9 *The Inter-war Commonwealth*

I

The transition from empire to commonwealth affected British
overseas territories in different degrees in the inter-war years. In
some cases the changing attitude towards empire both in Britain
and her dependencies was clearly marked by alterations in status
but so far as the underdeveloped countries, including India, were
concerned they would have to wait until the end of the Second
World War before they became emancipated. But even in these
countries the creation of new trade patterns, the disruption of
traditional rule through native councils and chiefs or princes, the
development of roads, all these changes were presenting problems
for British pragmatism. In a novel published in 1939 Joyce Cary
caught the atmosphere by a conversation between Rudbeck, a
young District Officer in Nigeria, and his superior, Bulteel :

'I suppose one mustn't talk about a plan,' Rudbeck says.
'Oh, no, no, no. They'll take you for a Bolshy.'[1]

On the whole the British Empire drifted into becoming the British
Commonwealth for at this time 'natural', so-called 'organic' growth
was preferred and politicians had still to decide that forward planning was respectable and could be non-revolutionary. As yet there
existed no clear concept of commonwealth structure and the term
still signified the revolution of the colonial planets around Britain
rather than any new sense of sharing resources and bearing the
burden of each other's needs.

Joseph Chamberlain's dream of an imperial economic common
market as the basis for political co-operation between Britain and
her overseas territories remained a dream. His son, Neville Chamberlain, when Chancellor of the Exchequer, took great pride in
introducing imperial preference in 1931 and the system was formally applied to the dominions by the Ottawa Agreement of 1932,
and further extended to the Crown colonies in the following year.

[1] *Mister Johnson*, London, 1968, p. 185.

But although this dropping of Free Trade under the economic blitz of the Depression represented a watershed in British political and economic history, it lacked the culminating importance which Neville Chamberlain attributed to it in a speech to the Commons on 4 February 1932 when he referred to 'setting the seal on the work which [my] father began but had perforce to leave unfinished'.[2] Joseph Chamberlain's vision, many years ahead of his own period, of welding the British Empire into an efficient political unit through economic co-operation had failed, and his son's efforts were too little and too late. But in the inter-war years the effects of this failure were masked by semi-religious devotion still paid to the British Crown and by similarities of background, breeding and education among British and Commonwealth leaders. Even after the Second World War these remained powerful factors dangerously hiding the lack of serious commonwealth co-operation as hybrid personalities like Nehru of India, caught between their own culture and that of the West, momentarily gave an illusion of new life to the Commonwealth. But in the late 1960s it was subjected to new strains as differences of policy on racialism emerged, and Britain sought to enter the European Economic Community.

In the late nineteenth and early twentieth centuries the British Empire had economic reality; it was a market for cheap mass-produced goods from Britain as well as for more substantial items such as railway lines and material. As Britain industrialized and exported, more and more capital flowed back home but it tended to flow outwards again not to the Empire but to more advanced countries such as the USA where purchasing power was greater. In economic terms therefore, leaving aside the question of imports of primary products, empire was becoming less attractive, more especially because the costs of imperial defence were rapidly mounting. But in the inter-war period British middle- and upper-class society was still firmly geared to an existence financed by the colonial outhouse system. Now empire was largely continued for social and defence reasons and not, as in the earlier period, so much for what was believed to be overall economic advantage. Yet even here change was occurring for as British domestic society altered and the class divisions became more blurred, this affected command abroad in the empire. The British domestic servant was a declining social type as labour was attracted away to better-paid and freer conditions in industry. It had formerly been an easy transition from

[2] K. Feiling, *The Life of Neville Chamberlain*, London, 1946, insertion after p. 204.

ordering about poorly paid servants to ordering about natives abroad, and so the check to one kind of social authority influenced the other.

II

As mentioned earlier the new commonwealth concept lacked elaboration, a typical feature of change in Britain, but this did not mean that it took place without some central decision-making. At the close of the nineteenth century, colonial conferences began to provide a forum for discussion of common British and imperial concerns such as defence and trade. This practice began in 1887 and primarily concerned the older and self-governing colonies such as Australia and Canada although the Crown colonies and India were represented at the first meeting. Such conferences took place again in 1897, 1902 and 1907, and it was in 1907 that it was decided in the future to call the conferences 'imperial' instead of 'colonial'; the aim was to mark the distinction between the self-governing countries—now to be known as 'dominions'—and the less politically and economically advanced colonies.

In 1911 the first imperial conference took the form of a meeting between the prime ministers with the British Prime Minister as chairman. This meeting, like those which followed, showed the need for closer imperial communications, but since the self-governing states were jealous of their political freedom, no provision was made for decisions to be binding nor for machinery to enforce any decisions which were reached. Everything depended on a truer consensus being achieved or, as critics argued, on an avoidance of awkward issues. In justification of the lack of system, it must be said that at a time when social and political attitudes were changing rapidly the very amorphousness of the Imperial Conference was its saving grace. The practical test of these meetings came in the First World War when Britain in her fight against the Central Powers was backed not merely by her colonies but also by her dominions. During this period imperial consultation went on, but it was not until 1923 that the main imperial conferences were resumed.

The effect of the First World War on the imperial association showed clearly. The dominions felt that their war effort and diplomatic training when attending the Versailles talks justified a clearer definition of their status and an *ex post facto* recognition of independent rights to negotiate and sign treaties subject only to the sanction of their own parliaments. Similarly, the non-self-governing countries within the British Empire, conscious of their share in winning the war and noting the progress of their autonomous colleagues, were strengthened in putting forward their own cases for an acceleration of progress to dominion status. But the twofold demands upon Britain set up a tension which was not altogether favourable in the inter-war period to the non-self-governing colonies. As the dominions ineluctably slid away to greater freedom, British policy on the less autonomous countries within the Empire became increasingly marked by a desire to temporize, and to seek, as in India, compromises on the way to autonomy which were less and less satisfactory.

During the First World War British and imperial co-operation had been achieved after numerous difficult struggles and when the war ended the dominions tended to fear that Britain might use her increased power to take retrograde political steps. In 1922 the Chanak incident occurred when the British Prime Minister, Lloyd George, and Winston Churchill, then Colonial Secretary, took action against the Turkish Nationalists which might have involved the dominions once more in major war.[3] This resulted in intensified demands from the dominions for clarification of their status. At the Imperial Conference of 1923 an indeterminate compromise was reached between the British centripetal tendencies and the centrifugal drives of the dominions. It was decided that the individual dominions could make treaties in their own right and validate them by laying them before their respective parliaments.[4] But it was also stated to be 'desirable' that member-states of the Empire should bear in mind their colleagues and the concerns of the Empire. As early as 1921, however, some of the dominions, such as South Africa and Canada, had pressed for clarification of dominion status, influenced by their greater independence in the immediate post-war period. Their pressure increased after 1922 when Southern Ireland, i.e. the Irish Free State, was granted the position of dominion, for she also wanted to know what her new status meant in concrete terms and not merely by reference to the position of earlier dominions.

In 1926 Canada's wish for a clarification of dominion status was

[3] F. S. Northedge, *The Troubled Giant . . . Britain among the Great Powers 1916–1939*, London, 1966, p. 151.
[4] Canada had already taken a lead here. Britain in 1920 had conceded to Canada the right of separate representation at Washington and in 1923 Canada signed the Halibut Treaty individually.

strongly intensified when the British Governor-General refused to grant a dissolution automatically. The Canadians considered that this refusal was forcing them back into a colonial or neo-colonial status. In 1926 there also occurred the Nadan v. Rex case when Canada lost her fight to prove that she could end the method whereby appeals were made to the British Judicial Committee simply by an act of the Canadian legislature. The Imperial Conference of 1926 considered how to reform these matters and proposals were worked out in detail partly by the Committee on Imperial Relations in the same year and also by the Conference on Dominion Legislation in 1929 and the Imperial Conference of 1930. Finally, the Statute of Westminster in 1931 set the seal on imperial reform.

III

Even before the Imperial Conference met in 1926 Britain was taking steps to come to terms with these new imperial aspirations to freedom and equality. In 1925 came the end of the old administrative system under which the Colonial Office dealt with all imperial territories except India (which had a separate department of its own) and certain areas like Egypt which, because they were not strictly defined as colonies, remained under the care of the Foreign Office. A new Secretaryship of State for Dominion Affairs was established to deal with the self-governing dominions, i.e. Australia, Canada, New Zealand, Newfoundland and South Africa, and also with the South African High Commission Territories of Swaziland, Bechuanaland and Basutoland, as well as self-governing Southern Rhodesia.[5] Similarly, when Britain signed the Locarno Treaty in October 1925 she took care, in view of the earlier desires of the dominions not to be over-closely identified with Britain's European policy,[6] to make a separate agreement clearly excluding them (see below, pp. 184–5).

When the Imperial Conference met in 1926, it had before it the report of the Committee on Imperial Relations drawn up under Balfour. The document was a careful but somewhat implausible attempt to paper over the difficulties of the imperial relationship.

[5] The association of the non-governing and self-governing areas was not logical but represented an administrative tidying-up which in later years would have offended dominion susceptibilies.

[6] Sir Austen Chamberlain, *Down the Years*, London, 1935, pp. 151 *et seq.*

Ancient feudal terms like 'allegiance', the precise meaning of which was abandoned, jostled with new terms which had sprung into prominence in connection with the League of Nations and the peace-making after the First World War, such as 'autonomous' and 'free association'. Although the term 'British Empire' was retained, and still needed since the non-self-governing territories were imperial in nature, the new term 'British Commonwealth of Nations'[7] appeared. 'Commonwealth' itself was a term of some antiquity[8] but as applied now was a restricted term since each state member of the association merely owed allegiance to the British Crown. The extent, therefore, to which 'Commonwealth' would mean 'commonweal' was left to be determined by the passage of time.

The Imperial Conference of 1926 was notable for its description of the dominions as 'autonomous communities within the British Empire, equal in status, in no way subordinate one to another in any aspect of their domestic or foreign affairs, though united by a common allegiance to the Crown and freely associated as members of the British Commonwealth of Nations'. But, equally important for the future although sometimes ignored, this conference also decided to recommend imperial preference to the governments concerned. Baldwin, then leading the Conservative Party, did not, however, win the 1923 General Election. In 1924 the Conservatives won the election but had pledged themselves 'not to impose new duties for preferential purposes'.[9] From 1924–29 the Baldwin administration as a result of their election policy only gave the empire limited preference by 'abolishing or reducing duties on imperial goods without reducing those on foreign'.[10]

The resolutions of the Imperial Conference of 1926 were considered inadequate legal security for the new status of the dominions particularly by South Africa, Canada and the Irish Free State. At that of 1930 a draft statute was drawn up for submission to the British and the dominions' parliaments. After the dominions' parliaments had given their approval the act was passed as the Statute of Westminster in 1931. The statute gave full legal force to the posi-

---

[7] This term was used in the Agreement of 6 December 1921 made with Southern Ireland.

[8] First use had been in modern times apparently by Lord Rosebery speaking to an Australian audience in January 1884, see Colin Cross, *The Fall of the British Empire 1918–1968*, London and New York, 1968, p. 171.

[9] James A. Williamson, *A Notebook of Commonwealth History*, New York, 1967, third edition revised and ed. by D. Southgate, p. 255.

[10] *Ibid.*

tion of the dominions as laid down by the Imperial Conference of 1926. For some years the dominions had in practice been free from British control and now theory also had been brought into line. The dominions were also now freed from the Colonial Laws Validity Act of 1865 for the Statute of Westminster 'provided that the powers of the parliament of a Dominion should include the power to repeal or amend any existing or future act of the Westminster Parliament applying to that Dominion as part of the law of that Dominion'.[11] The dominions were now free to order their own affairs both in domestic and foreign policy.

In the inter-war period the impact of the changes legalized by the Statute of Westminster was seen most clearly in relation to the domestic policies of the self-governing countries. But the equally serious effect of the changes on international relations—although far-reaching in their influence on the confidence of ministers conducting British foreign policy—tended to be masked, since the formal Commonwealth remained in existence as an institution. Not until after the Second World War was the institutional effect of these changes in the degree of Commonwealth adhesion to British foreign policy fully brought out by the rise of the super-powers, America and Russia, the reduction in British power, episodes such as the Suez crisis and the growing importance of the United Nations. Lastly, as the bipolarity of politics grew the Commonwealth countries became linked with regional (rather than British) defence pacts such as the South East Asia Treaty Organization (SEATO). The division was also stressed, as mentioned earlier, by divergent internal policies on issues such as racialism.

IV

The domestic impact of the changes was soon illustrated in the case of South Africa which quickly went ahead with the formal legal process of establishing her independence by the Status of the Union Act and the Seals Act of 1934, which recognized South Africa as sovereign and independent and also allowed for her secession from the Commonwealth, should she so choose. Now the South African government, in the words of Smuts' biographer :

> possessed sole executive authority, in foreign no less than in domestic affairs. Whether in any future war South Africa became

11 Williamson, *Notebook of Commonwealth History*, p. 261.

a belligerent or a neutral, or something in between, would depend solely upon the advice which the government of the Union tendered to the Governor-General. That in turn would depend upon the government's command of majority support in parliament.[12]

South Africa was passing into the phase of growing Nationalist Party power which was associated with the triumph of Afrikaaner views on the inequality, now and in the future, of the African natives. Smuts himself, then serving in the government of the moderate Nationalist, General Hertzog, opposed Nationalist racialism. But he was accused by Hertzog of wanting 'to turn South Africa into a Kaffir state' and counter-accused by English liberals of a 'lack of fighting spirit in the cause of racial justice'.[13] It was becoming clear in the 1930s that one of the major dominions was set on a path of racialism which would draw it more and more away from the rest of the Commonwealth.

Other changes followed the Statute of Westminster. Newfoundland, whose finances were severely distressed, chose to surrender her Dominion status in 1933 and became a Crown colony with Britain accepting responsibility for her financial solvency. Later, in 1948, a referendum was held and Newfoundland became a province of Canada in the following year. But the most important changes, apart from those affecting South Africa, concerned Ireland. The status of the Irish Free State had been defined by the Anglo-Irish Treaty of 1921. The technical status of this treaty was merely that of an agreement until 1922 when the Westminster Parliament passed enabling legislation to recognize the Irish Free State as a state. The 1921 agreement created the Irish Free State by separating twenty-six of the Irish counties from the remaining six counties in the north. The latter became Northern Ireland and remained linked with Westminster and under the politico-economic control of the Protestants.

When the Statute of Westminster was passed in 1931, it gave the Irish Free State Premier, De Valera, a legal basis for attacking the 1921 agreement. He started a vigorous campaign which included demands for abolition of the Governor-Generalship, separate Irish citizenship, and refused to pay Land Annuities as part of an economic war with Britain. These harassment tactics paid off in

[12] W. K. Hancock, *Smuts—The Fields of Force 1919–1950*, Cambridge University Press, 1968, pp. 255–6; Williamson, *A Notebook of Commonwealth History*, p. 262.
[13] Hancock, *Smuts*, p. 259.

1937 when the Irish Free State was altered into the Dominion of Eire. In 1938 De Valera negotiated with Britain for the return to Eire of three naval bases used by the former under the 1921 agreement, and during the Second World War Eire remained neutral.[14] South Africa almost followed Eire into neutrality from 1939–45 since General Hertzog believed that South African and British interests were not identified. When, however, his motion went before the South African Parliament eighty members voted in favour of Smuts' amendment to sever relations with Germany and to co-operate with the British Commonwealth of Nations while only sixty-seven voted for Hertzog's proposal against involvement in the war.[15] The importance of the narrowly won South African adherence to the Commonwealth's war effort was inestimable.

v

The growing independence of the dominions as they evolved along individual lines of policy increased their ability to pressurize Britain and hence win further constitutional freedom within the Commonwealth. But as this development went on other changes were affecting the non-dominion areas. Within these areas of the British Empire, tremendous disparities existed between the small wealthy élites—whose children sometimes to the third generation had been anglicized by attending British public schools such as Eton and then often reading law at a university—and the mass of the poor. These gulfs made it easy for the British to separate off the troublemakers and to ignore inarticulate desires for self-determination. The recipe for control of the non-self-governing areas in the inter-war period remained a mixture of social and educational assimilation of the élite, gaol for anti-British leaders and some compromises designed to train the indigenous inhabitants in democratic government. There was, in fact, a bewildering muddle of policies. The most useful line, training for self-government, was vitiated by differences between British and foreign cultures, problems of religion and caste, lack of money for spending on education and above all the way the British were determined to cling on to major financial and political control.

But opposition to imperialism was strengthening in Britain and pressure groups were linking up with those of similar thought in the

---

[14] Charles Duff, *Six Days to Shake an Empire*, London, 1966, p. 280.
[15] Hancock, *Smuts*, pp. 321–3.

empire. Some of the élite of the empire had learned enough about British freedoms and constitutional monarchy to want a similar devolution of power for their own countries. The new outlook was spread among some but by no means all members of the divided British Liberal Party, also the British Labour Party and particularly those connected with the Webbs either through the Fabian Movement or the London School of Economics; it was encouraged by inexpensively priced literature turned out by publishers such as Victor Gollancz and Sir Allen Lane, and was also at work among members of the British upper classes who could not stand urban industrialized Britain and chose to champion the underdog abroad. The self-determination mood gained additional strength from the state of the Labour Party after it was split by MacDonald in 1931. Anti-imperialism served as a useful differentiating factor when both Left and Right were at a low ebb as regards putting into practice new policies to get Britain out of the domestic economic crisis. The Left of Centre groups in Britain received an intellectual boost from the influx of academics, journalists and cartoonists exiled from central Europe by the Nazis. Also at work in the movement for colonial self-determination was the British Communist Party but it was split by internal difficulties over the various Moscow lines and deeply involved in a losing battle with men such as Ernest Bevin for control of the British workers.

'Self-determination' as a term had come to prominence as part of the British propaganda drive against the Allied powers during the First World War and had also been used both by Kerensky and the Bolsheviks. The term was like a snowball which as it rolled on picked up more and more strength and took on powerful idealistic overtones. President Wilson was influenced by it and used it in his Fourteen Points, notably in Number 12 concerning the many peoples of the Ottoman Empire and Number 13 on Poland. Self-determination thus became a major premise of the League of Nations, and was championed in Britain by members of the League of Nations Union.

Self-determination faced the League of Nations with a serious problem for although this international institution was called 'League of Nations' it was a 'League of States',[16] many of whom had powerful imperial interests. An attempt was made, as we have seen in the preceding chapter on the League, to harmonize the power of major imperial states as exercised in the underdeveloped

[16] Sydney Herbert, *Nationality and its Problems*, London, 1920, p. 144.

parts of the world with self-determination through the 'sacred trust' concept under the mandate system. Hence imperial states such as Britain and France now had a new preoccupation with the indigenous inhabitants of their empires.

In the case of Britain, as early as 1923 a White Paper known as the Devonshire Declaration was issued after His Majesty's Government had examined the Kenyan settlers' demands for self-government. The inquiry took into account the growth of white power in South Africa and Southern Rhodesia but stated that African interests were paramount. It admitted that there were other interests in Kenya—European, Indian and Arab—which must also be safeguarded, but concluded that 'in the administration of Kenya His Majesty's Government regard themselves as exercising a trust on behalf of the African population, and they are unable to delegate this trust, the object of which may be defined as the protection and advancement of the native races'.[17] Yet in the same year, 1923, Britain granted virtually complete self-government to the white settlers of Southern Rhodesia who were allowed to control both administration and army, leaving Britain only with residual legal powers to veto laws passed in Southern Rhodesia which might harm the Africans.[18] It has been argued that this discrepancy was because the Southern Rhodesian settlers were in a stronger position than those of Kenya, and that Britain feared a serious crisis such as had recently occurred in Ireland, i.e. a potential Unilateral Declaration of Independence (UDI) such as took place in 1965. But the important fact to note is the muddle of British compromises under the strain of colonial self-determination.

The Devonshire type of declaration has to be checked against development in individual colonies particularly as regards the amount of money spent on different levels of education, and the degree to which Britain retained political and financial control. The thinking of many British liberals in the inter-war years remained biassed in favour of 'Empire' rather than of 'Commonwealth', focussed towards enlightened colonialism rather than in favour of training the natives for political take-over. To a great extent this was because many Western statesmen were obsessed by European events, not just because so many important problems existed there but also because Europe was their intellectual and political theatre. Even devotees of the League of Nations trained their eyes on Europe

[17] Jennings, *The British Commonwealth of Nations*, p. 160, citing Cmd. 1922.
[18] Theodore Bull (ed.), *Rhodesian Perspective*, London, 1967, p. 13.

and thought about the working out of League concepts in relation to Europe rather than to the world generally. This sort of thinking shows in men such as Lord Cecil of Chelwood who nevertheless wished to keep Britain a degree or two apart from Europe and tended to fall back upon the problems of the Empire and Commonwealth when the French seemed to want too close a European association.[19] It must also be remembered that in so far as empire was concerned, the League of Nations had set up an emotional backlash; impetuous and self-willed figures such as Sir Winston Churchill opposed closing the gap between theory and practice in imperial decentralization. Lord Halifax, indeed, believed that but for the 'violent and obstructive opposition by Sir Winston Churchill and his friends [in 1935] . . . we might perhaps have got an all-India solution to the Indian problem before the Second World War'.[20]

VI

Traditionally India and Ireland were regarded as the keystones of the British Empire from the nineteenth to the first decades of the twentieth century. Hence when Ireland won free in 1921 retention of India became of even greater importance. The fight for the older, more developed British dominions was over and Britain had conceded defeat, but India was now the symbol of the new struggle just beginning in earnest for self-determination in the non-white and less developed areas of the British Empire. This importance derived in part from the size and politico-economic value of India to Britain and also occurred because the educated Indian élite were more numerous and more highly advanced than those now developing, say, in Africa. Moreover, it was evident that should trouble threaten in the Far East through the growth of Japanese ambitions, then India would be a strategic pivot and base for British and imperial resistance in war. Yet this latter military consideration should not be overstressed for, as has often been pointed out, Britain tended to turn a blind eye to the possibilities of Japanese aggression. This was symbolized by the fact that the guns of Singapore still pointed seawards, and that little or no preparation had been made for the likelihood of a Japanese motorized onslaught down through landward Malaya. In part this military blindness resulted from the way in which the major Western powers, and America—understandably

[19] *All the Way*, London, 1949, see especially pp. 253–6. See also below, p. 238.
[20] Lord Atlee, *Empire into Commonwealth*, Oxford University Press, 1961, p. 36.

preoccupied with storm signals from Europe—had stood by and allowed the Japanese seizure of considerable parts of China and mineral-wealthy Manchuria earlier in the 1930s. Modern Japan seemed to the politicians so much an admirable copy of Western industrialization and efficiency that the sleeping tiger of Asiatic hatred for Western imperialism was hardly discerned. In part because it was convenient to regard Japan as Western-oriented and in part because the Japanese seemed so busy with their industrial revolution, the British often talked about the strategic importance of India in relation to trouble in the East—and not-so-distant memories of the threat from Imperial Tsarist Russia were turned over—but the new military implications of India's strategic value were insufficiently explored.

The earlier and illusory steps towards giving Indians more political power in their own sub-continent have been mentioned (see Chapter 5, pp. 77–8); and their irritant value in promoting Indian demands for self-determination cannot be overestimated. Additional progress had been made at the close of the First World War when wartime promises given in order to prevent unrest—a wave of which hit India with news of the Bolshevik revolution in 1917—had later, at least in part, to be honoured.

Under the India Act of 1919 which was based on the Montagu-Chelmsford Report of 1918, structures of Parliamentary and local government were set up. Political and financial control of India, however, remained firmly in British hands because the Viceroy could issue laws in emergencies without consulting the Indian Parliament, and because the executive or government was appointed by the ruling British power and could not be got rid of by the Indian Parliament even if it had been constitutionally defeated within the two chambers. The frustration and irritation caused by this so-called constitutional reform can be imagined. But it was worsened by the fact that Montagu, as Secretary of State for India, had declared in the Westminster Parliament in 1917—when it was urgent to get Indian military aid during the war[21]—that India was to move to self-government;[22] in addition, Indian hopes had been encouraged when she had been given quasi-dominion recognition in 1917 on being allowed to attend the Imperial Conference.[23] Apart

[21] India sent approximately one million troops to aid Britain in the First World War.
[22] Williamson, *A Notebook of Commonwealth History*, p. 250.
[23] *Ibid.*

from these problems of disappointed hopes, the Government of India Act of 1919 got off to a bad start following the so-called Amritsar Massacre of April 1919.

This massacre occurred on 10 April when General Dyer, faced by a threatening mob (which had gathered to attend a forbidden mass meeting), allowed his troops to open fire, killing 379 Indians and injuring over a thousand. General Dyer was called upon to resign and was censured by the British government, and arguments continue to the present day concerning the decision to fire. But with general discontent present throughout India, lack of work for returned soldiers, famine and the influenza epidemic adding to a near-revolutionary situation, it seems that but for this sharp check to mass resistance to British rule, all India might have gone up in flames and slaughter since religious and communal antagonisms might well have been vented under cover of the revolt against the British. The Moslem community at this time was uneasy over the fate of the Sultanate of the Ottoman Empire and over its impending partition.[24]

After the Amritsar massacre, the Punjab, where the incident took place, and India settled into an uneasy calm. At this stage Mohandas Karamchand Gandhi, an Indian barrister who had already won a reputation as a campaigner for Indian rights in South Africa, began to play an increasingly important part in the struggle for Indian independence. He had returned to India in 1914 and by 1919 had won control of the Congress Party. When the British, as part of the Act of 1919, tied further grants of devolution of power to the degree of co-operation shown by Indians in working this Act, Gandhi refused to accept this link. He advocated a policy of non-co-operation with, and passive resistance against, the British in India. He was repeatedly imprisoned—in 1922, 1930, 1933 and again in 1942—but only became more and more convinced that India must receive her independence. He fully realized that independence would not be the millennium but as he once told a friend, 'Please try never to forget that it is the inalienable right of a people to misgovern themselves.'[25] Gandhi's policy of non-co-operation was not accepted by all Indian politicians, many of whom

[24] Williamson, *A Notebook of Commonwealth History*, pp. 249–50; see also Sir Percival Griffiths, *Empire into Commonwealth*, London, 1969, pp. 257–9. The latter writer stresses the effect of contact with the outside world on Indians who served abroad during the First World War and Moslem fears of Hindu domination under the reforms which Britain was bringing in.

[25] Letter, *The Times*, London, 6 May 1970, p. 11, from Mr. Evert Barger.

worked with the British in an attempt to use the provisions of the Act of 1919 successfully.

To indicate that the new policy of partnership and training for future independence was more than mere words, the British government in 1923 relaxed the economic bonds of imperialism. This was done by allowing India the right to protect her nascent industries through tariffs, a right which the other formal dominions had also won earlier. Indian industry thus had a firmer base from which to develop.

When the India Act of 1919 was passed it had contained provisions for the establishment of a constitutional commission to check on the progress of reforms after ten years. But it was decided to set up the commission as early as 1927 and it was headed by the Liberal barrister, Sir John Simon. While the Simon Report, which was published in 1930, made suggestions for further reforms such as the separation of Burma[26] from India and an intensified degree of responsible government, it did not go far enough to meet the pace of Indian desires for self-government. It continued the system mentioned already and crystallized in the Act of 1919 under which the central executive was not responsible to the central legislature which the provincial legislature was now empowered to elect. The problem which was emerging in India as Britain gradually relaxed her imperial grip was the need to develop central responsibility and to draw the provinces together. The Simon Report had not gone far enough in this direction. Further discussions and investigations were considered necessary and the Round Table Conferences on India met to carry out this work in London during 1931-2. In 1933 the British government issued a White Paper based on the conclusions of the Round Table Conferences that there should be a federated India composed both of the princely states and the British provinces. The acceptance of the federal principle, which was a departure from the Simon Report, marked a significant step forward towards Indian political unity and preparedness for independence. The White Paper also advocated continuance of the traditional system of provincial self-government combined with central British control although this was now relaxed except in regard to all-important matters such as foreign and defence policy, law, finance and religion. Under the provisions of the White Paper a parliamen-

---

[26] Burma was occupied by Britain in 1882, attached to India in 1886, given a degree of self-government in 1937 and finally achieved independance in 1948 when it then decided to leave the Commonwealth.

tary committee was authorized to draw up detailed proposals for Indian reform.

The reforms discussed in the White Paper of 1933 became law under the India Act of 1935 which made India a federal state, although politically it was a dyarchy since power at the centre remained divided between the Indian and British authorities, and the latter retained emergency powers which could be used without consent of the legislature. But, once again, the reforms came too late for the climate of Indian opinion and although the provisions for full responsible government in the eleven British provinces considered suitable were brought into force on 1 April 1937, the important provisions on the federal state were held up by Indian communal and religious disagreements.

When the Second World War began for Britain in September 1939, the Indians were still divided and the federal state existed only on paper. As mentioned earlier, defence and foreign policy, as well as traditional British imperial controls such as law, order and finance, remained in British hands. In addition Britain had retained important residual powers of unilateral action through the emergency provisions of the 1935 Act. Consequently, the British government involved India in its war against Germany and her allies in 1939 and this was fiercely resented by the Indian Congress Party which decided to pursue a policy of non-co-operation for the duration of the war. The difficulties which this policy created for the British government in its relations with India were exacerbated by the demand of the Moslem League made in 1940 that Pakistan should be their homeland, separate and independent from India. But Pakistan, like India, was a mosaic of Hindu and Moslem settlements and the danger of this proposal lay in the near-certainty that any attempt to grant the Moslem wish would lead to ejection of the Hindus from Pakistan and communal reprisals in India against the Moslems. Britain in 1939 was therefore faced by serious political and religious opposition in India and the wartime problem was whether the necessary degree of Indian co-operation could in some way be achieved.

VII

To sum up on the Commonwealth in the inter-war period, perhaps the most important fact to bear in mind is that the Empire and Commonwealth co-existed in this period. The dominions had obtained their political freedom from Britain in part through their efforts in the First World War to aid the mother country, and thereafter by their resolute will to sever the links—legal, defence and foreign—which had marked them as non-sovereign states subject to Britain's rule. But the less developed and largely non-white populated regions of the British Empire still had to win their freedom from Britain. It was to take the Second World War, and the political concessions which Britain was then to make, combined with the anti-colonialist thrust in the new United Nations Charter which the USA championed from 1945 to around 1960, to enable these regions of the British Empire to win through to independence.

During the 1920s to 1930s the British Empire and Commonwealth enjoyed advantages from and suffered difficulties because the British, although a great imperialist nation, never possessed a highly elaborated doctrine of imperialism. Imperialism for the British had been to a great degree an organic growth developing from trade, protection of trade and resultant theories of strategy. The advantage for the Empire and Commonwealth of this absence of a rigid doctrine of racial imperialism was that Britain, when challenged as by India, one of the members of the League of Nations, did make concessions. Admittedly, these concessions were—as we have seen—generally anachronistic by the time they were brought into constitutional practice, but they were steps downwards from the assumption of a divine right to sovereignty over other nations or peoples simply because these peoples were weaker economically, not developed technically through industrialization and in many cases were not organized on a state basis like the European nations.

This lack of an elaborated doctrine of racial superiority in British imperialism—notwithstanding the efforts of writers like Cromer and Milner to evoke highly emotive images of ancient Greece and Rome—also meant that Britain in the inter-war years often made quiet administrative concessions which were in some ways of greater significance than the much more publicized political concessions. One of these important changes occurred in 1924 when Britain decided to step up rapidly the Indian complement in the Indian Civil Service so that within fifteen years there would be parity between the British members and the Indians. As one British member of the ICS admits :

Many British members of the [Indian Civil] service, including those like the writer, who then took the inevitably parochial view of the District Officer, disapproved of that announcement, but there can be no doubt that the broader views of the Home Government led to the right decision.[27]

Yet the problem of an unconscious assumption of racial superiority remained a legacy from British imperialism and colonialism, and although the rising tide of self-determination, accompanied by an inability to cope with the economic and political problems which self-determination drives brought, was to lead Britain to resign her empire after the Second World War, this did not mean that racialism was also resigned.

In the inter-war period British rule over the Empire and association with self-governing dominions came to be broadly classed as the Commonwealth. But the sense of commonweal which this change of institutional title implies is misleading. The Commonwealth as an international institution was composed of vastly different economic, political and cultural units. So long as Britain was apparently sovereign, the conflicting tendencies within these units was masked, but by the eve of the Second World War when Britain's political power was being challenged even by the less-developed units of the imperial sector, the importance and strength of national characteristics, religious beliefs, traditionalism and inbred attitudes towards the conduct of public business were all reasserting their power.

Britain had given her Empire and Commonwealth a tradition of constitutionalism and uncorrupt public service, a focus in the monarchy, and in many cases political and national unity. But all this rested largely on British confidence in her right to govern and on the acceptance by indigenous populations of this assumption. This confidence was not steadily eroded, it rose and fell cyclically. After the shock of the American rebellion, many writers and publicists found it natural to compare colonies to ripening fruit which must inevitably fall off the parent tree. Yet the work of imperialism went on and was to revive later under the willing hands of Disraeli and the less willing hands of Gladstone. But even in the period when the quiet work of imperialism was continuing, before Disraeli made it fashionable once more, the Earl of Durham was considering the application of the principle of the English Whig revolution—constitutional monarchy—to the colonies. The devolution of power which in England led to constitutional monarchy in the colonies implied, as Durham saw it, responsible self-government. The way in

[27] Griffiths, *Empire into Commonwealth*, pp. 260–1.

which Durham worked out his understanding of the principle of responsible self-government in the colonies from the analogy of responsible government in Britain is matched over and over again in British colonial history, for as Britain herself made political advances so these advances were gradually passed on in varying degrees to her colonies.

By 1939 the ties which bound Britain to her dominions and colonies were slackening. The Second World War artificially tightened these connections again, but once this tension was relaxed the demands for self-determination were to rise in increased volume. Nations, as Gandhi put it, wanted the right to govern themselves and to misgovern themselves if this should be the case. Once these nations had won statehood the old Eurocentricity of international politics would be gone. But in 1939 the British Commonwealth still held together and Britain, partly through political firmness, partly through slender chances as in the case of South Africa, would once more be aided by men, money and resources from her far-flung lines of power and influence when the tocsin of world war struck again for Europe.

But would that hour have come again if Britain had been clearly backed by the Commonwealth and Empire in the inter-war years? For, as we have noted earlier, the self-governing dominions did not choose to give Britain a blank cheque in international relations. Hence Britain in the 1920s to 1930s was placed in a position of extreme difficulty in foreign policy. On the one hand, it could be argued that if Britain's time of need in a world war should come again, then the Commonwealth and Empire would in fact, as ultimately occurred, back Britain through the need for self-preservation. Yet, on the other hand, British statesmen in the inter-war years could never assume that the material and moral strength of the Commonwealth and Empire would underwrite British decisions concerning the tangled web of European politics. Possession of an empire had been considered necessary by writers such as Seeley in the late nineteenth century precisely because Britain *alone* would not be a strong enough economic and military unit to hold her own with America and Russia, let alone modern Germany. But by the 1920s to 1930s the situation which Seeley had dreaded had, in effect, arrived, for British foreign policy could not be made on the confident assumption that the Commonwealth and Empire would back it. This situation, masked as it was by the British love of tradition and weakness for platitudes, resulted from the inability of the British

G

to weld the Commonwealth and Empire into an *active* as distinct from a *passive* supranational institution. This task, the importance of which was only glimpsed by a handful of politicians and writers, was probably an impossible one, even had it been attempted; it would have required Commonwealth and imperial units which were just struggling up towards levels of sovereignty to abandon sovereignty before they had tasted its pleasures and its pains. As post-war history has shown, only states whose sense of sovereignty was badly depressed by the fortunes of traditional warfare, or later equally rough economic lessons, have been willing to consider creating *active* (as distinct from *passive*) supranational institutions such as the European Economic Community.[28]

When discussing the weakness of British inter-war foreign policy, it is customary to stress the violent emotional distaste for war caused by the extent of the First World War and the degree of casualties, combatant and non-combatant, once industrialization was applied to military matters. It is also usual to refer to the American decision not to enter the League of Nations, and the similar American decision not to share with Britain the guarantee to underwrite French security against Germany. Equally customary are allusions to the enfeebling effects of the financial and economic crisis of Western capitalism before the device of deficit-finance righted matters in part by substituting alternately creeping or rapid inflation for the earlier problem of mass unemployment. But to these factors we should add this additional argument that the weakness—or it could be argued the realism—of British foreign policy in the inter-war period was also rooted in lack of confidence concerning the relationship with the Commonwealth and Empire. For here it is not so much the question of what these areas would do to back Britain if major war should come again, but rather the need for the authority to conduct British foreign policy on the assumption, years before 1939, that Britain was backed in her daily dealing with the other major continental powers by the Commonwealth and Empire. But this confidence and hence the resultant authority were precisely what was lacking in the inter-war years.

It was mentioned earlier that when Britain signed the Locarno Treaty on 1 December 1925, she took care not to involve the self-governing countries of the Commonwealth (see above, p. 169).

[28] With the exception of the United Nations. But this supranational institution is in many ways more like the Commonwealth in its problems than the EEC in its powers.

Yet this treaty concerned arrangements to guarantee the Franco-German and Belgo-German boundaries as well as to safeguard the demilitarized zone of the Rhineland. Maintenance of these safeguards was central to keeping the inter-war peace, but Britain had been unable to win the dominions over to supporting a unified foreign policy. The failure to do so can be traced back to the Imperial Conference of 1923 which, one recent writer has claimed, the British hoped to use 'as second best peacetime substitute for the imperial war cabinet' and to 'formulate at least the broad outlines of policy for the whole Empire', producing in effect 'a single imperial foreign policy'.[29] If indeed British policy was so clear in 1923 then it ran aground against fears in the dominions that they might be involved in defending what were essentially British interests. Acceptance of such a central British role challenged the basic point which they were trying to establish, i.e. that freedom in foreign policy which is traditionally regarded as the hallmark of an independent state. The attitude of the dominions was well summed up by one of the advisers to Mackenzie King, then Canadian Prime Minister, who warned him in 1923 that 'a common foreign policy offers a maximum of responsibility and a minimum of control'.[30] All that the British achieved in the end was the hopeful statement issued at the Imperial Conference of 1926 that the foreign policies of Commonwealth countries although individually controlled would not endanger common objectives.

What these common objectives were, however, remained in doubt. But since the diplomatic representation of the dominions was still minimal they necessarily relied on the British Foreign Office for information and general assistance. Canada, for instance, was only diplomatically represented in three capitals in the inter-war years. In addition, since dominion levels of defence and general expertise were necessarily much less than those of Britain, such countries as Australia and New Zealand, as well as South Africa, expected to be protected by British naval forces. Undoubtedly, these two factors—residual British diplomatic aid and naval protection—imposed a tendency to co-operate with Britain for basic needs but equally certainly the lack of defined common objectives in foreign policy left Britain lacking in confidence in her conduct of international relations between the world wars.

The implications of the wishes of the dominions not to be

[29] Nicholas Mansergh, *The Commonwealth Experience*, London, 1969, p. 224.
[30] *Ibid.*, p. 223.

involved in Britain's European entanglements shown in 1922 over Chanak and again in 1923 at the Imperial Conference and concerning the Locarno Treaty in 1925 were worked out in similar episodes which followed. When Britain made a new agreement with Egypt in 1936 providing for maintenance of troops in the Canal Zone but for the progressive evacuation of forces from the rest of Egypt, despite the importance of the Suez Canal as the imperial naval link, the dominions took no part in the treaty. Early in 1939 when Britain was hastily improvising a patchwork of guarantees to east European countries such as Rumania and Poland as well as Balkan Greece, not one of the dominions joined in to back Britain in this attempt to buttress French efforts and so deter Hitler from using force in the East. As one writer puts it, 'while there was community in sentiment, there was no community in commitment'.[31] But even this expression seems too strong when we look back at, say, the narrow basis for the South African decision to back Britain in September 1939. In the end all the dominions, except as mentioned Eire, did back Britain in the Second World War, but this endorsement of British foreign policy came too late to prevent that war from being worldwide and intensely destructive. Had Britain received strong dominions' backing in the inter-war period, had a mechanism for thinking out common objectives grown out of the 1923 Imperial Conference, then the course of European and world history might have run along different lines; certainly, the conduct of British foreign policy would have been more confident.

The importance of this factor of the lack of British confidence in the conduct of international relations in the inter-war years can hardly be exaggerated. When the pattern of modern politics emerged in the latter part of the nineteenth century with the striving of five roughly equal states for economic and political power—Britain, France, Germany, Russia and the USA—it was essential for one of these states to operate as a fulcrum in the balance of power, and to play an essentially passive role in support of maintaining peace. Britain, the most mature state in historical terms, assumed this role. She did this through limiting war by her own non-participation or by encouraging others not to participate as in the Franco-Prussian War of 1870–71. After this war the problem of maintaining peace rested for about thirty years on Britain's ability not to side too decisively with either of the major alliances of the day, the Triple Alliance of Austria, Germany and Italy or the

[31] Mansergh, *Commonwealth Experience*, p. 283.

Dual Alliance of France and Russia. But by the early years of the twentieth century, this now traditional policy associated with Salisbury was falling into disrepute. Younger statesmen such as Lansdowne were willing to strike alliance bargains such as that made with Japan for naval co-operation in the Far East, which released Britain to make the early moves in policy which were gradually, unknown to the British public, to mesh her future in any war with France and Russia rather than with Germany who had been the customary British friend. Britain, her Empire and all her allies combined were to prove insufficient to carry the day against Germany and her allies in the First World War. The scale had to be tipped in their favour by the USA.

Against this background showing the importance of imperial aid for Britain in the First World War, and later that of the USA, the effect of the relative withdrawal of backing by Empire, Commonwealth and the USA on British confidence in the conduct of international relations in the inter-war years can be assessed. The problem of threatening war remained, but the temporary unity of the First World War was gone, leaving Britain and France, who, as the preceding chapter has shown, were divided on how to maintain peace, to carry the burden alone from day to day. During the inter-war years too, Britain was losing power as her imperial control slackened and she was in fact being reduced to a status slightly below that of countries such as Germany, France and Russia, since although she still carried the burdens of empire she no longer proudly possessed the power and confidence which these burdens had originally conferred. Yet despite this lack of superiority Britain in the 1920s and 1930s reverted to an attempted balancing role in international relations similar, although on a reduced scale, to that she had had the power to play from 1871 to 1904. Such a fulcrum or balancing role in international relations is possible if based on superior power, or even perhaps merely on equal power if conditions are favourable, but if such a role is attempted from a position of inferiority it cannot succeed. In this instance, it fooled no one but merely allowed Hitler to get much of what he wanted by threats of use of force as Britain made one retreat or another in search of appeasement. The dismal events of inter-war politics stress the need to know the real basis and extent of a state's power.

REFERENCES

Attlee, Lord, *Empire into Commonwealth*, London, O.U.P., 1961.

Cecil of Chelwood, Lord, *All the Way*, London, Hodder and Stoughton, 1949.

Chamberlain, A., *Down the Years*, London, Cassell, 1935.

Cross, C., *The Fall of the British Empire 1918–1968*, London, Hodder and Stoughton, and New York, Coward-McCann, 1968.

Duff, C., *Six Days to Shake an Empire*, London, Dent, 1966.

Feiling, K., *The Life of Neville Chamberlain*, London, Macmillan, 1946.

Griffiths, P., *Empire into Commonwealth*, London, Benn, and New York, International Publications Service, 1969.

Hancock, W. K., *Smuts—The Fields of Force 1919–1950*, Cambridge and New York, C.U.P., 1968.

Herbert, S., *Nationality and Its Problems*, London, Methuen, 1920.

Jennings, I., *The British Commonwealth of Nations*. London and New York, Hutchinson, 1967.

Mansergh, N., *The Commonwealth Experience*, London, Weidenfeld and Nicolson, and New York, Praeger, 1969.

Williamson, J. A., ed. D. Southgate, *A Notebook of Commonwealth History*, London and New York, Macmillan, 3rd Ed., 1967

10 *The Twenty-Year Armistice*

In the first chapter of this book we have described the nineteenth century—ending for our purposes in 1914, not 1900—as a 'century of total peace', at least as far as Europe was concerned. The twentieth century, or its first five or six decades, has been called by contrast 'the century of total war'.[1] This is true in that this century, as we have defined it, began with a four-and-a-quarter-year war which involved all the major states and many minor ones, mobilized all the belligerents' energies and resources for the struggle, and killed almost twenty million people either as war casualties or the victims of epidemic diseases which followed the war. There succeeded an armistice of twenty years, during the last eight years of which the European system of international relations crumbled with increasing speed, resulting in a second total war, this time of six years' duration. This, again, was total in its involvement of all the major powers and very many of the smaller ones, in its mobilization once more of all the belligerents' resources, in its geographical extent, which was far greater than that of the First World War, and its loss of human life, which has been put at thirty-five million. It has been estimated that, but for the Second World War, the population of the Soviet Union alone would have been thirty million greater in 1945 than it was in 1939. Since 1945, although there has been no major war, hostilities confined to particular regions have been almost continuous and, as part of the structure created to deter aggression, the major powers have remained in a permanent state of being prepared for war since 1945. Unprecedented proportions of the national budgets of America, Russia, Britain and France, ranging from 13% to 45% in 1969, are spent on armaments, amounting to some nine per cent of the yearly output of the world's goods and services. Even a small state like Portugal spends 40% of its budget on armaments.

Yet there is a sense in which the first half of the twentieth century marked the end of total war. First, there is no doubt that the utterly unforeseen scale of destruction in the First World War left

[1] The title of a book by Raymond Aron published in 1954.

its mark on all the belligerents, in the sense of a determination to avoid a similar bloodbath in future. In Britain, the dominant power in world diplomacy during the twenty-year armistice, fear of another total war took the form on the Left of reluctance to rearm against the danger of Nazi and Fascist aggression and, on the Right, a desire to go to the limit in placating the dictators. In France the political defeatism of the 1930s, which culminated in the actual military *débâcle* of 1940, was to a large extent an emotional refusal to suffer again the protracted horrors of 1914–18. Soviet Russia's whole political ideology, Marxism-Leninism, was based on revulsion against the capitalist system which allegedly had war built into it. America's isolation of the 1930s, in the face of the clearest signs of danger to her security, arose mainly from the feeling that her entry into the war in April 1917 had been a tragic mistake, the result of the machinations of American financiers committed to the Allied side. Italy's romantic dictator, Benito Mussolini, extolled war in writings and speeches, but did his utmost to avert it in 1938 and 1939, and only entered the Second World War in 1940 when victory for the Axis side seemed assured. Significantly, of all the belligerents in the First World War, only Japan, who had little or no fighting to do, entered the Second World War, for which her own expansion in China in the 1930s was the curtain-raiser, with anything like relish.

It may be argued that Adolf Hitler, often held to be the originator of the Second World War, despite A. J. P. Taylor's arguments to the contrary, was an exponent of total war, and an enthusiastic one at that. But the opposite is the case. When Hitler in his speeches in the thirties dwelt on his unpleasant experiences as a common soldier in the 1914–18 war, he was, of course, seeking to enlist the sympathy of the democracies by underlining his horror of war. But he was also speaking sincerely. Almost the last thing Hitler desired was that his Nordic youth should be slaughtered on European battlefields as they had been twenty years before. Hitler's conception of war—*Blitzkrieg* —was not total war, but its opposite : an attempt to avoid total war by terrifying the enemy into surrender through threats of total war with a pretended overwhelming military predominance on Hitler's side.

Hence the exaggerated importance Hitler attached to propaganda. *Blitzkrieg* was in reality propaganda war, a psychological rather than physical destruction of the enemy's will to resist. Hence Hitler's lies in the 1930s about the size of his air force, which deceived a man as shrewd and well-informed as Churchill. Hence, too, Hitler's failure to mobilize totally the German war machine until the autumn of 1942, when Speer was put in charge of war production. This happened in 1942 because Hitler then found himself in the very kind of war in Russia which it was the whole aim of his policy to avoid. In Russia's great plains the German army suffered heavy losses and with that came Germany's defeat and Hitler's suicide in blazing Berlin. Total war had proved that in modern conditions it cannot be used as an instrument of foreign policy. After the First World War total war was a catastrophe which might and did occur, but not a rational instrument of statecraft.

The invention of the atomic bomb during the Second World War, then the thermonuclear or nuclear bomb, followed by the intercontinental ballistic missile, and the incorporation of these weapons into the armouries of the present-day super-powers, the United States and the Soviet Union, with destructive force capable of killing all the world's population hundreds of times over, and later the spread of these weapons now to three, perhaps tomorrow a dozen, other states : all this has served merely to underline the lessons of the First World War that total war in the twentieth century is an impractical tool of foreign policy and not the extension of diplomacy as Clausewitz conceived it over a hundred years ago.

We must later consider in detail the effects of nuclear weapons on the working of the international system. It is sufficient to repeat here that it is not these weapons, but the first total war of the twentieth century, the 1914–18 war, which eliminated itself as a means of advancing a cause in international relations. Hitler's miscalculation, that he could overcome his enemies without fighting a total war, was a gamble which almost succeeded. The Second World War had to be fought to prove that it was indeed a miscalculation.

I

But this is by no means the whole truth about the origins of the Second World War or why the peace after 1918 proved to be merely a brief truce of two decades. The fact was that the European system of international relations collapsed, and that European system was indeed *the* system of international relations. The two world wars marked the end of Europe as the epicentre of international politics. Before 1914, before even 1939, decisions were made in Europe the effects of which were felt in distant continents outside. Since 1945 decisions have been made outside, the effects of which have been felt inside, Europe. Perhaps, as integration among the west European states proceeds and their relations with east European communist states improve, Europe may resume, if not its former primacy, at least some of its old power to influence world politics.

The years 1914 to 1945 represent, then, a continuous decline of Europe as the dominant focus of world politics. To some extent this had already begun by 1914; as we have seen in a previous chapter, by the time Europe plunged into the vortex in 1914, Japan had already begun her meteoric rise to a place among the paramount naval powers of the Pacific; had formed an alliance with Britain in 1902, the first occasion on which a dominant European power reached out into the non-European world for assistance against another European power; and in 1905 had overthrown one of the classic giants of the European system, Russia. Then again, the First World War could not be won by the Allies, after the German defeat of Russia in 1917, without the entry into the war of the United States, and this not only on account of America's actual contribution to the Allied victory in 1918, but because of her unmeasured potential strength waiting to be mobilized in future. Again, the European economic revival in the late 1920s, the basis, or one of the bases, of the Franco-German reconciliation symbolized by the mutual understanding of Aristide Briand and Gustav Stresemann, was eased by the flow of capital from the United States. The precipitate withdrawal of that capital in 1929 and 1930 knocked the bottom out of Europe's prosperity, with disastrous consequences for the whole international order.

During the entire inter-war period, as we shall see later, the extra-European world which Europe had dominated and financed, the passive object of diplomacy conducted in London, Paris, Berlin, Moscow and Vienna, was slowly coming to life, weakening the old European powers, setting them at one another's throats and providing them with new themes for their international debate. This usually, though not always, slow emergence of the non-European world was facilitated not only by the advent of national consciousness in that world, often after having originated in Europe, but by the adoption of the cause of colonial independence in Liberal and Left-wing circles in Europe, especially in Britain, as discussed in the preceding chapter. After the acceptance of the principle of national self-determination by the Allies during the 1914–18 war, if only in its application to the successor states of the old empires in Europe itself and the Arab portions of the Ottoman Empire, as we have noted it was difficult to see how it could be denied, first to the Irish, who received their independence from Parliament at Westminster in 1922, next to Egypt, over which Britain had extended her protection in 1914 and which received further instalments of independence by treaty in 1922 and 1936, then to India, the most precious jewel in the British Crown, which in 1935, after bitter struggles in the British Conservative party, received a limited form of autonomy for its provinces and which struggled continuously for complete self-rule during the Second World War.

There were other areas in which local pressures against European rule made their weight felt. In the Middle East the nationalist revolution led by Kemal Ataturk destroyed the Treaty of Sèvres which the old regime of the Sultan had signed in August 1920 and which amounted to the internationalization of the Dardanelles, or in effect the driving out of the Turks from Europe, and the partitioning of Anatolia among the Allied powers, especially Italy and Greece. In place of the Treaty of Sèvres the new Kemalist regime in Ankara negotiated and signed with the Allied powers at Lausanne in July 1923 a treaty which restored to Turkey its full political and economic independence, removed the old Capitulations or European extraterritorial rights in Turkey, ended the partitioning of Anatolia, much to the chagrin of Greece and Italy, and restored Turkish sovereignty over Eastern Thrace, thus giving back to Kemal a foothold in Europe, and over the Straits. The latter were demilitarized by the Lausanne Treaty, but by the Convention of Montreux in 1936 Turkey was allowed to remilitarize the Straits though under internationally controlled agreements on rights of passage through these waters.

The Arab portions of the old Turkish Empire, as we have explained earlier, became semi-independent states supervised by two European mandatory powers—France for Syria and Lebanon and Britain for Palestine, Transjordan and Iraq—answerable for the discharge of their mandates to the League of Nations (see above, Chapter 6, p. 107). The Arab states ought perhaps to have welcomed the mandates system until, as Article 22 of the League Covenant said, they were 'able to stand by themselves under the strenuous conditions of the modern world'; certainly that system was preferable to the pre-Kemalist Turkish regime. But they did not. They hated the French and French mandatory administration had to be established in Damascus first by military decree, then in

1926 by force. Given the choice, all the Arab states would have preferred Britain as the mandatory power. But they really wanted
neither. They assumed that by the correspondence between their
wartime leader, Sherif Hussein, and the British High Commissioner
in Egypt, Sir Henry McMahon, in October 1915, they had been
promised an independent Arab state or confederation of Arab
states extending from the eastern Mediterranean to the Persian
Gulf and the Indian Ocean to the south, except that the British said
that they could make no promises concerning Lebanon and western
Syria, where the interests of their allies, the French, were involved.
Moreover, when General Allenby's triumphant forces entered
Damascus, liberated from the Turks in November 1918, the British
and French governments had issued a declaration committing
themselves to self-determination for the Arabs. When the declaration was promulgated, it mentioned, as Britain desired, only Iraq
and Syria, although the declaration was officially circulated in
Palestine as in the other territories; Clayton, Allenby's chief political
officer, said people in Palestine thought it applied to them.[2] As
though this was not enough to damn the Allies utterly in Arab eyes,
Britain had uttered the famous Balfour Declaration on 2 November
1917 stating that she looked with favour on the creation in Palestine of a National Home for the Jewish people, though without
prejudice to the rights either of Jews living outside Palestine or of
other religious communities inside Palestine. The Balfour Declaration was evidently issued without consulting the Arab leaders,
though on any common-sense interpretation of the Hussein-
McMahon correspondence Palestine was never excluded from the
area allocated to the Arabs. Arab leaders at first did not object to
the Balfour Declaration; they considered, rightly, that it would bring
Jewish capital and enterprise into Palestine from which the resident
Arabs would profit. Indeed, early in January 1918 Commander
D. G. Hogarth had been sent to Jeddah with a carefully formulated
message from the British government to Sherif Hussein: 'so far as
Palestine is concerned we are determined that no people shall be
subject to another'.[3] With the growth of Zionist nationalism, however, and the efflux of Jews from Europe after the initiation of the
notorious anti-Semitic campaign of the Nazis in Germany in the
early 1930s, the long struggle of Jew and Arab for the control of
Biblical Palestine began, and with it the shifting of Arab sym-

---

[2] A. L. Tibawi, *A Modern History of Syria*, London, 1969, p. 275.
[3] Cmd. 5964, 1939.

pathies towards Germany, a situation full of the greatest peril for Britain, with its enormous economic, commercial and strategic stake in the Middle East.

All this growing stress and strain in the non-European world— we have already dealt with the growth of the Chinese nationalist movement and its effects on European power in the Far East in another chapter[4]—worked to the pronounced disadvantage of the two major victorious allies of the First World War, Britain and France. Apart from the problem of quelling unrest in their own colonies arising from the impact on their intellectual leaders of Wilsonian and Bolshevik doctrines, it set these two countries at one another's throats, parallelling the central tension between them concerning the enforcement of the peace treaties against Germany. It caused France to intrigue with Kemal Ataturk, returning to Turkey Cilicia and parts of northern Syria in return for mineral rights and French investment in the new Turkey.[5] The French saw no reason why they should continue to fight the Turks in 1921 and 1922 merely to ensure that Turkey would not be a threat in future years to British naval power in the eastern Mediterranean and the Black Sea. At the same time, British officers on the spot in the Middle East, if not always British ministers in London, derived a certain *Schadenfreude* from watching France's desperate efforts to establish herself as a mandatory in Syria and Lebanon. They were not slow to wring what political capital they could from this situation.

Britain and France had a third major ally in the First World War, Italy, and she came out of the peace negotiations of 1919–23 almost as disappointed as, if not more than, the defeated powers. In 1915 she had deserted the Dual Alliance of Germany and Austria-Hungary in the expectation of gaining, among other things, foreign territory at the peace settlement. This, consisting mainly of half of Dalmatia and islands off the Dalmatian coast, southern Tyrol from Austria, Trieste and most of Istria, territory in Asia Minor and Africa, was promised to her by Britain and France by the secret treaty of London signed on 26 April 1915. By the time the war ended, however, none of these promises could be fulfilled, except for southern Tyrol, inhabited by 300,000 Austrians, and the Dodecanese island group, which Italy virtually controlled before 1914

---

[4] Chapter 7, above, pp. 124–53.
[5] F. S. Northedge, *The Troubled Giant. Britain among the Great Powers, 1916–1939*, Bell and the London School of Economics, 1966, p. 146.

anyway. Her expected gains in Dalmatia were pruned down as a result of the formation of the triune state of Serbia-Croatia-Slovenia, later known as Yugoslavia, made up from former Serbia and the Slavonic areas of Austria-Hungary as the old empire fell to pieces in the closing stages of the war. Italy's expected gains from Anatolia were swept away when Kemal Ataturk forced a revision of the Carthaginian Treaty of Sèvres. As for Africa, none of Germany's colonies were handed to Italy as mandates; when Italian resentment against the alleged non-fulfilment of Allied promises at the end of the war reached a head with her invasion of Ethiopia in 1935, Mussolini was shocked to find that Britain and France, having built up vast empires in the past, now informed him that as a result of the new League of Nations, the colonization of non-European people was no longer tolerable to the conscience.

Here, then, was another great change in the conduct of international relations effected by the growing extra-Europeanization of the international system. Before 1918 it was altogether normal and natural for the great powers to compensate one another for the strains between the powers at the centre at the expense of colonial or semi-colonial people at the periphery. Thus Bismarck had urged France to take Tunis in 1881 to soothe the resentment left in Paris by his own victory over France in 1870–71. Thus Britain and France, by their Entente in 1904, had helped forge a political alliance later to stand them in good stead in their conflict with the central powers, by Britain recognizing France's paramountcy in Morocco and, conversely, France recognizing British supremacy in Egypt. Italy herself had been compensated for deserting the central powers and joining the Allies in 1915 by promises of extra-European gains at the peace conference. But by 1918 and afterwards the picture had changed. Not only were there by that time fewer places left on the map to paint with imperial colours, but the *ethos* of international life had changed : with the advent of the League of Nations any use of armed force was considered bad, but force against non-Europeans was far worse. And, after all, had the unknown soldier spilt his blood in the massacres of 1914–18 merely in order to put more foreign soil under the British, French or Italian flag? No wonder that Mussolini (and many Right-wing Frenchmen, too) threw up their hands in despair at the sanctimonious hypocrisy, as they deemed it to be, of the British who changed the rules of the game once they had acquired an empire larger than they could conveniently manage, and when British statesmen professed horror, in public at least, at Mussolini's violation of the League Covenant which few of them in their heart of hearts agreed with or had confidence in.

This extra-Europeanization of the international system continued throughout the inter-war period and culminated in the Second World War, in which all the strength of non-European or semi-European powers, the United States and the Soviet Union, was organized to overthrow the rogue elephant of the European system, Nazi Germany, and the non-European threat to the European order, Japan. But the process was also intensified by the policies and attitudes of the two giants of the post-1945 period, America and Russia. American isolation from 1920 until 1941, more marked in Europe than the Far East, more evident in the political and the military than the economic fields, was partly the consequence, as we have said, of an emotional recoil against the First World War in which Americans thought they had spent their blood and wealth in a traditional, incorrigible struggle between rival European imperialistic systems in which they had got caught up by mistake.[6] But it also expressed a refusal to take part in yet another slide towards war which, if it came, would be fought to save two imperialistic powers, Britain and France, from other less well-known examples of imperialism, the Axis powers. It is a curious fact that the Americans, so hostile towards Marxism in the years since 1945, should have so absorbed the Marxist analysis of war and international affairs generally during the inter-bellum phase. Yet such was the case. This American traditional anti-colonialism did not operate as an important factor weakening the European grip on the extra-European world, as it was to do after 1945. But it did prevent Americans realizing the implications of the European balance—or rather imbalance—of power for their own security.

American listeners to Franklin Roosevelt's appeals for efforts to halt the successive challenges to the *status quo* made by the dictators in the 1930s, including his famous 'quarantine address' in October 1937, supposed that he was merely asking them to go in and fight on behalf of Britain's dominion over palm and pine. Roosevelt himself was by no means immune to such thoughts. When he said to his Secretary of State, Edward Stettinius, at the Yalta conference in February 1945, 'remember, Ed, the British will seize land anywhere in the world, even if it is only a rock or a sandbar', this may have been something more than a merely private joke between the two

[6] Selig Adler, *The Isolationist Impulse*, New York, 1961, Chapter V.

of them. And it is significant that also at Yalta, Roosevelt said to Churchill, in all seriousness, that Churchill had four hundred years' acquisitive blood in his veins when the latter said China wanted Indo-China.[7] The probability is that the long mistrust by Americans of Britain's imperial record, even in a statesman as alert to international realities as Roosevelt, allowed old biasses to cloud his judgment. Hence it is not surprising that the United States entered the Second World War, not because in the first two years of that conflict Hitler came within an ace of dominating the continent of Europe and Britain as well, but because the Japanese had attacked their shipping and territory in Pearl Harbour on 7 December 1941.

A strange ally of the United States in this extra-Europeanization of the international system by breaking down European control of Africa and Asia was the Soviet Union. As the twenty-year armistice progressed, Russia turned in upon herself and became less of a European power. This was partly because the rise of Japan in the Far East, the slow emergence of China from its civil wars, and the conflict between Japan and China, which lasted intermittently throughout the 1930s, gave Russia the strongest interest in making her central Asian provinces the new heart of her industrial power so that it should be more accessible for the supply of her forces in the event of her being involved in war in the Far East; in 1932, for instance, the Soviets double-tracked the Trans-Siberian railway. At the same time, Russia's pathological fear of attack from the West, especially after the Locarno agreements of 1925, which seemed to attract Germany towards the Western powers, Britain and France, and away from the Rapallo treaty of 1922 by which the two pariah states, Germany and Russia, became friends, drove the Kremlin to make the trans-Caspian republics the most important areas of industrial expansion under the first five-year plan which began in 1928. Stalin's programme of 'Socialism in One Country' referred to a country becoming more Asian and less European.

Even before this shift in the industrial centre of gravity in the Soviet state, however, the Soviet government had tried and failed to shake Western imperial dominance in Asia. It was their second disappointment concerning the failure to spread the Communist revolution. Their first was the non-occurrence of red revolution in the main areas of Western capitalism, especially Germany, after the Bolshevik seizure of power in November 1917. Their next attempt was to smash Western capitalism in Asia. That, too, failed when

[7] E. R. Stettinius, Jnr., *Roosevelt and the Russians*, London, 1949, p. 212.

first Persia, then Afghanistan, after shaking off British protection, recoiled sharply against Communist penetration and thereafter remained, if not actively anti-Communist, certainly on their guard against Communism. It failed again in Turkey when, at the negotiations for the treaty of Lausanne in 1922–23, Lord Curzon, the then British Foreign Secretary, was able to drive a wedge between the Turks and the Russian Bolsheviks by spelling out, for the Turks' benefit, Russia's plans to dominate the Black Sea.[8] It failed in China when in 1926 Generalissimo Chiang Kai Shek began to persecute the Chinese Communists and drove out the Soviet advisory mission which the father of the Chinese nationalist revolution, Sun Yat-sen, had invited into the country. All these were warning signals to Stalin in his struggle for supremacy with Leon Trotsky, the advocate of permanent revolution, after Lenin's death in 1924. Stalin recognized, as Trotsky did not, that any active campaign by Soviet Russia to communize countries in Asia under Western capitalist control, or countries adjacent to such states, would in the long run have a boomerang effect in surrounding with enemies the highly vulnerable Soviet Russia, a great sprawling land mass with more neighbours than any other country. His political arguments against Trotsky, though no doubt primarily motivated by personal ambition, were eminently those of *Realpolitik* as against abstract ideology.

The effects of the Soviet campaign against the bastions of Western, especially British, rule in Asia were vastly exaggerated by Conservative governments in Britain in the 1920s, who feared that India and other British Asian possessions would be steadily eroded by Bolshevism; that the allegiance to the Crown of the British army and navy would be undermined by Comintern propaganda; that the prevailing industrial unrest, culminating in the General Strike in 1926, was fed by Moscow gold. Even if these larger nightmares never materialized, one Conservative M.P. told the House in the 1920s that the London poor were becoming demoralized as a result of drinking large quantities of gin purchased with Moscow gold.

Anglo-Soviet relations reached such a low point in 1927 that the British Foreign Secretary, Sir Austen Chamberlain, urged on by his back-benchers and against his better judgment, broke off diplomatic relations with Soviet Russia, though they were restored two years later by his Labour successor, Arthur Henderson, in 1929. Hence, Russia's campaign against European capitalist dominance in the

[8] The Treaty of Lausanne was signed on 24 July 1923.

extra-European world enjoyed no major success, but at least it kept European colonialist governments worried and preoccupied, diverted their time and attention from the central question of the balance of power in Europe, and provided some moral and intellectual encouragement for nationalist movements and their leaders in Africa and Asia. Above all, the bad blood created between Russia and the West over the former's efforts to weaken capitalist power in the non-European world persisted into the 1930s and helped to destroy confidence on both sides in the possibility of building a containing ring round Nazi Germany, with London, Paris and Moscow as the strongest links in the chain, on the eve of the Second World War.

II

Europe therefore throughout the 1919–39 period was losing its world primacy. In fact the Munich conference of September 1938 can be described as the last great meeting of the old Concert of Europe, even though the conference excluded Russia, a dominant member of the former Concert, and when the frontiers of an east European state, Czechoslovakia, were the main subject of the conference. Nevertheless, as late as 1939 the main decisions affecting world peace continued to be made in Europe. Hence we must now ask ourselves how the European international order collapsed, and resulted in another great war which led to the political eclipse of Europe for at least a quarter of a century following the end of that conflict.

Here we must inquire into the further question how order is ever maintained in any system of states at any time. That order we normally take for granted; we make arrangements to travel abroad, send letters or goods to other countries, lend money to other governments or establish businesses within the frontiers of other states, all in the expectation that mutual dealings between legally independent states will continue uninterrupted by violence or other manmade forms of disorder. When that international order breaks down and communications between states are broken off or fighting breaks out between them, we wonder whatever the causes can be, and books are written competing with one another in the different accounts they give of these causes and the explanations they provide of disorder in the world of states. But, considering that the member-states of the international system are equal and sovereign entities with no authority above them to keep them all law-abiding and peaceful, it is not surprising that from time to time they quarrel and fight, and order in the international system breaks down; the remarkable thing is that that order remains in being as long as it does. What we must inquire into is not why the international order broke down in the 1930s and resulted in a catastrophic world war, but why the forces which normally preserve order in the international system failed to act as they normally do during those years.

The forces referred to can be divided into two groups : the positive and the negative. A certain family of states will tend to commit themselves to live in harmony with one another and to settle their differences peacefully provided that the existing state of affairs offers them more satisfaction than they believe they could derive from forcefully upsetting it; this is the positive factor in the maintenance of international order—it need not prevail through every part of the international system, but there needs to be enough of it to counteract any tendency in the opposite direction. The negative aspects consist of restraints, especially perhaps military ones, which deter states from attempting to overturn the existing international system because the forces arrayed in defence of it are stronger.

In the first chapter of this book we have seen how in the nineteenth century an important factor militating against major war was the stake all the great powers had, and recognized that they had, in their expanding economies at home and abroad. As they counted the profits from the economic process, the entrepreneur classes had no wish to jeopardize these profits by pulling down the world about their ears; and working-class people, as their real standards of living rose, themselves felt that they had a certain stake in the international system. After the First World War this confidence in the profitability and the justice of the existing system waned, or rather collapsed. The defeated states, and in particular Germany, resented what the Germans called the harshness of the treaties imposed on them in 1919 and, encouraged by the sympathy extended to them by many people, even of the greatest eminence and even among the Allied nations, especially Britain, were confirmed in their determination to break the shackles of Versailles. In Germany, Hungary, Bulgaria and, to a lesser extent, Austria, millions of young men and women grew up to believe that all their sufferings and frustrations were the result of the peace treaties of 1919. And the fact that, at least as far as the Germans were concerned, the treaties attributed to them primary legal or moral responsibility for the tragic war led them to conclude, either that they must be a very powerful people indeed if they could let slip the dogs of war on such a massive scale, or that the whole treaty system was a gigantic lie resulting, not from a fairly fought struggle, but from the central powers having been stabbed in the back by treacherous forces at home.

On the Allied side there was a not dissimilar feeling that the existing system of world politics was wrong and not worth defending. Here we must contrast attitudes towards world politics during the inter-bellum period with those prevailing after 1945. After 1919 critics of the international system abounded in all the major powers, but they had little to compare that system with; international affairs for the ordinary person hardly seemed to exist before 1914—he did not know whether they were conducted badly or well. In 1945, on the other hand, men had the horrors of the 1930s and the Second World War to look back upon—the incredible bestialities of the Nazi regime, the extermination of the Jews and millions of other innocent people in the concentration camps, the hundreds of thousands of pitiful, nameless refugees fleeing from Japanese forces in China or from German dive-bombers in Spain, the cruelties of Mussolini's Blackshirts in Italy, the flabby weakness of democratic governments before the war, the crowning horror of Hiroshima and Nagasaki in August 1945. Hardly anything could be worse than that.

Moreover, the social system prevailing within the Western great powers in the 1920s and 1930s alienated almost the whole generation who grew to manhood in those years, shaping the literature they read and the plays they watched. The social system's massive unemployment, its extremities of wealth and poverty, the sheer want of houses, a very low standard of living and minimum security in times of illness or accident—all this was associated in the minds of the millions of readers of Marx and Lenin, G. D. H. Cole and Harold Laski, George Orwell and Upton Sinclair, with a moribund and cruel international system run by parliaments of 'hard-faced men who looked as if they had done well out of the war'. If war existed, it was due to the 'contradictions of capitalism'; if attempts to reduce the risks of war failed, it was due to the machinations of the 'merchants of death' who waxed fat on the profits of war. The play *Oh! What a lovely war!*, produced in London in the 1960s and dealing with the 1914–18 war, was watched with a certain wistful nostalgia by its post-Second World War audiences, but its savage indictment of the 'war system' would have been taken seriously by youth in the twenties and thirties.

And so the young men of Oxford voted in 1936 never again to fight for King and Country. So, too, these millions of rebels against the domestic and international evils of capitalism looked to Soviet Russia, more as a symbol of a better world than as a reality to be probed and examined, as a new Jerusalem in whose life there was 'a daily beauty that makes us ugly'. But, by the same token, those who dreaded the Soviet system, either through fear of their wealth being taken from them if that system should spread, or through more disinterested hatred of the tyranny Stalin had imposed on Russia, looked with sympathetic eyes on the tough legions of Nazism and Fascism who represented themselves as the true defenders of European civilization against the red peril, the spectre haunting Europe. 'Better Hitler than Stalin' was a phrase heard not only in the beer-cellars of the Rhineland and Bavaria, but in the stately homes of England.

By contrast, in the world since 1945, people in non-Communist countries have seen that the Soviet government can treat its own nationals almost as cruelly as Hitler or Mussolini did theirs, and can be almost as disregardful of the freedom and independence of other countries as the pre-war dictators. The Western powers which huddled together within the North Atlantic Treaty Organization in 1949 felt that their system *was* worth preserving and that worse things *could* exist, after their experience of Nazi, Fascist and Communist internal and external policies, than the economic and political regimes which they themselves lived under. Even the newly created African and Asian states formed through the decolonization process after 1945 were not as keen to follow the Communist formula for economic and social progress as many of their former European masters had feared. But they, or most of them, resisted Western efforts in the 1950s, chiefly inspired by the United States, to force them into self-defensive pacts against Communism; they also denounced loudly the continuing so-called 'neo-colonialism' of the Western powers. But the fact remains that the international system as a loose association of independent sovereign states they had no wish to renounce. On the contrary, the chief form which their foreign policies took, namely neutralism or non-alignment, was to preserve that system against the risks of its being dominated either by a capitalist or by a Communist world hegemony.

The inter-war political system, then, was repudiated with horror

by some of its finest minds and by millions of the younger generation. This revulsion was expressed by the poet Cecil Day Lewis, in
a poem called *Why there is no war poetry* written in the early
months of the Second World War :

> They who in panic or mere greed
> Enslaved religion, markets, laws,
> Borrow our language now and bid us
> To speak up in freedom's cause.

But the international economic system was also rejected with the
same contempt, especially after the disastrous inflation suffered by
Germany and other central European countries in the 1920s, the
great world-wide depression of 1929–32, and the persistence year
after year of the dead weight of mass unemployment which characterized the democratic states throughout the inter-war period. It
was not only that the world economic system was regarded as
indefensible if it could produce social evils on this scale. The fact is
that no one, not even the experts, seemed to be able to explain why
it was that millions were idle while the living standards of the
majority of people were pitifully low, or why coffee was burned as
locomotive fuel and fish thrown back into the sea while hundreds of
millions starved the world over. Governments, not in militarist
states but in the democratic states, applied, on the advice of their
expert economists, deflationary remedies which were even worse
than the disease.[9] In such a situation, in which the nations seemed
to have lost control over their own affairs, it is not surprising that
two things should have happened : *first,* that men, in searching for
the reason why they were plunged into impoverishment after having
lived for the most part comparatively virtuous lives, should have
dogmatically accepted the most absurd 'devil' theories of their
plight, and, *second,* that in seeking an escape from a world economy
which drew everybody except the rich minority down into the vortex
of disaster, states should first of all demand that they themselves
and their peoples should survive whatever happened to others
beyond their frontiers.

The first of these phenomena characterized both sides in the
ideological civil war which was fought in most European states, and

[9] The traditional economists worked on the fallacious analogy that the role of the
State in economic affairs was the same as that of an individual. Hence if an individual was in financial difficulties he must prune his expenditure, and similarly a
State suffering economic depression should make cuts in spending. This policy
worsened economic depression.

between them, in the shape of Nazism or Fascism against Communism and its less extreme partner, social democracy. Hitler, more in tune with the thoughts and emotions of the world-wide working and middle classes than the old-fashioned patriot, Mussolini, was able to convince millions, and not only in Germany, that the devil in the machine of international finance which had reduced them to destitution was Jewish capitalism working in an improbable combination with the Marxists. For millions more on the opposing side in the ideological war, the devil in the machine was the right-wing capitalist, who had financed the dictators in Germany, Italy and Japan, partly to ward off a dispossessing proletarian revolution, partly to reap rich profits from the wars the dictators, in their speeches at least, lusted after. No one could seriously pretend that these childish stereotypes of the 'enemy' were other than devices by which the frustrations, fears and smouldering hatreds of the masses whose minds they held in thrall could find relief. But at a time when the experts who were supposed to understand the international economy talked hardly more sense, who could really blame the man in the street for mentally sticking pins into his images of the devil in the machine?

Secondly, a less psychological outcome of the world-wide economic malaise was the determination that, if anyone were to suffer, it should be the other nation rather than one's own. If no one seemed to be in the driving seat of the international economy, then men of one's own stock, who 'talk the talk I am wonted to' and are 'used to the lies I tell', should be at the wheel of the national economy even if it meant collisions at every other minute of the journey. At Geneva in the 1930s the nations, or such as still remained members of the League, continued to conjure up the ghost of the old multilateral economic system; at home the god they worshipped was economic nationalism, no matter how it hurt the foreigner. The rules of the old system were simple and automatic in principle, intolerable in practice: earnings from foreign trade shrank, purchasing power must be reduced at home; that would lower the prices of exports and reduce the home demand for imports, you would cease to lose gold to pay for your deficit on the international trade account, and your currency, being based on gold, would return to its former value. But, for reasons beyond the wit of man to understand, the foreign trade of all countries was falling off, at first slowly in the 1920s and then precipitately after 1929. To expect a state on the gold standard to increase its already massive unemployment by deflating prices at home was more than flesh and blood could stand.

They did not stand it. The gold standard was put into cold storage. Britain, the age-old practitioner and exponent of free trade, introduced protection, not only for its own industries by the Import Duties Act of 1932, but for those of the Empire and Commonwealth as a whole by the Ottawa agreements of the same year, which gave the non-British parts of that vast association preferences in the still huge British market and *vice versa* (see above, Chapter 9, pp. 165–6). With the discovery, first by Adolf Hitler and Franklin Roosevelt, that the best cure for unemployment was for the government to pump money into the economy in times of depression rather than take it out, all the major states set the restoration of their own internal economies as their prime target. If this meant tariffs or quotas on the foreigner's exports or depreciating one's currency so as in effect to export one's own unemployment, that was a pity, but it was better than allowing one's economic system to rot, and millions of unemployed human beings with it. This economic nationalism, however, did nothing to alleviate international political frictions, rather the reverse. Nor did it do anything to win the allegiance of thinking people, or the many millions of more unthinking people, to the support of the world economic system, if such a word was deserved at all.

III

The positive factors tending towards international order were thus lacking in Europe between 1919 and 1939. But what of the negative factors, and chief among these the fear of using force which springs from the apprehension of retaliatory force being used on the other side : or, in short, the equilibrium, or balance, of power? We have argued in the first chapter of this book that in the nineteenth century the chief European powers, as well as having a positive stake in peace, were such that no one of them, even with an ally or two, could hope to overthrow the rest. But in the First World War Germany, with some assistance from Austria-Hungary, Bulgaria and the Ottoman Empire, though the principal effort was hers alone, was able to defeat almost all her European adversaries. Russia, that vast reservoir of manpower and untold spaces, she knocked completely out of the war. France was so mauled by German military might that after her reverse at the battle of the Aisne in April 1917, on which the French had pinned their hopes of finishing off the war, she was for almost a year *hors de combat*; had military justice been done, France should have come out of the war on the losing side in 1918. Italy, too, was knocked sideways by her great defeat at Caporetto in the Julian Alps in November 1917; she could barely struggle on to the end without assistance in equipment from sorely pressed Britain and France. Britain was almost starved into surrender by the German U-boat campaign in the same year, and when Haig launched his tragic Third Battle of Ypres in November 1917, it relieved the pressure on the French and killed off more Germans in what Winston Churchill called 'this great blood test', but was far from bringing the German war machine to its knees. As for the lesser European allies, Belgium, Rumania and Serbia, they might hardly have existed as factors draining the enormous strength of the central powers.

What terminated the war in 1918 for Germany was not so much the counterforce of her European opponents but the knowledge that, when fully committed and mobilized for the struggle, the United States could and was willing to fight on almost indefinitely (see above, Chapter 6, p. 109 n.1). America had entered into the European balance of power when she declared war on Germany in April 1917 when that balance, or equilibrium, against Germany could no longer be maintained in European terms alone. The New World had, in the interests of its own self-preservation, to be summoned into the European balance of power to restore equilibrium, or some semblance of it. *In other words, the European enemies of Germany could not contain Germany without extra-European help.* In that fact lies perhaps the major part of the explanation why the European international order collapsed in the 1930s, leaving the Second World War as its consequence.

The Allied victory in 1918 was in a certain sense a fake. The German army capitulated when it still occupied scores of square miles of enemy soil. It marched home as an integrated force, into a fatherland which, though naturally suffering from wartime shortages and the post-war continuance of the Allied blockade, was for all practical purposes unscathed by war. The Second World War had therefore to be fought again after twenty years in order to turn the fake Allied victory of 1918 into a reality. This could not be achieved without great extra-European forces, the United States and the Soviet Union, being called into the struggle. But, once having been called into it, they could not this time rest content with the technical defeat of German military forces on the battlefield. Germany's supreme political authority had to be smashed at its heart; German territory itself had to be split up and divided between America and Russia, with Britain and liberated France decidedly junior partners in the occupation. Not until 1945 was the disequilibrium caused by the massive superiority of Germany over all her European neighbours, excluding Russia, overcome by planting the frontiers of extra-European America and almost extra-European Russia contiguous to one another in the heart of Germany and its old capital, Berlin.

How then did Germany get into a position in which under Hitler in the late 1930s it dominated the European scene? First and most obviously, the United States retired decisively in 1920 from the enforcement of a peace which could never have been won without her assistance. Britain and France were left to control a disarmed Germany, but they could do nothing with her; they could enter Germany, as France entered the Ruhr in 1923, though in the teeth of British opposition, to enforce the peace, but, unless France was willing and able to take over the government of the whole country, her forces sooner or later had to march out again, and with the stigma of defeat branded on them. America, as we have seen, re-entered European affairs as the provider of capital for reconstruction with the Dawes plan of 1924 after the French occupation of the Ruhr and the disastrous German inflation which followed it, but only on condition that there would be no more occupations of the Ruhr or any other part of Germany. This was a purely economic American intervention and it might have been better for Europe had it never occurred, since the withdrawal of American capital, most of it being of a short-term nature, with the 1929 slump, took away the supports from beneath the shaky European structure.

But politically the United States was more distant from Europe in the 1930s than she had been during the European crisis of 1911 to 1914. Franklin Roosevelt's hands were shackled by the Neutrality Acts passed by Congress in the years 1935 to 1937; his proposal for the quarantining of the European aggressors made in his famous Chicago speech in October 1937 was vehemently rejected by the American press and public opinion, to the great jubilation of German newspapers whose headlines ran *Rusdruck aus Chicago*. In January 1938 President Roosevelt proposed an international conference to discuss a wide range of world problems. The incident is important since the discouraging reply received from the British

Prime Minister, Neville Chamberlain, was one cause of his quarrel with his Foreign Secretary, Anthony Eden, which ended in Eden's resignation from the National Government in February 1938. But when the American proposal is examined, its irrelevance to the political realities of the current European situation is apparent. There is some truth in Chamberlain's bitter comment : 'we can expect nothing from the Americans but words'. And the obvious conclusion might have followed :

> Sticks and stones may break my bones
> But words will never hurt me.

Then there lay between Russia, who had borne her share, and more than her fair share, of the fighting in the First World War until her retirement from the struggle in March 1918, and the Western states threatened by Germany, namely Britain and France, the deepest mistrust. First, the Soviet government throughout the 1920s lived with its nightmare of a combined capitalist invasion from the West, especially during the period of Franco-German reconciliation between 1925 and 1930. This was partly the consequence of the Allied military intervention in the Russian civil war which raged from 1918 until 1920, partly the result of Marxist-Leninist doctrine that capitalist states are driven by inexorable laws of history to seek to destroy their predestined successor, communist society. After the accession to power of Adolf Hitler in Germany in January 1933, Stalin sought to make common cause with the Western powers Britain and France. They agreed to facilitate Russia's entry into the League of Nations in 1934 and France allied herself with Russia in the following year. But this alliance was but a pale reflection of the great Franco-Russian alliance of the 1890s; it was hated by the French Right wing who saw its only usefulness in reducing the opposition of the French Communist party to the rearmament of their country against Hitler.

Thereafter Stalin saw Britain and France reluctant time after time to challenge the dictators—when Hitler announced German rearmament in 1935 and the remilitarization of the Rhineland in 1936, both in plain and unpunished defiance of the Versailles and Locarno agreements, when Hitler and Mussolini unashamedly helped General Franco into power against the Spanish liberal republic between 1936 and 1939, when Mussolini invaded Ethiopia with French, and to some extent British, connivance in 1935, when Japan began her war against China in July 1937, when Hitler forcibly brought Austria within the German Reich in March 1938, again in violation of the Versailles and St. Germain treaties of 1919. But the culmination of Stalin's disillusionment with the Western powers came in 1938 when Britain, lamely followed by France, agreed to the secession of the Sudetenland in Czechoslovakia to Germany, thus emasculating Czechoslovakia as one of the obstacles to Hitler's march to the east, and without so much as taking Russia into account or inviting her to the Munich conference.

When Hitler's promise of no more territorial claims in Europe after the absorption of the Sudetenland was falsified by his occupation of Bohemia, essentially non-German in population, on 15 March 1939, Britain, again without consulting Moscow, gave her guarantee against German aggression to Poland, a guarantee which could not possibly be implemented without Soviet co-operation. This was further food for Stalin's suspicion that Britain's paramount aim was to embroil Germany with Russia, thus getting rid of two enemies at the same time. Disbelieving British and French pledges to come to Poland's assistance if Germany attacked, contemptuous of their military capacity or national unity even if their intention was sincere, and desirous of turning the tables on London and Paris by provoking Germany and the democratic states into fighting each other, leaving Russia as the *tertius gaudens,* Stalin signed his non-aggression treaty with Hitler on 23 August 1939. This made war inevitable by removing from Hitler's mind the fear of war on two fronts, gave the Baltic states and half of Poland to Russia, and allowed the latter two years of neutrality in which to strengthen her defences and stand on guard against the swelling might of Japan in the Far East.

Mistrust of Russia was equally rampant in the West. Winston Churchill's famous statement 'Communism rots the soul' fairly characterized the attitude of ruling circles in Britain and France towards the Soviet regime during most of the inter-war period. Nevertheless, Churchill, without a moment's hesitation, welcomed Russia into the anti-Axis coalition when Hitler invaded Russia on 22 June 1941; after dinner on the 21st, he said to his private secretary, 'if Hitler invaded Hell I would make at least a favourable reference to the Devil in the House of Commons'.[10] To some extent the Russians had brought this mistrust down upon themselves by their unceasing propaganda warfare against the two Western powers and their unconcealed hope of destroying all bourgeois

[10] W. S. Churchill, *The Grand Alliance,* London, 1950, p. 331.

society after the immediate problem of dealing with Hitler's Germany had been disposed of. Furthermore, the terrible purges initiated by Stalin against many of his closest colleagues and his decimation of the Red Army's leading generals for suspected disloyalty to his regime, beginning in June 1937 with the investigation for treason and trial of Tukhachevsky, Putna and six others, convinced experts in Paris and London—in so far as they needed convincing—that Russia was a man of straw. When Hitler dispatched his legions into Russia's endless plains in June 1941 the maximum which the British press gave the Soviets was six weeks before they succumbed.

Hence mutual mistrust was a powerful factor preventing the formation of an Anglo-French-Soviet peace front during the negotiations in Moscow during the summer of 1939. Instead, the Russians signed the Nazi-Soviet pact and Britain and France were placed in the same perilous position as Britain was when Napoleon and Alexander I made their truce at Tilsit in 1807. But we must never forget that throughout the inter-war period Soviet Russia, besides being an ostensibly revolutionary state, was also territorially a revisionist power; the East European settlement of 1919 was imposed upon her as much as it was imposed upon Germany. Added to that was the fact that the militant Poland of Marshal Pilsudsky, backed by her ally, France, had thrust Bolshevik Russia's frontiers, at the moment of Soviet weakness in 1920–21, further east even than the Entente powers wished. Moreover, the East European states created in 1919 were, with the exception of Czechoslovakia, fiercely anti-Soviet, fearing Stalin as much as, or more than, they feared Hitler. Stalin visualized them as no more than Hitler's pawns; there was here therefore another reason for his revisionism in the 1930s.

Britain and France, however, after Hitler's annexation of Bohemia in March 1939 were supposed to be protecting the remaining East European states; indeed, it would have been impossible for the British government at least, in view of the state of Parliamentary and public opinion after 15 March 1939, to do other than guarantee Poland, Rumania, Greece and any other state in East Europe against Hitler's ambition. But hardly any of these guarantees could be made effective without the assistance of Soviet Russia, the very country which had grievances against them not very different in character from those of Nazi Germany. Accordingly, in his negotiations with Britain and France in Moscow in the summer of 1939, Stalin virtually demanded Western recognition of Eastern Europe as a Soviet sphere of influence, as it was to become as a result of the

Second World War, with Poland in particular as a kind of Soviet protectorate. This the Western powers felt they were in no position to concede and Stalin turned to Hitler, who had no objections to doing so.

With the United States and Soviet Russia thus either neutral or ambiguous in their attitudes towards the construction of an anti-German coalition, Britain and France were hardly in a state to challenge Germany, which they could only overcome in the First World War with substantial American and Russian assistance. To make matters far worse, Italy and Japan, allies of the Anglo-French entente in the 1914–18 war, were now on the other side. Italy, it is true, was no considerable military factor, as the Second World War was to show. But Mussolini made a lot of noise, scared the British Admiralty when they contemplated a war in the Mediterranean with the Italian fleet on the German side, and worried the French with the possibility of their having to fight a war on two fronts while it might take Britain many months to put anything like a substantial army across the Channel. The case of Japan was far more dangerous. Had the United States been willing to assist Britain in restraining Japan's militant policy towards China, culminating in open war in July 1937, the British government could have faced with more confidence the prospect of war in Europe, as they did in the First World War when Japanese forces harassed the Germans in the Pacific.

But President Roosevelt, though he was free to protest unilaterally to Tokyo against the infringement of American rights during the Sino-Soviet conflict, was not permitted by Congress or public opinion to act jointly with Britain. The British authorities therefore, not having the naval capability to fight wars in the Pacific and the seas surrounding Europe at the same time, hardly had any other option but to protest verbally, and without the force to make the words go home, even when the Japanese virtually blockaded the British settlement in Tientsin, China, in the early summer of 1939 and exposed its inhabitants to the kind of humiliations many other Asians had long dreamed of imposing on the white man.

All these combined strategic disadvantages made it hard, if not impossible, for Britain and France to take up Hitler's challenges in the 1930s, even without assuming any kind of surreptitious sympathies on their governments' side with the Nazi régime. To which must be added the state of near civil war in France in the mid-1930s, when that country became a battlefield for the contemporary warring ideologies of Nazism and Communism, to such an extent that the calumnies of the extreme Right had driven Roger Salengro, Minister of the Interior in Blum's government, to suicide. Before the French authorities, especially the Léon Blum Popular Front government formed in 1936, lay the spectre of civil strife such as threshed the Spanish republic if they moved to the Left in support of the Spanish government against Franco, and in opposition, arm in arm with Russia, to further Axis advances in Europe; or if they moved to the Right by abandoning the struggle against Germany and sheltering under the Nazi wing as indeed they did after France's military defeat in June 1940.

In any event France's international history had not been happy since 1919. She had secured an Anglo-American guarantee against renewed German aggression during the 1919 peace conference if she abandoned her demand for a separate Rhineland state; she complied, and the promised guarantee nevertheless fell to the ground when the American Senate failed to ratify the peace treaties. She had begged Britain to take the danger of a German military revival more seriously in the 1920s, only to be regarded in British eyes as paranoid. She had seen Britain take Germany's side at the disarmament conference in 1932–34; had failed to provoke Britain into joint positive action against the German reoccupation of the Rhineland in March 1936; had failed again to get from Britain a definite commitment to joint military staff talks even in the critical days of 1938, when Europe stood on the brink of war, owing to British suspicions that joint staff talks with the French before 1914 had dragged their country into war. Is it surprising that so many Frenchmen who felt that they could not carry on the struggle alone against the Nazi domination of Europe should have toyed with the idea of making the best private deal they could with the German Chancellor? Marshal Pétain's dilemma in June 1940 was a cruel one indeed : if all the cards seem stacked against an Allied victory, is it better to fight until your people are ground to dust under the conqueror's heel, or to make what terms you can for the survival of your country, or at least a half of it, under German rule with all that that implies?

It is often said that, despite this preponderantly unfavourable balance of world power against Britain and France in the 1930s, as compared even with the desperate situation in 1914–18, the Germans could have been halted at Munich when their military strength was less than that of Britain, France and Czechoslovakia combined—some even say less than Czechoslovakia's alone—and that the German generals would have implemented their plot to oust Hitler if Britain and France had decided to call the Chancellor's bluff. This is the argument of Winston Churchill himself in the first volume of his memoirs of the Second World War.[11] But the objection to this line of reasoning is surely obvious. Adolf Hitler was a politician whose mediumistic insight into other people's thoughts and feelings was little short of the miraculous. He foresaw—with the certainty of a somnambulist, as he often put it—that Britain and France would succumb to his demand for the cession of Czechoslovakia, and for a reason which will appear later; calculating this, he did not need a large army or air force—it was enough, as we have argued earlier, to threaten *Blitzkrieg*, a total war, which he might have been unable to fight, in order to bring Britain and France to heel. Had his insight told him that Britain and France would stand firm, he would not have attempted that particular move on the chessboard, or would have supplied the force, which Germany certainly had in reserve, to overcome their opposition if he must. But his insight that they would capitulate proved correct, as it had when he remilitarized the Rhineland in March 1936.

But why did Britain, which stood at the pinnacle of world power in 1919, with the largest empire mankind had ever known, stoop so low as to sacrifice a small country to Hitler's appetite in 1938 and naively believe his promise that this was his last territorial demand? It was partly because the empire was so large, too large for Britain to manage. As we have seen, the winds of national self-determination were blowing through the dependent empire and semi-independent states under British supervision, like the Arab states and Palestine in the Middle East. In the independent Commonwealth countries, the so-called dominions, Britain could no longer call the tune in foreign policy on their behalf; she had to take up challenges thrown down by the dictators which would seem vital to her and their existence in their eyes as well as her own. But, above all, there was the terrible, sad, unforgettable trauma of the First World War.

In Britain the idea grew up during the twenty-year armistice, more on the Left than on the Right, more among the young than among the old, but permeating public opinion generally, that the war had been a tragic mistake, that millions of young men, the 'doomed, conscripted, unvictorious ones', had died through the

[11] *The Gathering Storm*, London, 1948, p. 245.

blunders of incompetent generals sitting in safe châteaux miles
behind the front and in order to line the pockets of war profiteers.
After the war soldiers returned to what was sneeringly called 'a land
fit for heroes to live in', a land of poverty, unemployment, the dole
and the means test. A cruel conspiracy of capitalists, careerist

Germany—Territorial Gains, 1938–39

generals, crafty diplomats, had plunged Britain into an ocean of
blood and then made a peace almost as horrifying. No wonder that
British ministers in the 1930s determined that next time they would
not be accused of plunging their people into war without so much
as taking their wishes and opinions into account. Was Hitler seeking
to dominate Europe or merely asking for the application of the
Allies' own principle of national self-determination to the situation
of the Sudeten Germans? No one could be sure, and so long as the

H

merest particle of doubt remained, it would be wrong, British ministers felt, to set in train once more the measureless catastrophe of 1914–18. The British fought, without thought of surrender, in 1940 because they knew without a shadow of doubt that Hitler was an evil man and that there was no living in the same world with him.

Munich in 1938 may therefore be said to have made British resistance in 1940 possible. But there is a further consideration. Britain, with or without France, with or without Russia, could not hope to defeat Germany without American assistance. And she did not in the event do so. When she went to war against Germany in 1939, two years had to elapse before America came into the war, two years in which Britain survived by the skin of her teeth. Had Britain gone to war in 1938, on an issue where there was a shadow of doubt whether it was the right one, and had America still come into the war in December 1941, would Britain have survived in the three years between? No one can say.

Were, then, the causes of the Second World War Hitler's evil ambitions and British and subsequently Soviet and American determination to put an end to them? The question, after the reasoning of the present chapter, should sound absurd and is absurd. The whole balance of world forces, physical and psychological, was for the time being on Hitler's side. Having far more than the average ingredients of human greed and ambition, far more than the average human insight into the ways of men and the movements of affairs, it was altogether natural that he should take advantage of this situation.

REFERENCES

Avon, The Earl of, *The Eden Memoirs: Facing the Dictators*, London, Cassell, 1962.

Beloff, M., *The Foreign Policy of Soviet Russia*, 2 vols., London and Fair Lawn, New Jersey, O.U.P., 1947–49.

Bullock, A. L. C., *Hitler: A Study in Tyranny*, London, Odhams, and New York, Harper, 1960.

Carr, E. H., *The Twenty Years Crisis, 1919–1939*, New York, St. Martin's, London, Macmillan, 2nd Ed., 1958.

Dalton, E. H. J. N., *Memoirs 1931–1945: The Fateful Years*, London, Muller, 1957.

Medlicott, W. N., *British Foreign Policy Since Versailles, 1919–1963*, London, Methuen, 1968.

Northedge, F. S., *The Troubled Giant. Britain among the Great Powers, 1916–1939*, London, Bell for the London School of Economics, and New York, Praeger, 1966.

Selby, W. H. M., *Diplomatic Twilight 1930–1940*, London, Murray, 1953.

Taylor, A. J. P., *The Origins of the Second World War*, London, Hamilton, and New York, Atheneum, 1961.

Wolfers, A., *Britain and France between Two Wars*, New Haven, Conn., Yale U.P., 1940.

11 *Impact of the Second World War*

As already stated, the purpose of this book is not to recount the history of international affairs since 1870. Our aim is rather to focus upon changes in the system of international relations during these hundred years : in other words, how did the nature of international politics alter in this century, what changes took place in the structure of power in the international system, the methods of organizing and conducting international relations, the themes of international debate and so on?

Accordingly, we have no intention in the present chapter of sketching either the military or diplomatic history of the Second World War. That has been done many times in the years since 1945.[1] Our business is with the implications of that war for the international system itself and we shall be concerned with the military operations and the diplomacy of the war only in so far as these are relevant. The first notable change in the international system, then, which the Second World War effected or symbolized was the emergence of the two super-powers, the United States and the Soviet Union, as dominant leaders of the world political system and the parallel decline of Europe as the classic epicentre of world diplomacy. We have explained in the previous chapter the diminution in Europe's primacy in world politics from the end of the First World War to the beginning of the Second, and how the very causes of the latter struggle are to be found in the imbalance in the European system created by the preponderance of Germany and the failure of that imbalance to be corrected in European terms alone. Nazi Germany and Japan in the Far East could only be overcome by a coalition in which Britain, now the only surviving European power of any significance fighting against the Axis states, gave what assistance it could to the two giant powers, vast in resources and manpower, and continental in extent, which finally overthrew the Axis powers. It is significant that Germany, whose preponderance took two world wars to destroy, was to become, after its defeat in 1945, the main theatre of rivalry between its two giant conquerors,

[1] See bibliography at the end of the book.

which we shall describe in the following chapter. But first we must
see how the super-powers emerged to their eminence in the Second
World War, how the war affected their position and what the
nature of these powers was.

I

The Soviet Union was no willing party to the Second World War.
By his pact with Nazi Germany in August 1939, Stalin evidently
hoped to hold the line against any German expansion to the east
while watching the Nazi regime and the Western powers, Britain
and France, bleed each other to death in the west. Stalin had good
reason, as explained in the previous chapter, to mistrust the Western democracies and understand their hostility towards the Soviet
Union. At the same time, he could not discount the possibility of
being involved in a war on two fronts, one with Germany, the other
with Japan. If such a war were to occur, Russia's vast spaces,
though a source of strength in being able to absorb foreign invaders
and drain their spirits before reaching the industrial heart of Russia
in Central Asia, was also a source of weakness in so far as the supply
of Soviet armies in two such widely separated theatres of war was
concerned.

As the reward for his neutrality in the European sector of the
war, Stalin received the eastern half of Poland, thus recovering
territory lost in the Soviet-Polish war of 1920–21, and German
recognition of the Soviet absorption of the Baltic states, Latvia,
Lithuania and Estonia. During the duration of the Nazi-Soviet pact,
from 1939 until June 1941, Russia took from the dismembered
Czechoslovakia the tip of Sub-Carpathian Ruthenia, with its substantial Ukrainian minority, northern Bukowina from Bulgaria, and
Bessarabia, another Soviet loss at the end of the First World War,
from Rumania. Stalin also made known to Germany in the negotiations leading up to the Nazi-Soviet pact his hopes of establishing a
kind of protectorate over the Dardanelles, an ancient goal of
Russian foreign policy, with its preoccupation with the acquisition
of ice-free ports for winter use. The potential annexation of the
Dardanelles was temporarily achieved in February 1915, when
Britain and France agreed to cede the Straits and Constantinople
to Tsar Nicholas II when the war was won; that was naturally nullified by the separate peace the Bolsheviks made with Germany in
March 1918. Hitler was given to understand by Stalin that the

Middle East, in the Soviet leader's eyes, was also a Soviet sphere of interest. At the other end of Russia's western borders, Stalin wrested from Finland, against whom he fought the winter war of 1939–40, the northern territory of Petsamo, which gave Russia a common frontier with Nazi-occupied Norway, the Porkkala promontory, and achieved the thrusting back of the Russo-Finnish border in the area adjoining Leningrad by a distance of thirty miles.

Thus, in the two years' duration of the Nazi-Soviet pact Stalin had succeeded in establishing the limits of Russian power in the west, not as they had been in 1914, when the whole of Finland had been under Russian rule, but not far short of that. With the onset of the Nazi invasion of Russia on 21 June 1941 these gains, or most of them, fell into Hitler's hands and the German *Wehrmacht* thrust into the heart of Russia until it stood in the suburbs of Leningrad and Moscow, dominating the industrial Ukraine in the south, the Crimea and the oil-rich Caucasus. Russia's resistance, though not without the mass desertions to the Germans of hundreds of thousands of Soviet refugees from Stalin's tyranny, won the admiration of the democratic world, especially Britain, which now felt the fury of Germany's military might turned away from itself to Russia. During this period of Anglo-Soviet wartime collaboration, from June 1941 until the American entry into the war in December, the myth of Soviet military weakness which had made Britain and France so uncertain about the merits of an agreement with Stalin to stop Hitler was gradually turned into the myth of Soviet invincibility.

The result was that after the German surrender in May 1945 the British and American people tended to overestimate Soviet military power, just as they had underestimated it all the years since the Russian military collapse in the First World War, and to forget the terrible bloodletting Russia suffered during Hitler's attack. The latter weakness the Soviet leaders had every incentive to conceal since they still feared an Anglo-American capitalist invasion at the end of the war, as they had in the 1920s. Indeed, one of the chief obstacles to closer military co-operation between Russia and the two Western powers, from June 1941 until the end came for Germany in 1945, was Stalin's fear either that Britain and America would leave Russia to bleed to death at Germany's hands—hence his sustained pressure on the Western powers to open a second front in Europe in 1942 and 1943—or would reach a secret agreement with the Nazis by which the Germans, as they neared defeat, would join the democracies for the final destruction of the Communist state. After all, had not Churchill dreamed of such a possibility at the end of the First World War?[2]

The problem as the war neared its end was to secure from the two Western powers a recognition of Russia's gains during 1939–41, which in the event they conceded without much hesitation, and also to re-establish Russia in the Far Eastern position which she had occupied under the Tsars. When the British Foreign Secretary, Anthony Eden, visited Moscow in December 1941 in order to agree with the Kremlin on the substance of the Anglo-Soviet Treaty which was signed in May 1942, both he and Prime Minister Churchill wished to incorporate into the agreement a recognition of Russia's claims to territorial revision in the west after the war. They considered it wiser to have these claims discussed and embodied in a solemn agreement while Russia was still dependent upon aid from the two Western powers than to wait until the end of the war when Stalin, if his armies were eventually victorious, would be virtually able to dictate his terms for a territorial settlement in eastern Europe. President Roosevelt, however, like President Wilson before him, was averse to agreements on the division of the loot while the result of the war still hung in the balance. Moreover, he had signed with Churchill in August 1941 the Atlantic Charter and Stalin himself had endorsed it on Russia's behalf in January 1942. This document recorded the two democratic leaders' agreement not to accept any territorial claims which did not accord with the 'freely expressed wishes of the peoples concerned' (see below, Chapter 13, pp. 273–4).

It was not until the Yalta conference of Churchill, Roosevelt and Stalin in February 1945, marking the high tide of tripartite Allied unity, that agreement was registered that Russia's western frontier should be advanced to the middle of Poland, not much further in fact than the Western Allies had themselves agreed at the end of the First World War by the adoption of the so-called 'Curzon line', though without the slightest by-your-leave from Russia's new Bolshevik leaders. As compensation for Poland, it was agreed at Yalta that German territory in Silesia as far as the Oder and Western Neisse rivers should be placed under Polish administration pending the signature of a final peace treaty with Germany. The effect of this was to make any future Polish government, whatever its political complexion, dependent for all practical purposes upon the Soviet Union, since Moscow would always in future be free practi-

[2] See W. S. Churchill, *The World Crisis: The Aftermath*, London, 1929, p. 25.

cally to destroy Poland by agreeing with Germany to restore the Polish-German frontier as it stood in September 1939. In addition Churchill and Roosevelt agreed that Russia should further be compensated by—besides the Baltic republics—the eastern half of East Prussia, including the ancient German city of Königsberg. Then, concerning the Far East, Roosevelt agreed—and of this Churchill was little more than a spectator—that Russia should be rewarded for her willingness to enter the war against Japan (after Germany's defeat) by the southern half of Sakhalin, which she had lost as a result of her defeat by Japan in 1905, and a lease of the naval base of Port Arthur, an ice-free port as contrasted with Russia's summer port of Vladivostock, north of the Korean peninsula, and known throughout the Soviet navy as 'sacred Russian soil'.

The question was how these territorial changes were to be effected 'in accordance with the wishes of the people concerned', as the Atlantic Charter promised. One solution, applied by the Poles at the end of the war to the nine million Germans inhabiting the territories assigned to Poland beyond the Oder and Neisse rivers, was to drive the people bag and baggage back into their original homeland and hence their wishes would not have to be consulted. As for Stalin's Far Eastern gains, Roosevelt made the extraordinary commitment at Yalta that he would make himself responsible for securing General Chiang Kai Shek's agreement when the proper time came. This reflected his wish at all costs to keep on friendly terms with Stalin, regarding Soviet-American good understanding as the essential key to peace in the post-war world, and also his desire to have the Russians switch their war effort to the Far East in order to defeat Japan when Hitler's war machine had been broken. This was a time, it must be remembered, when the Americans, though pressing on with the manufacture of the atomic bomb, had no assurance that the device would work, and American Chiefs of Staff gave horrifying estimates of American casualties if an invasion had to be mounted on Japan's home base itself.

But the problem of securing local agreement to Stalin's territorial claims in Europe was far more difficult because these claims were not confined merely to frontier changes. Russia—and Britain and France, too—had suffered much from the self-assertive vagaries of Polish foreign policy between the wars. The Poles, while being necessarily dependent for their very existence on the good will of either Germany or Russia, if not both, had managed at different times to alienate both these two powerful neighbours, to say nothing of quarrelling with Lithuania over Vilna, which the Poles forcibly seized in 1920, and with the Czechs over the district of Teschen. In 1939, as we saw in the previous chapter, Poland's refusal, even in the very shadow of a German invasion, to accept a military agreement with Russia ruled out the only expedient which might have deterred Hitler from war. Stalin was therefore determined, not only to rectify his post-war border with Poland, but to have a government in authority in Poland after the war which would be responsive to his will. Thus, when Warsaw rose in rebellion against German occupation in August 1944, partly through being urged to do so by Moscow Radio, Stalin, though his armies were within striking distance of the city, did nothing to help and even prevented British and American aircraft using Soviet-occupied airfields in order to drop supplies on the besieged Poles in the capital. It seems likely, though other explanations have been offered, that Stalin hoped that in this way Polish resistance leaders would be eliminated and hence Stalin's own hand-picked Polish Communists based on Lublin would stand a better chance of becoming the future Polish government.

Thus Stalin evaded the agreement reached at the Yalta conference that the Lublin regime should not be accepted as the provisional government of Poland until it was broadened by exiled Poles from abroad and other Poles in Poland. Churchill, on returning from Yalta, undertook that Poland would not become a 'projection of the Soviet state', but added that the British guarantee to Poland in 1939 was a pledge concerning its independence and not its frontiers. Nevertheless, Russia's armies at that time occupied Eastern Europe and Eastern Germany and there was little or nothing that Britain and America could do about Poland, short of making war against Russia, which would have been politically impossible. Churchill and Roosevelt had, it is true, persuaded Stalin at Yalta to sign a 'declaration on liberated areas' which promised respect for fundamental rights and freedoms, free elections and so on, in those areas. But it was clear that Stalin would not allow such conditions in Poland in view of the kind of government the Poles could be expected to elect after their long history of suffering at the hands of Tsarist and Christian Russia, to say nothing of what they could expect at the hands of Communist and atheist Russia. However Roosevelt may have regarded the declaration on liberated areas, it is hardly likely that Churchill signed on any other assumption than that it would come in handy as proof of Soviet duplicity when

Stalin's true intentions in regard to Poland and eastern Europe as a whole became known.

Russia, then, in the summer of 1945, though desperately weakened by invasion, had restored much of her territorial position, and especially the paramountcy in eastern Europe which the Tsarist regime enjoyed before the First World War. Her ambitions in regard to the Middle East, however, met with greater resistance. First, Churchill had agreed with Stalin at their meeting in Moscow in October 1944 that, while Russia should be predominant in Poland, Bulgaria and Rumania, with Yugoslavia as a kind of buffer state between British and Soviet spheres of interest, Greece would be predominantly under British influence; this agreement was respected on the Soviet side during the civil war in Greece immediately after the end of the German occupation in the winter of 1944, when Stalin refrained from giving all the assistance he could to the Greek Communists. Moreover, Stalin's efforts to establish a separate, though Soviet-protected Azerbaijan in northern Iran petered out when the Iranian government, with firm support from the United States at the newly founded United Nations Security Council, demanded the withdrawal of Soviet troops. The same applied to the Soviet demand to Turkey for joint Soviet-Turkish defence of the Straits. The American proclamation of assistance to Greece and Turkey under the heading of the Truman Doctrine in March 1947 effectively put a stop to Soviet expansion towards the eastern Mediterranean, as also did Yugoslavia's defection from the Soviet camp in 1948. At the 'Big Three' meeting at Potsdam in August 1945, Russia had proposed, though somewhat half-heartedly, that she should have a trusteeship over the former Italian colony of Tripoli, only to be ignored by the two Western powers. The Soviet Union, thus retiring from the Mediterranean and the Middle East in 1947–48, was not to return until the Soviet bloc arms deal with Egypt in September 1955 and the re-establishment of Soviet naval strength in the eastern Mediterranean in the 1960s.

Western views on Soviet foreign policy at the end of the Second World War varied from those who considered that Stalin, like Lenin at the end of the First World War, saw the world as ripe for Communist revolution, with Russia as its historically determined leader, to those who regarded the Soviet Prime Minister as thinking primarily in terms of Russian national interest, or rather the restoration of Russia's imperial position as under the Tsars of the eighteenth and nineteenth ceturies. There are strong arguments for both points of view. Certainly, the language of the Cominform, the organization established by Moscow in 1947 for co-ordinating policies and attitudes between the Soviet Union, the Communist regimes she successively imposed on eastern Europe between 1945 and 1948 and Communist parties elsewhere, was as full of denunciations of Western capitalism and imperialism and messianic prophecies of its early demise and succession by Communism, and as ideologically determined as that of its predecessor, the Comintern. The latter Stalin had abolished in 1943 as an irritant in relations between himself and the British and American peoples. Certainly, too, no one like Stalin and his closest colleagues, such as Foreign Minister Molotov, after their many years of training in Marxist thought, could fail to see the external world through any but Marxist spectacles.

Again, the Soviet Marxist in 1945 could have little reason for doubting that the Communist cause was a rising tide in world affairs. Communist Russia, with, as the ordinary Soviet citizen thought, only marginal assistance from the Western democracies, had overthrown the mighty spearhead of bourgeois capitalism, Nazi Germany; in China, with its six or seven hundred million people, the Communists, under Mao Tse-tung, were winning more and more of the peasantry over to their side and within four years of the end of the Second World War, the red flag would fly over China's vast spaces in friendly alliance, as from 1950, with the Soviet Union; in European countries, too, the Communist parties had played a leading role in resistance movements and in the driving out of Nazi and Fascist invaders; France and Italy in 1945 seemed poised on the brink of a Communist take-over and throughout the West many intellectuals, though by no means committed Communists, believed that Communism represented the 'wave of the future'.[3] Very little, in short, in the world political scene as it appeared from Moscow seemed to contradict the Marxist-Leninist messianic dream, and, as new states were formed out of the old European colonies in Africa and Asia, it was not difficult to believe that these would take the same Communist road as Russia had done to strength and power through centralized economic planning for public good rather than for private profit.

At the same time, the Second World War, hard and cruel as it was on the eastern front, did a great deal to revive the simple, old-fashioned nationalism or patriotism which seems endemic in the

[3] See E. H. Carr, *The Soviet impact on the Western World*, London, 1947.

Russian people and led them to entitle the struggle against Nazism 'The Great Patriotic War'. Stalin's appeals to the Russians in the dark days of 1941 and 1942 to remember 'the great heroes of our race'—Ivan the Terrible, Peter the Great, Alexander Nevsky, Dimitri Donskoi and others—his identification of himself with the cruel but heroic Tsars of the past, his touchy concern for the dignity and status of Russia and its recognition as a leader among the world powers at the Yalta and Potsdam conferences, the Russians' flashy display of military power at their May Day parades : all this suggested that the war had done something to stiffen the Russian nationalistic backbone and to induce them, if not to impose their form of society on the whole world, at least to exact acceptance of Russia as a world leader. Moreover, they had suffered a traumatic experience during the war; never again, if they had any say in these matters—and their achievements during the war gave them that say—would they allow the states of eastern Europe to act as a corridor for Central European forces to pass into the Russian motherland. Never again would they allow a regime to grow up in Germany which had hostile designs on the Soviet state. Rather than permit that, they would attempt to Communize all Germany, but if that were impossible or if it were thought undesirable as giving Germany the chance to rival Russia as the centre of the Communist world, they would keep Germany permanently divided and retain their control of the eastern part of Germany beyond the river Elbe, which held within its territory, a hundred miles from the Western-occupied zones of Germany, the old German capital, Berlin, also under four-power control. The division of Germany and, with it, the division of Europe thus became and, evidently at least until 1970, remained permanent principles of Soviet foreign policy.

The United States was by contrast almost the complete opposite of the Soviet Union except for its continental extent and its two hundred million or so racially mixed population. It had no frontiers except those with friendly or weak states, Canada and Mexico. It had never been invaded except for the trivial skirmishes with British forces in 1812. It, too, like the Soviet Union, had strong and long-standing interests in the Pacific and the Far East; but these took the form of concern with the balance of power at sea in that area, whereas Russia, as in Europe, was preoccupied with the security of immensely long land frontiers. America, moreover, had never been concerned with European politics or the balance of power in Europe, except for a short period during and immediately

after the First World War—indeed much of the American population had been directly recruited from people who were fleeing from
the political, social and economic evils of Europe and had no desire
to revisit them—whereas Russia had been immersed in European
politics and diplomacy from time immemorial, and not only by
reason of ambition, but because her own survival depended on the
European balance of power.

Besides, America's economic system was ostensibly based on
private enterprise, though state control had grown rapidly in the
Roosevelt 'New Deal' era of the 1930s; Russia's economic system
was based on collective ownership and centralized planning. The
American system gave priority to individualism, while being without the relatively rigid class consciousness of Britain, whereas in
Russia the emphasis from distant times was on the community, the
mir, to be outcast from which was considered a form of spiritual
death. America was, while deeply religious, at least in upper levels
of society, a materialistic civilization, holding in high esteem the
man or woman who had made a fortune by his own energy and
enterprise; in Russia the technological accomplishments of Communism were regarded with childlike wonder by simple country
folk, but there had also in the Russian mind been the idea that
materialism was a soul-destroying force and that without spiritual
values, especially those to do with the welfare of the local community, the pursuit of wealth eliminated all that was noble in man.

Both these super-powers, however, had one thing in common, and
this was the idea that there was something deeply at fault with the
prevailing international system. American criticism of international
relations concentrated on the 'power politics' and the imperialism
of the world system, its oppression of small states by great (not that
the United States had been entirely innocent of that) and its tendency to set a low value on the common man's welfare and freedom
to shape his own future. Between 1917 and 1920 Americans, or at
least the followers of President Wilson, imagined that they were
building a better world, based upon human rights, national self-
determination and the collective restraint and renunciation of
force. The Bolshevik Russians, on their side, entertained somewhat
similar hopes of overthrowing the international system in 1917–20
and replacing it by the brotherhood of working men, except that
their ideal society was to be based, like early Christianity, on the
renunciation of private property. Like the Americans, though in a
different sense, the Russians suffered a rebuff with the restoration

of capitalism and the old Euro-centred diplomatic system by the Allies after 1918. But, unlike the Americans, the Russians could not retire into themselves, vast as their homeland was, when their hopes of a transformation of the international system failed. They had to remain in that system and to develop much the same diplomatic practices, the same alliances and balance-of-power principles of the system. In fact, in 1939 or 1945 it was difficult to see how the external behaviour of the Soviet Union differed in its motivations from that of any other state, except perhaps in Stalin's determination to regard other countries near to his own territory as mere pawns in the game of Russia's survival and restoration to world eminence.

In 1941–45, therefore, when the United States was for the second time reluctantly forced to take a leading role in the international system, there were certain curious affinities between herself and her Soviet ally and later bitter adversary. First, the Americans respected the scale of Russia's vast war effort and the valour of its armies, just as the Russians seemed sneakingly to admire the physical prowess of the fully mobilized United States, such prowess in fact that in 1944, when America was spending on the war an amount of money equal to its whole pre-war national income, private consumption in that country did not fall below its level in the 1930s. Secondly, the United States and the Soviet Union wished to use the Second World War, not merely as a means of re-shaping the international system to prevent war breaking out again, but to create a new world order. The American and Soviet images of what this new order should look like were strikingly different, of course, but there was enough vague resemblance between the two for them to be confused, at least on the American side, in the warm spirit of wartime companionship. Both wished to break up the old European overseas empires; Roosevelt and Stalin were united on this at Yalta against Winston Churchill, who stood for an outmoded Victorian imperialism in the sight of both. Both sought a peace dedicated to the rights of the common man, though it was not apparent to the Americans until later that they themselves conceived these rights as meaning in the main freedom *from* government control, whereas the Soviets saw them as liberties safeguarded against invasion by private wealth and power *by* governmental control, and governmental control inspired by one set of revealed political principles only.

The American administration at the end of the Second World War was loath to agree that Stalin was inspired by fundamentally different principles from their own; they brushed aside Churchill's arguments that the balance of power still governed international relations and that once a power vacuum had been created in the heart of Europe by Germany's unconditional surrender, on which the three Allies had insisted, nothing but firm Western opposition could prevent another country's power flowing into the vacuum. The Americans, somewhat like the British in the early 1920s, but totally unlike the Russians and the continental Europeans, were apt to distinguish sharply between war and peace; war, they appeared to think, was caused by irresponsible military despotism, and once the despot had been deposed, the victor could return home and resume his right to life, liberty and the pursuit of happiness. Thus Roosevelt told Churchill, to the latter's horror, that American troops could stay in Europe no longer than two years after Hitler's defeat.

Churchill did not regard the Russians as aggressive by nature, though he continued to detest their Communist system; but he considered it inevitable that once a great power is overthrown, there must, almost by a law of nature, be a struggle between the surviving victors for the portioning out among themselves of that great power's territory, resources and influence. Nothing, he thought, could prevent the redistribution of German might in Europe turning out to be in Russia's favour except some counterbalancing force, of which the United States must be a considerable part. The Americans, on their side, refusing to believe that conflict is inevitable in international relations without an effective equilibrium of power, supposed that the British Prime Minister must be attributing ill-will to Stalin; they could not, in the exhilaration of victory, share this view and 'gang up against Uncle Joe'. They prepared therefore to return home from Europe, but found they could not because Stalin began to act in the very way Churchill had prophesied. In their bitter disappointment that the great world conflict had not ended war for all time with the defeat of Hitler, Mussolini and the Japanese militarists, they suddenly turned on Stalin's Communism with the hatred which the idealist tends to feel when his assumptions about a necessary harmony of interests between the peoples of the world are falsified. Democracy, George Kennan once wrote, is like a palaeolithic monster which is slow to anger, but which, once aroused, lays about itself with such force as to wreck its habitation. This proved true of the American democracy during the immediate aftermath of the Second World War. When that happened, it was by a strange irony Winston Churchill and other British statesmen who felt it their duty to urge restraint upon their American ally, as they had urged vigilance before.

II

Such were the giant powers which the Second World War left dominating the international scene in 1945. The European states which had formed the nodal points and communication centres of international affairs before the war, Britain, France, Italy and Germany, were exhausted, if not actually militarily defeated, and it seemed that many years would have to elapse before their recovery was complete. Of the four, Britain seemed least affected by the war; though the heavy bombing of her cities was something new in her experience, it was not nearly as devastating as had been feared by those who presumed to know in the 1930s. British military casualties, too, owing to the main brunt of the fighting in the closing stages having been borne by the United States and the Soviet Union, were not comparable with those of the First World War.

Moreover, Britain had never lost its sovereignty to a foreign state as most countries in east and west Europe had lost theirs to Hitler by 1941 and as Germany and Italy lost theirs to conquerors at the end of the war. This, together with the great prestige Britain had gained through its lonely defiance of Hitler in 1939–41, gave it the opportunity in the years 1945 to 1948, when the movement towards political and economic unity in western Europe was beginning, to give it a lead; this was strongly urged by Churchill, the then leader of the Opposition as a result of the general election of July-August 1945 which gave the Labour Party its first clear Parliamentary majority in British history. But the facts, first, that Britain had remained sovereign and independent throughout six years of war; secondly, that the British, forming a politically unitary state, had little understanding of the notion of sharing sovereignty with another state; and, thirdly, that the Labour government under Clement Attlee's leadership had no wish to surrender to a federal Europe the levers of economic power which they had come to control after so many years in the political wilderness : all these meant that Britain, together with the Scandinavian states, was a non-participant in the movement towards federalism in western Europe in the later 1940s. Thus Britain refused to assign to the Council of

Europe, created in 1949, the 'limited but real powers' which its advocates had asked for. It refused, too, to attend the Paris conference in the summer of 1950 for the pooling of west European coal and steel industries which the French called for under the name of the Schuman Plan—Robert Schuman being at that time the French Foreign Minister—and hence were excluded from the European Coal and Steel Community (ECSC) when it came into existence in 1952.

The Conservatives, Churchill in particular, criticized Labour Ministers for their negative attitude towards European unity. But they themselves, when they returned to office in October 1951, there to remain for thirteen years, proved no more favourable to federal tendencies in western Europe, as distinct from closer international co-operation on the traditional model with the sovereignty of the participating states unaffected. Accordingly, they failed to persuade the six west European states which formed the ECSC, Belgium, France, Holland, Italy, Luxembourg and West Germany, to base themselves on old-style *international* rather than new-style *supranational* principles. They also refused to join in the French plan of 1952 for a common west European army, the so-called European Defence Community (EDC), and partly for this reason the French National Assembly rejected the EDC treaty when it was presented for ratification in August 1954. This failure left the Western powers with no option but to assent to the formation of an independent West German army. This was, however, to be controlled, as to the weapons available to it, by the West European Union (WEU), a body formed among the west European states, with British membership, which had signed the Brussels pact in March 1948 for collective defence against the possibility of aggression from Soviet-dominated east Europe. Italy, too, joined WEU, and Italy and federal Germany, an independent state formed from the British, French and United States occupation zones in Germany, also joined the North Atlantic Treaty Organization, which we shall discuss in the next chapter.

Hence, too, the British Conservative government refused to attend the Messina conference in 1955 at which the West European Six drew up their plan for a European Common Market of Economic Community (EEC) or to sign the Rome Treaty which actually created EEC in 1957. Again, as in the case of the Schuman plan, Britain attempted to modify the proposals for an EEC in order to retain the principle of national sovereignty, and especially national control of a member-country's external tariff. But this once more proved unacceptable to the Europeans.

British pride in its uncontaminated sovereignty during the war and a certain disdain for west European states which had failed to retain theirs were thus important factors in the shape taken by the movement towards west European unity. But there were others. One was the physical detachment of Britain from the European continent, long-standing but by no means as old in its political implications as the British often supposed. During the early eighteenth century, for example, a British commander, Marlborough, had fought victories as the head of a European force against French armies in the heart of central Europe. A century later another British commander had done the same, again opposing French armies. It was in fact the expansion of the British Empire in the late eighteenth and the nineteenth centuries which committed Britain to a policy of balancing the powers of Europe one against another so that she herself would be free to cultivate her imperial estate. Many British leaders, Churchill in particular, thought that these imperial threads could be taken up again after the Second World War. But this was not to be. First, the Labour Government was faced with a demand that Britain should quit India, which the Indian Congress party had campaigned for throughout the war. After Britain's failure to reconcile Moslems and Hindus to the idea of one nation within the Indian sub-continent, partition was agreed to between Jawaharlal Nehru and Mohammed Jinnah, and independence came to predominantly Hindu India and the two widely separated East and West wings of predominantly Moslem Pakistan in August 1947. The independence of Ceylon and Burma followed almost immediately.

These developments, together with the Labour Government's refusal to use force against Iran when it nationalized the Anglo-Iranian Oil Company in 1951, were denounced by Churchill as 'scuttling from Empire', but Britain, exhausted by a six-year war in which she had fought longer than any other belligerent, was in no position to hold down 450 million people in India against their will. Churchill himself advised the Attlee government to give back to the United Nations the British mandate for Palestine in August 1947 when, after endless negotiations, no formula could be found to reconcile Jewish and Arab nationalism; Israel, as a predominantly Jewish state, was thus to emerge in 1948 after its first great post-war military defeat of the surrounding Arab states. Again, Churchill himself liquidated the massive British military base in the Suez Canal area in 1954 by agreement with Colonel Nasser's revolutionary nationalist regime which had displaced the Egyptian monarchy of King Farouk in 1952; he also granted independence to the Sudan in an agreement with Nasser made in the same year. The Suez base was moved to Cyprus, touching off a struggle for independence there, which was finally conceded in 1960. After taking over the premiership in 1957 from Churchill's successor, Sir Anthony Eden, following the ill-fated invasion of Egypt during the Suez crisis of 1956, Harold Macmillan initiated a rapid process of decolonization of British Africa which began with the grant of independence to Ghana in 1957 and ended with the illegal declaration of independence by Rhodesia under a government led by Ian Smith, which Britain disapproved and opposed (though not with arms) since the declaration excluded from political power the native African majority, in favour of political supremacy by the white minority.

By 1970 the mighty British Empire, which, already in 1870, was the most extensive and populous that the world had ever seen, was reduced to a few scattered outposts which clung to Britain either because they were not viable as independent states or through fear of being brought within the sovereignty of some neighbouring state which they had no wish to join. But the wonder was not so much that this great act of decolonization, vastly accelerated by the Second World War, was achieved with the minimum of bloodshed, as compared, for instance, with France's struggles in Indo-China and Algeria, but how Britain, with the least possible amount of military force but the maximum amount of confidence, had held together this enormous conglomeration of different races scattered throughout the world.

Out of the Empire sprang the Commonwealth, or rather the dependent Empire and the old Commonwealth, consisting of the old white dominions—Australia, Canada, New Zealand, and South Africa—and Britain herself, became all Commonwealth and practically no Empire. The new Commonwealth was highly acceptable to the British Labour party because it symbolized the party's old desire to see all colonial empires whittled away, and because it held out the hope of resolving, owing to its multi-racial character, what many on the Left thought to be the greatest problem of the mid-twentieth century : the struggle for racial equality. Conservatives, too, though never entirely at ease at post-war Commonwealth Prime Ministers' conferences in which white, black and brown government leaders mingled freely with the traditional white faces, nevertheless welcomed it as a typically informal British institution and one which promised to give Britain access to many diplomatic ears throughout the world, and especially to the new world of decolonized states then coming into existence.

Hence there sprang up, after the breach between the Western powers and the Soviet Union widened in the late 1940s, the Churchillian conception of British foreign policy being played out within three overlapping circles: Europe, in the affairs of which Britain could never disinterest herself, the Commonwealth, and the Atlantic community. By the last term British politicians were really referring to the 'special relationship' which had developed between Britain and the United States during the Second World War, though it had its earlier roots, an association much more warm and intimate than that between either country and their seemingly churlish and remote ally, Russia. British interests, in both Conservative and Labour eyes, seemed to lie in keeping these three circles strong and effective, while not becoming so closely integrated as to compel Britain to choose between one circle and another. In the early years after 1945 the three-circle conception worked well enough. But it was not long before, in the middle and late 1950s, British governments felt that they might have to choose between Europe, on one side, and the Commonwealth and American ties, on the other. There were even times when Commonwealth sentiment, especially in non-aligned India, clashed with British adherence to the Atlantic alliance in the world-wide struggle against Communism and when, in the mid-1960s, British support for United States policy in Vietnam made many in the Afro-Asian Commonwealth countries wonder whether the Commonwealth any longer had meaning for them.

Moreover, the three-circle conception presupposed that Britain, if not quite equal in power or status to the two super-powers, still remained a country with world-wide interests. This was reflected in British representation at all heads-of-government meetings of the anti-Axis powers during the Second World War; British participation, along with American, French and Soviet, in the four-power control and occupation of Germany and, at least formally, of Japan after their defeat in 1945; the British presence, along with that of the other three and China, as a permanent member of the Security Council of the United Nations, founded in 1945 as a successor to the old League of Nations; Britain's possession, along with that of

America and, as from September 1949, Russia, of independent nuclear capability, that supreme symbol of great power status in the post-war world which France and China were later to acquire. But it was difficult even for the most optimistic to see how these world-power pretensions could be long sustained in view of the interrelated economic and psychological consequences for Britain of the Second World War.

In 1945 and the years following, there seemed little that the mass of the British people wanted more than a quiet and prosperous life. They had fought two terrible wars within a space of thirty years and there were few times in the period between the two wars when their armed forces were not in action in one part of the world or another. Yet, in return for these efforts, they had had to endure unemployment, malnutrition, bad housing, economic insecurity in times of sickness or when the family grew in size. Small wonder it is that in 1942 British public opinion snatched eagerly at the Beveridge Report, with its provision of social security for all, the war-time coalition's undertaking in 1944 to assume government responsibility for full employment after the war, and in 1945 the chance to vote massively for a Labour government which undertook to make life richer for all than it had ever been in the 1920s and 1930s. The British almost welcomed the loss of empire after 1945 as the laying down of a burden, and although in the 1960s all three political parties, Conservative, Labour and Liberal, talked vaguely of 'setting the people free' and 'getting the country moving again', it was the parties' promises of higher living standards which were listened to most intently.

Yet the problem remained of how Britain, a country which normally exported a fifth of its gross national product to pay for the fifty per cent of its food and raw materials, which it consumed as imports from abroad, was going to pay its way. To finance the war, it had had to sell most of its foreign investments, worth some £3,000 million in 1939, dividends from which had paid for almost a half of its pre-war imports. In addition, it had accumulated considerable debts abroad for the upkeep and supply of its forces there, and these—the so-called sterling balances—had to be repaid by unrequited British exports. It was estimated that the real value of British exports would have to rise by something like 74 per cent over the pre-war figure merely for Britain to pay its way in the world; and this had to be done, first, when foreign purchasing power was low, especially in Europe, owing to the dislocation of all economic

systems by the war, and, secondly, when defeated countries like
Germany, Japan and even Italy, seemed, after a period of dependence upon the occupying powers, to have had some new industrial
dynamic bestowed upon them by the war and the necessary fresh
start.

At first, the Labour Governments of 1945–51, like most British
people, considered that the lack of foreign currencies, especially the
dollar, with which to buy necessary supplies from abroad was a
short-term post-war phenomenon which could be cured by a temporary injection of dollars. This was granted by the American authorities in the form of a £1,000-million loan, repayable at a 2 per cent
rate of interest, in December 1945, on condition that sterling be freely
convertible on the world money markets after two further years had
elapsed. But no sooner was the loan received than it was spent; and
no sooner was sterling made convertible in 1947 than it had to be
restored to control because its value shrank dramatically in world
markets. Only with the supply to Britain and other west European
states of massive instalments of dollar funds under the American
Marshall plan of 1948–52 was Britain able to balance her foreign
trade account; but even this did not prevent the country being
thrown into insolvency again as a result of the great programme of
rearmament forced on Britain following the outbreak of the Korean
war in June 1950, when Britain joined with other United Nations
members, led by the United States, to assist South Korea against
attack from North Korea, an event which alarmed all the Western
powers about the possibility of a similar Communist attack in
Europe.

From then on Britain's international economic situation was
crisis-ridden year after year; no sooner was there a spate of business
investment intended to modernize Britain's somewhat old-fashioned
industrial equipment than prices rose, and with that came the
inevitable balance of payments crisis, earnings on foreign trade
account falling below spendings. Economic expansion was then
purposefully slowed down, Britain fell further behind her trade
competitors in industrial growth and efficiency, and business investment was resumed to cope with this decline; then again export
prices rose and the dreary round of economic 'stop-go' was resumed
once more. Some relief was afforded by the devaluation of sterling
by 15·4 per cent in November 1967, but it was not long before
Britain's competitors began to creep up on her again, while the
prices of her goods continued to rise. Was there something funda-

mentally wrong with the British economic system, or even with the British way of life?

The rate of growth of the gross national product was lower in Britain than in any other advanced industrial country, certainly less than in the European Economic Community, which Britain, belatedly and vainly, tried to join, only to be vetoed by France's President de Gaulle in 1963 and 1967. A new start was made on the attempt to join the EEC in 1970 but this time with British public opinion more depressed than ever about the expected costs of entry. British foreign policy moves—such as the armed action jointly with the French against Egypt when President Nasser nationalized the Suez Canal company in July 1956; the failure to bring the Smith regime to heel after UDI in November 1965; the inability to exercise any influence as a mediator in the Vietnam war or in the Nigerian civil war in the late 1960s—all this suggested that the British might have lost that political flair which had swayed the world for so long. One of Britain's American friends, Dean Acheson, a former secretary of state, described Britain as having lost an empire without finding a new role. The British response to such painful remarks, namely that others, like Philip of Spain, Napoleon and Hitler, had underestimated Britain, to their own cost, in the past, sounded hollow and unconvincing.

Other leading European states had their difficulties, but for a variety of reasons these did not seem to shake the national nerve as Britain's did. France, whom Britain played a chief role in raising out of its humiliations of the Second World War and endowing with a place once more among the leading powers, experienced a succession of governments reminiscent of the Third Republic before 1939 and was almost brought to the brink of civil war by the disastrous defeat of her army at Dien Bien Phu in March 1954 by the Vietminh forces of Ho Chi Minh, when France was seeking to establish firmly a friendly regime in South Vietnam, all Vietnam having formerly been a part of her Indo-Chinese empire; and again, and more seriously still, by her unavailing struggle to crush the nationalist movement in Algeria, where the French *colons* or white settlers implacably held on to what they had in the country. It required the immense authority of General de Gaulle, summoned back to power in May 1958 to win the Algerian war, to solve the problem by giving Algeria its independence and then crushing the opponents of decolonization in France, the secret OAS movement.

Subsequently, the former French colonies, especially in Africa, were kept under French influence, partly through their assimilation of French culture, while former British dependencies, with the possible exception of India, never bore to the same extent the stamp of the British way of life, partly through massive French economic assistance, compared with which British aid to former colonies was meagre, and partly through France securing for them associate status within the EEC, which she dominated. But France, quite unlike Britain, had another string to her bow besides empire, and that was her mission as the leader of and driving force behind the idea of a united Europe, a mission incidentally which had more than once in the past brought her into bitter conflict with Britain. Under Napoleon I, the French Third Republic at the end of the First World War and Aristide Briand, with his plan for European Union in 1930, the French had dreamed of *le rayonment de la France,* the drawing together of the threads and sinews of European life beneath the shining lustre of Paris. During his Presidency (1958–69), Charles de Gaulle himself used the mystical and rationally meaningless term 'Europe from the Atlantic to the Urals' as the goal of his policy, a loose association of European states freed from the 'twin hegemonies' of America and Russia, and always with France as its leader.

In 1963 de Gaulle signed a friendship treaty with Chancellor Konrad Adenauer of the Federal German Republic, which the three Western powers, Britain, France and the United States, formed in 1955 as an independent state out of their zones of occupation in post-war Germany as a result of the failure to reach four-power agreement on a united Germany (see below, Chapter 12, p. 259). In this partnership, which was continued, after Adenauer's retirement in 1966, with his successors, Chancellors Erhard and Kiesinger, until de Gaulle himself resigned in 1969 following fierce student riots in May and June 1968, France was clearly the dominant partner. De Gaulle, for example, shut the door on Britain's first application to join the EEC in January 1963 and again in November 1967, after Britain had made her second application, without apparently taking into account Germany's views or interests. Again, in the autumn of 1965 de Gaulle was on the brink of breaking up the EEC when France's views on financial and agricultural policies were not acceptable to the other five countries; it was France again which refused to surrender sovereign powers to the EEC's Commission, despite the readiness of the other five to go further in this direction. De Gaulle, while not refraining from praising the achievements of the German army in building up that nation, once France's bitterest enemy, conducted an entirely independent foreign policy; he cultivated closer ties with the Soviet Union and Communist east Europe, acting as an agent for Federal Germany in this, when the tension between East and West began to diminish in the 1960s; in 1966 he took his forces out of the integrated command structure created under the North Atlantic Treaty, which the Western powers signed in 1949, when he judged that the danger of Communist aggression in Europe had dwindled almost to nothing; he recognized Communist China in 1964, toured Latin America and roused it to fight against 'domination' by the United States, took the Arab side, like the Soviet Union, in the continuing Arab-Israeli struggle, and showed undisguised pleasure when the United States found itself plunging deeper and deeper into a profitless commitment to defend South Vietnam against North Vietnam and the Vietcong guerrillas.

This defiance of the United States, who had become the champion of western Europe against the Soviet Union in the late 1940s, and disregard for the wishes of the Federal German Republic, his closest ally, was possible for de Gaulle because he knew that in the last resort America would come to the assistance of France if she were the victim of aggression, despite de Gaulle's behaviour, and because Federal Germany still carried on its shoulders the burden of guilt, which it had not yet appeased, for the Hitler regime and all its unspeakable horrors. The Germany which emerged from the Second World War, utterly defeated, leaderless, demoralized and entirely at the mercy of the four occupying powers, became a divided Germany, with its old capital, Berlin, still under four-power occupation, situated, as mentioned earlier, a hundred miles to the east of the limits of Western occupation and control. The three Western powers, partly to shed the burden of occupation when all attempts to reach agreement on a four-power basis for Germany as a whole failed, partly to make western Germany the armed front of the Western alliance facing Communist east Europe under Soviet control, began as early as 1949 to form a separate state in their occupation zones, a process as we have noted already which was completed in 1955 when Federal Germany entered the North Atlantic pact and was given authority to rearm, though still under the control of the West European Union.

This symbolized a great victory for Chancellor Adenauer's policy of westernizing the Federal Republic. The policy was criticized by the western German social democrats under leaders like Schumacher and Ollenhauer on the ground that it hardened the division between East and West Germany and ruled out the prospects of German reunification. Dr. Adenauer replied by extracting in 1955 from the three Western powers, Britain, France and the United States, a commitment to work for German unity on the basis of free all-German elections; not to recognize the German Democratic Republic, a Communist-dominated state which the Soviet Union had created as her client in the Russian zone of occupied Germany; to recognize Federal Germany as the truly representative voice of all Germans; and to regard the Oder-Neisse line agreed to at Yalta as a merely temporary border with Poland pending the final conclusion of a peace treaty with a united Germany (see above, p. 22). In addition the three Western powers reaffirmed their determination to keep their forces in the Western sectors of Berlin and to preserve freedom of communication between these sectors and Federal Germany.

These were very considerable and, as later proved, embarrassing commitments for the three Western powers to undertake considering that in 1954 and 1955 Federal Germany had hardly any other option available to her in foreign policy than to side with the Western powers. That they were undertaken at all was partly through fear that Federal Germany might follow the example of Weimar Germany's manœuvre in making a pact with Soviet Russia at Rapallo in April 1922, which was repeated by Hitler, with disastrous results for the West, in August 1939. But it was also due in some degree to Konrad Adenauer's skill in statecraft. One of Adenauer's strongest fears was a revival of extremist nationalism in Germany, a development which could only have the effect of bringing the Western powers and Russia together to suppress it. Moreover, he knew well enough that the strongest safeguard for Federal Germany, so long as the revival of Nazism there was feared by the east Europeans, Communist and non-Communist alike, and prophesied, morning, noon and night, by the Soviet Union, was the firm support of the United States, with its forces and medium-range nuclear missiles stationed in western Germany and facing east.

Hence Dr. Adenauer devoted his best efforts to winning over the allegiance of the West Germans, especially the younger generation, away from nationalism and towards the idea of a united Europe, in which Germany must in the long run play a leading role, if second for the time being to France. With Federal Germany firmly enclosed within the three west European communities, the ECSC, Euratom and the EEC, the last of which had a carefully worked-out programme of integration to be achieved when the economic systems of the six participating states were virtually combined to form one, the idea of German unity based on a dissolution of the two German states and the formation of a new, single Germany with free and impartially supervised elections receded into the indefinite future. The Soviet Union and most, if not all, east European states would stick at nothing to prevent it. Even the Western allies of Federal Germany seemed to regard German unity as a kind of heaven, another and better world devoutly to be wished for, provided it did not come for a long time yet. But, as the Germans reconciled themselves to that situation, as their guilt for Hitler's misdeeds receded, and especially when France lost her dominating, wilful leader, de Gaulle, in 1969, Federal Germany's inferiority to France in the European communities diminished.

The victory of Herr Willy Brandt, the Social Democratic leader, over Dr. Kiesinger's Christian Democrats in the Federal elections in September 1969 was a reassurance to Europe that the new Germany was firmly committed to democracy; at the same time the fear of her swallowing up the smaller states of western Europe declined, thus making easier the acceptance of Federal Germany as France's future successor as the leader of the west European communities. Thus emboldened, Chancellor Brandt determined to carry forward the policy of *Ostpolitik* initiated by his predecessor, Kurt Kiesinger, by opening up lines of communication with East Germany, Poland and Czechoslovakia, and even, in the summer of 1970, with the Soviet Union herself. What the Communists sought in these exchanges was a Federal German acceptance of the *status quo* in eastern Europe and a commitment to renounce force as a means of changing the *status quo* there, while Herr Brandt seemed to pursue the rather more modest aim of improving ease of access between the two parts of Germany and Berlin.

Thus, Britain's two major partners on the Continent, France and Federal Germany, did not appear to experience her own malaise, her lack of self-confidence and uncertainty as to where her place in the world was to be. For Britain the Commonwealth was gradually losing such economic, political and strategic unity as it ever had; the fourth post-war Labour Government, for example, determined in January 1968 to terminate its military position east of Suez by the end of 1971, and its successor, the Conservative government formed by Edward Heath after his electoral victory on 18 June 1970, adopted a more favourable view of South Africa and Rhodesia than Labour ministers, and this tended to alienate the British Right wing from the coloured Commonwealth countries. Hence, Britain increasingly found herself in a position in which only the Atlantic community and Europe were left out of the old three sacred circles of foreign policy. But the former waned as more and more Americans considered that Britain could best serve Western purposes, as well as alleviate its chronic economic ills which weakened it as a member of the Western alliance, by joining the west European community. Yet the price expected to be paid, both in financial terms and in the form of loss of independence, seemed almost beyond the willingness of British public opinion to disburse as negotiations began about British entry into Europe for the third time in the autumn of 1970. It was difficult to avoid the impression that Britain was seeking to join the movement towards European integration, not from genuine belief in the correctness of that development, but because the other options before her were becoming less and less convincing. This fact might have the effect of reducing opposition to British membership of the European communities among leaders of British public opinion, but it did nothing to lower the price the west European Six were keen to exact for British membership. They could perhaps be excused for thinking that Britain came to Europe principally because she no longer had anywhere else to go.

The smaller west European states, Belgium and Holland, had joined Luxembourg to form a customs union—Benelux—at the end of the Second World War, and Italy had suffered as much as any European state from the effects of the Second World War. Italy had been forcibly compelled to discard its African colonies by the peace treaty of 1947, although, through sheer failure among the victors to agree on any other solution, she was given a mandate over her old colony, Libya, under the United Nations. Otherwise Italy was gently treated at the 1946–47 peace conference in Paris; Russia recognized the country as falling mainly within the Western sphere of influence and did not complain even when the powerful Italian Communist party lost the elections in 1948, American aid and influence playing no small part in this turn of events. The Western powers were able to relieve Italy of heavy reparations and allowed her to retain South Tyrol, with its 300,000 Austrian inhabitants, even though Austria had played a far less willing part on the Axis side in the Second World War than Italy. But a Communist Italy, with a Communist Yugoslavia on the eastern side of the Adriatic, would have placed the greatest difficulties on the Western powers in the Mediterranean; hence Italy was liberally provided with American funds to keep her, though at times somewhat precariously, within the liberal democratic scheme of things. As a member of the supranational European community Italy prospered, though the ancient division between the richer, industrial north and the poverty-stricken, agricultural south remained, and was marked in the autumn of 1970 by riots in southern towns such as Battipagua and Reggio di Calabria.

As for Belgium and Holland, both were affected positively and negatively by the American aid-to-Europe programme, the Marshall plan. Both were able to overcome the ravages of war with American aid; Holland's plight was particularly hard owing to the dikes having been opened to flood the country when the German invasion came in June 1940. The Dutch, in consequence, loved the Germans even less than did the Belgians, though the latter had suffered another German invasion thirty years before. But the decolonization of the empires of both countries was also helped along by American efforts. When the Dutch were fighting the Indonesian nationalists who formed an independent state based on Java in the Dutch East Indies almost before the Japanese had left the country in 1945, the United States partially suspended Marshall Aid to the Netherlands as a form of pressure on the Dutch to concede full independence to the nationalists, and in this it was successful. Again, when the Belgians granted independence to their vast colony, the Congo, on 1 July 1960 without having given their Congolese subjects any preparation for independence and the Congo began to break up into separate states, it was the United States which helped a force sent to the Congo by the United Nations (ONUC) to suppress the secession of Katanga, a province rich in mineral wealth in which Belgian business interests were heavily involved.

Both of these were examples, of which post-war history was full, of American power and wealth being employed to sway events in areas distant from American territory, and also of the conflicts in the American mind between loyalty to European allies and the traditional American mistrust of imperialism, now sharpened by competition with the Soviet Union as to which of the super-powers was the more anti-imperialistic state. In this conflict more often than not it was the latter force which won. Nevertheless, having unburdened themselves of empire, the mass of the Belgian and Dutch people were no worse off, indeed were in many ways much better off, than they had been before. Thus, accidentally and against their will and expectations, the old European states found that they had been misled by inaccurate popularizations of works by thinkers like Marx into looking upon overseas empires as a source of national wealth. If they had observed Hitler's attitude towards colonies, or even General de Gaulle's, they might have realized that, so far from their being in modern times a source of enrichment, they are, as Adam Smith argued, more of a millstone round the national neck.

III

Thus the Second World War had left the international system divided into two opposed sub-systems, each dominated by one of the world powers, the United States and the Soviet Union, and with Europe, now a passive object of extra-European forces, divided between them. It almost seemed as though the prophecy made by Stalin in his *Lectures on the Foundations of Leninism* had come true : 'thus in the course of the further development of international relations two centres will form on the world's surface, one centre drawing to itself the countries that gravitate towards capitalism, the other drawing to itself the countries that gravitate towards socialism'. But, as Nikita Khrushchev, one of Stalin's successors, was to point out in the early 1960s, this was to omit another sector of the international system—the Third World, which sprang into being mainly from the process of decolonization and the members of which professed to belong to neither camp, but to follow policies of neutralism or non-alignment.

Neutrality, meaning a legal state of impartiality in any armed conflict between state-members of the international system, had of course long been recognized in international law and diplomacy. Certain European states, notably Belgium, Luxembourg, Sweden and Switzerland, were known as the traditional neutrals; many of these, Sweden being a striking exception, had been neutralized by agreements among the great powers, which meant that the powers were under an obligation not to infringe on their neutrality. In the twentieth century, however, neutrality as a voluntarily adopted position in time of war lost much of its appeal.[4] It was doubtful whether it could be reconciled with membership of such bodies as the League of Nations and the United Nations, which provided for the collective enforcement of peace, and in any case great powers fighting total wars in which their very existence was at stake had little respect for the traditional rights of neutrals. After the Second World War, however, Sweden and Switzerland retained their neutrality, the latter not even wishing to compromise itself by joining the United Nations. Austria, after ten years' wrangling among the four powers which had occupied it along with Germany after the latter's defeat in 1945, was eventually neutralized in May 1955.

However, after the Second World War a new concept came into the vocabulary of international relations : neutralism. This referred to a state of non-involvement in the collective defence treaties which developed as a consequence of post-war tensions between East and West, which became known as the Cold War, while no legal state of war existed between them. Moreover, neutralism referred to a political attitude which could be shared by individuals, as well as to a state's foreign policy. Thus one could speak of the existence of neutralism, meaning an attitude of mind prevailing in certain sectors of public opinion, even in states like Britain and France which were not, as states, officially neutralist, being bound together, after April 1949, in a collective defence agreement, the North Atlantic Treaty Organization. But one could speak of neutralist states as well, in which the government's attitude was one of non-involvement in the Cold War, the best known examples of this in Europe being Finland, which the Soviet Union refrained from bringing under her control, as she had with other east European states in 1945–47, provided the Finnish government followed policies which were not positively hostile to Soviet interests; and Yugoslavia, which broke away from Stalin's camp in 1948 without, however, showing any indication of willingness to join the Western military alliance.

But neutralism was also used to describe the policies of the great mass of new African and Asian states formed in the process of decolonization of the European overseas empires, though non-alignment was the term they actually preferred to use owing to the alleged overtones of indifference to great moral issues in the former expression. Non-alignment can be defined as an unwillingness to participate in the collective defence agreements which sprang up in

[4] See Nils Ørvik, *The decline of neutrality*, Oslo, 1953.

the Communist and non-Communist worlds as the rift between the two widened (see below, Chapter 12). Not all decolonized states opted for non-alignment. Some, like Iraq between 1955 and 1958, joined the West's collective defence treaty for the Middle East, the Baghdad Pact, later known as the Central Treaty Organization (CENTO), because they genuinely feared Communism either as an internal or external force; others, like Pakistan, joined CENTO and the South-East Asia Treaty Organization (SEATO) because they wanted Western military and economic assistance against a neighbour, in Pakistan's case India. But most of the new states did opt for non-alignment.

This partly reflected the external attitudes of all new countries, such as the United States in the 1780s, which was warned by George Washington in his Farewell Address to avoid 'entangling alliances'. It was partly the sheer poverty and desire for economic advancement and modernization of the new states, which gave them an incentive to avoid heavy military expenditures and to receive economic aid from both sides in the Cold War. Again, in part non-alignment reflected the emotional aversion of the new states from entering into defensive arrangements with their old colonial masters. In part, too, non-alignment in the East-West struggle was preferred because some of the new states had enemies nearer home—the Arab states in Israel, the independent African states in South Africa—while the threat of Communism was more remote.

The new states were far from bringing into existence a new international sub-system, with some degree of coherence of policies and co-ordination of attitudes. Attempts were made, notably at the Bandung (Indonesia) conference in April 1955, to agree upon a common philosophy and programme for the Third World, but these soon gave way to the same kind of frictions and differences between independent states which have always characterized international relations, all the more so as the non-aligned states, being new, cherished their hard-won independence and often had difficult problems of internal cohesion, which could sometimes be overcome by adopting hostile attitudes towards other states, whether old or new. Nevertheless, the new states or, to use the common euphemism, the developing countries were courted for some time by the super-powers, either as potential voters on one or the other super-power's side at the United Nations, or as potential members of its alliances. Often the rival super-powers would, openly or clandestinely, support opposing factions within the new states, as in the Congo or

Vietnam. This was a great change from the attitudes of the European great powers of the nineteenth century towards the non-European world. In those days the powers would more often than not stand together in defence of white civilization against the coloured world. Now the supreme powers intrigued against each other to win the support of African and Asian people against each other.

But this phase did not last for long. As the new states began to dominate the UN General Assembly in sheer numbers, they also passed beyond the control even of the United States, who, immediately after the Second World War, began to use the General Assembly as an instrument of political warfare against the Soviet Union. Moreover, the improvement in Soviet-American relations which began about 1962 made it less necessary for either superpower to solicit support in the Third World against each other. In fact, as the *détente* developed between America and Russia, both states began to recognize that each had a right to do as it pleased in areas vital to its own security, or in other words, in its sphere of interest, even if these zones included states forming part of the Third World. By 1970 it was still unclear how relations between the new states and the old would develop. But no one could doubt that one of the greatest issues in mid-twentieth century international relations was the rift between the poorer, southern half of the world and the richer, northern states, which now included the Soviet Union and its east European allies. That rift might in time make the East-West conflict, which dominated post-war international politics for at least sixteen years, seem insignificant. It is to this struggle, however, that we must now turn.

REFERENCES

Balogh, T., *The Dollar Crisis*, Oxford, Blackwell, 1949.

Bullock, A. L. C., 'Europe Since Hitler', *International Affairs*, January 1971.

Calvocoressi, P., *World Politics since 1945* (U.S. title: *International Politics since 1945*), London, Longmans, and New York, Praeger, 1968.

Feis, H., *Churchill, Roosevelt, Stalin*, Princeton, N. J., Princeton U.P., and London, O.U.P., 1957.

James, L., *World Affairs since 1939*, Vol. I, *Europe*, Oxford, Blackwell, and New York, International Publications Service, 1965.

Marlowe, J., *The Seat of Pilate: an Account of the Palestine Mandate*, London, Cresset Press, and Chester Springs, Pa., Dufour, 1949.

I

Merkl, P. H., *The Origin of the West German Republic*, New York, O.U.P., 1963.

Opie, R., et al., *The Search for Peace Settlements*, Washington, Brookings Institution, 1957.

Price, H. B., *The Marshall Plan and its Meaning*, Ithaca, Cornell U.P., and London, O.U.P., 1955.

The Royal Institute of International Affairs, *Documents on European Recovery and Defence, March 1947–April 1949*, London, 1949.

Vinacke, H. M., *Far Eastern Politics in the Post-War Period*, New York, Appleton-Century-Crofts, 1956.

12 *Birth and Death of the Cold War*

We have seen in the previous chapter how, for about fifteen years
after the defeat in 1945 of the principal Axis powers, Germany
and Japan, international relations were dominated by continuous
rivalry between the super-powers, the United States and the Soviet
Union, each with its pack of friendly but subordinate smaller states.
This state of affairs was known as the 'Cold War'—the phrase was
coined by Walter Lippmann—and was characterized by extreme
hostility between the two factions, psychological warfare and uninterrupted mutual vilification, especially in public international
organizations such as the United Nations, but with little actual
fighting, and this, where it occurred, was mainly between one super-
power, normally the United States, and an ally or client state of the
other. During these fifteen years there were repeated crises in which
war seemed imminent. Yet, with the development of nuclear
weapons and intercontinental missiles for the delivery of these
weapons to the most remote area of the other side, the super-powers
began to recognize a strong common interest in the avoidance of
war and this produced a period of *détente* between them which was
still vigorous in 1970. With this came a tendency for the tight
bipolarity of the Cold War to be transformed into a multipolar
pattern of international relations which had traditionally characterized the international system.

I

Some students would place the origins of the Cold War as far back
as 1917, when the Bolsheviks came into power in Russia and not
only defied all the established proprieties of diplomacy, such as the
avoidance of propaganda directed at the people as distinct from the
government of another state, but expressly committed themselves to
the overthrow of bourgeois society the world over and the bourgeois
international system with it. Relations between Britain, then the
dominant capitalist power of the day, and Soviet Russia deteriorated
to the point at which diplomatic relations were suspended by the

former in 1927, an event which never occurred between America and Russia in the period since 1945. But this pre-war tension between Russia and the West never looked like ending in total war between the two, except in the minds of the more doctrinaire xenophobes on the Soviet side, whereas on two or three occasions since 1945 a shooting war between Russia and the West looked like a distinct possibility. Moreover, tension between Moscow and the West in the 1920s and 1930s did not have the effect, as it did in the post-1945 period, of organizing the major members of the international system into rival hostile camps 'in the state and posture of armed gladiators'. Anglo-Soviet relations remained touchy and tense throughout the inter-war years, but relations with the Soviets were only a part, and by no means a major part, of Britain's total international relations. Since the Second World War, on the other hand, the struggle between Communism and Western political ideas, each embodied in powerful armed coalitions of states, has tended to cast its shadow over all world politics. The Cold War in the 1950s, in short, had all the appearance of a struggle for mastery of the globe, which the pre-1939 tensions caused by the mutual fears of Russia and the West never seemed like becoming.

We may say then that the Cold War which began about the time of the three-power Potsdam conference (Britain, America and Russia) in July-August 1945 reflected the twenty-five-year-old mutual mistrust of Russia and the West, but that its more immediate roots lay in the particular circumstances in which the Second World War ended. First, it is almost a law of history that victorious great powers fall out among themselves when the conflict which brought them together ends; it happened in 1815 and in 1918 and, while everyone knew that peace in the post-1945 world would depend on good understanding between the two super-powers, the historical pattern was almost bound to reproduce itself after the German and Japanese surrenders in 1945. These feuds arise partly from quarrels about the distribution of the benefits of victory, but their main cause is no doubt the fact that opposing interests among the victors, which have been subordinated to the task of defeating the common enemy, now come to the surface when the enemy is no longer there to unite the victors. It is more than possible that even if the Soviet Union had been miraculously whisked off the face of the earth in 1945, differences would have sprung up between the United States and its other wartime allies when victory was won. It is hard to recall now, but it is nevertheless true, that at the end of the First

World War the strongest resentment was aroused in Britain over the growth of the American navy; and from the intensity of the Anglo-American naval arms race in the 1920s, one might have imagined that war was in the offing. It is not unlikely that such resentments, along with American antagonism to the British Empire and a few other crumbs in the American-European bed, might have resulted in a 'Cold War' between the United States and its European wartime allies had Russia not been there on which to focus the hostility of both.

Secondly, there was the enormous problem of the future of Europe, and especially the future of Germany, the country which had played such a momentous role in the affairs of Europe since the twentieth century began. At the Potsdam conference a system of four-power occupation of Germany and Berlin and the settlement of Germany's future borders, except for the Polish-German frontier which was left for a definitive demarcation at a future peace conference, were agreed, together with some general principles for the future unification of a disarmed and 'democratized' Germany. But, in contradistinction to the situation in 1919, when Germany remained a united, though defeated state with a sovereign government competent to undertake the legal obligations of the Treaty of Versailles, in 1945 German sovereignty for all practical purposes passed into the hands of the victors; in Winston Churchill's dramatic phrase, 'a headless trunk had fallen on the table of the conquerors'.

Now, there had always been, since Germany was united into one national state in 1871, the strongest rivalry between Russia on one side and Britain and France on the other for the friendship of Germany, arising from the simple fact that experience seemed to show that he who controls Germany controls the balance of power in Europe. Germany and Russia came together, with the former predominant, by the Treaty of Brest-Litovsk in March 1918, which gave the Bolsheviks the release from the First World War they were seeking. After 1918 Britain did her best, by favouring lenient treatment for Germany, to pull her away from the allurements of Communism, to which the British Prime Minister, Lloyd George, predicted at the Paris peace conference in 1919 that she would otherwise fall victim. France, having suffered most from Germany during the war, took the opposite course, with the result that the ostracized Weimar Republic reached agreement with the ostracized Soviet Russia at Rapallo in April 1922 and this enabled Germany illicitly to rearm on a limited scale by building munitions factories on Soviet soil. At the Locarno conference in 1925, however, Germany was won for the West and there was panic in Russia at the loss of her only ally. When the Nazis came to power in Germany in January 1933, Hitler assumed an anti-Communist posture, intended no doubt to offset any fears in the bourgeois West of a resurgent German nationalism. Still, in August 1939 Russia and Germany came together once more in the Nazi-Soviet pact, making a European war inevitable. Now, in 1945, Russia was in occupation of eastern Germany beyond the Elbe and disposed of a massive land army which she did not demobilize, as Britain and America did their own forces, when the war ended.

Even if the Western powers and Russia had had identically the same ideology, they would still probably have been divided over the question of which way was the future Germany to lean : to the East or to the West? If to this is added the basic ideological rift between Russia and the West on such issues as the rights of the individual as against state control, freedom to speak and write as one pleases, and to organize alternative political parties to that of the government in office, liberty for the ordinary man to find his own way to salvation as against 'guidance' by the exponents of one purportedly true faith, the seeds of a desperate struggle for the body and soul of Germany are well and truly planted. The next twenty-five years of European, if not world, international relations were to be devoted to that theme.

Thirdly, there was the fact, as we have seen in a previous chapter, that the Soviet Union was territorially a revisionist state, both in relation to eastern Europe, the Far East and, at first, the Middle East. The two Western powers, Britain and America, had on the whole little difficulty in accepting these claims on the ground that if, as far ahead as one could see, the world was to be governed by the victorious triumvirate of Yalta and Potsdam, it was better that all three powers should accept the international system they were supposed to uphold, rather than allowing consensus among the three to be eroded by the territorial dissatisfaction of one. After all, even the United States benefited territorially from the Second World War, in the sense of strategic trusteeships in the Pacific as well as the island of Okinawa, though the 'residual sovereignty' over the latter still technically remained with Japan. Again, a stronger Russia in Europe and the Far East would be in a better position to prevent any resurgence of a revanchist Germany and Japan, a problem with which, strangely enough, many people in the West were preoccupied during the Second World War. But Russia was also politically revisionist; she wanted, that is, new territory handed over to her own control to be communized, and she wanted countries in eastern Europe adjacent to her western borders to be communized, too, though not at once. By February 1948 this had been achieved in Bulgaria, Czechoslovakia, Hungary, Poland and Rumania,

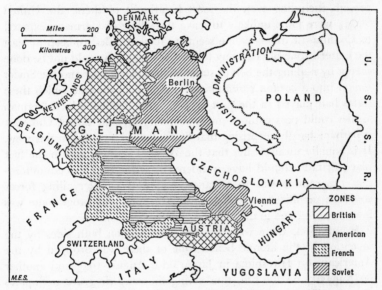

Europe in 1945

despite the Declaration on Liberated Areas signed by Stalin at Yalta in February 1945 which promised fundamental rights and freedoms to the second and fourth of these states, and the peace treaties, insisting upon the same rights, which had been signed in Paris in 1947 with the first, third and fourth of these countries.

It is hard to be sure why Stalin took it upon himself to force Communism on eastern Europe between 1945 and 1948. The reason may be the obvious one that he was an acquisitive, and old-fashioned, imperialist of the worst kind, and also that, being the leader of the world's first Communist state, he wished to see Russia's example followed elsewhere. This, however, was bound to meet with the hostility of the Western powers and bound to compel the United States to abandon the isolation it wished in 1945 to return to, and to force it into a powerful anti-Communist alliance opposed to further such Communist advances. This now seems to have been a heavy price to pay for the expansion of the Communist ideology, to which, as it happens, Stalin and his successors since his death in March 1953 have made very few concessions at the expense of determinate Soviet national interests. It seems rather more likely that what Stalin was chiefly concerned about in 1945 was the future of Germany. When he realized, between 1945 and 1947, that the Western powers, including even the most isolationist of them, the United States, were most unlikely to leave the whole of Germany exposed to Communist influence, he seems to have decided to keep at least the eastern zone of Germany for himself. But this could not be done except by making the belt of states between Germany and the Soviet Union into a *cordon communiste*. Considering the role which these states had played in the past as a corridor through which German armies could pass without much difficulty into the Soviet Union, it is perhaps hardly surprising that Stalin should have taken this view. It is equally unsurprising that the Western powers, and in the first place Britain, should have wondered how far Stalin's communization programme was to advance, and how countervailing forces could be mobilized on the other side in case that programme was intended to extend to the Atlantic.

In addition, there were the fears aroused on both sides by the invention of the atomic bomb. One of these was dropped by the Americans on Hiroshima in Japan on 6 August 1945 and another on Nagasaki on the 8th, thus giving the *coup de grâce* to Japan's already failing war effort and handing to Stalin all the gains in the Far East promised to him at Yalta in return for less than three weeks of Soviet fighting in Manchuria. It is well known how President Truman, who succeeded Franklin Roosevelt on the latter's death on 12 April 1945, told Stalin about the successful explosion of an atomic bomb in America at the Potsdam conference in August 1945 and how the Soviet leader appeared to pay little attention to this extraordinary news. It may be that Stalin still considered war in traditional terms, one mass army struggling against another, which no new-fangled weapon could change. Nevertheless, in the following year the Russians refused to accept the American so-called Lilienthal plan for the international control of atomic energy, the United States government insisting that no state which agreed to the plan would be able to use the veto to protect itself against sanctions if it manufactured atomic bombs illicitly; this Soviet rejection of the Lilienthal scheme may have been because Stalin *did* take the discovery of nuclear power seriously and considered that the American plan for subordinating it to an international authority would freeze the nuclear *status quo* to Russia's disadvantage. However that may be, the Russians did not neglect to press ahead with their own nuclear programme and, with the assistance of some famous physicists who defected from the West, were able to explode their first atomic bomb in 1949 and their first hydrogen bomb in 1953.

From that moment on the world, and perhaps more particularly the super-powers themselves, became filled with dread of a nuclear war, all the more horrible because the precise form it might take could not be imagined. A vast, terrifying and immensely costly machinery of deterrence was erected on each side. The arms race between the two supreme powers was accelerated as each strove to insure itself against a devastating surprise nuclear attack from the other side. At the same time the security curtain surrounding each camp was drawn tighter until the two worlds were practically sealed off from each other.

This growth of the two armed camps proceeded against the background of a still weak, demoralized and economically devastated Europe. At first American assistance was poured into it through the United Nations Relief and Rehabilitation Administration (UNRRA), but the United States Congress soon tired of assisting states in Europe which Russia was dominating, and eventually in June 1947 Secretary of State George Marshall announced in a speech at Harvard University a new programme of aid to Europe, the Marshall Plan, as it came to be called, which lasted from 1948 until 1952. Although in his speech Marshall claimed that his programme extended to all Europe, Communist and non-Communist, including the Soviet Union, he must have been relieved when, at a conference in Paris between Britain, France and the Soviet Union, Molotov, the Soviet Foreign Minister, withdrew from the whole operation on the ground that the condition on which the United States offered the aid called for some form of all-European co-operation in making use of it. This, in the Soviet view, offended against the sacred principle of national sovereignty. Not only that; the Soviet Union even refused to allow the states of eastern Europe to participate in the plan.

The Marshall Plan symbolized the divided paths which liberal democratic western Europe and Communist-dominated eastern Europe were now following. Western Europe, including the Western-occupied zones of Germany and Austria, were coalescing and con-valescing with the help of American economic strength. The international agency by which the needs of western Europe were considered as a whole was the Organization for European Economic Co-operation (OEEC), now called the Organization for Economic Co-operation and Development (OECD), since both the United States and Canada have now joined it. The OEEC was not, and the OECD is not, a supranational organization; the principle of national sovereignty was firmly rooted in both. Nevertheless, the OEEC gave a further impetus to those in western Europe who wanted to go beyond the nation-state in the fields of international co-operation in which they felt the need for some authority higher than that of the nation-state.

Even before this, however, the United States had gone yet a step further in shielding non-Communist states against Soviet expansion. This was in March 1947, when President Truman applied to Con-gress for authority to give assistance to 'free' peoples threatened by Communist aggression. Although this authority was sought and granted on the basis of the general principle of helping the weak stand up against the strong, it actually arose from the notification to Washington by Britain in February that she was no longer capable of giving financial assistance to Greece and Turkey. The former faced Communist pressure on the government from within, though this was encouraged by Communist states to the north of Greece, while Turkey was facing external pressure from the Soviet Union in the form of a demand for joint Soviet-Turkish defence of the Dardanelles Straits and a Soviet military base in the Straits.

Accordingly, the first countries to be assisted under the general authority accorded to President Truman were those two near-eastern states, the whole development being known, in the American-style vocabulary of international affairs, as the 'Truman Doctrine'. In one sense, however, its author, or rather the man who created much of the American mental background into which the Truman Doctrine fitted, was George Kennan, of the foreign-policy planning staff of the State Department, who, in pseudonymous articles in the American journal *Foreign Affairs,* analysed current Soviet policy as definitely a form of doctrinal imperialism and urged the United States to adopt a counter-policy of 'containment', that is, the con-struction of strong-points around the vast periphery of the Soviet Union to hold its expansionist propensities in check.

The Marshall Plan and the Truman Doctrine—it might have been better for East-West relations if they had been introduced in that order in time, with the Marshall Plan coming first—therefore marked a fundamental change in American foreign policy from intermittent intervention in European affairs to set matters right, as the Americans conceived it, followed by retirement into isolation, to a permanent, or seemingly permanent, commitment to hold in check Soviet imperialistic tendencies by putting new heart into non-Communist countries encircling the Soviet state through both economic and military assistance. The Plan and the Doctrine also marked the passing of the leadership of the Western democratic nations from Britain to the United States. How well, if at all, could the latter fulfil that role? Many asked that question, and most who asked it were in the United States.

II

The new spirit of active intervention in world affairs on the part of the United States was reflected in the famous Vandenberg resolution adopted by the Senate on 11 June 1948. Arthur Vandenberg had been a Republican leader of almost unshakable isolationist convictions before the Second World War, but the weakness of the democratic nations in Europe before that conflict, the almost ostentatious *Gleichschaltung* of eastern Europe by Stalin, as well perhaps as the urgings of men like Winston Churchill, had persuaded him that, in the air age, in the era of atomic bombs and missiles, the notion of 'fortress America' was obsolete. Hence his Senate resolution began with a statement of support for the United Nations, followed by condemnation of excessive use (the user did not need to be named) of the veto in the Security Council, now a well-established grudge of the West, and then it associated the United States with the maintenance of peace 'by making clear its determination to exercise the right of individual and collective self-defence under Article 51 [of the United Nations Charter] should any armed attack occur affecting [America's] national security'.

What had converted old isolationists like Vandenberg into interventionists, apart from the imposition of Communism on Czechoslovakia in February 1948 and the American recognition that with mid-twentieth-century means of warfare no country lives in a fireproof house, was—perhaps more than anything else—the deteriorating situation in Germany and the utter failure of the four occupying powers to reach any agreed solution to the riddle of

German unity and a German peace treaty. By the end of the dead-locked London conference in December 1947 of the Council of Foreign Ministers of the four powers, created by the Potsdam conference to reach agreement on the basic issues in the German question, following a similar failure in Moscow in March 1947, the Western powers decided that there was no alternative but to form their three zones of occupation into a separate state, to be called the Federal German Republic.

The basic issues which remained unresolved between East and West were five. First, as to reparations, the Russians pursued a policy of denuding their zone of all industrial or agricultural equipment left standing, while demanding, as they were entitled to by the Potsdam agreements, a share in reparations from current production in the Western zones. The Western powers, on their side, were finding the burden of keeping their zones financially solvent beyond their strength; certainly this was true of Britain, which fused its zone of occupation with that of the United States in December 1947 in order to even out the heavy burden of maintaining a dependent sector of Germany. They therefore soon reached the decision that they must end reparations and reconstruct their zones so as to make them economically self-supporting. Secondly, there was the commitment at the Potsdam conference to treat Germany 'as an economic whole'; on this the Western powers claimed that Russia was preventing the farm surpluses from the agricultural east which had traditionally fed the western areas of Germany from doing so; hence they protested that they themselves were provisioning western Germany with food while Russia was taking a proportion of its industrial products away as a form of reparations—the situation was somewhat like that of a farmer who fed his cows while somebody else drew off the milk. Thirdly, as to denazification, another principle for the treatment of Germany agreed to at Yalta and Potsdam, both sides accused the other of giving encouragement and employment to former Nazis. Fourthly, there was no agreement as to the form to be taken by the new all-German government which would one day be formed; at first, the Soviet Union wanted a centralized government, no doubt hoping that it would be Communist and hence under Soviet control. The West, on the other hand, especially France, argued in favour of a federal form of government. Later these positions were reversed, the West seeking all-German elections in order to form a democratic all-German government, while Moscow preferred a confederation between the two German states which had come into existence *de facto*. Finally, while the Soviet Union pressed for the neutralization of a united Germany, the Western powers considered that Germany should be free to choose the alliances it wanted to join; they did not do so, however, in the expectation that a united Germany would prefer to join the Soviet side in the developing international argument.

After the failure of the Moscow and London conferences, the Western powers, Britain, France and the United States, had no further doubt that their interest lay in the formation of a separate and independent west German state. The Soviet response was to amalgamate the political parties in her eastern zone of occupation into the Communist-dominated Socialist Unity Party (SED), and then to begin the formation of a parallel separate state in the eastern zone, called the German Democratic Republic (DDR). It is worth noting that, whereas subsequently the Soviet Union adhered to the principle of the permanent division of Germany while the West still strove for German unity, at this stage the trend towards the creation of two separate German states was set by the West. The DDR was not formally established until 1955 whereas the Federal Republic in the west had the basis of its independence laid as early as 1949 and was declared fully independent by the London and Paris agreements of 1954. The second Soviet riposte to Western moves towards an independent west German state was to impose in June 1948 a blockade on all access routes to Berlin from west Germany across the hundred or so miles of Soviet-occupied Germany except for the air routes, and by using these the Western powers were able, to the surprise of all, including themselves, to keep the two million Berliners in the Western sectors of the city provisioned. At length, in May 1949 Stalin had to admit moral defeat by agreeing to remove the blockade, while the West lifted its counter-blockade, on condition that another round of four-power talks were held about German unity. These were held in due course but ran true to form in proving sterile.

The Berlin blockade, coming hard on the heels of the fall of Czechoslovakia to Communism in February 1948, was the final move which brought the North Atlantic Treaty Organization (NATO) into effect on 4 April 1949. This treaty, based on Article 51 of the United Nations Charter, which permits the use of force in individual and collective self-defence against armed attack, was in essence the addition of the United States and Canada, together with five other states, Denmark, Iceland, Italy, Norway and Portugal, to the Brussels treaty for collective defence which Britain, France and the three Benelux countries had signed in March 1948. In the course of time an elaborate superstructure consisting of integrated military, naval and air commands, a Council representing participating governments, a military committee and subordinate agencies of many kinds, was built on the basis of the 1949 treaty. But the North Atlantic pact remained essentially a military alliance, its central feature being the undertaking given in Article V to consider an armed attack on any of the parties in Europe or North America (subsequently amended to include Turkey) as an attack against all and to assist the victim state or states 'by taking forthwith . . . such action as it deems necessary, including the use of armed force, to restore and maintain the security of the North Atlantic area'. The undertaking in Article 2 to seek 'to eliminate conflict in their international economic policies and . . . encourage economic collaboration between any or all of them' never progressed much further than was necessary to ensure rough justice between the signatories in shouldering the economic burden of collective defence; and the notion, entertained by some enthusiasts, that from NATO could spring a politically integrated Atlantic Community remained unrealized. The fact that the pact was a military alliance directed defensively against the Soviet Union was underlined by the emergence of frictions within the alliance—between the United States and her European allies, between Greece and Turkey, both of which joined the alliance in 1951, over Cyprus, between France and the Anglo-Saxon powers which resulted in the French withdrawal from the integrated command structure in 1966, and between Britain and Iceland over fishery rights in the seas surrounding the latter— almost as soon as East-West relations improved and the imminent fear of Soviet aggression diminished.

As the Vandenberg resolution showed, the Atlantic pact and the defensive umbrella which the United States now threw over the countries of western and southern Europe threatened by Communism were necessary only because the United Nations had failed to provide a convincing defence for countries like Czechoslovakia, Greece, Iran and Turkey; and the most important reason for this was the inability of the permanent members of the UN Security Council, especially Russia and the United States, to see eye to eye together on the current sources of international tension. The Communist *coup* in Czechoslovakia, in American eyes, was an act of aggression, if only indirect, which should have been declared such by the Security Council under Article 39 of the Charter, and action should have been taken by the Council to halt it; in Soviet eyes, on the other hand, it was an act of liberation from bourgeois oppression.

There was one occasion, however, when the Security Council did take action to suppress an act of aggression, and that was in June 1950, when it voted to support Western-oriented South Korea against invasion by Communist-dominated North Korea. Like Germany, Korea, formerly part of defeated Japan's empire, was divided into Communist and Western-occupied zones after the Japanese surrender, and in these appropriately politically inclined regimes were established. In the Korean crisis the Security Council was able to act only because the Soviet Union, which was then boycotting the Council in protest against the UN's non-recognition of Communist China, was absent and her absence was not counted as a veto. Even so, the Security Council only felt able to *recommend* action in defence of South Korea to member-states, and only 18 states, out of 50 or so, responded to the Council's appeal, by far the greatest contribution during the three years of the war being made by the United States. In fact, this episode illustrates the point we have made about collective security in a previous chapter, namely that it is most likely to be effective when in accordance with the everyday foreign policies of the states practising it. Would the United States have been as quick to defend Communist North Korea as it was to defend South Korea?[1] It seems doubtful.

III

However that may be, the Korean war had the most profound effect on the Cold War, amounting almost to a climacteric in its development. There was immediate fear in the West of a Soviet attack in Europe, the assumption being that the North Korean attack had its master-mind in the Kremlin where the ultimate aim was to divert attention from Europe, in which its principal blow would be struck. This led NATO to adopt a forward strategy of bringing its defensive capability as near to the Elbe—the dividing line in Germany—as possible. The inevitable consequence of this was pressure, particularly from the United States, for the rearmament of West Germany, and an almost equal resistance to this pressure from most of the European NATO allies; there was even opposition in Federal

[1] See above, Chapter 8, p. 163.

Germany itself from those who feared that the effect of German rearmament must be, like all Dr. Adenauer's policies, to relegate to the infinite future the achievement of German reunification. We have seen in the previous chapter how the device invented by the French Defence Minister, M. Pleven, to circumvent the objections to the creation of a national German army, namely the formation of a European Defence Community (EDC), failed to secure the approval of the French National Assembly in August 1954, and how, as a substitute lighted upon by the British Foreign Secretary, Anthony Eden, Germany was allowed to rearm but under the control of West European Union, formed from the Brussels Pact states, and Italy and Germany. Federal Germany was also admitted into NATO, Britain placating French fears of a German military revival by undertaking the revolutionary commitment to maintain an army and a tactical air force permanently in Germany unless British national needs demanded their re-deployment elsewhere (see above, Chapter 11, p. 231). At the same time, the existing NATO powers undertook to work for German unity and the fulfilment of German national aims as already explained (see above, Chapter 11, p. 240). NATO accordingly became an instrument, not merely for the defence of its participating states from armed attack, but for the achievement—though by diplomatic, not military, means—of certain national German aims, about which some of its member-states, not least Britain, had the strongest reservations.

Again, there came a shift in Soviet policy, following the now established pattern of Soviet moves responding to Western initiatives. Stalin had died in March 1953 and, following the expected intrigues among his successors, Bulganin eventually emerged as Prime Minister with the ebullient Nikita Khrushchev in the more important post of Secretary-General of the Soviet Communist Party. Their policy seemed to be, as Khrushchev later described it, 'to draw a line under World War Two', particularly by accepting the division of Germany as a *fait accompli* which it might be undesirable for both sides to try to change, the river Elbe marking the dividing line between East and West. First, the Russians formally established, entered into diplomatic relations with and tirelessly canvassed the world-wide recognition of the DDR. At the same time the Soviet government recognized the Federal German Republic and invited Chancellor Adenauer to Moscow in 1955. They also made a formal peace with Japan in the same year, having refused to sign the American-sponsored Japanese peace treaty concluded in

San Francisco in 1951. Secondly, the Soviet Union entered into the Warsaw defence treaty with her seven east European client states—East Germany, Poland, Czechoslovakia, Bulgaria, Rumania, Albania and Hungary—in 1955, this arrangement being an almost exact replica of the North Atlantic Treaty except that it made provision for a general European security treaty in the future, embracing both Communist and non-Communist states. Moscow campaigned vigorously on behalf of such a treaty in the late 1960s.

The Soviet government, too, reversed their attitude towards Yugoslavia after the breach with that country in 1948 by as good as apologizing to Marshal Tito for the split, and, more dramatically still, towards Austria. Having stalled for years in the negotiations for a peace treaty with Austria, Russia now gave way on most of the points about which she had formerly prevaricated and agreed to the creation of an independent, neutralized Austria, possibly hoping in this way to enhance the allurements of neutralization for West Germany which had just joined the NATO alliance. Finally, as part of a more placatory attitude towards the West, the Soviet Union agreed to most of the important points in the Anglo-French disarmament plan in the sub-committee of the UN Disarmament Commission in May 1955, only to find the United States withdrawing its support for the plan in September and beginning with quite a new approach to disarmament through President Eisenhower's so-called 'Open Skies' plan. The Soviet Union also evacuated Port Arthur in 1955 and the Porkkala promontory acquired from Finland in 1940. Altogether it seemed in 1955 that a new era of cordiality had begun for East-West relations.

By the end of the first decade following the Second World War, then, a certain degree of stabilization had entered the Cold War, with the two blocs still facing each other watchfully, each wishing neither to extend the area in Europe it controlled nor to disturb the precarious equilibrium which had now been reached. In the following year, 1956, the Soviet authorities suppressed with the greatest brutality a nationalist uprising against the Communist government in Hungary. Even so, despite the undertaking of the American Republican party whose candidate, General Eisenhower, won the Presidential election in 1951 and selected the intransigent anti-Communist, John Foster Dulles, as his secretary of state, that they would 'liberate' eastern Europe from Communism, no effective action was taken by the American government. In other words, as was shown again in August 1968, when the Soviet Union and other

Warsaw Pact states sent their forces into Czechoslovakia to stop the liberalization process initiated there by Dubcek, Secretary-General of the Czech Communist party, the United States had by now come to respect eastern Europe as a Soviet sphere of interest. President Nixon, a Republican, who entered the White House in January 1969, said in a speech delivered in February 1970 on American foreign policy for the 1970s that 'the time is past when any power would seek to gain strategic advantages in eastern Europe against the USSR'.

A fact of even greater importance which lay behind this change in American foreign policy was that in October 1957 the Soviet Union launched into space man's first artificial satellite to circle the earth and send back messages to its launchers. This event, besides filling Americans with a quite unnecessary dread and envy of Russia's temporary technological superiority, showed that no spot on the globe was too remote for the Soviet Union to reach with its nuclear-warheaded missiles, despatched with unerring accuracy. As America speedily caught up in the missile race and as both super-powers buried their intercontinental missiles deep in concrete silos and in submarines which could disappear beneath the seas for months without surfacing, America and Russia now achieved second-strike nuclear capability. Neither super-power could henceforward launch a surprise nuclear attack on the other and leave it entirely without the nuclear capability to retaliate with devastating effect.

IV

These developments had the most far-reaching political consequences. They meant that neither super-power was quite so depen-
dent on its allies as it had been in the past since both now had the means of striking directly at each other. At the same time, taking into account the quite unparalleled destructiveness of all-out nuclear war, the issues on which the super-powers were willing to fight each other to the death were gradually reduced until the only one left was that of their own national security. 'I cannot imagine', said Christian Herter, who succeeded Dulles as secretary of state on the latter's death in May 1959, 'any circumstances in which the American President would order the firing of our nuclear arsenal except in defence of the continental security of the United States.' These words, and the later repetition of them by other American spokesmen, were heard by America's forty-two allies around the

world, linked together in the great pacts encircling Russia and Communist China—NATO, the CENTO treaty for the Middle East, the south-east Asia Treaty Organization (SEATO), which the United States had created in September 1954 to hold that area safe against Communist penetration after the French defeat at Dien Bien Phu in North Vietnam in March 1954. They were heard, too, by states like Japan and by the Chinese national regime in Formosa, with which the United States had bilateral mutual security treaties. Some of these allies, like France, drew the conclusion that they should free their military hands from NATO and develop an independent nuclear capability which they could use in any part of the globe. Others, especially the Federal German Republic, began to wonder whether, now that fear of premeditated war was lessening in Europe and the super-powers were acquiring something of a common interest in keeping the *status quo* undisturbed, they should no longer rely upon the United States for the advancement of their national objectives, but should try to see what they could do for themselves.

But there were still wider consequences of the hardening of the *status quo* between the two super-powers. One of these was the search to maintain the military balance of power and the whole costly structure of deterrence at a lower price and with lower risk of this whole apparatus going up in atomic smoke. This was attempted, though without success, at a four-power heads of government meeting (Britain, France, the Soviet Union and the United States) in Geneva in July 1955, followed by foreign ministers' meetings in the same city in November. A further 'summit' meeting was to have been held in Paris in May 1960, when, for some unknown reason perhaps connected with internal Soviet politics, Khrushchev, then the Soviet Prime Minister after the displacement of Bulganin, no sooner arrived in Paris than he departed, making an excuse out of the American despatch of a U2 spy plane which the Russians shot down over the Soviet Union.

In all these East-West negotiations at the end of the 1950s three basic issues remained unresolved. First, no progress could be made with German reunification, which all four great powers, Britain, France, the Soviet Union and the United States, professed to consider vital for a settled Europe; the West wanted free all-German elections with a resulting united Germany free to choose its alliances, while Russia still demanded a confederation of the two German states which would be neutralized by international agreement, like Austria. Secondly, no agreement could be reached on the many different proposals for the thinning out of forces on both sides of the line dividing East and West in central Europe or, as the Poles proposed in their Rapacki plan (named after the then Polish Foreign Minister, Adam Rapacki) for the denuclearization of central Europe, that is to say, the prohibition of nuclear arms in the two Germanies and in the whole or part of the east European states. Owing to the proximity of the Soviet Union to the area in which these formulae for disengagement were to be implemented, these plans were resisted by NATO Commanders. The West Germans also objected on the ground that balanced force reductions in central Europe would discriminate against them by thinning out troops and weapons on their own soil.

The third issue on which agreement seemed to elude the powers was disarmament, or (to give it its post-war name) arms control. Despite the disappointing results of disarmament negotiations in the inter-war period, despite, too, the relatively low priority given to disarmament in the UN Charter as compared with the League Covenant, negotiations on arms control between Communist and non-Communist states were almost continuous after 1945 in one international forum or another, the propaganda function of disarmament plans being considerable on both sides in this exercise. From all this talk only a few definite agreements emerged : the agreement among the super-powers in 1961 not to place nuclear weapons on the sea bed, the nuclear test ban agreement, prohibiting the testing of all nuclear devices except that carried on underground, which was signed by America, Britain and Russia in August 1963 after five years of negotiation, and the nuclear non-proliferation treaty signed in 1968 by which the three mentioned nuclear powers agreed not to pass on nuclear weapons to countries not possessing them and many non-nuclear countries agreed by adhering to the treaty that they would neither manufacture nor acquire such weapons. It is significant that the only arms control negotiations which did not receive vast publicity appeared at the time of writing (summer 1970) to be meeting with most success, and those were the Soviet-American talks in Helsinki and Vienna on the limitation of strategic nuclear weapons and delivery-systems (SALT negotiations).

While the two sides naturally blamed each other for this relatively dismal record of disarmament negotiations, the real obstacles seemed to be two : first, the difficulty of detecting in a vast country like Russia or America the presence of deadly weapons, especially lethal gases and bacteriological weapons, which might be quite small in size, even if the Russians had been willing to allow inspection of their territory by the other side, and, second, the feeling on both sides that powerful weapons like nuclear missiles, no matter how frightful to contemplate, had, by their sheer horror, induced some stability into international relations, the like of which had not been seen before.

Another effect of the stabilization of the positions of both sides in Europe was to shift Soviet attention, at least temporarily, away from that continent to the non-European world. This had already begun with Bulganin's and Khrushchev's visit to south-east Asia in 1954 and their support for the conference of non-aligned states in Bandung a year later. In 1955—almost, it seemed, in response to the Western-sponsored Baghdad pact (Britain, Iraq, Pakistan and Turkey) which split the Arab world and alienated radical national states like Egypt from the West—the Soviet Union stepped into the Middle East by supplying arms to Egypt through Czechoslovakia. She also provided economic aid for the Egyptian Aswan Dam when Britain and the United States, who had promised to finance the dam, withdrew their offer in June 1956. Henceforward, in the Suez crisis in 1956 and the six-day war between Israel and the Arab states in June 1967, the Soviets constantly supported, armed and rearmed the Arab states and echoed their denunciations of Israel as a spearhead of American imperialism. At the same time, by doing so the Soviet Union was acquiring a military and naval foothold in Egypt, the Eastern Mediterranean and the Indian Ocean, which began to be viewed with alarm by the United States in 1970, since it seemed to threaten the southern flank of NATO and the supply of Arab oil to Europe.

Meanwhile, Khrushchev was making further efforts to consolidate the *status quo* in Europe until his fall from power in October 1964. First, as a means of protecting the DDR against the economic consequences of its massive loss of manpower to the West through Berlin, he sent the Western powers a note on 27 November 1958 proposing to make West Berlin a demilitarized free city, thus ridding it of Western military protection, and threatening to turn over Soviet responsibilities in East Berlin to the DDR if agreement was not reached on the demilitarization proposal within a period of six months. This time-limit, however, was successively deferred. The Western powers, while offering concessions to the Soviet Union and

East Germany which would make life easier for them in Berlin, stood firm on their right to be in that city at a four-power foreign ministers' meeting in Geneva in summer 1959, and this right was eventually conceded in a public statement by Khrushchev. In June Khrushchev met the young President Kennedy in Vienna and apparently formed the impression that he could be pushed without too much difficulty. Perhaps for this reason the Soviet Union and the East German authorities constructed a wall on 13 August 1961 between the two parts of Berlin, with no free access between; they also sealed off West from East Germany by building a rampart, guarded day and night, along the 850-mile border between East and West Germany. On both occasions, the proposal for demilitarizing West Berlin and the building of the Berlin wall were made on the assumption, wrong in the first case but definitely right in the other, that the Western powers could not violently react. Nor did they react much in a physical sense during the Soviet destruction of the Hungarian revolution in October–November 1956.

Khrushchev then went a step further and began to cultivate the Cuban Communist leader, Dr. Fidel Castro, who had succeeded in ousting the corrupt Batista regime in the island in January 1959, and then devoted himself to a struggle against the anti-Communist forces behind American pressure on the Latin American states. Possibly to defend Castro against United States threats—a United States backed invasion of Cuba failed in April 1961—but more likely in order to create a thorn in America's side, as West Berlin was a thorn, or so the Russians said, in their side, Khrushchev began to install missiles in Cuba capable of striking at the United States, only some ninety miles away. Whereupon President Kennedy established a doubtfully legal blockade of Cuba, having local naval superiority in the Caribbean sea, and Russia was compelled to withdraw her missiles, her only compensation being a vague undertaking by President Kennedy to respect Cuba's sovereignty in future. Thus, the super-powers had, by 1962, come to respect each other's sphere of interest and hence 1962, when the Cuba crisis occurred and quickly subsided, may be regarded as the true beginning of the end of the Cold War, or the start of the East-West *détente*, though some would date this from the construction of the Berlin wall in August 1961 and the Soviet-American agreement of that year not to place weapons of mass destruction in outer space.

v

The East-West *détente,* which occupied most of the 1960s and was
expressed in a decline of mutual vituperation, a lessening fear of
war and a growing number of economic, cultural and technological
agreements across the dividing lines between the Communist and
non-Communist worlds, was sustained at two levels : the Soviet-
American and the European. Both were interrelated in that Europe,
the original birthplace of the Cold War, was also the theatre of its
demise, and in that the Soviet-American understanding created the
conditions for states situated immediately on both sides of the
ideological divide to come somewhat closer together.

At the Soviet-American level it is easy to see what the causes of
the diminishing tensions were. At the top of the list must be placed
the fear of thermonuclear war, which could annihilate both sides,
and the determination to avoid the kind of confrontations between
the two super-powers from which thermonuclear war could spring.
The most striking example of this came in the summer of 1970 when
the United States and the Soviet Union, without abandoning their
basic support for their friends in the Middle East, Israel and the
Arab states respectively, joined their efforts to try to end the deadlock between them following the six-day war in June 1967. The
reason for this, not surprisingly, was that both super-powers realized
the dangers of being drawn into a shooting war between themselves
while defending their respective protégés in the area.

A second factor in the Soviet-American *détente* was the widening
range of common interests between the two super-powers, apart
from their joint interest in the avoidance of nuclear war. Both
states, for instance, were concerned to maintain their primacy as
super-powers. This gave them a joint stake in the treaty, which both
fought so hard to achieve, to stop the spread of nuclear weapons in
order that no other country, apart from Britain, China and France,
which had already slipped through the net, would be able to join
the nuclear club. All these five, incidentally, were the permanent
members of the United Nations Security Council, except that when
America thought of China she thought of the Nationalists in Formosa, whereas Britain, France and the Soviet Union recognized no
China except that represented by the Communists in Peking. Again,
rising living standards in the Soviet Union probably gave that
country a strong interest, like America's, in reducing the massive
scale of arms expenditure in the Cold War by arms control agree-

ments, in increasing its lagging technology by agreements with the Western powers to make their skills and equipment available to Russian industry, and, perhaps above all, in keeping the *status quo* stable in eastern Europe, when it was threatened by the liberalization programme of Dubcek of Czechoslovakia. This programme Russia felt obliged to reverse by force in the summer of 1968, lest Dubcek's liberal ideas should spread to other countries, the Soviet Union herself included, and hence undermine the whole basis of the Communist empire.

A final important factor in the Soviet-American *détente* was the emergence of China as a world nuclear power, especially after the turmoil of the 'Great Cultural Revolution', which began in 1966, had subsided. Both America and Russia feared China. America feared Chinese expansionism in south-east Asia. Dulles considered that he could put a stop to that by the formation of SEATO in September 1954. Later, under President Johnson's administration (1963–68), the United States became deeply involved in a cruel and seemingly endless war in defence of South Vietnam against Vietcong guerrillas and North Vietnamese invaders, both of whom, in American eyes, were agents for Communist China. But Russia had even stronger reasons for hating and fearing China. China contested Soviet supremacy in the Communist world; and Communist states at a low level of economic development, like Albania in Europe and North Korea in the Far East, sided with the Chinese against the comparatively rich, conservative, almost bourgeois state which the Soviet Union had become. Above all, Russia had a 4,500-mile-long border with China where fighting between the troops of both countries was intermittent, the Chinese never being able to forget the fact that large areas of Russia's Far Eastern provinces once belonged to China. Russia and America were thus united in a common hatred of China. At the same time each could not but fear that one day the other might make a secret deal with China, the effects of which might be to shift the whole balance of world power in its favour.

Compared with the Soviet-American level of *détente*, the European level was comparatively undramatic. It consisted in the first place of attempts by the odd-man-out in the Western camp, President de Gaulle, to enter into commercial and technological agreements with the east European states, especially Rumania, whose independent position in the Warsaw Pact resembled the French position in NATO. Britain and Italy in the 1960s followed up with similar agreements. But the most far-reaching of these encounters across what was once the Iron Curtain was the *Ostpolitik* initiated by the Federal German Chancellor, Dr. Kurt Kiesinger, but carried much further by his successor, Willy Brandt, after his victory for the Social Democratic party at the Federal German elections in September 1969. Brandt first developed the Kiesinger theme of opening up relations with East Germany and, without going nearly as far as the recognition of the DDR, committed himself to the revolutionary description of the German situation as being that of 'two German states in one German nation'. But, finding the East Germans utterly adamant in demanding recognition, Brandt turned to the Soviet Union itself; the non-aggression treaty which Brandt signed with the Soviet Prime Minister, Kosygin, in Moscow on 12 August 1970, though it still fell short of the Federal Republic's recognition of Eastern Germany while accepting the Oder-Neisse line as for all practical purposes permanent, was in many ways a turning point in East-West relations in Europe. It was the end of one era and the opening of another. West Germany had in this treaty gone far to give the Soviet Union the recognition she sought of the *status quo* in eastern Europe; Russia on her side abandoned her long-standing condemnation of Federal Germany as a neo-Nazi, revanchist state.

Had then the Cold War been all in vain? Had it all been a mistake? Certainly each side had exaggerated the wickedness of the other. Certainly the West was not the paragon of freedom it said it was; nor were the Communist states a worker's paradise. But it is equally true that, considering the hates and fears of both sides, the terrible weapons of destruction with which each was armed, the hair's breadth which seemed to stand between war and peace in the Berlin and Cuba crises, twentieth-century man had achieved something in merely avoiding a catastrophe of quite measureless proportions. 'What did you do in the Great War, Daddy?' asked the child. 'I survived, my son,' replied the man. Unfortunately troubles do not cease with survival either in private life or in international relations.

REFERENCES

Bluhm, G. R., *Détente and Military Relaxation in Europe*, London, Institute for Strategic Studies, 1967.

Fitzgerald, C. P., *Revolution in China*, London, Cresset Press, 1952.

Fleming, D. F., *The Cold War and its Origins*, 2 vols., London, Allen and Unwin, 1961.

Goodrich, L. M., *Korea: Collective Measures against Aggression*, New York, Carnegie Endowment for International Peace, 1952.

Halle, L. J., *The Cold War as History*, London, Chatto and Windus, and New York, Harper, 1967.

Hunter, R., *Security in Europe*, London, Elek Books, 1969.

Luard, E. (ed.), *The Cold War: a Reappraisal*, London, Thames and Hudson, 1964.

Lukács, J. A., *A History of the Cold War*, New York, Doubleday, 1961.

Northedge, F. S., *British Foreign Policy: the Process of Readjustment*, London, Allen and Unwin, 1962, Chapters 3 and 8.

Seaburg, P., *The Rise and Decline of the Cold War*, New York and London, Basic Books, 1967.

Seton-Watson, H., *Neither War Nor Peace*, London, Methuen, and New York, Praeger, 1960.

Snow, E., *Red Star over China*, New York, Random House, 1938, and London, Gollancz (rev. ed. 1969).

13 *The United Nations and World Politics*

In the closing years of the Second World War Britain and her allies began discussions on a successor institution to the League of Nations. The impetus to create such a successor was part of the upsurgence of hope in human affairs which tends to follow a period of major disaster. But the proposal was also a practical necessity since a number of inter-war problems—such as the final peace settlement of boundaries particularly in east Europe, and especially in the case of Poland—had created difficulties in the relations between the Western allies and the USSR. It was therefore hoped that the League's successor would help to sort out such problems. The Western allies and the USSR also wanted to prevent such a collapse of world trade and finance as had followed the First World War, and they were looking to what became the United Nations to assist in stabilizing the world economy.

The origins of the future UN were closely linked with Anglo-American determination that the post-war reconstruction of the world should bear a Western imprint and not be stamped too decisively with the Hammer and Sickle. At the time when Germany attacked Russia in June 1941, thus forcing Stalin to take sides against Hitler and putting Russia into harness with Britain and her allies, America had still not taken up the fight against Nazism. American forces, however, were already operating on the basis of 'All aid short of war', and the 'lend-lease' system had been initiated early in 1941 to provide Britain with material backing. But once Russia was precipitated into the Second World War by the German attack, Churchill and Roosevelt realized that they must draw up a general programme of post-war aims since these would vitally influence the conduct of the war, and could be designed to exercise, it was hoped, some restraint on the powerful Soviet state.

Churchill and Roosevelt held a series of meetings on board ships in Argentia Bay, Newfoundland, from 9–12 August 1941. They drew up an Anglo-American declaration of principles concerning the conduct of the war and their hopes for the future. This declaration was endorsed by Britain's allies, including Russia, and was published on 15 September 1941. Both powers formally renounced the seizure of territory and other forms of aggrandizement, and added that they were opposed to territorial alterations made against the will of peoples. Britain and America also stated that they respected the right of other peoples to choose their own form of government. The powers also promised to support arrangements which would give access to economic resources for all states on equal terms, and would generally aid growth of economic co-operation. The peace which would end the Second World War must provide not only freedom from fears caused by want but also freedom from fears of war which crippled the nations with heavy armaments bills. In order to achieve the desired peace the nations must disarm, or be disarmed, so that a general and permanent system of security could be established. To reinforce the fact that what became popularly known as the Atlantic Charter constituted the basis of the Allied aims, on 1 January 1942—after the Japanese attack on Pearl Harbour in December 1941 brought the USA into the war—a joint declaration was put out by the twenty-six states now fighting the Axis powers affirming their loyalty and support for the declaration.

But it was already evident from Soviet wartime diplomacy, and particularly in her desire to set up a militarily reliable *cordon communiste* of states in eastern Europe, that the Atlantic Charter required hard work and effort if it was ever to be translated from theory into practice. Western statesmen such as Churchill were fully aware of the danger of an increase of Russian power in eastern Europe and possibly in Germany itself. There was little, however, which they could do about this alteration partly because of the debt which the Western powers owed to Russia which bore the brunt of German arms and partly because, as mentioned earlier, they needed to retain Russian good will for the expected long-drawn-out struggle to overcome Japan in the Far East after Hitler had been crushed in the West. At later wartime conferences Stalin was not tardy in reminding his Western allies about Russian losses, especially since they were slow to launch the Second Front. As a result east European states such as Poland were to all intents and purposes already subject to Russian neo-territorial aggrandizement—via Communist puppet régimes—by the close of the Second World War. Meanwhile the dropping of the atom bomb prevented the long hard slog in the

Far East by Russia against Japan, the assumption which had lain behind much of the Western complacency towards Russia, but by then Russia had consolidated her position in eastern Europe.

Despite these contra-indications for the success of a new international institution to breathe fresh life into the work attempted by the League of Nations from 1920 onwards,[1] most of the nations fighting on the Allied side in the Second World War favoured the establishment of the United Nations. Whatever the Russians thought of such Western-derived institutions, they were willing to allow grandiloquent declarations to be made on their behalf.

A conference was held in Moscow on 1 November 1943 attended by representatives of Britain, America, Russia and China (then controlled by Chiang Kai Shek's Nationalist government) to discuss the future international institution. The communiqué issued afterwards stated that the four powers recognized 'the necessity of establishing at the earliest practicable date a general international organization, based on the principle of the sovereign equality of all peace-loving states, and open to membership by all such states, large or small, for the maintenance of international peace and security'. It was agreed to hold another meeting on the subject and this took place from August to October 1944 at Dumbarton Oaks, Washington, between representatives of the same four major powers. At the Dumbarton Oaks Conference the four powers agreed to set up the United Nations as a body similar to the League of Nations but with important differences.

It was realized that it was essential to prevent the United Nations from being weakened as the League had been either because major powers like America refused to join or because they felt that their interests were slighted and so decided to leave the association. In order to strengthen the United Nations in this way it was agreed that five major powers (France was now added to the other four) should operate as the controlling or management committee of the UN, which was to be termed the Security Council. These five states would be permanent members of the Security Council and would be aided in their task by six other states elected each for a two-year term by the General Assembly. This solution to one problem of the League created its own major problem. The point was nicely made by the cartoonist, David Low, on 25 September 1944 with a drawing of four policemen's uniforms labelled Britain, America, Russia and China (with France omitted as a make-weight) and captioned

[1] The League formally ceased existence in 1946.

'Who's to police the policeman?' If this fear troubled the public, it also troubled the three main powers, Britain, America and Russia. At the Yalta Conference between Stalin, Roosevelt and Churchill from 4 to 11 February 1945 it was agreed that the permanent members of the Security Council should be enabled to protect their interests by voting individually against a resolution. One vote, therefore, could veto a resolution on substantive or important matters even if the necessary affirmative vote of seven members could be achieved by the voting together of the other permanent and non-permanent members of the Security Council.

The Yalta Conference also saw an agreement reached that procedural matters along with other preliminary issues should be discussed at San Francisco in April 1945. This meeting took place from 25 April to 26 June 1945 and drew up the UN Charter and also the Statute of the International Court of Justice, the main judicial organ of the UN. Earlier at the Dumbarton Oaks Conference, Russia had tried to persuade the Western powers to grant a seat in the General Assembly to all the republics which were members of the Union of Soviet Socialist Republics. At this time there were sixteen such republics, but now Russia, feeling that her position at the UN was safeguarded by the veto in the Security Council, agreed that the Russian republics should only have three seats in the General Assembly and thus three votes there. The three states so represented were Russia itself, i.e. the Russian Soviet Federal Socialist Republic, the Byelorussian Soviet Socialist Republic and that of the Ukraine.

By June 1945 the preliminary conference on the UN at San Francisco had completed the draft charter of the UN which was then signed by the forty-six allies of the Western powers. On 24 October 1945 the UN entered into formal existence with fifty-one member-states. The close links between the phenomenon of world war and the UN were brought out clearly in the preamble to the Charter which stated that the peoples of the UN—and not, as might have been expected, the 'states'—were :

determined to save succeeding generations from the scourge of war, which twice in our lifetime has brought untold sorrow to mankind.

These 'peoples', however, were also determined to respect human rights, equal rights for men and women and also :

to establish conditions under which justice and respect for the obligations arising from treaties and other sources of international law can be maintained...

In addition, the peoples were 'to promote social progress and better standards of life in larger freedom'. In order to achieve these aims the peoples would practise tolerance to one another, would 'unite our strength to maintain international peace and security', would use methods in international politics excluding use of arms 'save in the common interest', and would also 'employ international machinery for the promotion of the economic and social advancement of all peoples'.[2]

In 1945 the Western powers and their allies had grounds for feeling euphoric. They had won a major war which, whatever their precise motives for involvement, had constituted in almost all cases a serious threat to the continued existence of their traditional states. But, as can be seen, the hard facts of power politics were already intruding into the development of the UN which at this stage was in part an institution embodying serious long-term hopes for controlling the anarchy of international relations through the concept of 'a common interest' and disarmament, and in part simply a postwar pact to maintain the wartime co-operation of the Western powers and their allies and to ensure that fascism was not merely trodden underfoot but rubbed out in the dust. Russia had already taken the lead, which other major powers behind the scenes were willing to benefit from, in obtaining veto power in the Security Council which not only prevented any decision being taken which ran counter to the wishes of a major power but also gave those major powers far greater institutional competence within the UN than was granted to the General Assembly even though it was composed of a greater number of states. The basic argument for this decision, as mentioned above, was that nothing of any importance could be done in a major international crisis unless the great powers were agreed. It was also evident that the UN needed a small executive committee like the Security Council for it already contained fifty-one states and would clearly grow if the decolonization emphasis of the Charter—through its stress on the equal rights of peoples and self-determination—was followed through. An even more basic

---

[2] References to the UN Charter text are taken throughout from H. G. Nicholas, *The United Nations as a Political Institution*, Oxford University Press, 1967, pp. 208–39.

point was that both the financial and military strength of the UN would clearly depend for the most part on the contributions of the major states, and since the UN was a voluntary contract, the good will of the major states in these respects was essential if the organization was to function at all.

But these points can also be regarded as merely positive statements of fundamentally negative positions in so far as the 'common interest' was a UN aim. In practice these factors meant that little or no action would be undertaken by the UN which was not approved of by all the main powers. There have, of course, been exceptions to this rule, such as the UN operation in Korea, but these exceptions depended in part on chance factors—such as Russia's momentary absence from the Security Council, or on either the General Assembly or the Secretary-General, and sometimes both, playing a stronger role in UN politics than originally designed for them. This is not to say that such departures from strict practice are wrong in the terms of wider politics, but they must always be fortuitous and are not to be relied upon since such operations are open to criticisms of illegality from the purists and depend in practice on concatenations of circumstances or the individual personality of successive Secretaries-General.

The UN was in theory an organization in which all states were equal but, in fact, as in ordinary life where people are concerned, the differences between the types of states were often more apparent than the similarities. The UN in 1945 began as an equal association of all its member-states but the hierarchical ranking according to power, economic, social and political, was already apparent. Under these circumstances the probability was that national power, backed by words, weapons and men, would often but not always defeat the general principles of equality outlined in the UN Charter. Hence decisions and actions of the UN although emanating from an 'international' institution are often not truly international but merely 'para-international', that is to say they represent a convenient and widely accepted method for making decisions by the major powers palatable to contemporary egalitarian taste.

Yet statesmen in their national councils are different from those same statesmen when gathered together in the UN forum or discussing matters off-stage. Taking nineteenth- and twentieth-century international relations as a whole it is evident that the tradition of conference or parliamentary diplomacy is a growing one. The informal Concert of Europe gave way to the League of Nations and that in its turn gave place to the much stronger UN. Talk can serve as a mimic form of warfare and prevent weapons going off. Since 1945 the UN has reduced international tension through providing men with an important and well-publicized forum for verbal release. World War III has so far been avoided. But when we look at the wider context of changes in international politics, it becomes clear that the role of the UN, although evidently useful and growing, should not be exaggerated. The relative stabilization of drives in international relations evident in the period 1945–71 owes much to the danger of nuclear warfare and the consequent nuclear balance achieved between the Russian and American super-powers. It also owes a great deal to the re-shaping of Europe carried out by Russia at the end of the Second World War, that is the division of Bismarck's modern Germany into two *de facto* states, the westernized democracy of West Germany and the communized one-party state of East Germany, along with the subjection of all the east European states to Russia's will either through the Warsaw Pact or by economic subordination through Comecon.[3] These factors, the nuclear balance, the territorial satisfaction or neo-territorial gains of Russia, the division of modern Germany into two manageable politico-economic units, and the military balance of East-West forces through the Warsaw and Nato Pacts, have cooled down the central European heartland which twice in less than fifty years triggered off world war.

II

Bearing in mind the existence of these other important factors, we may now examine the role played by the UN as an agency for the peaceful settlement of international disputes, which helps the world community. In the period 1945–70 there have been many such disputes, and the method of settlement has fallen into five main categories : (1) those settled by agreement; (2) those settled by force or a threat of force; (3) those settled tacitly by changes in relevant factors which have taken the heat out of the problem, mostly because the disputants have become distracted by other preoccupations; (4) those settled by economic sanctions or some form of economic pressure; (5) those which remain unsettled, with a high actual or potential tension level, and with active consideration still being given to the problem by the parties concerned. During the

[3] Council for Mutual Economic Assistance set up in January 1949.

K

period in question about half of the international disputes which occurred were ultimately settled without the use or threat of military force, and only some 14% were so settled. About 24% of the disputes were settled by agreement, and these were cases which—to use the term made familiar by Professor Roger Fisher of Harvard University—were capable of being *fractionated* or divided into negotiable elements. About 18% were settled by changes in relevant factors, 6% were settled by economic pressures while about 38% remain (1970) unsettled.[4]

Of the cases which remain unsettled many of these are old disputes and particularly intransigent to settlement. The main conclusion which can be drawn from these approximate figures is that the basic material of international-relations disputes is not so resistant towards peaceful settlement as is sometimes stated. But whether or not such peaceful settlement can be achieved through an international institution like the UN is a different matter. It is clear, however, that while the value of negotiations in relation to disputes should not be overlooked, the high percentage—some 18%—of cases where tension was alleviated by changes in relevant factors does suggest that it would be better for the states concerned, and the UN, to try to get results not by frontal negotiations (which probably only harden attitudes) but by modifying contextual factors. It is also evident that economic sanctions tend to be a relatively weak international weapon, either because states fear the damage which may hit their own economies, or because there are doubts about whether the necessary high degree of implementation can be achieved.

III

We may now consider more closely what the UN's role has been in the settlement of disputes and crises during the twenty-five years of its existence. Undoubtedly, the organization's peacekeeping role is, and is bound to remain, a difficult one. It is an *international* institution attempting to put into practice a code of behaviour laid down in the Charter; but it is composed of *nation states* whose sovereignty, however diluted, still includes the claim to independent decision-making in foreign policy. Put in these simple terms the UN

---

[4] These remarks are based on an article by M. J. Grieve, *Political Studies*, Oxford University Press, 1970, No. 1, Vol. XVIII, March 1970, 'The United Nations and the Settlement of International Disputes', pp. 126–33.

seems an unworkable institution and yet it works. The reason is that the nations, although they still jealously guard their right to say 'no', realize that they do *need* the world organization. Proof of this acceptance of the UN can be seen in a variety of different ways. UN membership is prized, for almost every month new members take their places and others apply to join, while none of the major states has left the institution. Indonesia left the UN in January 1965, only to return later. Also, in the 1945–70 period, some 80% of the world's disputes came before the UN for scrutiny.

Often, however, the UN simply served as an arena where protagonists discharged their accumulated anger and bitterness. But it would be foolish to dismiss this function—the importance of having one's case heard on the international public scene—as mere propaganda-making. Man does need to communicate his thoughts and feelings and to act them out. This aspect of the UN's work has been brilliantly caught by Conor Cruise O'Brien :

> Why, men often ask, does the United Nations not *act*? The answer is that it seldom does anything else : it is acting all the time. Almost all action, of course, involves an element of acting, in the theatrical sense; sociologists remind us of the number of *roles* we all play in our daily domestic, social and professional lives. National politics also, whether democratic or authoritarian in form, has always required play-acting, symbolism and ritual.[5]

The public debates of the UN are in some ways equivalent to the psychiatrist's couch where the patient 'talks away' his problems, and in the process acquires a new identity. The time spent in public talk can allow some of the heat to escape from acute crises.

The mimic-war aspect of UN debates has been mentioned earlier. One writer who made a detailed study of the Cyprus problem from 1954–58 commented that 'the Assembly thus becomes an arena of conflict-harmonization or a center of harmonization-conflict'.[6] Apart from its public forum, the UN in addition provides the scene for off-stage, private and probably more productive talks. Delegates in such talks are free from the need to take up postures for the world press, free also from the need to make propaganda; they can engage in serious dialogue with their opponents. Ministers can visit the UN to see the Secretary-General and can then also see their colleagues

---

[5] *The United Nations—Sacred Drama*, London, 1968, p. 9.
[6] Stephen G. Xydis, *Cyprus—Conflict and Conciliation, 1954–1958*, Ohio, 1967, p. 540.

from other countries in freedom from the pressures which attend state visits. Modern history has many ironies and few pleasant ones but one of the latter is that President Wilson's concept of 'open diplomacy' should have led in the course of time to an international agency which provides, behind its public façade, some of the pre-conditions for successful private diplomacy.

Critics of the UN who are irritated because it functions through its anomalies rather than the forms prescribed in the Charter often ask why it does not act or do more in relation to international crises. Often this question is asked by people who are sympathetic towards the UN but fail to realize to what a great extent it was a limited creation of the major powers, and hence hampered from the beginning in playing a truly independent role in world politics. The UN is criticized as though it had the powers of a non-territorial super-state. But if it were such an institution the UN would have independent powers such as the right to levy taxes to pay for its plans and the right to enforce disarmament so that peacekeeping operations could succeed, and so that major powers as much as minor powers were subject to the UN will. It would also have its own supranational force and not, as at present, small forces raised on an *ad hoc* basis once a crisis has developed. But when the UN began it was set up by the victorious states which had just won a major war and whose sense of statehood was thereby enhanced. These states were willing to make large promises in the name of their 'peoples' but they were also determined to leave the fulfilment of those promises to chance.

From its early years one vital factor inhibited the UN's success in peacekeeping. The premise of the UN, like its predecessor, the League of Nations, was that while it was agreed by Article 2 (3) that 'All Members shall settle their international disputes by peaceful means in such a manner that international peace and security, and justice, are not endangered', this must be accompanied by progressive disarmament. During the war years and up to 1945, disarmament was taken to mean reductions by balanced quotas in the conventional weapons by which territorial gains were made. Had war technology remained at this level, it is conceivable that the lessons of two world wars within twenty-one years might have had an effect in facilitating disarmament. It is important to remember that it was this sort of traditional military technology which lies behind the military clauses and collective security theme in the UN Charter. The Charter was not designed in the light of modern military technology, that of the atom bomb and all the variations later developed, although it is probable that the restraints on war caused by possession of these weapons have contributed to a major degree to the creation of general peace which has given the UN some chance of success.

Bearing this caution in mind we can now look at the military provisions of the UN Charter. It was carefully drawn up to reserve rights of individual or collective self-defence against armed attack (Article 51). This assumed that states would retain their own armed forces and also allowed them to enter into bilateral or multi-lateral collective security arrangements 'until the Security Council has taken measures necessary to maintain international peace and security'. Similarly, because a number of regional organizations already existed, or might come into being, the function of such organizations, both as regards collective security and peacekeeping, was accepted 'provided that such arrangements or agencies and their acitivities are consistent with the Purposes and Principles of the United Nations', and also provided that 'no enforcement action shall be taken under regional arrangements or by regional agencies without the authorization of the Security Council' except in self-defence or relating to the ending of the Second World War. These arrangements, as can be seen in Articles 52–54 of the Charter, indicated that in so far as these clauses went the UN role was to be supervisory and of first and last resort, but not itself taking action. In effect this meant that since the UN was a new international institution, its control or influence over such regional organizations might be small. If we look at the operations of the Warsaw Pact and its NATO counterpart, it can be seen that the UN influence is in fact small. In respect of regional organizations the UN Charter expressed the pious hope that these organizations would work with the UN for peace and not against it.[7]

The novelty of the UN thus did not lie in the provisions relating to individual or collective self-defence nor those concerning regional organizations. The novelty or hopes for future improvements in international collective security lay in the clauses which concern action of the UN itself 'with respect to threats to the Peace, Breaches of the Peace, and Acts of Aggression'. Unlike the Council of the League of Nations, the UN Security Council had principal respon-

[7] One side effect of the acceptance of regional organizations, and the encouragements to disputants to try to settle matters without prior recourse to the UN, is sometimes to harden and complicate the dispute. This effect of Article 33, paragraph 1, has been noted by one writer on Cyprus. See Xydis, *op. cit.*, pp. 532–33.

sibility for maintaining international peace and security. It is the duty of the Security Council to 'determine the existence of any threat to the peace, breach of the peace, or act of aggression' and to recommend what action should be taken (Article 39). Initially the Security Council can call on parties at issue to take provisional steps to cool the situation and can call on the UN members to undertake general sanctions against the offenders, including 'complete or partial interruption of economic relations and of rail, sea, air, postal, telegraphic, radio and other means of communication, and the severance of diplomatic relations' (Articles 40–41). If the economic and other sanctions provided for in Article 41 prove insufficient, the Security Council may call for action including 'demonstrations, blockade, and other operations by air, sea, or land forces of Members of the United Nations' (Article 42).

The UN force which the Security Council was to use should these measures prove insufficient was to be provided by units of the member-states' forces which were to be kept in readiness for UN action. The UN force, it must be noted, was not to be maintained separately from national forces. This decision was in keeping with the fact that the UN was not a super-state or world government. It meant, however, that in so far as the provisions in Chapter VII of the Charter have been implemented, UN forces are *ad hoc* forces, created in times of emergency and with all the difficulties which this implies. Often, as for instance in Cyprus and in the Congo, these UN forces have worked together extremely well after an initial nerve-racking period for commanders caused by different kinds of military training, command systems and language problems. Some UN officials prefer this *ad hoc* method of raising forces and make a merit of necessity since they feel satisfaction in being able to rise to the necessary levels in a crisis. But it is hardly a system to be commended. Often, quite apart from budget problems, such *ad hoc* forces as UNFICYP or the UN force in Cyprus operate with contingents barely within a margin of safety because nations have promised forces or sizes of forces which do not materialize,[8] either because the state concerned was over-optimistic, or due to national crises which have taken up most of the available state forces.

Even countries like Britain, whose ministers tend to take pride in supporting the UN, in practice find that their defence ministers

[8] James A. Stegenga, *The United Nations Force in Cyprus*, Ohio, 1968, p. 84. Britain was one of the main offenders whose forces did not reach the planned target, but she was also one of the *handful* of states which provided UN contingents.

show little interest in UN forces. As one recent book by a soldier who served as Chief of Staff to UNFICYP from 1966–68 has shown, the British Ministry of Defence seemed indifferent. The writer comments that 'Apart from one visit in the month before I was due to give up my post, no military member of the Army Board or head of a senior department of the Ministry of Defence visited either the British contingent or UNFICYP headquarters throughout my twenty-seven months as Chief of Staff'. But such members and such ministers frequently made top-level visits to the sovereign bases in Cyprus. Nor has the British Army undergone any specialized training for its UN work, and the writer found that, contrary to common opinion, the British soldier was not particularly suited to UN work since he was more accustomed to aiding civil powers than playing a neutral role between disputants. The same neglect is indicated by the fact that while other nations have carried out detailed studies on the participation of their military units in UN work, no such British work has been done.[9]

No doubt other or similar weaknesses would be found if contingents apart from the British were examined, since the central problem is clearly the pull between national and regional commitments on the one side, and on the other the less firm commitments made by nation-states to the UN. Harold Wilson, the British Prime Minister, addressed the United Nations Association's Annual General Council on the occasion of its twenty-fifth anniversary held from 17–19 April 1970. Amongst other pledges of British aid to the UN, he mentioned that large contributions of men and money had been made to UNFICYP and that in future Britain would offer up to six battalions of logistic backing for UN peacekeeping. But these sorts of statement are not binding commitments and, in any case, electoral changes also must be allowed for, so the problem between requirements for peacekeeping and fulfilment of promises—such as this British one—remains. Clearly, from the military angle of peacekeeping, the UN would be better served by its own body of men, trained specially for UN work, rather than miscellaneous national units sometimes headed by superannuated unworthies. But any UN decision is a political one, and this military matter remains as determined in 1945 because the UN member-states still do not trust each other sufficiently to wish to set up a strong UN military body, even one designed specially for peacekeeping.

[9] Michael Harbottle, *The Impartial Soldier*, Oxford University Press, 1970, pp. 184–5. See also pp. 189–90.

When these arrangements for providing a UN force were being drawn up in 1945, it was evident that both the political importance of any military action by the UN and the type of force to be provided necessitated establishment of some central military control. The form chosen was the Military Staff Committee which was 'to advise and assist the Security Council on all questions relating to the Security Council's military requirements for the maintenance of international peace and security, the employment and command of forces placed at its disposal, the regulation of armaments, and possible disarmament' (Article 47(1)). The highly important composition of the MSC was to be determined in two ways : firstly, it was to 'consist of the Chiefs of Staff of the permanent members of the Security Council or their representatives'; secondly, 'Any Member of the United Nations not permanently represented on the Committee shall be invited by the Committee to be associated with it when the efficient discharge of the Committee's responsibilities requires the participation of that Member in its work' (Article 47(2)). The MSC was to be 'responsible under the Security Council for the strategic direction of any armed forces placed at the disposal of the Security Council'. It was also agreed by the same article, (47(3)), that 'Questions relating to the command of such forces shall be worked out subsequently'. In addition, under Article 47(4), the MSC could be authorized by the Security Council 'and after consultation with appropriate regional agencies' to set up 'regional sub-committees'.

It is important to note that no UN force was ever put into action under the MSC system of control.[10] The MSC question was discussed from 1945 to 1948, but as the Cold War developed difficulties in reaching agreement between East and West multiplied and work ceased in July 1948.

One of the problems involved concerns establishing an agreed UN definition of 'aggression'. How to define 'aggression' has been a matter of study since the time of the League of Nations. The matter has been discussed intermittently by the UN, and a General Assembly Resolution 2330 (XXII) of 18 December 1967 was passed in favour of setting up a Special Committee on the Question of Defining Aggression. The Special Committee first met in the

[10] One result of the check to the MSC's work has been that there is UN civilian co-ordination of military operations. This has been criticized on military grounds but there are, of course, political factors involved, so perhaps this criticism is misplaced.

summer of 1968 and its work was extended to allow for a further session in 1969. In 1968 the Committee's work was affected by the Warsaw Pact powers' invasion of Czechoslovakia, since the Western members of the UN tended to refer repeatedly to this case of 'aggression'. The USA had doubted the value of trying to define aggression and now argued that even if it were defined this would not stop aggression. The east European states which had shown most interest in arriving at a definition of aggression were then forced on to the defensive, and interchanges became counter-productive. The attitude of the USSR has remained that it was important to define aggression since this will enable fuller application of the relevant articles of the UN Charter concerning collective security and would also strengthen international law. Various draft definitions were considered by the Special Committee in February 1969, but this session ran into procedural problems. A working party was set up, but it merely adopted an ambiguous report, and aggression remained undefined.[11]

IV

A similarly extensive and intensive debate has gone on since 1945 on the role of peacekeeping. The term itself denotes a static function, maintenance of the peace, but this begs the question of change and development which break up the peace. As mentioned earlier, the main emphasis of the UN Charter in so far as military action was concerned related to the major powers of 1945, the winners of World War II. Hence the peace to be kept was the peace they had won and the peace they were to establish.

The views of the USSR on peace were threefold. First, peace in eastern Europe meant, primarily, securing Russia against the possibility that a revived Germany could ever again stab Russia through the weak line of states set up under the Treaty of Versailles. Russia's determination to have military security, the *cordon communiste*, meant that early in the war, she had pre-empted eastern Europe and was staking out her claims by supporting Communist governments in exile. Thus from 1945 the USSR was not willing to allow the UN to interfere with her military security in east Europe. From the beginning continental Europe was divided in two and the UN's peacekeeping writ would not run in the eastern half. In pursuit of military security, the Russians also divided into two parts modern

[11] See *International Conciliation*, New York, 1969, September 1969, No. 574, pp. 175–9.

Germany, Bismarck's overpowerful creation, which had thrice pre-cipitated important wars—two of them world wars—in less than seventy years. In fact on the Russian interpretation of matters, Germany was split into three parts, since the Russians argue that West Berlin and West Germany are two separate entities.

While to Russia peace in eastern and central Europe meant essentially maintaining the *status quo* established at the end of the Second World War, the second and third aspects of Russia's foreign policy—concerning south-east Asia and new states in continents such as Africa—were less defined. Caution was the Russian watch-word towards the rise of other socialist or Communist states, and Russian policy was not based so much on Communist ideology as on traditional power politics. The ambiguous Russian attitude towards the rise of Communist China illustrates this approach,[12] and it has become increasingly clear in the late 1960s that Russian fears of China as a powerful Far Eastern competitor state for the moment outweigh ideological Communist ties.

None the less what can be described as Russia's passive rather than active support for potentially nascent Communism in Africa and Asia has from time to time posed serious problems for UN peacekeeping in these regions, not least in Egypt. Perhaps the most important effect of the divisive influence of the Russian Communist bias in foreign policy and the American capitalist drive has been that these super-powers have segmented the globe into regions which are tactily understood to be their spheres of influence. Latin America, despite the existence of the UN, remains under the Ameri-can aegis in the tradition of the Monroe Doctrine just as east Europe is within the Russian sphere.

In Africa and Asia the situation is more ambivalent. America has shown comparatively little interest in Africa and has concentrated on checking Communism in Europe, the Far East and Latin America. America has seemed willing, after having helped to defeat her old imperial ally, Britain, during the Suez crisis of 1956, to allow Russia to fall heir to British influence in north Africa generally. In south-east Asia Russia has been content to see America waste her substance and destroy her moral prestige by warring against Com-munism in Vietnam and Cambodia. But it is one thing to tolerate an unsuccessful American war in south-east Asia and another altogether if America seemed to be winning. But, so long as America

[12] Russia gave little or no aid to Mao Tse tung in the years before he won China for communism in 1949.

loses, Russia seems willing to allow the local Communists to be slaughtered and to leave active intervention, whether in terms of men or propaganda, to her more revolutionary Communist colleague, China.

China has also tended to make the pace in Africa below the Sahara desert. The Africans, however, intent on their own problems, have been willing to take aid wherever it is offered, but have kept their own counsel. They also have become resistant to UN peacekeeping, fearing that it makes their disputes a microcosm of Communism versus capitalism, and the OAU, or Organization of African Unity, in effect put up a 'keep out' sign over the Nigeria-Biafra conflict, and was more willing to see the dispute ended by war, and arms supplies from Britain, the former imperialist power, than to allow UN involvement. Thus regionalism poses a serious problem to UN influence and action. As mentioned earlier, the UN was based on a recognition of *de facto* conditions prevailing in international power politics and from the start accepted regional organizations provided that they did not act contrary to the aims of the UN (see above, p. 283).

Thus it can be seen that UN peacekeeping operates, if at all, under severe limitations. It was never intended to be able to control the main powers, particularly those represented permanently on the Security Council, unless they acquiesced. The UN lacks the power to do this but it is possible that some fortunate combination of circumstances might at some future date allow the ethical principles of the UN to triumph and influence a dispute between major powers or even super-powers. This is possible but it must also be admitted improbable. The consequence of this limitation on UN powers is that when a major confrontation occurs as over the Cuba missile crisis between Russia and America in 1962, there is little that the UN can do to influence the situation. Yet to that mythical figure, the man in the Western street,[13] the main reason for the existence of the UN is fear of war, major or minor, apart from economic and social work. The expectation that the UN is or should be able to discipline the major powers is also constantly reinforced by UN statements criticizing or condemning selfish unilateral acts by these powers. But although the direct ability of the UN to con-

---

[13] As one American writer noted, while the Western world tends to rate the UN according to its ability to deal with threats to the peace in many other countries, in the emergent world, 'an emphasis on economic and social problems might get first rating'. Maurice Waters, *The United Nations*, New York, 1967, p. viii.

trol major powers engaged in a dispute is weak, we must also remember the more impalpable factor of long-term UN influence exerted in favour of justice in international relations. This influence is not easy to judge and therefore it is all too easy to forget or dismiss it, which would be wrong.

We have seen that the UN was not intended, and is not able, to act effectively in disputes between major powers. There has been one important exception to this rule, but the Suez crisis of 1956 must be studied carefully. It is clear that the UN played a significant role both during and after this episode and the reasons why it was able to do so are important. America decided not to back Britain whose serious aim of maintaining free passage of international waterways had been muddied over by Anglo-French-Israeli collusion[14] and Prime Minister Eden's desire to topple Nasser from power in Egypt.[15] It was America which finally put the screws on Britain and made her back down by making it clear that she would not continue to support the pound sterling. There were other problems such as the military weaknesses shown by Britain in the operation. More important, America and Russia were for once agreed on the policy to pursue, and were backed by an exceptionally wide range of world opinion, including many of the Commonwealth countries. There was also a serious crisis of confidence in Britain itself, and all in all the disputants were willing to back down. The moral of the Suez crisis was that the super-powers if agreed can most effectively control major powers and can use the UN as a mechanism to clear up a difficult and embarrassing diplomatic situation. This conclusion was the original justification for creation of the UN Security Council in the form chosen, but it is a rare example.

v

We have seen that the UN cannot exercise much direct influence during a crisis between the super-powers and also that super-power agreement to discipline major powers through the UN is a rare occurrence. This process of elimination leaves the minor states to

[14] On this subject, see Anthony Nutting, *No End of a Lesson*, London, 1967; Hugh Thomas, *The Suez Affair*, London, 1967; D. C. Watt, *Documents on the Suez Crisis*, London, 1957; Alan James, *The Politics of Peacekeeping*, London, 1969.
[15] Nutting, *No End of a Lesson*, and Sir A. Eden, *Full Circle*, London, 1960.

be considered. The exercise of UN peacekeeping in relation to minor states has been principally of two types. Firstly, the UN in its earlier years was mobilized by America as an agency to help it in its struggle against world-wide Communism. Secondly, the UN was also used by a wide spectrum of its member-states, old and new, to accelerate or control the process of decolonization.

Of all the cases coming before the UN from 1945–70, the UN has played a significant role in four main instances, i.e. the Korean War, the Suez crisis and those concerning Lebanon-Jordan and the Congo. The Korean War was the first of the four cases in which the UN played a major role, and like the other three cases it concerned an aspect of decolonization which in this case was complicated by the Communist question. Three important factors go a long way to explaining why the UN was able to mount the Korean operation : Russia's fortuitous absence from the Security Council, dissatisfaction in the General Assembly with the so-called 'veto' of Security Council powers in checking UN action, and American anti-Communist feeling. As a result a UN force took the field in Korea, largely provided with American military manpower and officered by General MacArthur.[16]

The Korean campaign demonstrated what was to be a continuous difficulty for American foreign policy in the 1950s to 1960s, whether acting independently or through the UN, that although America might have military strength—including the atom bomb and later the nuclear bomb—the political restraints operating in non-total war would prevent such a war being waged to the extent necessary for military success. In this case when General MacArthur, faced by heavy inflows of Communist Chinese troops, wished to raid their bases in Manchuria, to call on Chiang Kai Shek for aid from the nationalist Chinese forces and even seemed to threaten use of the atom bomb, he was recalled by President Truman in April 1951. An armistice was signed on 27 July 1953 and Korea remained divided into two countries along the 38th parallel which had been the situation before the Communist North Koreans had invaded South Korea. A demilitarized zone was established between the two states and observation of the armistice is carried out by the Supervisory Commission of neutral states. Periodically the armistice is violated and disputes occur, but up to 1970 the situation, although not finally settled by a peace agreement, has been contained. As one authority on the UN concludes :

[16] James, *The Politics of Peacekeeping*, pp. 197–8, 376–81.

Thus the latter end of the Korean affair, inevitably, was a good deal less resounding and, from the point of view of the U.N., less heartening than its beginning. Nevertheless, it could be claimed, with reason, that although the war did not result in the full attainment of the U.N.'s objective of a unified, democratic, and independent Korea, it did demonstrate that aggression could be halted and an invader thrown back.[17]

The closing of the Korean War by the armistice agreement of 1953 caused Communist ambitions to be diverted from that region into Indo-China where they were already operative. When the French gave up the battle in Indo-China, the USA took up the struggle and has found it similarly a ploughing of the sands. One of the lessons of the Korean War had been that America would almost certainly have taken action against the North Koreans even had there been no UN. When she was drawn into the attempt to hold back Communism in Indo-China, the USA did not draw the UN with her although individual states such as Australia have sent contingents of troops and other states such as Britain have associated themselves with her anti-Communist action, or more accurately have failed to disassociate themselves from it. After the Korean episode, changes in the membership of the UN with the inflow of the Afro-Asian states, many of whom were trying to pursue neutral non-aligned policies in the Cold War between East and West, rendered the atmosphere in the General Assembly unfavourable towards any American attempt to repeat the UN's involvement in a direct clash with Communism. This alteration tended to concentrate the UN's peacekeeping work on aspects of decolonization.

The most notable of these cases, leaving aside the Suez crisis, was the Congo operation of 1960–63. This case of active UN peacekeeping—as distinct from later and lesser exercises in holding the ring between disputants as in Cyprus—occurred just before the wave of UN successes petered out, and in itself contributed to this change. Dag Hammarskjöld, the most influential Secretary-General to date, was killed in a plane crash. From the peacekeeping angle, the UN's action in the Congo was extremely successful, especially in view of the *ad hoc* nature of the operation. But the UN's very success was turned into a weapon against it, partly because of traditional pacifist types of view that somehow the UN should win

[17] Nicholas, *The United Nations as a Political Institution*, p. 55.

battles without bloodshed, but even more because the Congo episode showed the difficulty of external forces taking sides in civil war.

Major peacekeeping action of this type by the UN was rendered unlikely to occur again in the near future because the operation caused a serious UN financial crisis, and powers such as the USSR and France which had not approved intervention later refused to pay their share of the costs. The new Afro-Asian states also were not induced to expose their territories to similar UN peacekeeping should future disputes occur because they had seen the Congo become a battlefield of Communist and capitalist ambitions on a reduced scale. It was also apparent to them that UN peacekeeping in some ways was a brand of weakness in the immediate post-colonial period, and as time passed and they became more confident, they preferred to turn to their own organizations such as OAU, or even, as mentioned earlier, to rely on decisive aid from former colonial powers such as Britain in the case of the Nigeria-Biafra war of 1967–70 or France in relation to her former African states. The check to future UN action of this type was also indicated by the USSR's proposed 'troika' arrangement, i.e. the suggestion that there should be three Secretaries-General, representing respectively the Communist, Western and non-aligned states. This proposal was not pressed through but clearly the fact that it had been made rendered it likely that U Thant, the new Secretary-General, would play a less active role than his predecessor. The importance of the keying-down of the Secretary-General's influence in relation to the more passive UN policy since the early 1960s cannot be overlooked. This loss of dynamic, combined with the fact that the earlier UN operations tended to be against left politics in new states and the rise in the number of new left-ist governments in the UN, has produced in the later 1960s a relatively static UN.[18]

[18] Perhaps the deadlock may now be easing slightly. In 1969 a working party of the Special Commitee on Peacekeeping Operations (Commitee 33) studied Model 1 peacekeeping concerning UN military observers. The June 1969 progress report of the working party indicated that agreement had been reached on 'authorization, establishment, and composition of observer missions created by the Security Council'. Private talks have given ground for belief that the USSR may be willing to allow study of Model 2 peacekeeping, including matters such as 'the participation of military contingents'. See *International Conciliation*, September 1969, No. 574, pp. 43–6.

VI

The success or non-success of the UN does not relate so much to good or bad use of the functions permitted under the Charter, but rather to historical changes in international politics. In its early stages the UN, if it took any peacekeeping action at all, tended in practice—whatever the original aim—to support right-wing international politics. The most significant single factor accounting for this right-wing bias was that America was not only the UN's most powerful supporter but was also much more active than Russia in trying to develop the UN as a successful international institution. Possibly if the USA had not provided the main force behind the UN's dynamic, it might by now have become as ineffective as the League of Nations. But while not depreciating American good will, it is evident that when the UN was successful, this occurred because the USA had decided that it should be so, and gave the decisive economic, military and political backing. This finding, like the earlier conclusion that the UN's main role permitted in the first twenty-five years of its existence by the world community is in decolonization, is a further severe limitation on the UN. If, in fact, as seems possible the USA intends to pursue a less active foreign policy and to concentrate more on domestic problems, UN peacekeeping of a major type is likely to decline although the need for it may rise.

It is also likely to contract because, as mentioned earlier, the new Afro-Asian states are now unwilling to expose their territories to the hazard of major UN peacekeeping, i.e. they are afraid that their regions may become miniature disaster areas for the working out of East-West tensions. If, however, the much spoken of but little realized East-West *détente* materializes further then this might provide one of the contextual factors necessary for major UN peacekeeping.

But, writing in 1970, the future of UN peacekeeping seems to lie in minor but important peacekeeping such as that which is being carried out at the moment in Cyprus by UNFICYP, while major issues of international disputes—such as that between the Arabs and Israel—tend increasingly to be dealt with by the main powers whose work, although linked sometimes with the UN, is largely by-passing it.

Both of these trends contain dangers. Probably the most serious issue of our day is the struggle for control of south-east Asia, yet both in relation to Vietnam and now Cambodia the UN is ineffective. Although it may be argued that the UN should concentrate on minor peacekeeping where it can hope to be successful, this argument cannot be accepted by those who wish to see the UN as an international peacekeeping institution become stronger. Even if this argument—in favour of minor peacekeeping—is merely criticized on its merits, we can see that it has problems. Discussing the Cyprus operation one writer commented :

> However, UNFICYP *is* vulnerable to the charge that it may very well be inhibiting settlement. By helping to protect and thus consolidate the abnormal *status quo* and by reducing the sense of urgency felt by both sides, the Force may actually be making a negative contribution to what in the long run is the most important requirement, a viable political order.[19]

Indeed, the very idea of 'holding the ring' between disputants, which is the UN function *vis-à-vis* the Cypriot Turks and Greeks, tends to encourage third parties to emerge, in this case Archbishop Makarios, for whom 'to a great extent the violence he precipitated in December of 1963 has paid off'.[20] In the case of Cyprus, however, the rule of Makarios is probably the only possible solution unless extensive bloodshed and fighting were permitted.

But will the third party solution always be the best result? This seems doubtful. The third party effect of UN intervention can be seen also in the case of the Congo, although this involved major and not minor UN peacekeeping. During the troubles the left leader, Patrice Lumumba, was maltreated and later murdered, while the right secessionist leader, Moïse Tshombe, was ultimately exiled and died in prison. UN peacekeeping, therefore, if successful, can be said to produce rulers who support the middle way, which is perhaps one of the reasons why it is not currently popular.

The present stalemate of the UN in peacekeeping, resulting from the balance of power between the USA and USSR, might have been broken by a swing towards supporting left-wing international politics. But this has not happened for the new Afro-Asian states try to maintain their role as a 'third force' in the General Assembly and the USSR cannot automatically count on their support nor are these new states necessarily left-wing. The stalemate has con-

[19] Stegenga, *The United Nations Force in Cyprus*, p. 186.
[20] *Ibid*, p. 154.

tinued since the early 1960s because the earlier trend towards using
the General Assembly as a means of initiating action if the Security
Council was blocked by the 'veto' ground to a halt as the super-
powers and intermediate major states realized that majority decisions of this type might just as easily go against as for them. In
practice this has meant that only one major UN peacekeeping
operation was started through the 'uniting for peace' resolution of
1950, i.e. the Korean case.[21] The other main cases of UN peacekeeping,[22] Suez-Gaza strip 1956–67 (UNEF), the Congo 1960–64
(ONUC), Dutch West Irian 1962–63 (UNTEA), and Cyprus 1964
to the present (UNFICYP) were initiated in the normal way
through the Security Council and with assent from the General
Assembly. There were, of course, dissenters in most of these cases,
but the resolution in favour of setting up UNFICYP was adopted
unanimously by the Security Council.[23]

The check to any hopes which the USSR may have had that the
American-oriented phase of the UN (due to the structure of the
General Assembly in the early days) would be followed by a
Russian-oriented UN (as the new Afro-Asian states became members) and would allow an increase of Russian action through the
Security Council was paralleled within the General Assembly itself.
For it soon became apparent that the new Afro-Asian states voted
according to individual needs and pressures and that these did not
form any strong pattern. To take one instance of this, these nations
have backed the fascist Franco régime in Spain because Franco
seemed willing to push the anti-colonial issue to the limit in the
case of Gibraltar. Not only were fears of a Soviet-controlled Afro-
Asian bloc proved wrong, but in addition it became clear that the
divisions within the Afro-Asian bloc itself in the General Assembly
meant that it did not operate along any united policy line and so
could not be said to have a clear and distinctive influence on UN
politics.

The difficulty of agreeing upon action through the UN leads not
infrequently to a would-be self-fulfilling diplomacy which is insufficiently based on study of the realities in international relations.
Policy, as over racialism for instance, degenerates into a series of
gestures designed to convince the African states that something is
being done and so to discourage them from independent action.

[21] Nicholas, *The United Nations as a Political Institution*, pp. 52–3.
[22] Leaving aside a number of smaller observer and other units.
[23] Stegenga, *The United Nations Force in Cyprus*, p. 70.

The Rhodesian sanctions are a case in point.[24] Applied too late and still too ineffectively, these sanctions are continued despite widespread African disbelief in their efficacy. Similarly, the selectivity of countries like America and Britain over racialism means that little is done against apartheid in South Africa. British trade and investment with South Africa, combined with the Simonstown Naval Base, allegedly make good relations with this country too important to interrupt. Britain and America have therefore refused at the UN to class South Africa as a threat to international peace but acquiesced in using this formula as the basis for the UN sanctions operation against Rhodesia. A large state, it seems, can get away with racialism but a small state will be pilloried for it. The UN will not grow stronger if such selective judgments persist.

The UN as it exists at present is not an international but merely a para-international institution, a halfway house on the way towards an institution which will have sufficient power, either granted to it by the nation-states or accepted by them as part of an agreed international code. Meanwhile the failure to achieve substantial disarmament and likewise to establish a permanent UN force has made the UN rely on the power of states such as the USA. This power has been expressed in many ways to aid UN operations. It was, for instance, a commonplace before the Cyprus peacekeeping to claim that without the help of the USA air force a peacekeeping operation could not get under way.[25] Sometimes the American pressure was economic as in the Dutch-Indonesia case of 1947 when the Dutch realized that Marshall aid would be cut unless their policy was altered. At other times the American method was diplomatic persuasion and as one writer on the Cyprus case comments, 'it is a reasonably safe speculation that American warnings to Turkey's leaders probably were as much of a deterrent as UNFICYP's presence on the island'.[26] At all times, whether American pressure to aid a UN peacekeeping operation or initiative was military, economic or political, beneath these levels it was largely American funds which kept the UN operative. To take only one case, that of Cyprus, America provided 44% of the funds needed for this peacekeeping operation. In addition, concerning the Cyprus case, although Russia, Nationalist China and France voted

---

[24] See M. J. Grieve, 'Economic Sanctions—Theory and Practice', *International Relations*, III, No. 6, October 1968.
[25] Stegenga, *The United Nations Force in Cyprus*, p. 157.
[26] Stegenga, *op. cit.*, p. 184.

for the UN operation, they have made no contributions towards it and none of the Communist countries has provided money or troops.[27] As this case, which is now generally considered the model for future UN peacekeeping operations, shows the American contribution is fundamental, and the need to rally other major states to act up to their commitments to the UN is pressing.

Initially, this need for the UN to rely on American help meant that the line between UN policy and American policy was blurred as in the case of the Korean War. Later, this difficulty was partly avoided because the main powers agreed tacitly that Cold War disputes or cases involving major problems with Communism should not come before the UN. Thus the difficulties in south-east Asian and the problems of east European states, such as Hungary in 1956 or Czechoslovakia in 1968, have been—token references apart—outside the UN cognizance as far as practical action is concerned. On the other hand, Russia has not been slow to remind the Western powers that should there be a danger of neo-Nazism or ultra-right-wing policies with their emphasis on frontier revision then Russia would invoke Articles 53 and 107 of the UN Charter to justify military action in West Germany to restore the *status quo*. More recently, as the Cyprus case indicates, Russia may vote in the Security Council for a UN peacekeeping operation but may then do nothing to help the UN carry out the authorized action. Although the Cyprus peacekeeping operation is not so much concerned with a theme of American policy as was the Korean War, the Russian abstention—at a time when Russia is seeking better relations with Greece—could be attributed partly to this aspect of her national diplomacy, but also may reflect the view that this UN operation is a 'save NATO' action in that Cyprus is a bone of contention between the two eastern Mediterranean pillars of NATO, Greece and Turkey.

Against a background of this complexity it is not surprising that UN peacekeeping operations, setting aside the vexed problem of inadequacies of mediation caused by lack of money, are weak on the negotiation side. It would be difficult for a UN peacekeeping operation to be strong on this aspect since this would require a political decision on the line of settlement to be pursued and this is precisely what is lacking. Hence the problem here for UN peacekeeping operations apart from their tendency to stabilize instability—as in the Cyprus case—is that they may bog down the UN for very long

[27] *Ibid.*, pp. 167-8.

periods of time, be costly, and encourage the view that continuance of a mission is a sign of effective peacekeeping which it clearly is not. The aim of any UN peacekeeping is to facilitate the emergence of a viable political settlement, not mere continuance of a peace-keeping mission.

VII

The Cold War, and the ever-present although currently muted East-West tensions, have made it well-nigh impossible for the UN to perform the expected assimilation function concerning divergent national aims in international relations. The constant need to rely upon the USA for one form of assistance or another has meant a sacrifice of ideals or of the desired international code. One of the assumptions underlying the creation of the Security Council was that the more power which a state had the more responsible it would be in the exercise of that power. But this argument of necessity ignored the fact that both the USA and the USSR were compara-tively new states and as such still exhibit strong aggressive drives. So, of course, do new states in the Afro-Asian bloc, although since their aggression is verbal rather than active, and is expressed in drives encouraged by the UN Charter, this aggression tends to be overlooked. Paradoxically, if the UN were more powerful, its revo-lutionary theme of change might lead to more rather than less international disputes and aggression.

The UN Charter is a battle hymn of change, but change can cause international crises and war. The pull between the theory of UN peacekeeping and change is only partly resolved by the synthe-sis 'good change'. In practice the UN member-states have been engaged since 1945 in setting limits to this process of change wher-ever it might conflict with national interests. The USA has been at work in Latin America using economic power and diplomacy, partly on a pragmatic basis and partly through the Organization of American States (the OAS), founded in 1948, to check the growth of Communism or left-wing governments. She has pursued the same task but with less success in Cuba and in south-east Asia.

Both Russia and America have preferred to keep the south-east Asian imbroglio away from the UN. Similarly, Russia has retained and strengthened her control over the east European states in the *cordon communiste,* with this process culminating in the Warsaw

Pact forces' invasion of Czechoslovakia in 1968 when Dubcek wanted to develop 'socialism with a human face'. The determination to retain power in these countries was expressed in Russia's Brezhnev doctrine, i.e. that no Communist state has total sovereignty but that sovereignty is limited in the interests of Communism.

America in pursuit of her aim of calling a halt to Communism persisted up to the spring of 1971 in her opposition to the entry of Communist China into the UN, and other states also have reservations on China's entry.[28] The difficulty lies not merely in the intransigence of recent Chinese foreign policy with its emphasis on repeated domestic revolutions and the export of revolution, but also in the fact that Nationalist China, which holds China's seat in the General Assembly, also holds a seat in the Security Council. Yet, clearly, China with its immense population (reaching about 800 million by 1970) and its capacity to cause problems in international relations should be in the UN. Sometimes those who oppose Chinese entry argue that China is not interested in becoming a member of the UN. But it is hardly surprising—in view of the repeated snubs to China when the annual resolution concerning her entry comes up and is turned down—that her public statements should show lack of interest, or indeed that they should condemn the UN as a tool of the USA. Yet China is interested as is shown by her interest in trying to create an Eastern-oriented rival to the UN during the Indonesian crisis. In addition, during 1969 the Chinese let it be known that they were interested in becoming a member of the UN.

The other major problem here is the question of Nationalist China. It has been suggested that one solution to the problem of Communist China's membership would be if she accepted the existence of Taiwan or Formosa by acquiescing in Chiang Kai-shek's government retaining a seat in the General Assembly. During the closing months of 1969 the Nixon administration tried to sound out the Chinese on this approach by referring to American willingness to accept the 'two Chinas'. But it is extremely difficult for the Communist Chinese to accept this solution since their national

[28] Typical voting figures were:

1966—proposal to seat the Chinese People's Republic:

     in favour—46; against—57; abstaining—17; absent—1;
1967—   ,, —45; ,, —58;   ,, —17; ,, —2;
1968—   ,, —44; ,, —58;   ,, —23; ,, —1.

In 1968 a proposal to set up a study commitee to report back to the General Assembly on the question of China's potential UN membership was also defeated by 67 votes to 30, with 27 abstentions and 2 absences.

pride is intense. It is known that during 1970 they made approaches themselves to the Nationalist Chinese government to see if some formula for the return of Taiwan to Communist Chinese suzerainty can be arranged. The question of Chinese entry to the UN may, therefore, have to be deferred until the Taiwan problem is settled, although American policy by 1971 favoured China's membership of the U.N.

VIII

To conclude, the political and peacekeeping functions of the UN remain underdeveloped in face of the vitality of nation states and their success in setting up zones of influence which severely restrict the UN's work : that of the USA in Latin America, western Europe and less successfully in south-east Asia, of the USSR in eastern Europe, and, more recently there have been indications—in relation to Nigeria—that the Organization of African Unity intends to keep the UN away from dealing with civil wars in new African states. If this trend continues the activity of the UN in peacekeeping will decline even further.

As a result of these checks, some theorists would prefer a less idealistic and more functional UN. But to attempt such a major change might merely destroy the very real degree of international- ization of economic and social assistance which the UN has achieved through its agencies (see Chapter 14).

Yet some reforms are needed and speedily. The élite division of power between the Security Council and General Assembly is out of date and should go; instead there should be one chamber with weighted voting. This method of voting, as the EEC example has shown, encourages attempts to obtain real consensus decisions and not the anodyne common denominator resolutions which so often mark UN history, and which are well-nigh unenforceable. In any case, serious consideration of weighted voting must come in the near future as it has been estimated that there about fifty micro-states, with populations of less than 100,000, which may soon reach independence and seek UN membership. Although these states would have such low incomes that they could play little part in financing or policing the peacekeeping obligations of the UN, they could amount to about one-third of the membership within the General Assembly. Attention has been drawn to this problem by U Thant in 1965 and 1967.

Setting aside this problem of micro-states, the advantage of weighted voting would be that it should encourage greater responsibility in regard to acceptance of UN peacekeeping obligations than exists at present. The change could pave the way for 'international' and not 'para-international' decisions, and states might be willing to encourage resumption of the vitally needed military staff committee work which stopped in 1948. It is also evident that the UN tends to be viewed by the USSR and the Afro-Asian states as a Western imperialist institution, and this image is coloured by the siting of the UN in New York. It would be better, therefore, if the UN's headquarters were re-established in central Europe and if regular meetings were held in turn in different capitals. Other obvious weaknesses, such as the exclusion of Communist China, should also be remedied.

At present, the UN tends to fail in dealing with international disputes because it is such an external factor. It seems unlikely that a significant reduction in war can result from such an external para-international institution. If use of war to achieve political ends is to decline, it is more likely to come through changes in society precipitated by economic and technological developments. One such change has been seen already in the way in which the nuclear weapon has acted as a deterrent on use of war by the super-powers. In relation to war between small or intermediate states probably the best that the UN can achieve is to 'freeze' the dispute rather than settle it, although in some cases involving relatively small areas —such as Cyprus—the UN may act as a catalyst and encourage a middle or third solution to emerge; whether the latter result is desirable remains to be seen. But this more limited role in peacekeeping is important since it allows time for other relevant factors to work on the situation and draw the tension out of it. For this reason the economic and social work of the UN ranks in importance with more formal attempts at peacemaking, and to this we now turn.

REFERENCES

Goodrich, L. M., Hambro, E., and Simons, A. P., *The Charter of the United Nations—Commentary and Documents*, New York, Columbia U.P., 3rd Ed., 1970.

Harbottle, M., *The Impartial Soldier*, London, O.U.P., 1970.

Higgins, R., ed., *United Nations Peacekeeping, 1946–1967*, London and Fair Lawn, N. J., O.U.P., for the Royal Institute of International Affairs, 1969, Vol. I, *The Middle East*; Vol. II, *Asia*.

James, A. M., *The Politics of Peace-Keeping*, London, Chatto and Windus, for the Institute for Strategic Studies, 1969.

Jenks, C. W., *The World Beyond the Charter in Historical Perspective*, London, Allen and Unwin, and New York, International Publications Service, 1969.

Nicholas, H. G., *The United Nations as a Political Institution*, London, and Fair Lawn, N. J., O.U.P., 1967.

O'Brien, C. C., *The United Nations: Sacred Drama*, London, Hutchinson, and New York, Simon and Schuster, 1968.

Stegenga, J. A., *The United Nations Force in Cyprus*, Columbus, Ohio State U.P., 1968.

Waters, M., ed., *The United Nations*, New York, Macmillan, and London, Collier-Macmillao, 1967.

Xydis, S. G., *Cyprus—Conflict and Conciliation, 1954–1958*, Columbus, Ohio State U.P., 1968.

14 *The United Nations and World Economics*

In the preceding chapter we have seen that the United Nations is a hybrid international institution, partly composed of truly international themes, such as support for self-determination and the checking of aggression, and partly designed to give a respectable multilateral façade for use of power by major world states. The contrast between the desired role of the UN in world politics and that which the UN achieves is great, and a similar discrepancy exists between the economic needs of the world as seen by the UN and what the organization can achieve. The modern economic system was created by two main factors : the impact of the old world on the underdeveloped new world, and industrialization particularly as this concerned the application of power, mass production and the need of the more developed world to use the less developed world as the source from which to derive primary products.

Up to 1945 and in some cases thereafter, the relationship between the developed and underdeveloped world is usually called 'imperialism'. By this term both political and economic dominance by one country over another country or over another group of countries is understood to exist. Although the heyday of imperialism, from the late nineteenth century up to the inter-war period, concentrated attention on the political aspects of this relationship between the developed and underdeveloped world in the sense that dominance of one race over another was sought for and prized as a mark of racial superiority, of better political and economic development or even as a distinguishing favour bestowed by God himself, the economic relationship was the keystone of the imperialist structure. Hence, divorcing the term 'imperialism' from the idea of racial superiority, it can be realized that basically the term merely expressed the idea that one state as a unit was more highly developed than another and that its impact on the less developed state would encourage a sense of superiority because the more powerful state would, in economic matters, colonize or cannibalize the less powerful unit.

I

The UN Charter states that the organization is concerned to aid self-determination, or in other words to end imperialism or, again, to promote decolonization. To aid self-determination is basically a political goal, i.e. to help a people to move towards self-government or to rid themselves of the political trappings of imperialism, like external control of finances, and imperial apparatus such as Governors-General decked out in military uniforms of the early nineteenth century, and above all to reject the idea that any one race—through its particular level of skills in the march of history— has the right to dominate another. Broadly speaking, the phrase 'to promote decolonization' means the same as encouraging self-determination, for decolonization is concerned with the need to remove from the dominated race the inhibiting label of inferior or colonial status. But when we look at the task of ending imperialism, the matter becomes much more complicated, for although racialist attitudes are on the whole now much attenuated—with certain rare but notable exceptions such as in South Africa—imperialism in the basic sense of an economic relationship between countries which are more highly and powerfully developed than others still exists, and, indeed, can in economic terms be said to be increasing since the developed world is accelerating more and more swiftly away from the underdeveloped world in terms of income per head, generation of wealth and general economic development.

The wave of anti-colonialism which swept the world after the Second World War took with it when it receded much of the political apparatus of imperialism and even the formal economic subordination of many less developed countries to the more developed, but it could not, in the nature of things, destroy the fundamental economic disparity between the developed and the underdeveloped regions of the world. Thus, in many cases, while colonialism may be ended, economic imperialism—in the sense of a relationship which consistently discriminates unfavourably towards the less powerful economic states[1]—is still with us. It is difficult to see how this economic and political discrepancy can be smoothed out. The task is evidently one for centuries and not decades, and against the back-

---

[1] This is as true of the economic and political imperialism of the USSR over the satellite states of eastern Europe or Egypt as of the more commonly discussed economic imperialism of the Western world over the Third World.

ground of such economic superiority, the efforts by the UN to improve matters necessarily seem small although important.

One writer who has concentrated on interpreting world economic history to telling effect is Pierre Jalée whose most recent work, *The Third World in World Economy*, was published in 1969.[2] Jalée's passion for social justice sometimes leads him into colourful exaggerations, but on the whole he is accurate in his view that 'Political decolonization has done nothing to alter the system of pillage. Change has no more come to pass in Africa and Asia than it has in Latin America, where national governments have had the appearance of power for 150 years.'[3] Basically, if the West or capitalist world was seriously interested in improving the rate of economic growth of the new world, it would have to accept cuts or at least retardation in its own standard of living since this level is based on a world system of international trade which pays the primary producers much less than it pays to producers of finished goods. As Western politicians generally now base their election manifestos on the assumption that they can improve national standards of living, and achieve this by a pattern of controlled inflation with some productivity increases, it is unlikely that the peoples of the West will even be aware of the relative insignificance of their economic contribution, or willing to help the Third World. Hence Western economic effort to aid developing countries[4] is at present so minimal, whether bilateral or multilateral, done on a national scale or via the UN or other world agencies, that it can only be palliative and not remedial. Soviet (and Chinese) aid-trade is growing, is politically oriented, and—in the case of the former[5]—is now recognized as a complicated economic matter although the political jargon continues to be simplified.

But why should we regard the question of improving economic conditions in the Third World as of so much importance? Fundamentally, the answer to this question lies in the dangers of world war springing out from some civil broil or frontier dispute between states of very different levels of economic development which are

[2] Translated from the French by Mary Klopper (New York and London).
[3] *Ibid.*, p. 130.
[4] The term 'developing countries' succeeded the more accurate term 'underdeveloped countries' in response, it is claimed, to the susceptibilities of the Third World; but the earlier term was more accurate and the newer term no doubt eases embarrassment of the developed world as much as that of the underdeveloped world.
[5] Robert S. Jaster, 'Foreign Aid and Economic Development—The Shifting Soviet View', *International Affairs*, July 1969, Vol. 45, No. 3.

supported by mutually hostile super-powers. The UN itself exists principally because of this fear of war. But over and above such questions of war and peace, the economic and moral aspects of the relationship between the capitalist West, the developed USSR economy and the Third World must be explored further. The original outburst of creativity which started off Britain—and later the rest of the West—on the process of industrialization is, clearly, a complex matter; as more and more economic research is undertaken, the old simplicities such as the 'Industrial Revolution' or its agricultural counterpart have been discarded. The evolving interpretation of economic development necessarily includes attention paid to the importance of the capital which flowed back to Britain from her entrepôts and territories abroad. This was part of the vital stimulus which made Britain into the workshop of the world. It is often asked, well, why can't these new African and Asian states reach economic take-off alone? After all, it is frequently added, Britain did it alone. But this is precisely what Britain did not do : she was enriched by the wealth flowing in from trade abroad. In terms of economic morality, the New World supplied a vital part of the capital which geared the outburst of agricultural and industrial activity which began in the eighteenth century and created modern Britain and the modern world. The old or developed world has thus both an economic and a moral duty to repay the new or underdeveloped world, and to give it the chance of reaching economic take-off. Whether, in fact, the old world will fulfil its economic and moral duty in this respect remains seriously in doubt.

II

Towards the middle and the close of the 1960s many indications of current dissatisfaction with the levels of aid and trade with new countries existed. On the one hand, the underdeveloped countries noted the insufficiency of economic effort by the developed states, and, on the other hand, spokesmen for business in the developed states more and more frequently expressed the view that aid in particular was just a waste of scarce resources. On the first attitude, it is useful to quote Diori Hamani, President of Niger, not merely for the interest of his statement but also because it contradicts the conventional assumption that all is well with the former French colonies and other new states linked with the European Economic Community. Diori Hamani expressed his disappointment with the benefits gained through this link in a statement published in *Le Monde* on 1 November 1966 :

> For our part, we, the African states, have loyally implemented the Yaoundé Convention. But, on the European side, we notice more and more : (1) That bilateral aid to our countries is decreasing or, at best, stagnating; (2) that the prices of our agricultural products are steadily declining; (3) that the prices of industrial products continue to rise.
>
> Moreover, several of the Six have imposed taxes on the products we export to them.[6]

The Yaoundé Convention was made between the Six states of the EEC and the former colonial territories of Belgium, France, Italy and the Netherlands on 20 July 1963. It replaced earlier arrangements made at the time of the Treaty of Rome, which founded EEC, and was signed in 1957 although the EEC did not function until 1 January 1958. The Yaoundé Convention provided for an increase of EEC aid to these new states from $18 to $730 million ($620 million of which was given as outright grants and $110 million as loans), and $70 million was granted to the remaining territories which were not yet independent. The EEC signed a similar agreement with Nigeria in July 1966 though this does not include provisions for aid which Nigeria wished to exclude.[7] Similar statements to that made by the President of Niger have been made by other statesmen connected with the EEC through the Yaoundé Convention.[8] On the other hand, Western criticisms of aid levels or the impact of aid also abound. Towards the end of 1968, John Davies, then Director-General of the Confederation of British Industry and since July 1970, typically claimed that financial aid to less prosperous countries has proved 'an absolute busted flush'.[9]

This kind of Western statement is based on realization that the politico-social infrastructure, vitally necessary if aid is to be successfully utilized, is often lacking in new countries. Hence aid is often wasted if not squandered, and not infrequently in the past merely went to line the pockets of the traditional or emerging élite of new states. It is admitted that there has been—despite much

[6] Jalée, *The Third World in World Economy*, p. 134.
[7] John Calmann, *The Common Market*, London, 1967, p. 22; see also, Uwe Kitzinger, *The European Common Market and Community*, London, 1967, pp. 131–50.
[8] Jalée, *The Third World in World Economy*, pp. 134–5.
[9] Davies was appointed Secretary of State for Trade and Industry by the Conservative government in July 1970.

valuable work done—waste of aid and corruption; even Lester
Pearson himself has alluded to the secret unnumbered bank
accounts held by the élite of new states in Switzerland. But attention need not be focussed exaggeratedly on the waste or squandering

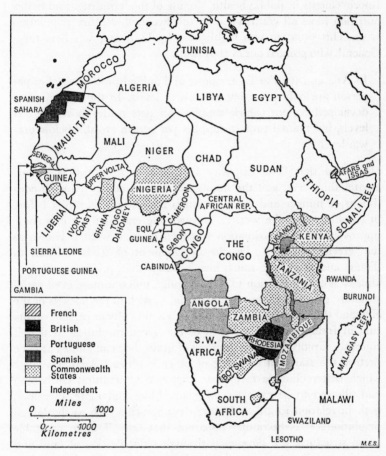

Africa, 1971

of earlier aid, although clearly the question of pre-aid investigation
and the need to realize whether or not a developing country has
the infra-structure necessary to take advantage of aid must be
thoroughly explored. It is, however, more important to realize that
much of the apparent loss from earlier aid results from other and
more intransigent factors than corruption or inefficiency.

III

One of the most important of these factors, leaving aside the vital need to build up the infra-structure, is the population explosion. Improvements in public health, the use of modern drugs and better nutrition have all contributed to the twentieth-century population crisis. This situation was highlighted by U Thant, UN Secretary-General, who pointed out in 1961 that :

> In Asia and the Far East, calorie and animal protein supplies per person are only just back to pre-war levels. In the other under-developed regions calorie supplies per person are above pre-war levels, but animal protein supplies per person are still below pre-war levels.

He added that 'The disparity in standards of nutrition is now greater than ever, and the number of human beings living in conditions of hunger and malnutrition is now larger that ever before in the history of the world'. Towards the end of the 1960s some improvement in this situation was seen through what is known as the 'green revolution', i.e. the development of seeds resistant to disease and producing much heavier crops than previously. But, as already noted in relation to aid generally, unless a more even social structure can be developed profits tend to stick in the pockets of the élite and the peasants gain little. This is a difficulty at present occurring in India. Another problem of the 'green revolution' is that if countries rapidly become exporters of grain they can almost at once destroy the standard of living of other south-east Asian countries which better climatic factors or improved agricultural cultivation had allowed to be exporters of grain. More and more, therefore, both in relation to aid and other developments such as the 'green revolution', it is becoming apparent that only if more equitable social structures are developed through redistribution of land and wealth can advantage be taken to improve effectively the standard of living of the mass of the people in underdeveloped states. Alternatively, it can be argued that if a state is relatively small and with new and high income levels from natural resources such as oil, mass standards of living could be effectively raised through autocratic paternalism, such as exists in some of the Arab states. But whether such politically structured states can survive in the long run is doubtful.

The population crisis makes it essential to consider other methods, apart from increasing food yields, of easing the world situation. The trend towards high population continues despite attempts made by individual countries such as India, now with the long-delayed official blessing of the UN,[10] to promote birth control. It has been estimated that at present average rates of population growth (about 2% per annum) 'world population is expected to reach about 7·5 billion in the year 2000, with 80% in the developing countries'.[11]

This rate of population growth neutralizes other economic gains from agriculture or industrialization, thus 'For example, although the average annual rate of economic growth in developing countries was 4·5% during the period 1960–65, per capita growth was only 2%. Such low per capita income growth rates may well mean perpetual poverty.'[12] In 1967 the UN responded to the need to try to control the population explosion by setting up the UN Population Trust Fund to extend earlier work on the population problem. Administration of the fund was taken over in 1969 by the UN Development Programme in order to strengthen this work.

As far as international relations are concerned, the explosion of population has increased the tendency towards political, economic and social co-operation, and in so far as common aims have been projected, is an influence moderating the power of the nation-state. One recent indication both of the effect of population growth and industrialization is the UN Conservation Year of 1970 which developed from realization of the need to preserve natural resources (and to restock where possible) as well as knowledge of the serious extent to which the world was becoming polluted in one way or another. A striking instance of this occurred in mid-1970 when the explorer, Thor Heyerdahl, who was voyaging on a papyrus raft from Africa to South America, recorded that even far from the shipping lanes oil slicks and sediment could be noted nearly every day in the Atlantic Ocean.

Earlier a statement made by U Thant in 1961 on world nutrition problems was quoted. In the same report U Thant went on to indicate just why the developed countries must aid those less favoured. He said :

[10] Before 1965 the UN pursued an ultra-cautious attitude on the population problem partly because of Catholic pressures and partly because the UN lacked facilities to promote large-scale birth control policies.

[11] *International Conciliation*, No. 574, September 1969, p. 124.

[12] *Ibid.*, pp. 124–5.

L

The rise in agricultural productivity is not sufficient at the present rate to provide the surpluses which are essential if the industrialization of the under-developed countries and accelerated growth of national incomes are to be achieved.

This statement stresses the vital aspect of the world problem that if there is to be even a provision of basic living standards for people in the developing countries, this can only be achieved either if the developed sector pays more for primary products—which is very difficult to achieve—or if industrialization can be promoted more rapidly in the new countries. It is only industrialization which can give a sufficiently rapid capital return and hence the desired improvement in income per head. Agriculture, however, must not be neglected and recently there has been greater emphasis on this aspect of development, partly because of a reaction against grandiose and unsuitable projects—such as roads, harbours or airports—financed in earlier stages of aid-trade with developing countries on the assumption that trade would develop on a great enough scale more quickly, but also because the agricultural aspect had been pushed aside. But the reaction against aiding industrialization must not be carried too far, since in the long run it is this sector which will carry a new country forward not merely economically but socially, educationally and politically. This argument is reinforced by the fall in the price of primary commodities from the early 1950s onwards. An additional difficulty in primary goods prices is the accelerating tendency for the developed sector to produce replacement materials synthetically through the plastics industry in particular—plastic replaces rubber and even in some cases metals; it can also replace jute—and there are many other instances of this sort of change.

IV

In 1961 the UN General Assembly designated the 1960s as the Development Decade and called on all member-states to join in a sustained effort to break through the cycle of poverty, hunger, ignorance and disease which still afflicts two-thirds of the world's population. The primary aim of the Development Decade was to attain by 1970 a minimum annual growth rate of 5% in the annual income of developing countries. Half-way through the decade it became clear, however, that the gap between the rich and poor countries was not only still wide but was widening. In the mid-1960s the annual income in the developed states rose by $180 to $720 per head while in the developing states it went up only by $7.20 to $72.00 per head. To take another example to illustrate this situation, Robert McNamara, America's former Defence Secretary, who became President of the World Bank in 1968, commented in November of that year that 'Another measure of the same point is that the rich nations have expanded their annual income within the last eight years by an amount that exceeds the total annual income of all the developing nations'.[13] Overall, it is probable that the developing countries taken as a group will not have fallen far short of reaching the target of 5% growth rate as regards income and output, but individual variations are great. Taking 1960–67 'while the annual percentage growth rate of per capita gross domestic product in all developing countries taken together was 2·1, the growth rate was 1·5 per cent in Africa, 2·2 in Asia and 1·8 in Latin America'.[41]

There were also large variations in individual national performances; for example, Pakistan had a rise of 3·8% in growth rate while Indonesia recorded a fall of 0·6%.[15]

Towards the close of the 1960s preparations began for a second UN Development Decade to run from 1970 onwards and stock was taken of results from earlier aid-trade. Three major reports were commissioned, the Prebisch, Pearson and Jackson. The first study was set on foot by the Inter-American Bank which has requested the Prebisch Commission, named after its chairman, Dr. Raul Prebisch, to 'evaluate what international collaboration has represented for Latin America in the recent decade'.[16] Dr. Prebisch, former Secretary-General of UNCTAD, had already produced a hard-hitting analysis of aid-trade in his study *Towards a New Trade Policy for Development* published by the UN in 1964.[17] Secondly, the World Bank in August 1968 appointed an independent commission under Lester Pearson, the former Canadian Prime Minister, to study aid-trade in the 1950s and 1960s, and to 'assess the results, clarify errors and propose new policies'.[18] The report was published

[13] Quoted in interview in the London *Sunday Times*, 3 November 1968, p. 36.
[14] *International Conciliation*, No. 574, September 1969, pp. 114–15.
[15] *Ibid.*, p. 115, n. 1.
[16] *International Conciliation*, No. 574, September 1969, p. 117.
[17] For an analysis of this, see Richard Bailey, *Problems of the World Economy*, London, 1967, pp. 165–6.
[18] *International Conciliation*, op.cit., p. 117.

on 17 October 1969 under the title, *Partners in Development, Report of the Commission on International Development.*[19]

The report made ten main points. Free trade must be encouraged by the dropping of tariff barriers or excise duties in developed countries, and the initial aim should be a network of tariff preferences by 1971. Foreign private investment should cease to be inhibited in developing countries. The aim of aid is to allow the developing countries to reach self-sustaining economic growth. A reasonable target would be an increase in the annual growth of GNP in the Third World to 6%, i.e. an increase of 1% over the existing figure of 5% p.a. UNCTAD II had set an aid target of 1% of GNP in 1968 and this figure should be reached by donor states in 1975 'at the very latest'. Reduction of interest charges or debt relief on aid loans should be considered as a form of aid. A major conference on the checks concerning aid should be held between donors and donees in 1970, and should concentrate attention on 'untying' aid, i.e. cutting it free from both the exports and political or military requirements of the developed states.[20] Technical assistance had often been insufficiently adapted to the real needs of developing countries and inadequately co-ordinated with capital assistance. A UN Commissioner for Population should be appointed and there should be international co-operation on birth-control research. Aid in education should break away from its existing pattern of reinforcing traditional methods of teaching. By 1975 at least 20% of official development aid should be funded multilaterally through the International Bank for Reconstruction and Development or IBRD, and the Development Banks for Africa, Asia and the Inter-American area.

Although all these matters are important, they are also well-rehearsed themes in the aid-trade problem. Criticism of the Pearson Report was, therefore, possible on the grounds that it did not make a dynamic enough contribution to the deteriorating development situation[21] under which between 1967–68 there was a fall of 8% in total official aid, from 62% to 54%. Thus, as E. McCammon Martin, Chairman of the Development Assistance Committee of the

[19] London, 1969. A neutral assessment of the report is given by Caroline Miles in International development co-operation: the challenge of the 1970s, *The World Today*, London, February 1970.

[20] This has not been held at the time of writing.

[21] Michel Monroe (a pseudonym), 'A Lost Opportunity—A Comment on the Pearson Commision Report', *International Affairs*, January 1970, Vol. 46 No. 1. The fact that Monroe felt it necessary to write pseudonymously speaks for itself.

Organization of Economic Co-operation and Development (OECD), stated in November 1969, the fact that there had been a rise of 15% in the total amount of capital exported to developing countries was due to a rise in private investment. Under these circumstances, it would have been expected that the Pearson Report might have taken up vigorously the point made earlier that unless the developed countries radically alter their attitude to aid-trade by far more intensive efforts to move away from economic imperialism (that is the continuing economic exploitation of the underdeveloped world by the developed) by deliberate policies such as higher payments for primary products and encouragement of manufactured imports from the underdeveloped states, resentment between the new and the old states is bound to grow. At the same time, the Pearson Report failed to tackle the root causes of irritation by developed countries which see aid-trade running to waste because of factors such as the caste system in India—said to be increasing and not declining—or the existence of social and political patterns which foster corruption.[22]

The Pearson Report noted, however, that four countries, USA, Britain, Belgium and Italy, were falling behind in that the percentage of GNP which they allocated for aid was declining. The British case highlights a characteristic reduction of interest in aid. Even before the Conservative Party replaced the Labour Party as the governing administration at the General Election of 18 June 1970, the real decline in aid had become an issue in British politics. Reginald Prentice who resigned as Minister of Overseas Development on just this matter has written :

> In fact, aid has been going up slightly in cash terms, remaining static in real terms and going down as a proportion of GNP. Government aid, leaving aside private investment, was 0·53 per cent of GNP in 1968. On the figures announced by Mrs. Judith Hart [his successor at ODM] it is likely to be about 0·47 per cent in 1973–74.[23]

It is important to bear in mind in this connection that about 90% of official aid is still funded bilaterally.

The third important report was *A Study of the Capacity of the*

[22] *Ibid.*, p. 35.
[23] More Priority for Overseas Aid, *International Affairs*, January 1970, Vol. 46 No. 1, p. 2.

United Nations Development System made for the Governing Council of the UN Development Programme by Sir Robert Jackson of Australia.[24] The Jackson report surveyed the full range of UN agencies and other administrative or consultative units concerned with development work. It noted that there were severe organizational problems in that the development work depended on piecemeal tackling of situations, and as each new UN initiative occurred either an existing unit would be expanded or some new method of carrying out the work would be applied. This resulted in functional dislocation and overstraining of the UN mechanism and the report suggested that the machinery must be carefully overhauled, lines of communication and power cleared, along with general simplification, if a single strong organizational weapon was to be produced in order to carry out the proposed UN Development Co-operation Cycle over the following five years.[25]

But, unlike the Pearson Report, the Jackson study was more frank about the nub of the aid-trade problem. Would the developed states, and indeed all states members of the UN, have the willingness to make the necessary surrender of national power needed if aid-trade was to be worked out as a truly international form of economic justice?[26] This is indeed the vital question for as we have seen earlier in relation to the political, and particularly the peacekeeping, work of the UN, the failure to surrender national sovereignty has been the decisive stumbling block. It is, of course, possible that the countries of the world may be willing to make such a surrender in the economic and not the political sphere, but as Sir Robert Jackson concluded, 'the forces of inertia resisting change are very great'.[27] In practical terms the Jackson report proposed that the UN Development Programme (UNDP) should be given major power over the other units involved and should become the brain and decision centre of development.[28] But UNDP in order to achieve the work must become part of an independent specialized UN agency, just as the International Monetary Fund (IMF) and the World Bank (or International Bank for Reconstruction and Development, IBRD) already are. In effect the revised UNDP would be to the UN system as a basic and important nationalized industry is to the domestic system of a nation-state. The work of the new UNDP, which should

[24] United Nations, 1969, 2 volumes.
[25] *Ibid.*, Vol. II, p. 147.
[26] *Ibid.*, Vol. I, pp. v–vi.
[27] Jackson report, I, p. vi.
[28] *Ibid.*, pp. 33–4, 43.

probably be renamed as UN Development Authority or Agency,[29] would be much strengthened by better and more regular financing and use of a higher calibre of personnel.[30] If matters are allowed to slide, the Jackson report concluded that UN development work would be limited to a capacity to deal with about $200–250 million p.a., and it was doubted whether even this amount would be dealt with effectively.[31] The alternative to fundamental revision of UN development work would be that

> the present monster will continue to propagate, the UN system generally will deteriorate, and the economic and social development of the 'Third World' will be frustrated at the very time when a unique opportunity exists to expand it significantly.[32]

v

It is important to remember at this stage that, as mentioned above, about 90% of official aid is still funded bilaterally and not multilaterally through agencies such as the UN. Aid takes four main forms : first, loans either bearing little or no interest, that is soft loans, or hard loans with normal, i.e. high, rates of interest; second, outright grants of money; third, technical assistance of all types;[33] fourth, sales or gifts of surplus or obsolete products of the developed areas. The last type of aid is very common and often enables a developed country to get rid of supplies of outdated military equipment and this also serves the secondary but important object of tying the donee country to the donor country when repair tools or spare parts for the machinery or equipment are needed. Overall, bilateral aid has tended to be given by developed countries in order to link donee states with their ideological or military requirements. Hence, America armed up Pakistan to the detriment of neutralist India and created a need for India to spend scarce resources on military needs. It has been estimated that through interest and tying of aid to the advantage of the economy of the donor country,

[29] *Ibid.*, p. 51.
[30] *Ibid.*, Vol. II, Chapters 8–9.
[31] *Ibid.*, Vol. I, p. 18.
[32] *Ibid.*, p. vi.
[33] In Britain such valuable technical assistance has been given mainly through nationalized industries such as the National Coal Board or through governmental secondment schemes. and private industry needs to join more fully in this work. The failure of private industry generally in regard to the Third World is highlighted in the article by Monroe (p. 33) cited earlier.

both bilateral and multilateral aid 'yearly drains from the Third World three times as much capital as it puts into it. Sometimes the hunt is in private preserves, sometimes the spoils are shared, but pillage it remains'.[34] The importance of this economic inferiority in stoking up the fires of hatred, distrust and antagonism of the underdeveloped towards the developed countries can hardly be overestimated. Western statesmen in particular, who may be satisfied with the current economic *status quo*, need to ask themselves whether the economic and political polarization which this situation creates can, in the long run, be anything but detrimental to maintenance of the capitalist system which they support.

It is often stated that in discussing the economic development of new states, a careful division must be made between aid and trade, and it is currently fashionable—rather as industry is now being demoted in favour of promoting the 'green revolution'—to stress the greater value of trade over aid both in economic and political terms. But this approach begs the question : trade with underdeveloped countries is fundamentally based on whether or not developed states are willing to grant preferential agreements, or in other words, to allow their own privileged position to be notched down or held back a degree or two. Hence even trade with underdeveloped countries is, in view of the relationship of economic inferiority between the developed and underdeveloped, a form of aid. Thus it can be argued that for Western capitalist states at least, since the political motivation is clearer for Sino-African deals like the August 1970 one between China and Zambia with Tanzania for £169m. linked to railway building,[35] commodity agreements with underdeveloped countries can artificially inflate prices for primary products and make them a form of subsidy.[36] But, equally, one can argue that the underdeveloped countries subsidized the developed for many years when monopoly capitalism dictated the low level of primary prices such as cocoa. The important point, however, is that the would-be clean distinction between trade seen as a straightforward commercial matter and aid seen as tied with strings of one sort or another does not, in practice, exist.

The relative failure of the first half of the Development Decade by the mid-1960s led the UN General Assembly to take a new initia-

[34] Jalée, *The Third World in World Economy*, p. 131.
[35] For which, China may need to purchase rolling stock from third countries such as Britain.
[36] Argued notably by A. R. Conan in the National Westminister Bank *Quarterly Review*.

tive to hasten development programmes, and this step was linked with trade. The UN joined together its earlier Expanded Programme of Technical Assistance set up in 1949 with its Special Fund established in 1958 to found the new agency, the UN Development Programme (UNDP) which has been discussed earlier. This move was in part a response to the fact that the UN Economic and Social Council (ECOSOC) was felt by many incoming Afro-Asian states to be too musclebound and over-weighted in favour of the developed world.[37] UNDP does not provide capital for development projects in new states since this work is done through the World Bank or International Bank for Reconstruction and Development (IBRD)[38] and associated units such as the International Development Association (IDA)[39] and the International Finance Corporation (IFC).[40] Instead UNDP stimulates investment in developing states by pre-investment assistance such as encouraging studies of the potentialities for industrial growth and setting up training centres to turn out skilled workers. UNDP also advises developing states on how to get the best out of any new product and aids governments in economic planning. By January 1967 when the Development Programme had been in operation for 15 months it was estimated that $1,688m. had already been invested in some 150 countries and territories as a direct result of pre-investment studies sponsored by UNDP.

Following the new trend to ensure that the practicalities of aid maximization were no longer neglected, the UN General Assembly set up the Industrial Development Organization to speed up industrialization in new states in 1966. UNIDO replaced the earlier Industrial Development Committee which came under ECOSOC's control. The change, made after the IDC had operated from 1960,

[37] Walter R. Sharp, *The United Nations Economic and Social Council*, New York, 1969, p. 177.

[38] IBRD commonly called the World Bank was set up in December 1945 following on from provisional work done at the Bretton Woods Conference of July 1944. On the institutional side of this UN specialized agency, see D. W. Bowett, *The Law of International Institutions*, London, 1964, pp. 52, 56, 94–119 *passim*. On functioning, see Fred Hirsch, *Money International*, London, 1969, pp. 540–2; on reforms, see Jackson report, II, pp. 304–5.

[39] IDA was set up on 26 September 1960 and commenced work on 8 November 1960 in an attempt to raise capital on terms less onerous than customary in order to aid developing states. On functioning, see Hirsch, *op. cit.*, pp. 540–4, 549; as an institution, see Bowett, *op. cit.*, pp. 96–119 *passim*; on reforms, Jackson, II, p. 295.

[40] IFC began work in 1956 and is a specialized agency of the UN although set up by IBRD. Its main function is to encourage the flow of private capital to the underdeveloped countries. See Bowett, *op. cit.*, pp. 96–119 *passim*.

followed the indication by new UN member-states that they wanted more intensive action on development. UNIDO is an autonomous organ of the General Assembly and has a status midway between that of a Council and a specialized agency. One of UNIDO's main tasks is to carry out rapid appreciations of new industrial projects and to assist governments in decision-making.

VI

But all this emphasis on aid maximization in order to improve economic growth in new states means little unless the benefits of trade are internationalized so that developing countries can reach the point of self-sustaining growth. To Marxist or neo-Marxist analysts the possibility that the developed capitalist states will seriously want or be able to help new states to reach this stage and so compete with their own economies is ludicrous. Jalée considers this unthinkable :

> In these circumstances, how can it be suggested that the peoples of the Third World can rise from their underdevelopment without first breaking the chains of imperialism? What desperate self-deception could make anyone believe that imperialism could ascend to, or even promote, the economic emancipation of the countries whose exploitation is a condition of its own survival? This is the key to the problem : imperialism does not pillage the Third World diabolically or for fun, but because of *vital necessity*, because it could not survive otherwise.[41]

But Jalée's argument is carried too far. Capitalism in developed states has shown remarkable ability to adapt itself in order to survive and—if Third World pressures are great enough—will no doubt make similar compromises. The inter-war crisis of capitalism was met in a variety of states in different ways but most of the solutions, imperfect though they were, contained a mixture of deficit financing, i.e. with the state assuming an innovatory finance and credit creating role, and large-scale planning both to occupy the unemployed and to go some way to meet the demand of the working class for better economic and social conditions. Special Drawing

[41] *The Third World in World Economy*, p. 131. The 'survival' aspect, in view of technology's ability to produce substitutes, is exaggerated. The 'pillage' continues because the developed world is following lines marked out under formal imperialism.

Rights on the International Monetary Fund are a similar recent international compromise. After the Second World War developed economies, such as the British, attempted moderate forms of nationalization, but found them politically unpalatable and economically vulnerable to change when governments fell. The transition was made in states like Britain and France to the mixed economy, which meant economic trial and error, and a combination of forms of national activity with private enterprise. Democratic socialism has thus further underpinned capitalism and continues to do this daily by the use of state money to promote industrial activity and change. These sorts of national adjustment will, no doubt, have international equivalents.

Moreover, Jalée writes of the need for new states to overthrow imperialism if they wish to progress economically and to make the political and social gains which would accompany this. But how would he achieve this? His own work demonstrates clearly how economic and financial imperialism cannot be got rid of more or less overnight like political imperialism since, as argued earlier, economic imperialism is merely the expression of the inequalities existing between the developed and the underdeveloped world. If Jalée merely means that new states rather than tie themselves up with monopoly capitalism after independence would be better advised to nationalize foreign assets, offering as has often occurred national bonds only financially realizable at some future date as compensation, he is arguing a weak case. Clearly, this policy might be best from the standpoint of a new state if it did not have to rely on the marketing services of big business in the developed world and if co-operation among new states was sufficiently high to see that the developed world did not get any desired primary products except at an agreed figure. However, since both of these necessary preconditions for full nationalization are lacking, any new state which takes this action either runs the danger of becoming over-dependent on aid from abroad or may tie its economy just as tightly and unwisely to a Communist or more highly developed economy which, revolutionary slogans apart, will cannibalize or imperialize the new state both economically and financially, just as much as any Western developed state would do. A leader of a new state who followed Jalée's advice would find that his state had merely exchanged one set of economic and political masters for another, unless his economic position was extremely fortunate and he possessed, say, an oil or mineral monopoly. This unfortunate trend of events has already occurred to a large extent in Egypt. What is needed is better internationalization of trade throughout the world and not an increase in politico-economic bloc trading. Meanwhile new states must pursue a policy of balancing aid-trade from a political mixture of developed states.

The desirability of better internationalization of trade was fully realized at the close of the Second World War by economists who had studied the lessons of contracting trade and bilateral tendencies in the inter-war period.[42] The initial organization concerned with this economic work which has so great an impact on international relations was GATT, the General Agreement on Tariffs and Trade.[43] GATT was set up after talks were held by most of the states of the world at Geneva from 10 April to 30 October 1947. It had been intended that a stronger organization to co-ordinate internationalization of trade would be set up. To this end the Havana Charter was drawn up at a UN Conference on Trade and Employment which took place from 21 November 1947 to 24 March 1948. Under the agreements referred to in the Havana Charter, an International Trade Organization would have been established in order to expand and liberalize world trade. But the USA Congress refused to ratify the Charter and instead of the strong ITO agency, work to internationalize world trade fell instead to the weaker GATT. GATT came into operation from 1 January 1948 and has tried to internationalize world trade through useful but limited methods, notably encouraging bilateral tariff reductions and the Most Favoured Nation principle. The theory is that working out from these beginnings, gradually lower tariffs would prevail and a degree of free trade would develop. But, as will be realized from GATT's two main methods, its work is not innovatory enough and dissatisfaction with its results encouraged the moves towards regional economic free trade blocs such as the EEC.

During 1969–70 the USA, now finding problems as regards expanding its own hitherto well-guarded domestic market, showed interest in reactivating GATT; American governmental spokesmen referred to the bad effect of regional economic blocs in the long term and the possibility that they might contract rather than expand world trade. By 1970 fears of contracting trade led to a pro-

---

[42] One of the best books on this period is H. W. Arndt, *The Economic Lessons of the Nineteen-Thirties*, London, 1963; first published 1944.
[43] See [Kenneth Dam, *The GATT—Law and International Economic Organization*, Chicago, 1970.

tectionist America Trade Bill being considered by the American
legislature which firmly rejected it. But the ambiguous American
line on trade expansion is clearly a case of too little and too late,
and what is really needed is a revival of some form of the earlier
discarded ITO. Yet GATT could prove a useful interim economic
institution in the struggle to internationalize world trade. It has
powers to organize consultations, to mediate on problems arising
from its work and, particularly valuable, can prevent tariff reductions being negated by domestic policies such as taxation, customs
dues or import and export duties.[44]

The failure to set up ITO has meant that, GATT apart, efforts
to internationalize world trade have been sporadic and piecemeal—
depending too much on the economic vacillations of major trading
nations. To mention one example, an International Commodity
Trade Commission was set up by ECOSOC but in 1965 its work was
transferred to UNCTAD I, the UN Conference on Trade and
Development. This UN body met in Geneva in March 1964, and in
December 1964 the UN General Assembly recognized it as a
specialized UN agency. UNCTAD I had a board representing 55
nations which operated and represented it between conference
sessions, and its Secretary-General in the 1960s was Dr. Raul
Prebisch. His report on the trade problems of developing countries
(mentioned above, p. 313), dealing specifically with 77 of these
states which were represented at the Geneva Conference in 1964, is
one of the best on this subject. Following on from the Geneva meeting, the developing nations met again at Algiers in October 1967
and produced a list of ideas which was called the Algiers Charter.
This document was debated at UNCTAD II which took place at
New Delhi in the spring of 1968. The New Delhi meeting dealt with
eight groups of issues ranging from tariff preferences for the exports
of developing nations to the problem of expanding and diversifying
their manufactured exports. The agenda of the conference was
massive but the results have been less striking.

This comparative check was partly related to the size of
UNCTAD II: 132 states were represented and there were 1,400
delegates which made complicated negotiations difficult if not
impossible. Again, the developing nations, only too conscious of
their economic and social problems, raised the level of their demands
upon the developed states beyond even the ideas of the Algiers

---

[44] GATT in 1969 noted more sophisticated concealed checks such as health and
packaging requirements and government-fixed insurance rates.

Charter, which made it easy for the latter to find explanations for not making further concessions. Despite these checks, however, UNCTAD II remains the world's chief instrument for placing the needs of the developing countries before the attention of the developed. The need to keep up this work is indicated by the fact that although world exports have increased in value by an average of 7% in the 1960s, the share of world trade held by the developing countries is still declining although not so quickly as in the 1950s when the value of primary products fell abruptly.

VII

Yet grave doubts exist about the ability of the machinery of the UN, through the agencies already mentioned, as well as others such as the UN Children's Fund (UNICEF), the Food and Agricultural Organization (FAO), the UN Educational, Scientific and Cultural Organization (UNESCO), the World Health Organization (WHO), the International Labour Office (ILO), and numerous other smaller units, to carry forward the development programme at a sufficient speed. In part the problems are technical and administrative, there are so many committees and bodies, some linked centrally with main specialized agencies and some—like the World Bank and the International Monetary Fund (IMF)—operating as independent specialized agencies. A plethora of policy-making takes place and much of it is not merely unco-ordinated but may even conflict not only in technical advice, but also because of the pull between state, regional or international oriented programmes. The basic problem, however, is not merely the need to reorganize the piecemeal UN system for development, but whether, in fact, the developed world has the will to accept the conclusion of the Pearson Commission that we do live in one world and that the developed world cannot indefinitely isolate itself from the problems of the developing world.[45]

To conclude on the economic attempts to promote development in new states, firstly, it is apparent that the developed sector does not yet realize the dislocation in attitudes of privilege necessary if fundamental alterations in the world economic system are to occur, or, if realizing this, rejects the attempt because it would erode

[45] For criticism of this approach defined as 'infantile internationalism', see Susan Strange, 'International Economics and International Relations', *International Affairs*, April 1970, Vol. 46 No. 2, pp. 309–10.

economic and financial privilege. Secondly, can the system change? Can the developed world which is for the most part based on capitalism buttressed by democratic or bourgeois socialism alter its ethos to the extent necessary for fundamental rethinking to occur? As we have seen, so long as development aid-trade is seen in the context of the present economic inferiority or new imperialism of the mid-twentieth century, it is likely to be minimal; in this way at present the UN and multilateral agencies overall only channel about 10% of official aid.[46] Thirdly, unless aid-trade for the developing countries is linked with attempts to base society more equitably, the division between rich and poor is merely perpetuated at new levels. Fourthly, the interim solution to the world economic problem of a more just distribution of wealth and resources has since the 1950s tended to be regional economic groups. These communities such as the EEC have played a notable, although as mentioned earlier insufficient part in channelling aid-trade to the underdeveloped sector. But their value in the short term must not be underestimated. The comparative success of the EEC in this field[47] highlights the comparative failure of other former economic pivot states such as Britain to do the same for her Commonwealth.[48]

But in the long term the impact of regional economic groups based on trade preferences is not likely to be salutary. They may encourage multistate hostility fed by economic disadvantage. Even more important, these groups can pick and choose which developing states to benefit with their aid-trade. Yet all these states need such aid-trade and for this reason a truly international effort to adjust world inequalities must be made through an international

---

[46] Individual variations are great, however, and Britain in 1968–69 gave 44% of her aid multilaterally, '17 per cent through international institutions and 27 per cent through co-ordinating mechanisms such as consortia'. See 'Britain, the developing Commonwealth, and the EEC', by Carol Ann Cosgrove, *The World Today*, June 1970, p. 254.

[47] Much of the political acidity of Commonwealth countries towards British foreign policy can, the race issue apart, be traced back to the fact that they see the former French colonies receiving much more infra-structure aid. This stifles African criticism of French arms sales to South Africa in so far as former French colonies are concerned.

[48] British official aid totalled £65m. in 1957–58, £170m. in 1961–62, £225m. approximately in 1966–67. The similar approximate figures for 1968–69 was £219m. and the estimated figure for 1970–71 was £227m. See *Economic Aid: A Brief Survey* (COI reference pamphlet 77, HMSO 1966), *British Development Policies—Needs and Prospects 1968* (ODI Review—2, 1968), and 'More Priority for Overseas Aid', by Reg Prentice, M.P., *International Affairs*, January 1970, Vol. 46 No. 1, p. 1.

institution such as the UN. Similarly, regional economic groups in the long run may restrict the growth of international trade rather than encourage it, as they may stifle competitive growth in order to maintain their privileged economic position.

Although the enthusiasm of the 1950s to late 1960s about the possibilities of aid-trade, bilateral and multilateral, has declined, we must now consider, in summing up, what has been achieved lest in the current welter of pessimism a further decline of aid-trade is encouraged through misapprehension. The UN *World Economic Survey* for 1968 provides evidence[49] showing that, as briefly alluded to earlier, the original target of 5% set for the growth of income and output in developing states may well be reached. It must be remembered that when this figure was originally set many doubted whether it was realistic. In dealing with developing countries which necessarily have very different rates of progress it is essential to look at the individual figures. In the years 1960–67 twenty new states reached the 5% growth figure and in 1967–68 there were still sixteen states in this bracket. If we look at the individual figures we can see the striking variations: Taiwan in the latter years achieved 10% growth, the African Ivory Coast 8%, Korea 7.9%, Iran 7.7%, Thailand 7.6%, Mexico 6.6%, Trinidad and Tobago 6.5%, Iraq 5.7%, Pakistan 5.5% and Honduras and Bolivia 5.4%. In the same years, 1967–68, petroleum-rich Libya reached a growth figure of 21%. We have looked earlier at the weaknesses of aid utilization in the developing countries but these successes must receive due value.

VIII

Up to this point we have been concerned with the facts and criticisms of aid-trade, but now, with the background sketched in, we must consider the impact of economic activity on this type of international relations. First of all, it is apparent that as aid-trade has grown to be a major preoccupation of governments in the developing countries and as their demands have increased, the attitude of the developed world has hardened. No longer able to stress the outmoded 'charity' approach to aid-trade with its emphasis on self-congratulation, a colder outlook has developed with the stress on questions such as 'Well, what after all has been achieved? Is it worth it?' or, even more flatly, 'It has *not* been worth the effort'.

[49] Usefully summarized in the Jackson report, Volume II, pp. 19–20.

The latter statement is clearly wrong, not merely in humanitarian terms of suffering and hunger alleviated but also in relation to the growth pangs of new states. The political impact, both domestic and in international relations, is more significant than the volume of aid-trade might suggest. But, unfortunately, this impact was often due to the negative aspects of aid-trade rather than the positive ones. Much of the earlier aid-trade was given or not given at the crucial time of imperial change-over. It could well be argued that the failure of democratic two-party political systems was not caused by the fashionably stressed failure of the Westminster type of democracy to transplant but was the result of the failure of former imperial powers to give sufficient economic stability, combined with educational and medical aid, to new regimes. Evidently, other important factors were at work, notably tribalism with the associated problem of secession, and the influence of outside business interests often involved in encouraging the richer segments of new states to secede in order to transfer their wealth more easily to the capitalist sector rather than see it spread thinly around the new large states. Yet in the final analysis it was the sense of national crisis, the possibility that the aftermath of obtaining freedom might be staffed by deaths through hunger or factionalism, which often forced post-revolutionary leaders to suppress opposition. As a young trade unionist from East Africa, studying at Ruskin College, Oxford, said in 1968: 'We can't afford your luxuries of dispute and time-wasting since there are so many problems, starting with just keeping people alive.' Insufficient as the effort of the developed countries is in relation to the developing ones, it nevertheless remains clear that the aid-trade then given helped many new states over the worst stage of post-independence.

The classic example of the failure to provide the necessary assistance was the Belgian government's abnegation of duty when leaving the Congo in 1960. A bloodbath ensued, marked by excesses of tribalism, left and right political polarization, massacres, rape, starvation and attempted secession. Later in 1960 the UN started its major operation to stabilize the situation and this continued up to 1963. Militarily the UN operation was a success, but it was marked by deep dissensions amongst the members of the UN and left the organization with a serious financial crisis since Russia and France, which did not approve of the UN action, refused to pay collectively for it. A serious political crisis caused by these attitudes dragged on long after 1963, but was ultimately passed over, rather than settled, by the traditional UN device of letting a matter drop unresolved.[50]

A similar but more severe crisis in international relations caused by inadequate aid-trade assistance occurred earlier in 1956. The genesis of the Suez crisis was in some ways similar to that of the Congo. Egypt was in the maximum revolutionary stage in the 1950s: in July 1952 the Army, acting as the means of reform, forced the abdication and later departure of King Farouk, and talks were begun with Britain for the ending of the British military occupation of Egypt. In 1954 the Anglo-Egyptian Treaty of 1936 was brought to a close and this left at issue the question of British forces in the Suez Canal Zone who were not to leave until June 1956. Egypt had been declared a republic in June 1953 and in 1954 President Neguib lost effective power to Nasser who became Prime Minister in the same year; in 1956 he became President, a post which he held until his death in September 1970. The new regime was under strong pressure from its people to deliver the economic and social fruits of revolution swiftly. Attention was concentrated on the Aswan High Dam project which, if realized, would irrigate more land, provide more food and work, and also supply the hydro-electricity needed to industrialize. At this juncture, relations between the Egyptians and the Americans, who had advisers in the country, were good, and to all appearances America was intent on building up Egypt to help it over the initial hard years after the revolutionary *coup* and to prevent the new regime swinging too far left.

The Suez Canal in the 1950s was of far greater economic importance than it is today when the development of supertankers and super cargo ships, the draught and length of which are too large for the canal, dominate the flow of goods between East and West. It was then still regarded by Britain, one of the main canal users, as not only her major economic but also her most important strategic line of communication. The British, like the French although to a lesser degree, were also both at state and private levels shareholders in the Paris-based Suez Canal Company. Anxiety was felt and expressed concerning not merely the financial security of these shares under the Nasser regime, but also whether once the British troops left the Canal Zone in 1956, the Egyptians might not take over the canal itself and prove incapable of running and managing

[50] See Claude Leclerq, *L'O. N. U. et l'affaire du Congo*, Paris, 1965; W. J. Ganshof van der Meersch, *Fin de la souveraineté belge au Congo*, Brussels, 1965; Crawford Young, *Politics in the Congo*, Princeton and Oxford, 1965.

this vital international waterway. It had long been a tenet of Egyptian nationalist thought that the milking of Egypt's wealth from the canal, then one of her few assets, by the Western developed nations should be stopped. But whatever President Nasser's long-term views on the status of the canal, he was not, in the mid-1950s, pressing strongly on the issue and in any case the canal was due to revert to Egypt in 1968.

Apart from the strategic and financial importance of the canal, the Egyptian situation was further complicated for the British and the French by other colonial factors. The British had helped to create modern Israel whose passage to formal statehood blessed by the UN occurred in 1948, but had been accompanied by multistate Arab attack throughout 1948–49 and thereafter plagued by raids along non-viable frontiers.[51] The French for their part resented the fact that Algerian freedom fighters were receiving assistance and encouragement from the Egyptians. Matters were brought to a head when the Egyptian government turned from the Western states[52] which were unwilling to help it build up its arms supply in favour of a deal with the Communist sector under which the USSR bought part of the Egyptian cotton crop and the Czech government supplied arms in return for cotton, rice and other Egyptian produce. Nasser announced and justified the Czech arms agreement on 28 September 1955 and the Western states, although disliking the situation, appeared to accept the policy shift. Coincidental with the Egyptian difficulties, America was engaged in a periodic phase of retrenchment concerning overseas commitments and on 19 July 1955 the Egyptians were abruptly informed that the USA could no longer take her expected share, along with Britain and the World Bank, in financing the Aswan High Dam. As the World Bank's scheme had been contingent on quotas coming from America and Britain the whole project now collapsed. This in turn triggered off the Egyptian take-over of the Suez Canal Company on 26 July, which in turn set off the Anglo-French-Israeli collusive attack on Egypt inspired by the ideas of toppling Nasser and teaching Egypt to keep her place in Middle East politics.

[51] Non-viable in the sense that Israel's frontiers invited Arab attack because they were not drawn on good strategic lines.

[52] Britain and France had refused arms supplies; America claimed that she was willing in principle to supply arms, but that the deal was not possible since she did not want the cotton or other produce on which Egypt wanted the deal to be based. This was a fine distinction since it was clear that Egypt had no other resources on which to base the deal.

The early unfortunate system of having important projects financed by one or two main states in this case provoked a major international crisis which almost completely destroyed British influence in the Middle East, nearly wrecked the Commonwealth, made Israel even more the target for Arab resentment, and now in the 1970s has led to Russia's having such a degree of military, air and naval control over Egypt[53] that that country is in effect—despite many Egyptian denials—as much a Russian satellite as Czechoslovakia. The lessons of the Suez crisis and its aftermath were that international financing of major projects must be managed more carefully, and one recent new device of importance which spreads not only the economic but the political load is use of consortia, a combination of business groups and multilateral financing, often combined with traditional loans from individual states. Thus India for example had, by August 1970, been promised $197m. for 1970 from Western states and agreements had been signed with America, Britain, Canada, Japan and Austria as well as the World Bank (IBRD). But apart from this promised $197m. The Aid India consortium had set itself a target of $1,100m. for 1970 with $400m. of this allocated for specific developments. In 1969 India received $812·96m. from the World Bank and the Aid India consortium.[54]

To conclude on the work of the UN and world economics, one of the two main functions of this international institution has been to try to soften the economic disparity between the developed and the less developed world. As we have noted, the amount of funds for multilateral aid-trade is still relatively small but as has also been seen the achievements have been considerable in view of the amount of money spent. In this chapter we have mainly been concerned with the aid-trade problem of the developing countries. But the UN has also played a second main function in world economics since 1945, i.e. general economic and currency stabilization work concerning traditional world finance through Specialized Agencies and notably through the International Monetary Fund (IMF).[55] Although much of this work has related to the developed economies,

[53] A report in the London *Times* on 17 December 1970, p. 6, claimed that Russian personnel in Egypt (troops and technicians) had risen to 20,000.
[54] *The Guardian*, 3 August 1970, p. 2.
[55] On the more traditional work of the IMF see Shigeo Horie, *The International Monetary Fund*, London, 1964; Joseph Gold, *The International Monetary Fund and International Law, IMF*, 1965, monograph; Robert. A. Mundell (ed.), *Monetary Problems of the International Economy*, Chicago, 1969; J. Keith Horsefield, *The International Monetary Fund*, IMF, 1970; Fred Hirsch, *Money International*, especially pp. 584–5 on SDRs.

it does, however, affect developed and underdeveloped equally for it is particularly important to expand the world supply of credit—through such devices as the IMF Special Drawing Rights mentioned earlier—since insufficient liquidity restricts the growth of world trade. It is important, moreover, to remember that capitalism itself is fragilely balanced, as the financial and economic crises of the 1960s have shown, for all its apparent superiority when compared with the weaknesses of the economies of developing states. Europe, too, has its problems, and is subject to irrationality in economics, as well as to the need somehow to fit together the new larger economic needs with the nation-state structure. In the next chapter we will look at the problems accompanying the transcendence of sovereignty.

REFERENCES

Arndt, H. W., *The Economic Lessons of the Nineteen-Thirties*, London, Cass, and New York, Kelley, 1963, first published 1944.

Bailey, R., *Problems of the World Economy*, Harmondsworth and Baltimore, Penguin, 1967.

Bowett, D. W., *The Law of International Institutions*, London, Methuen, and New York, Praeger, 1964.

Calmann, J., *The Common Market*, London, Blond, and New York, International Publications Service, 1967.

Dam, K., *The GATT—Law and International Economic Organization*, Chicago, Chicago U.P. 1970.

Gold, J., *The International Monetary Fund and International Law*, I.M.F., 1965.

Hirsch, F., *Money International*, Harmondsworth, Penguin, Pelican, and New York, Doubleday, 1969.

Horie, S., *The International Monetary Fund*, London, Macmillan, 1964.

Horsefield, J. K., *The International Monetary Fund*, I.M.F., 1970.

Jalée, P., *The Third World in World Economy*, New York and London, Monthly Review Press, 1969.

Kitzinger, U., *The European Common Market and Community*, London, Routledge and Kegan Paul, and New York, Barnes and Noble, 1967.

Mundell, R. A., ed., *Monetary Problems of the International Economy*, Chicago, Chicago U.P., 1969.

Sharp, W. R., *The United Nations Economic and Social Council*, New York, Columbia U.P., 1969.

15 *The Transcendence of Sovereignty*

Throughout this book we have been concerned with the development over the past hundred years of the international system. This system is not older than two or three centuries; its origins may be placed during the Protestant Reformation which converted the emerging states of Europe from associated agents in the governing of a single whole, Christendom, into entities whose whole *raison d'être* was their own continued existence and welfare. The modern international system is merely the latest answer which man has given to one of his perennial problems, namely, how peoples differing from one another in race, language, culture, religion or other respects are to live together and enjoy the potential riches of the earth without destroying or irremediably weakening themselves in conflict. Our international system lacks the order, law and peacefulness of, say, the Roman Empire, but it gives to its separate units, the different states, more equality *inter se* and more independence than any previous formula for the co-existence of unlike peoples.

The system is called international, suggesting that its units are nations, that is, sizeable groups of people who enjoy a feeling of oneness through the possession of certain common cultural attributes such as language or religion, and who also perhaps share a common historical experience and a common aspiration to form some day a state, that is, a legal organization wielding supreme legal competence over its members, if they do not already do so. The traditional unit within the so-called international system has, however, always been the sovereign state, no matter how many non-self-governing nations were governed by the states' executive and legislative authorities. Thus, at the beginning of the hundred years covered by this book, 1870, Austria-Hungary, Prussia and Russia, three of the five great powers of the then international system, contained within their borders several (in the case of Russia, many) self-conscious nations, the Poles, for example, that had been divided between these three great powers since the partitioning of Poland at the end of the eighteenth century. As for Britain and France, the other two great powers in 1870, these, like smaller European states such as Belgium and Holland, ruled millions of people in Africa, Asia and Latin America, who, if not exactly divided along national lines as understood in Europe, were later to acquire something in the nature of a national consciousness transcending tribalism and local differences in language. This sense of national identity became a primary force in their secession from the old European empires after the Second World War.

Since the French Revolution of 1789, however, it has been an article of the Liberal faith that, as far as possible, every self-conscious nation should form a state of its own, or that, again within the limits of the possible, the political map should coincide with the ethnographic map of the world. This is the moral principle called national self-determination, carried by the armies of the French revolution, and, after 1801, of Napoleon, from one corner of Europe to the other and embodied in British Liberal theory by J. S. Mill in his *Principles of Representative Government*. With the best will in the world, the theory had to bow to certain limitations, notably the viability of the resulting nation-state whenever the principle was applied and, secondly, the interests of the great powers.

As for the former, a nationally homogeneous state might lack access to the sea and territory inhabited by people of a different nationality may have to be incorporated within it in order to provide that access; thus, when Poland was re-born at the Paris Peace Conference in 1919, a corridor to the Baltic Sea, inhabited mainly by Germans and cutting through East Prussia, was awarded to the revived state. Again, at the same conference, the new Czecho-slovakia, itself a patch-work quilt of nations, was given the mountains of Sudeten Germany, half-surrounding Bohemia, in order to provide it with a defensive frontier to the west. J. S. Mill argued that the nationality principle was a factor making for peace in that no self-conscious nation could ever be content for long in subjection to a state predominantly controlled by another nation. But, considering that national self-determination had always to be squared with the principle of viability and hence could never be applied to perfection, neither could national minorities incorporated in the interests of viability in a state predominantly populated by another nationality long remain content with their situation, especially if incited from the outside, as the experience of Czechoslovakia and Poland in the late 1930s showed.

As for the second limiting factor on the principle of national self-determination, the interests of the great powers, this will clearly act as a barrier to the realization of the Liberal dream, even if the great powers are professed, or even genuinely convinced, adherents of the doctrine. No one has more enthusiastically espoused and made sacrifices on behalf of the nationality principle than the United States, the traditional enemy of imperialism, which is the exact opposite of the principle of national self-determination. Yet even the United States after the Second World War, when it bestrode the world like a colossus, refrained, on grounds of self-interest, from asserting the national principle forcefully against the Soviet Union when the latter was trampling upon it in Hungary in 1956. And, to give merely one of an infinite number of less dramatic examples, the United States agreed that Italy should retain the 300,000 Austrians in her Alto Adige district when peace was made with Italy in 1947 because America was anxious that Italy should remain firmly in the Western camp as the opposing blocs became solidified in the Cold War. As with all other moral principles in international affairs, national self-determination must stand aside whenever the policies and interests of the greatest powers are ranged against it.

Nevertheless, the principle of nationality has undoubtedly helped to shape our international environment during the last two centuries. Today, the nationality of a people is felt to be a highly relevant criterion in determining in which state the inhabitants will live or exactly where international frontiers are to be drawn : the United Nations Charter itself imposes on member-states the obligation to respect the national self-determination principle, without granting nations, which have no *locus standi* in international law, the right to claim it. At the same time, national self-determination has re-shaped the political structure of the world, breaking states and making new states in the process. During the nineteenth century the national principle blew like a tornado through the fabric of the *ancien régime*, rehabilitated in Paris in 1815 in defiance of the French Revolution and Napoleonism. There resulted the division of Belgium from Holland, joined by the Vienna treaty, in the 1830s, the liberation of Greece from Turkey in the same years, the formation of Bulgaria and Rumania from the rotten structures of the Ottoman Empire and finally, as the supreme monument to the national principle, the unification of Germany and of Italy in 1870.

The First World War, especially after the United States joined the Entente powers in April 1917, was rapidly transformed into a struggle to emancipate the so-called enslaved nations of Europe from Austro-Hungarian and Prussian rule, while in Russia the Bolsheviks, for reasons in which Wilsonian conviction and national weakness were combined, made no effort to retain their own national minorities, Estonians, Finns, Latvians, Lithuanians and Poles, when these peoples threw off Romanov rule and established themselves as independent states. The Ottoman Empire, as we have seen, succumbed to its own national revolution led by Kemal Ataturk, and this, with the aid of the Allies, gave a Bolshevik-like farewell to its Arab subjects which then claimed independence only to have a much restricted form of it foisted upon them in the form of British and French 'A' mandates within the League of Nations.

At the Paris peace negotiations in 1919 President Wilson confessed that when he issued his call for national self-determination (or rather 'autonomous development') for subject peoples in his Fourteen-Points address of 8 January 1918, he never realized how many people, Egyptians and Gypsies among them, would come to the Paris Conference to cash the cheques of independence the President had issued to them in his speech. The spirit which the Sorcerer's Apprentice, Wilson, had evoked in his call for national freedom never ceased to vex the great imperialist powers in the inter-war years as the Irish, Egyptians and other Arab peoples, the Indians and African nationalist leaders demanded for themselves what the new states of eastern Europe had achieved in 1919.

Wilson's successor in the Second World War, Franklin Roosevelt, was even more confident that his mission was to reduce the European empires, especially the British, to their supposed national fragments. The only occasion, it seems, when he had a conversation to make a specific proposal to the British Ambassador in Washington, Lord Halifax, during the Second World War was for the purpose of expressing his wish for the 'liberation' of Hong Kong from British rule.[1] At the Yalta Conference with Churchill and Stalin in February 1945 Roosevelt believed he could work with Stalin, whatever the British thought, in extending national self-determination from its strictly European environment of 1919 to a world-wide scale. The disestablishment of almost all that remains of the great European empires in Africa and Asia in the quarter-century since Yalta bears witness, not only to the strength of the anti-colonialist movement in the United Nations, but to the force of

[1] The Earl of Halifax, *Fulness of Days*, London, 1967, pp. 249–51.

national feeling among non-European peoples whether or not they possess the attributes of nationhood as understood in Europe.

II

This is not to say, however, that many, even among those who have every sympathy for the new nation-states in Africa and Asia, do not deplore, not only the kind of deification of the nation-state which inspired the German and Italian dictatorships of the 1930s, but the allegiance most of us render up to the nation-state even at the cost of wider international interests. From time to time in this book we have had occasion to reflect on the limitations placed by national sovereignty on the kind of collective efforts which mankind might undertake in the interests of greater security from war and the exploitation of human and natural resources for the betterment of human life everywhere. Yet we must be careful to distinguish between nationalism and national sovereignty. Most people would no doubt agree that there is nothing wrong in nationalism, if by this we mean merely the pride men take in the habits, customs, *mores*, outlook and culture of those of their own kind. In a world increasingly dominated by the materialistic *ethos* of Western man, reflected today all over the world in the standard pattern of architecture, music, art, food, who would wish to restrict the diversity represented by the different national types? But the argument of most people is that when nationalism is yoked to state power, when it becomes the legitimate basis of sovereignty, which knows no law but its own interest, it becomes a danger to the survival of mankind. 'The wars of nations', prophesied Winston Churchill, 'will be far more terrible than the wars of kings'! The divorcement of nationalism from the divided sovereignty now characterizing the international system seems to many people the ideal.[2]

Not merely that, but some authoritative writers prophesied, almost as soon as the Second World War ended, that the national state was bound to be superseded by larger units as the scale of modern technology increased. Notably E. H. Carr in his *Nationalism and After* (1945) forecast that the two needs which the nation-state formerly satisfied—military and economic security—could no longer be met by that instrument, and that the road was now opened to larger multinational units, one of which, curiously

[2] See the conclusions of *Nationalism*, a study by a group at the Royal Institute of International Affairs, London, 1938.

enough, was in Carr's view the Commonwealth. Other writers, the American scholar, John Herz, being a notable example, though he later revised his original views, did not see how the nation-state could survive in a world of nuclear weapons.[3] Others foresaw the displacement of the nation-state by other forces : the super-powers, America and Russia, which would reduce all other countries to the status of client-states or satellites without an effective will of their own; international or supranational institutions like the United Nations or the European Economic Community (EEC) respectively which would more and more take over the role of the chief 'actors' in the international system; or giant business corporations or inter-national revolutionary movements which would soon make the national state seem like national parliaments as seen through the eyes of Undershaft, the armaments manufacturer, in Bernard Shaw's *Major Barbara* : mere talking shops, the real decisions being taken elsewhere.

To take the first of E. H. Carr's criticisms of the nation-state, its inability to solve the economic problem of our own day, it is true that the modern state exists within an ever-thickening network of trade and other economic relations between similar states so that all its economic policies have to be decided in the light of their possible effects on these multinational economic systems. This has been particularly true of Britain with its economic stresses and strains of the past two decades : even our internal policies have to satisfy the 'gnomes of Zurich' before they will make available the necessary credit to overcome recurrent financial crises. Moreover, we in Britain have found that unless we attach ourselves to larger econo-mic groupings like the EEC we run the risk either of more and more of British industry being owned by American capitalists, or of our being unable to manufacture the more expensive and sophisticated equipment such as supersonic aircraft which is a symbol of member-ship of the club of advanced industrial nations.

At the same time, it is evident from British public reactions to the negotiations on British membership of the EEC that economic efficiency is by no means the only test a nation applies when it con-siders amalgamation with other nations.[4] The fear of loss of control of the national economy, even the national 'way of life', is a con-siderable argument even if the case is clearly made out for the economic benefits of a nation-state committing suicide, so to say, in

---

[3] J. H. Herz, *International Politics in the Atomic Age*, New York, 1959.
[4] Written in December 1970.

order to be reborn in a larger multinational unit. Moreover, the economic case against the nation-state has by no means impressed the Afro-Asian states these last few years. Poverty-stricken and lacking almost all the infra-structure of a modern economy as most of them are, this has not encouraged them to return to the multinational empires which they so enthusiastically left, or to form larger integrated economic units of their own. The newly decolonized states seem to have concluded that they were more likely to achieve their economic take-off *outside* the European empires than within them, and although there has been some degree of regional economic co-operation among these countries, most of them seem to think that their economic aims can be achieved by their own separate efforts, backed in appropriate cases by aid from individual rich countries or multinationally through United Nations agencies.

As for the second argument of critics of the independent state, that nuclear weapons have rendered it obsolete, this is on even weaker ground. When the then British Home Secretary, Sir John Anderson, began a broadcast on the BBC Home Service on 6 August 1945, the day the first atomic bomb was dropped on Japan, with the words : 'a new door has been opened on the future of mankind', it seemed indeed that the international system (or lack of system) would have to be scrapped forthwith and a more secure world order substituted for it, if man was to save himself from a highly probable self-destruction. But after the immediate flash of the atomic bomb, nothing of the kind happened. The states of the world, even in crowded and vulnerable Europe, did not hasten to abandon their sovereignty and form a federal club, strong enough, if any political organization ever could be, to defend itself against nuclear attack. On the contrary, the twenty-five years of the nuclear age following the bombing of Hiroshima and Nagasaki in 1945 have constituted an epoch in which more independent nation-states have been created that ever before in the whole history of international relations. Moreover, most of the new decolonized states cling all the more tenaciously to their independence because they believe that too close an involvement with the politics of the great powers, their former masters, might implicate them in the latters' future atomic conflicts.

Nor have nuclear weapons had any distinctive federalizing effect on these older state-members of the international system; the 'united Europe' movement which emerged after the Second World War owed more to fear of Communism than of nuclear death. Some think nuclear weapons have consolidated world peace, others that they have enhanced its tensions. But in either event these terrifying forces have entrenched rather than undermined sovereignty as the basic principle of the international system. For example, in so far as nuclear weapons have lessened the risk of war between the major powers, it has made integrative arrangements such as the NATO and Warsaw Pact systems less urgent. Who would endure the restrictions on national independence involved in membership of one of these bureaucratic military alliances, if there is no real danger of armed attack? The mavericks, General de Gaulle and Ceaucescu of Rumania, gave the answer: a nuclear-induced *détente* between East and West is the father of polycentrism.

But even if nuclear weapons, or rather the latest devices, anti-ballistic missile systems and multiple-targeted re-entry vehicles, have a destabilizing effect on the central balance of power between East and West, the implications for the sovereignty of those states involved remain, paradoxically, the same. For the more massive the scale of nuclear destructive power and the greater the risks of full-scale nuclear conflict between the super-powers, the less willing are they to risk total destruction on behalf of their weaker allies; and the more determined are their allies, as they draw the obvious conclusions, to rely upon their own deterrents, nuclear if possible, conventional if not, against attack. In the last resort Britain and France acquired their own deterrent forces, ineffective as these might be in a full-scale global nuclear conflict, because they could not be one hundred per cent confident that the United States would come to their aid if attacked, and every year in which the nuclear arms race has become more intricate and costly, the more their initial scepticism was justified. Moreover, the logic which Britain and France have applied to the arms race applies to all other countries. The odd conclusion seems therefore inescapable that whether nuclear weapons succeed in making the world a more or less dangerous place to live in, they have strengthened rather than weakened the argument for national sovereignty.

Again, some writers and certainly many less articulate people have also tended to assume that the super-powers—the Soviet Union and the United States today, no doubt China tomorrow—are so outstripping all other states in economic strength and military capability that they alone are the truly sovereign states and that other countries can do little more than try to make the best of the world which the super-powers are making for them.[5] The force of this argument lies in the facts that the two super-powers are by every test head and shoulders above all the allies which have huddled, or been forced to huddle, around them during the Cold War; that they have it in their hands, because of their wealth, to put the developing countries on the road to their economic take-off; that there is scarcely an international problem in any part of the globe in which they are not in some way involved; and, above all, that they literally have it in their power to determine, not only whether civilized life will continue on the globe, but whether any kind of human life will do so.

But it would be a serious mistake to postulate too direct a relationship, in any kind of social system, between freedom to do as one pleases and power, whether measured in the crude form of men, money and ships, or their equivalents today, or equated with influence or the capacity to evoke deference from others. Today, simply because the super-powers have such unimaginable capability of destruction under their control, they are obliged to move much more cautiously than the smaller states in their foreign relations. Neither of the super-powers, for instance, can use military force outside their own territories without carefully weighing the possibility of touching off an avalanche which could engulf themselves as much as the countries against which that force was used. Thus, when the Soviet Union joined with some of her Warsaw Pact allies to invade Czechoslovakia in August 1968, she took the precaution of notifying the Western powers as she did so, for fear that her action might be regarded in the West, not as a short and sharp discouragement of liberalization tendencies in Czechoslovakia, but as a prelude to a general Warsaw Pact invasion of western Europe. Moreover, the Russians were anxious to bestow a certain legality on the invasion by devising the so-called Brezhnev Doctrine which purported to give the Warsaw Pact states the right to intervene in any state in east Europe in which socialism's very existence was in jeopardy. That same year, 1968, saw the highly humiliating experience of the United States when one of her spy ships, the *Pueblo*, was captured by North Korea, the North Koreans arguing that the ship was within their territorial limits. For twelve months the United States was in the position of being unable to recover the spy ship because of the sheer dread of the possible escalation which

[5] See for example R. J. M. Wight, *Power Politics*, The Royal Institute of International Affairs, London, 1946.

might follow on the use of force. Eventually the spy ship's crew were released in December on condition that the captain signed a declaration admitting responsibility for infringing North Korean territorial waters; this he did, and immediately afterwards said that his 'confession' was null and void since it was signed under duress, this being one of the few cases in which duress can be regarded as invalidating a legal agreement.

One can imagine a great power of the nineteenth century wasting no time in taking a cold and brusque line with any such tiny state which crossed its path. But today there is the risk of escalation arising from a local resort to force; there are the serried ranks of Afro-Asian countries which are always ready to condemn vociferously at the United Nations a powerful country's attack on a smaller state. To which must be added the fact that, in this day of public relations and foreign policy conducted as public relations, no state can throw its weight about without losing some good will and sympathy somewhere in the international system. It may be, too, that the small country which has a great power as a friend cannot militarily be brought to heel even by the weapons now available to developed states. For all these reasons, the world has seen the extraordinary spectacle of little North Vietnam, with its underdeveloped economy and 17 million people, holding at bay for more than six years the greatest military power in the world, the United States, with its population of over 200 million and its untold economic and military strength. And this was after the Communists in North Vietnam had for twenty years before made their country a graveyard for the generals of that military colossus of the older European international system, France.

Small states, on the other hand, often because of their very weakness, can afford to take risks in their foreign policy which are denied to the giant states. This has been particularly so in the bipolar pattern of power which characterized the post-1945 international system. The fear of the two super-powers that one or other of their client states, if geographically well situated to do so, might bolt to the other side, has held the Leviathan states' hands when on the point of punishing the smaller state. The United States since 1959 has had to put up with that thorn in its side, Castro's Cuba, for fear of driving it too deeply into the Soviet Union's arms. The Soviet Union, after its anathematization of Yugoslavia in 1948, has had to be watchful about treating too harshly states on its perimeter lest they seek succour in the other camp.

In fact, the late President Nasser of Egypt said more than once quite openly that he did not fear the loss of his country's independence to Russia as a result of receiving financial aid from Moscow, because in any creditor-debtor relationship the debtor often has more freedom of manœuvre than the creditor, since the latter simply cannot afford to let the former be destroyed lest he lose his whole investment in the debtor. Similarly, it has often been said that certain small countries, not only among the new states, have been able to get support from the United States for almost anything they wished to do because unless their wishes were heeded, there would be a Communist revolution and the United States could not possibly want that. In fact, it has been rumoured that such small countries have habitually 'borrowed' each other's Communist parties in order to strengthen their case for more aid or more freedom of action from the United States.

It must not be taken for granted, therefore, that all modern states have ceased to be sovereign or self-governing entities and that sovereignty only belongs to the great powers. Part of the confusion here derives from a misunderstanding of the meaning of sovereignty itself. Many people are inclined to think of sovereignty in terms of supremacy, or rather being 'above the law' and able to do whatever one wants. Internally this may well be the case in all settled states, but even here there is a division between theory and practice. For Jean Bodin (1529–1596) sovereignty meant the final law-making power : '*majestas est summa in cives ac subditos legibusque soluta potestas*'. In speaking of this internal aspect of sovereignty, we can ask the question : Where does it lie? Who has it? What person or agency has the capacity to make supreme law in the community? We know well enough that sovereignty in the United Kingdom lies with the Queen in Parliament. As we have no written constitution or Supreme Court with power to review and approve the constitutionality of what the Sovereign does, the Queen in Parliament can make and unmake any law. But this is in the realm of legal theory only, since sovereignty is a matter of legal theory. In practice one knows that the Queen in Parliament has only limited capacity to make law affecting powerful associations or groups which constitute the web of society; any Act of Parliament to make smoking or drinking alcoholic liquor illegal would probably break down through the smoking and drinking public's refusal to observe it. Nevertheless, the fact that Acts of Parliament have behind them what Bagehot called the 'dignified parts' of government, that is, the

pomp and circumstances of sovereign organs, is probably an important reason why most of us defer to them unthinkingly and as a
matter of habit.

Now, in speaking of the *external aspects* of sovereignty, we are
thinking, not of certain persons or organs within the stage, but of
the state as a whole in relation to other states. External sovereignty,
in other words, while still being a legal attribute, though an attribute of the state as a whole, presupposes the existence of an international society or international system, the members of which are
sovereign states : their sovereignty can only be defined in terms of
the society which the states collectively constitute. So conceived,
external sovereignty connotes the legal equality of one state with
another, which is why the UN Charter speaks of *sovereign equality*
as one of its basic principles. To be a sovereign state is not to be
above the law; it is to be subject, from the moment of its foundation, to all the existing rules and obligations of international law,
and only sovereign states and, to some extent, international institutions can be so bound since other entities have no *locus standi* in
the sight of international law.

Just as internal sovereignty is a formal legal conception which
only partially corresponds with factual reality, so the formal legal
external sovereignty of states is not wholly consistent with reality.
Clearly, the states of the international system, while legally equal,
are very unequal one to another in other respects. But this does not
mean that formal equality does not have important practical consequences; it was to enjoy the practical benefits of theoretical
sovereign equality that the Smith regime in Rhodesia strove so
earnestly for Rhodesia's recognition as a sovereign state after its
unilateral declaration of independence in November 1965. Nor does
the equal enjoyment of legal rights and equal subjection to legal
obligations which are implicit in the notion of external sovereignty
mean that a state can in practice do what it is legally entitled to do
or that it will in practice do what it is legally bound to do. Every
sovereign state is entitled to do what it thinks fit within the limits
set by international law. But it may, and not only because it is
physically strong, do things which are not permissible within the
limits of international law and suffer no damage as a result; conversely, it may be prevented, by a thousand and one limits in the
practical world, from doing even those things which it is legally
entitled to do.

The most obvious limitation on the practical enjoyment by states

M

of their legal freedom is the will of other states. Almost every external action of a state, and many internal ones, too, requires the co-operation of other states, and this may not be forthcoming except at a price which the state is unwilling or unable to pay. This places a severe limit on the theoretical freedom of even the greatest powers, or perhaps especially the greatest powers. The security of Britain in effect depends upon the co-operation of at most fourteen other NATO countries; the security of the United States requires the co-operation of forty or more allies in all parts of the globe. Then there are limitations imposed by resources. Ernest Bevin, the British Foreign Secretary in the 1945–51 Labour governments, once said that his task would be much easier if he had another 30 million tons of coal, and for coal may be substituted all the multifarious resources on which states depend in order to implement abroad foreign policy decisions made at home.

Thirdly, there are limits imposed by public opinion and the national mood, especially, of course, in the liberal democratic states. It would make the Foreign Minister's tasks much easier if he knew that the decisions he made in the national interest, in so far as he understood it, would be accepted and implemented by the nation in the way that decisions on internal matters tend to be. But the public has less experience of and less training in recognizing the implications of events happening thousands of miles away. Hence President Franklin Roosevelt, though well aware of the dangers to American security of European Nazism and Fascism of the 1930s, was so far from being able to swing an isolationist public opinion and Congress to his side in a policy of facing up to them that he was not even allowed to allude to them publicly. Similarly, with the coming of the affluent society in the West since, say, the mid-1950s, NATO states have found themselves unable to persuade their public opinion to accept lower consumer spending in the interests of a more adequate defence posture. But the illustrations are endless; the fact is that sovereign states, so far from being legally and practically free to do as they like, face innumerable limitations on their freedom to do even those things they are legally entitled to do.

These limits to the freedom of states to act as they please tend to be overlooked by the critics of the independent state, with the result that they reach the pessimistic conclusion that there can be no peace or order in the world so long as states are perfectly at liberty to do exactly as they please. But, as we have seen, sovereignty, even in theory, does not mean absolute freedom to act as one likes, and moreover sovereign states are normally prevented from acting even within the limits of their legal freedom by a host of restrictions surrounding their making of foreign policy. In fact, a good case can be made for saying that states, even the most powerful, do not make foreign policy *ab initio* : what they do usually is to choose one or two alternatives from a limited range of choice which is for all practical purposes dictated by circumstances. Moreover, the issues which the policy-maker has to decide are not of his, or his state's, making. They come to him from abroad, out of the ever-changing flow of international affairs; moreover, the manner in which the issue is eventually resolved is not necessarily as he would have it, but represents a consensus between states, some more powerful and influential than his own; and his own state may be only one of the many which determine the ultimate outcome.

But to add to all these factors making for a far less independent role of the sovereign state than its critics tend to suppose, there is the fact that over most of the hundred years covered by this book, and certainly in the period since the First World War, efforts have been made by the international community itself to restrain the free exercise of national sovereignty and hence to reduce the inconvenience and dangers of living in a society in which power is not concentrated into the hands of a common superior authority, but is unequally divided between the 130-odd states now comprising the international system. We may briefly consider some of these efforts before examining certain proposals for carrying the free exercise of national sovereignty even further.

First of all, it has always been accepted that when states have common interests and common aims a more or less formalized machinery for international co-operation must be created. Those common aims and interests may be as simple and pedestrian as the transmission of mail from one country to another or as complex and intricate as the joint military defence of a certain frontier. But, however complex the need and the organizational apparatus created to fulfil it, it is clear that some restriction on the freedom of the co-operating states to do as they please is necessarily involved. When one contemplates those intricate structures for international co-operation, the Specialized Agencies of the United Nations, whose scope covers the whole range of national activities from education to pest control, it is evident that few sovereign states could exist without the help of some or all of these agencies and that help is not available without some limitation of a state's freedom. We have dealt in previous chapters with the work and problems of the two great universal international organs of the twentieth century for general international co-operation, the League of Nations and the United Nations. These bodies, as we have stressed, represent essentially international rather than supranational agencies for international co-operation, except that the UN Security Council, when dealing with threats to or breaches of the peace under Chapter VII of the Charter, has the power legally to demand from member-states compliance with its decisions. Nevertheless, the body of international legislation built up by these two organizations on the rules of good behaviour in the international system, to which we must add the ban on war as an instrument of national policy embodied in the Briand-Kellog Pact of 1928, is, both actually and potentially, a distinct limitation on the freedom of states to do exactly as they please in their international policies.

The point is indeed well taken that a powerful state bent on the use of force, either offensively or defensively, is not likely to be dissuaded by recommendations or rules of the United Nations. But, over a period of time and taking into account the daily flow of decisions on matters of foreign policy great and small, a state which persistently flouts UN principles or resolutions may well find, as South Africa has done from time to time, that the good will shown towards it by the states of the world as a whole is a rapidly wasting asset. Naturally, much will depend on the sophistication and sensitivity to external pressures of its national public opinion and the relative importance of that opinion in the making of foreign policy. But it is already clear that few states, if any, positively relish condemnation by UN organs; to the extent to which they seek to avoid it by acting in a law-abiding way as a UN member-state, the world organization will act as a brake on their liberty to do as they please.

Something similar may be said of the regional arrangements, for defence and other purposes, which have grown up since the Second World War. Some of these, like the Atlantic Pact of 1949 and the Warsaw Pact of 1955, have been developed under the aegis of Article 51 of the UN Charter which recognizes the right of individual and collective self-defence if for some reason the Security Council is unable to ensure international peace and security; some are recognized by Chapter VIII of the Charter as local agents for carrying out the general work of the UN, including the peace-enforcement work of the Security Council. These agencies have proliferated so much in the last twenty years that there can be few states today which are not members of one or other of the regional sub-systems.

Most of them, with the exception of the supranational communities now functioning in western Europe, are international in character in that their decisions are not deemed to be binding on states which have not voted for them. Nevertheless, as already stated, a country which profits from participation with other states in any more or less permanent organization is bound to find that its freedom to do and say what it likes is more restricted than before it joined. Considering all the sensitive toes which are likely to be trodden upon by any considerable modern state which acts in a cavalier fashion towards its fellow-states in some or all the international organizations of which it is today normally a member, its freedom to do as it pleases is becoming increasingly eroded.

III

All this gives rise to the question whether and how this transcendence of national sovereignty can be consciously carried further in the interests both of greater order in the international system as a whole and the more efficient exploitation of the world's economic resources. Few people would doubt that a once-for-all abandonment of national sovereignty by all peoples and the creation of a world state is not now, and is not likely to be in the foreseeable future, within the scope of practical politics. It is not merely that, to provide the consensus necessary to support a world government, the existing differences between the various states would have to be so reduced that a world government would not be necessary in order to achieve world security. An even stronger argument against the feasibility of world government is that the essential agreement on the ideological basis of such a government is wholly lacking. Rather than live under a Communist world government, most Americans, to say nothing of most Europeans, would rather die, on the principle of 'better dead than Red'. Rather than live under a capitalist world government, most Chinese, it seems, to say nothing of Russians, would rather die, on the principle of 'better dead than anything but Red'.

This still leaves the question whether the closer integration of states is not feasible on some less than universal basis, as for instance within some distinct geographical region. It must be said that so far, despite all the alleged dangers and inconveniences of a world divided into so many separate states, integration even of this

M*

kind has made painfully slow progress. However alluring the example of the US federation of the late eighteenth century, the integration movement has gained little ground elsewhere; there have been short-lived unions of states like the United Arab Republic embracing Egypt, Syria and Lebanon, and the Ghana-Guinea federation, but even in Europe, where the philosophic vision of United Europe is at least three centuries old and was once partially achieved under the Romans, integration on a voluntary basis even today (1970) has been confined to the six western states, Belgium, Federal Germany, France, Holland, Italy and Luxembourg; and Britain's first two attempts to gain entry into their integrated communities in 1961 and 1967 ended in miserable failure, due to the French veto. According to some economists, it is even a matter of doubt whether the European Economic Community of the Six (EEC) created by the Rome Treaty of 1957 has noticeably increased the economic performance of the six member-states, with the possible exception of Italy. As for political union developing out of the three West European supranational communities—the Coal and Steel Community, dating from 1952, and Euratom and the EEC dating from 1957—this seems as distant a dream as ever.

Hence there cannot but seem something artificial about the debate between advocates of federalism and functionalism as rival roads to the integration of states. The federalist argues for the head-on attack on sovereignty, proposing a once-for-all fusion of sovereign powers within a supreme constitution which would distribute authority between the federal centre and the peripheral states. The functionalist replies that this is to deal with sovereignty at its strongest point, the emotional attachment of a people to its symbolic trappings of independence; it also results, he says, in a federal constitution too rigid for a rapidly changing age.[6] His recipe is a growing network of functional organizations which link states together for specific types of international co-operation, in the fields of transport, agriculture, marketing, building, and so on. Thus, the functionalist argues, the different countries are knitted together by stealth, so to speak, in such a way that all become part of a single community without realizing it. Instead of states competing like peacocks for the age-old values of prestige and power, they would join together in the single task of promoting the welfare of all. In that process of closer functional integration more and more of their

---

[6] The classic statement of the functionalist case is David Mitrany's *A Working Peace System*, first published in London in 1946.

people would find that they had a vested interest in the continuance of the functionalist framework as it was gradually constructed.

The history of integration in western Europe since 1945 gives no clear answer to this debate : perhaps progress should be made along both paths at the same time. The crisis in the EEC in September 1965, when General de Gaulle challenged the power of the Community's Commission to take decisions over the governments' heads, seemed to show that functional integration must in the final resort always depend upon the willingness of governments, acting from political considerations, to let it go forward. At the same time, the viability of the west European communities despite many prophecies of their early demise—'We are condemned to succeed', remarked a Belgian diplomat after an EEC meeting—seems to show that at the time of writing (December 1970) too many people in the six countries have too great a stake in the future of the communities to allow them to fail.

But whether or not the argument between federalists and functionalists on the basis of west European experience since 1945 is inconclusive, the fact remains that the dent which the movement for wider integration has so far made in the sovereignty principle is small and partial indeed. All the evidence seems to show that, however the sovereignty principle is criticized as dangerous and anarchical, however states, with modern world economic and technological developments, become mixed up in their affairs, man's desire to 'run his own show'—even if simply an illusion—remains strong. If, as all fervently hope, the threats to world peace continue to be kept at bay, confidence in the principle of national sovereignty is likely to remain strong. It is a perhaps paradoxical but nevertheless true fact that the more man's prayers for peace are answered, the more the institution many hold responsible for war, namely the sovereign state, is likely to be strengthened.

REFERENCES

Beloff, M., *New Dimensions in Foreign Policy*, London, Allen and Unwin, 1961.

Brzezinski, Z. K., *The Soviet Bloc : Unity and Conflict*, New York, Praeger, 3rd Ed., 1967.

Camps, M., *European Unification in the Sixties*, New York, McGraw Hill, and London, O.U.P., 1966.

Haas, E. B., *Beyond the Nation-State*, Stanford, Stanford U.P., 1964.

Haas, E. B., *Tangle of Hopes*, Englewood Cliffs, N.J., Prentice-Hall, 1969.

Herz, J. H., *International Politics in the Atomic Age*, New York, Columbia U.P., 1959.

Hinsley, F. H., *Sovereignty*, London, Watts, and New York, Basic Books, 1966.

Jessup, P. C., 'The Equality of States as Dogma and Reality' in Olson, W. C., and Sondermann, F. S. (eds.), *The Theory and Practice of International Relations*, Englewood Cliffs, N. J., and Hemel Hempstead, Herts, Prentice-Hall, 2nd Ed., 1966.

Laqueur, W., and Labedz, L., *Polycentrism: the New Factor in International Politics*, New York and London, Praeger, 1962.

Osgood, R. E., *NATO: the Entangling Alliance*, Chicago and London, University of Chicago Press, 1962.

Twitchett, K. J., and Cosgrove, C., *The New International Actors*, London, Macmillan, 1970.

Vital, D., *The Inequality of States*, Oxford and Fair Lawn, N. J., Clarendon Press, 1967.

16 *Conclusion*

I

Perhaps the most important conclusion to be reached at the close of this study of a century of international relations is that there is no conclusion, in the sense of an end to our story. The political process, whether within the frontiers of a state or between states, has no termination, or even beginning. 'In political activity', Professor Michael Oakeshott wrote, 'men sail a boundless and bottomless sea : there is neither harbour for shelter nor floor for anchorage, neither starting place nor appointed destination.'[1] The year 1870, the beginning of our story, began nothing essentially new; 1970, its ending, is not the closing of the account. In all the battles, verbal as well as military, which punctuate the unfolding of this tale, each time the defeated finds that he, or his descendant in the hereditary states of the world, lives to fight another day; the victor, more often than not, discovers that if there is one thing worse than failure it is success. New generations take up the story, the grass grows again over concentration camp and battlefield, new divisions spring up between old wartime comrades while scars of conflict heal and the children of enemies marry and produce new generations with their own affinities and differences, loves and hates.

It would perhaps be unnecessary to make such an obvious point, were it not for the temptation for men and women, especially in times of great social or international conflict, to imagine that, with a little more effort, one more heave, the present struggle will be won, and, what is more, that peace will reign for ever and the lion will lie down with the lamb. 'Comrades ! Come rally', runs the socialist anthem, 'the last fight let us face : the *Internationale* unites the human race.' It is easy to smile at such naive messianism in time of peace and plenty, but when a political party or movement and, much more, an entire nation girds itself for a great struggle, it seems essential to the maintenance of morale to believe that this indeed is the final effort after which the messianic age of perpetual peace

[1] *Political education. An inaugural lecture*, Cambridge, 1951.

will dawn. British soldiers marching to the monstrous slaughter of the Somme in 1916 in the belief that this was the final assault which would end the war, and not merely *the* war, but *all* war, or Winston Churchill holding out the vision in 1940 of an emergence on to the 'bright uplands of peace' once the Nazi beast had been downed, are merely two examples of the flight into eschatalogical fantasy which men and nations indulge in as the brunt of the battle is borne.

But not merely is it historically unreal to entertain these hopeful notions of a conclusion to the story of international relations; their ultimate and inevitable falsification only serves to embitter those relations even more than they might otherwise have been. The myth that an epoch of international affairs, which may have been violent and full of conflict, can have an end, in the sense of permanent freedom from violence and conflict, is inevitably shown to be the folly that it is. But this is not the conclusion that men usually draw about their own fantasies. They are far more likely to infer that if the dream of perfect peace and understanding which sustained them during the dark days of conflict vanishes with the break of day, this must be because of the ill-will of somebody else, and now he must be stopped in his tracks before true peace will really come.

Russians who suffered in the Second World War struggles against the Nazis imagined in 1945 that only the bourgeois states now intervened between them and a world order undisturbed by conflict. Western nations which had laboured as comrades of the Russians during the war against the *last* enemy, Nazism, could not but think that sheer, doctrinaire Soviet obstructionism stood in the way of lasting peace. Rather than admit that states which submerge their differences of interests to fight a common foe are bound to find those differences emerge when the foe is defeated, former allies of war will destroy themselves under the influence of the fatal illusion that the other country, not *la condition humaine*, is the cause of it all.

If a study of any period of international relations has no conclusion in the sense of a close or finale to the human drama, neither has it (though this is more controversial) conclusions in the sense of lessons from the past which may be profitably applied to the future conduct of international affairs. We have, it is true, already suggested one such lesson: namely, that it can be inexpedient, if not possibly dangerous, to pitch too high our expectations from the successful outcome of a particular national endeavour, or to exaggerate the catastrophes which could follow its defeat. But, apart from this, the lessons of history are few and far between; history, it has been said, does throw a beam of light on the dark waters sailed by the ship of state, but it projects it over the path the vessel has already traced rather than the calms and storms ahead.

What is more, the lessons which men draw from their history may be true enough according to the unique circumstances of the past, but can lead them badly astray when they face the new circumstances of today and tomorrow. Everyone knows how Sir Anthony Eden (as he then was) was haunted by the spectre of Munich and the years of 'appeasement' of the 1930s and determined that President Nasser, another Hitler in Eden's, and for some time the Leader of the Opposition, Hugh Gaitskell's, eyes, should not be allowed the easy triumphs for unilateral *faits accomplis* as the dictators were two decades before. Possibly the spectre of Munich has haunted the mutual attitudes of both the Communist and non-Communist worlds in the Cold War after 1945, to the grave disadvantage of both.

But perhaps the aptest example of the dangers of applying to the present lessons (or conclusions) derived from the past is that of the formulae devised for the collective maintenance of peace after great wars which have rocked the international system. Tocqueville wrote of the political nostalgia of his own day :

> The first duty which is at this time imposed on those who direct our affairs is to educate the democracy; to rearm its faith, if that be possible; to purify its morals . . . to adapt its government to time and place and to modify it in compliance with the occurrences and actors of the age. A new science of politics is indispensable to a new world. This, however, is what we think of least; launched in the middle of a rapid stream, we obstinately fix our eyes on the ruins that may still be descried upon the shore we have left, while the current sweeps us along, and drives us backward towards the gulf.[2]

When writing this passage, Tocqueville could have been thinking, *inter alia*, of the Quadruple Alliance of November 1815 between Austria, Britain, Prussia and Russia which had defeated his own country, France, at Waterloo and was then devoted to preserving the peace in Europe by, among other means, keeping Napoleon and his heirs permanently from the throne of France. The effort badly

[2] Alexis de Tocqueville, *Democracy in America,* ed. by H. S. Commager, London, 1946, pp. 6–7.

misfired. When Napoleon I's nephew, Louis Napoleon, became the French Emperor in 1852 he was universally mistrusted. So much so that in the Franco-Prussian War in 1870 European, and especially British, sympathies were on Bismarck's side. This was one of the circumstances which concealed from Europe's eyes for forty years the implications of German unification for the balance of power in Europe.

An even more telling example of the mischief wrought by lessons of history being wrongly applied in the post-war construction of international machinery to keep the peace is the case of the League of Nations. In 1919, when the League Covenant was framed, every-one was conscious that in 1914 there had been a resort to war through the armed crossing of frontiers; much in the Allies' mind naturally were Germany's armed crossing of French and Belgian frontiers and the violation of Serbia's frontiers by Austro-Hungarian forces. But suppose, on the eve of these invasions, all the belligerents had been bound to undergo a process of inquiry and delay. Suppose, too, that a country resorted to war without conforming to this pro-cess or made war against another country which did, would it not be pointed out before the eyes and ears of the world as deserving of ostracism from the international community? Hence the opening words of the famous sanctions Article 16 of the League Covenant ran : 'Should any Member of the League *resort to war* [author's italics] in disregard of its covenants under Articles 12, 13 and 15, it shall *ipso facto* be deemed to have committed an act of war against all other Members of the League, which hereby undertake immediately to subject it to the severance of all trade or financial relations. . . .'

Was the German attack on Belgium and France and Austria-Hungary's attack on Serbia in 1914 a 'resort to war'? Indubitably. If they had not complied with the procedures for peaceful settle-ment laid down in Articles 12, 13 and 15 in the League Covenant, would they have deserved the application of League sanctions against them? Certainly. But was the Japanese attack on Manchuria in 1931 and its subsequent conversion into a puppet state of Japan a 'resort to war'? The case was not so clear. The Japanese called it an 'incident' and European League member-states that felt dis-inclined to make a fuss about it recalled the civil-war conditions in China and Japan's right in those conditions to defend her property, the South Manchuria Railway, which she had virtually to establish law and order in the whole country to do.

Was Mussolini's invasion of Ethiopia in October 1935 a 'resort to war' within the meaning of Article 16 of the League Covenant? Certainly, and almost the whole League and British public opinion said so : the only question, according to the British Foreign Secretary, Sir Samuel Hoare, was whether sanctions, economic or military, could be effective unless applied by the League as a whole, without any backsliders. But was Hitler's reoccupation of the Rhineland in March 1936 and his incitement of the Sudeten Germans in Czechoslovakia to demand secession in order to join the Third Reich 'resorts to war'? The first was certainly illegal and the latter recklessly provocative, but 'resorts to war'? Yet they, or even the former alone, were far more dangerous threats to European peace than Mussolini's Ethiopian enterprise, immoral as this may have been from any angle. Could it be that the framers of the League Covenant, by singling out 'resort to war' as the offence meriting collective punishment, had signalled to potential breakers of the peace much more insidious and dangerous methods of smashing the prevailing international order which did not fall under the League's interdiction? (See above, Chapter 8, p. 163.)

The present United Nations Charter is another such example. It seems almost as though the dominating idea at the San Francisco conference in 1945 which finalized the Charter was to avoid the mistakes of the 1930s, especially the failure of Britain and France to secure the assistance on suitable terms of the United States and the Soviet Union when the Europan dictators threw down their challenges to the democracies. It was an almost perfect example of *l'esprit d'escalier* : the reconstruction in the mind after the event of a disastrous encounter, but this time with all the cards stacked in the victim's favour. Although provision was made in Articles 53 and 107 of the Charter for preventive action against the former Axis Powers outside the scope of the UN Organization, it was as though the great victorious powers—Britain, China, France, the Soviet Union and the United States—were saying at the San Francisco conference : just let the circumstances of the 1930s return again and Hitler, Mussolini and the Japanese militarists will find us ready for them next time ! In other words, while we would not wish to underestimate the important work the United Nations is doing in all its various branches, it is difficult not to believe that the only circumstances in which it might act effectively to preserve the peace are the very ones which are most unlikely to occur : namely, a revival of the anti-democratic front of the dictators of the 1930s.

We are chary therefore of drawing 'lessons' from the hundred years' experience of international relations described in this book which may assist in the handling of those relations in the future, though some such indications will be given before this chapter ends. Our more important, and more legitimate, concern is to summarize the major changes which the international system has experienced during the last century. Though this may offer only limited guidance as to developments in the next century, or even the next decade, it is of vital importance to understand the earlier forms of conducting relations between independent states from which our present-day system emerged.

The first in importance of the changes which overtook the international system in the century covered by this book is without doubt the transformation of a traditional, essentially European system of states into the world-wide system which is part of our familiar international environment of the present day. Indeed, this globalization of the old international system raises the question whether one can continue to speak of a single international system today. Is not the position one in which, in contradistinction to the relatively simple and territorially restricted Concert or 'comity' of Europe of the nineteenth century, we now have a world-wide system of states formally linked together by such universal institutions as the United Nations and temporary or more enduring *détentes* between the super-powers, but in fact fragmented into a series of sub-systems, as for instance the Western or Atlantic grouping, the Warsaw Pact bloc, the Arab League, the African states grouped together within the Organization of African Unity, the Organization of American States and so on?

We would ourselves, however, prefer to describe these regional groupings as sub-systems of a single global international system rather than as separate international systems in their own right. Our reasons for preferring this approach are threefold. First, there can be no doubt that within these regional sub-systems states manifest much the same kind of motivations, interests and patterns of behaviour as they do in the world system as a whole; for them the local regional group represents little beyond a more convenient theatre of diplomacy than the global system as a whole. Secondly, it is equally obvious that the extent of cohesion in these regional sub-groups reflects, and must reflect, the state of relationships within the entire global international system. It has become clear, for example, that the solidarity and sense of common interest within the North Atlantic and the Warsaw regional defence systems have varied in direct proportion to the intensity of the hostility between Communist and non-Communist states as a whole; the greater the danger of the East-West conflict terminating in actual military hostilities, the more the member-states have huddled together in mutual self-defence, while an easement of international tension has slackened the bonds between them. Thirdly, it remains true, whether disagreeable or not, that the state of the central balance of power between the Leviathan states of the international system is still the determinant of whether these regional sub-systems can continue to survive or whether they will be swept away, along with the rest of us, in the final *dies irae, dies illa* of nuclear war. For all these reasons, we agree that the modern state, as distinguished from its forerunner in 1870, tends to live in two worlds : the regional world of limited alliances and alignments, and the great globe itself. Naturally, the extent to which global international developments affect it will be governed by its general power ranking and the geographical extent of its interests. But we are inclined to think that today, in times of great international strain, even the smallest states must more anxiously scan the global horizons of world politics than affairs within the regional sub-system with which they are identified.

There is no need to recapitulate here in detail how this extra-Europeanization or globalization of the international system occurred and the forces and factors behind it. As we have seen in discussing European imperialism in Asia and Africa in the quarter-century following 1870, the increasing wealth of the European powers and the incentives they felt to utilize it in expansion into the non-European world, the improvements in techniques and communications which made this possible, and the nineteenth-century myth that no power could genuinely describe itself as great without a fair group of appropriately coloured areas on the maps of Asia and Africa, signifying its elevation to the senior rank of states, were all important forces spreading the European impact abroad. Along with Europe's military power, commercial goods, loans and the religion of the West, however, went Western ideas, including the essentially Western idea of national self-determination. The European great powers nursed in their bosoms the viper of nationalism which was ultimately to destroy their empires.

This could not be done at once. The European Empires were too strong in, say, 1900 to be shaken by such powerless protests as the Chinese Boxer Rebellion. But once Japan had overthrown Russia, a military giant among the European powers, in 1905, the myth of the inviolability and permanence of European power outside Europe began to fade. In the Second World War Japan smashed the bastions of European imperialism in Malaya, Singapore, French Indo-China and the Dutch East Indies, and the grip of Europe on east Asia and its outlying islands and archipelagoes, once broken, could never thereafter be restored.

To which we must add the inevitable effect on the primacy of Europe in international relations of the two great wars of the twentieth century which ravaged Europe and left it gasping for breath. We have argued earlier in this book that the unification of Germany in 1870 and its subsequent industrialization created a military force in central Europe of superb self-discipline and technical ingenuity, to say nothing of its key strategical situation, which could not be overcome, neither in 1918 nor again in 1944–45, by any European combination even including Russia, though the immensity of Russia's spaces and the spirit of her people made her a vital force in the defeat of Germany in 1945. Given that Germany could not be finally conquered without the joint efforts of the United States and the Soviet Union, both only partially European in politics or geographical position, the post-Second World War period was bound to be overshadowed by these two and the struggle between them. As it happened, both were confessedly enemies of European imperialism, though Russia could only make this claim with tongue in cheek. Both vied with each other to stimulate the revolt of Asia and Africa from the war-devastated and war-weary old European powers—Belgium, Britain, France and Holland. Is it surprising that the new nations, if such they could be called, seized with both hands the opportunities which history had created for them to break the bonds of Western imperialism and extend the international system to the whole world itself by making themselves independent and self-governing members of it?

But it is the effects of the globalization of the international system on the functioning of that system which concerns us here. First, there is, of course, the remarkable increase in the number of state members in the international system, from 50-odd at the end of the Second World War to some 130 today, some of which, like Germany, Korea and Vietnam, are still divided either as a result of the Cold

War or, as in the case of Vietnam, the decolonization process. It could be argued that the greater the number of states, the greater the the number, by geometrical progression, of potential international conflicts; on the other hand, the case could equally well be made out for saying that the fewer the states the more bitter are likely to be the conflicts between them, on the principle that any given level of tension in the international system as a whole has to be distributed among the existing states, and the more numerous the states, the more thinly the prevailing amount of tension has to be spread. But this is an unconvincing mathematical method of dealing with amity and discord between states. It may be said, however, that when a large number of new states are admitted into great international organizations such as the United Nations, the tendency is for resolutions to be adopted there which represent a definite majority of national opinions but not necessarily of world power. Since 1945, and perhaps even since 1919, states have been called upon to make decisions within international organizations about issues geographically remote from them or involving interests which are neither directly nor indirectly their own. Whereas in the nineteenth century conferences were called 'between the states immediately concerned', today merely being a state and being recognized as a member of the UN entitles any community to participate in a process of exercising power, if only in symbolic form. Hence there come into existence UN resolutions which the organization is not able to implement, precisely the situation which the framers of the Charter in 1945 most wanted to avoid.

Secondly, the globalization of the international system reduced and then finally extinguished the areas into which the great powers could expand, with the general consent of their peers, in order to compensate themselves for frustrations of policies between themselves. We have noted in a earlier chapter how it was a characteristic practice in the European system for the major powers to induce any of their number who felt dissatisfied with the situation at the core of the system to compensate itself at the expense of the periphery (see above, Chapter 10, pp. 196–7). Thus Bismarck encouraged France to take Tunis in 1881; thus the Entente powers in 1915 welcomed Italy, then an ally of the Central powers, to enter the war against them on the Entente side by offers of territorial expansion in south-east Europe, Anatolia and Africa. By 1900, however, the non-European areas were acquiring the strength to resist European expansion: the defeat of Italy by Menelik of Ethiopia at

Adowa in 1896 is one example, the defeat of Russia by Japan in 1905 another. Moreover, with the creation of the League of Nations, the idea began to take hold among League supporters that no state, in Europe or outside it, should be fair game for any dissatisfied European great power to annex. This notion received dramatic expression in the world-wide recoil of horror against the Italian attack on Ethiopia in 1935 while Mussolini, having been led to believe by Pierre Laval of France that he could do as he wished with Ethiopia so long as he maintained the Stresa front against Germany in Europe, was astonished at the British government's attempt to placate pro-League opinion by abolishing the old practice of compensation at the expense of the non-European world.

Together with the filling in by independent nation-states of the non-European world during the decolonization process after the Second World War, came a further change. Before 1914 there was an almost instinctive solidarity among the European powers against the non-European world if the latter gave any sign of resistance to European control; the collective self-help of the European powers to protect their position in China during the Boxer rebellion of 1900 is a striking example. Behind this joint defence of European rule in Asia and Africa lay the much older tradition of European unity against the Turks in Europe, of which Gladstone, for example, was an outstanding exponent. Since 1945 the situation has been exactly the reverse; instead of the world powers, Russia and the United States, combining to resist any challenge to their primacy from the new Third World of decolonized states, each until recently has tried to curry favour with Third World states as possible allies in the struggle against the other. One result of this which would have shocked the mid-Victorian statesman is the competition between the two super-powers and their respective allies to show that their opposition to racialism is more genuine than the other side's. Race was never an issue between the old European powers because all shared the same common notion of the white man's superiority to coloured races. Today professions of freedom from race prejudice on one's own side and allegations of race prejudice on the other side are common elements in the political warfare between East and West.

The second important change in the international system since 1870, which is partly bound up with the extra-Europeanization of that system, is what may be called the 'democratization' and 'socialization' of foreign policy. The former word stands for the increasing tendency for statesmen to be aware of the 'public-relations' aspect of their policies—the amount of public support at home and abroad they are winning for those policies—and the latter for the tendency of foreign policy to be geared to certain economic goals, especially economic growth in the case of the developing countries, as well as older aims such as the acquisition of territory, the military strength and security of the state and so on. Since Woodrow Wilson and the Russian Bolsheviks at the end of the First World War called for the abolition of the old practice under which foreign policy was the exclusive and private concern of an inner circle within the Cabinet, every word or gesture of a minister, even of a totalitarian state, before the world-wide audience of today, with its countless television and radio sets, has to be weighed carefully with respect to its effects on public attitudes throughout the world. Just as the mass media of communications have converted internal state politics into a rivalry between 'images' rather than between formulated policies, so modern states in their relations *inter se* seek more and more to create a mood in the world-wide public mind rather than negotiate legal agreements with one another. Again, the socialization of foreign policy has caused more departments of state than the foreign office or ministry to be concerned with foreign relations; international relations and negotiations to cover a much wider range of matters, including the economic and commercial, than the strictly political; and advanced and developing countries alike to judge policy options more and more in terms of whether they are likely to retard or advance the economic policies of the nation.

The causes of these great changes are to be found in many different developments. The devastating impact of war on the ordinary people made it essential for foreign policies to be explained to the ordinary person and his or her consent to the broad lines of policy to be sought; another factor tending in the same direction was the increasing literacy and political awareness of the masses resulting from spreading education and the great mass media : the popular press, broadcasting and television. As for the developing countries, the expectations in those states of a richer life after the bonds of colonialism had been shattered imposed on their governments acute concern with economic development and compelled them to make a show, at least, of using foreign policy as a means of raising economic levels. To which must be added the increasing refinement and costliness of modern weapons. The wholesale destruction implicit in these weapons and the need to keep them fully abreast of new technology in the condition of permanent war-preparedness in which the major states have lived, at least since 1950, have placed a premium on other means of changing the mind of other states so as to accord with one's own : means such as propaganda, psychological warfare, the active, unceasing attempt to operate on the minds and emotions of other people; subversion and sabotage, including the entire complex apparatus of attempting to undermine other states from within, or at least to soften them up so that if in the end one has to apply military force the costs and repercussions can be deliberately minimized; and alterations in the style of warfare, such as the introduction of *Blitzkrieg*, guerrilla warfare and the use of paramilitary forces, all of which are attempts to secure the aims of war, which, according to Clausewitz, is to 'compel our opponent to do our will by using violence against him', at lower cost in human life and resources.

One of the most important effects of the democratization and socialization of foreign policy is what may be called the bifurcation of diplomacy; this is the division of diplomatic activities into two types, one being the traditional manner of communication between one government and another, the other being the direct appeal to the peoples of the world over the heads of their governments. When Lenin and the Bolsheviks tried the latter after their seizure of power in Russia, and when President Wilson, during a deadlock in the negotiations with the Italian representatives at the Paris peace conference in 1919, threatened publicly to appeal to the Italian people over their government's head, the effect was shattering on statesmen like Lloyd George and Clemenceau. They had grown up in a world in which, so far from fomenting a revolution from below in another country, the European powers stood together in opposing revolution from the lower orders. Nevertheless, the appeal to disloyalty against one's own government, the search to break apart the social forces binding the other side together, has been a mark of international relations ever since.

Third among the major changes which have overtaken international relations since 1870 is the prolific growth of permanent international institutions covering almost every branch of political, economic, strategic, social and cultural activities proceeding within the modern state. We have already described the inter-governmental machinery for the settlement mostly of political questions in 1870 as rudimentary and informal in the extreme : the Concert of Europe is the classic, and almost the only, example (see above, Chapter 4, p. 64). The Concert had no written constitution, secretariat or other methods of recording proceedings, nor even a permanent meeting-place. There were courts of arbitration set up entirely on an *ad hoc* basis and the beginnings of both governmental and non-governmental bureaux and agencies for functional co-operation, as we would call it today, in specialized and technical fields. And that was about all. The need for the further development of international organizations was not felt to be pressing, both because the volume of inter-state relationships was limited, though rapidly growing, and because various social forces combined to keep the peace without the special need of international organizations to enforce it (see above, Chapter 1).

In the 1970s the picture has changed entirely. With the foundation of the League of Nations in 1919, the world habituated itself to international machinery not much less complex than the political machinery of one of its member-states. The League had its constitution, its regular Council sessions and annual sessions of the Assembly, its permanent headquarters in Geneva and its permanent secretariat, a full-time, paid international civil service to prepare agenda for meetings, to keep records, to implement the decisions of the various League organs when requested to do so, and generally to act as a link or channel of communication between the League and member-states. Moreover, the League had its court, the Permanent Court of International Justice at The Hague, and a host of departments dealing with subjects as diverse as the mandates system and intellectual co-operation, finance and economics and the traffic in drugs.[3]

The United Nations has a similar constitutional structure, but far more complex, with a bigger budget, a larger secretarial and administrative staff, even a larger, and much more verbose, basic constitution, the Charter. Its membership is more than twice that of the old League and from the League's modestly sized specialist commissions and committees have sprung, as principal organs of the UN, the Trusteeship and Social and Economic Councils, the latter having four regional commissions, and a score of Specialized Agencies, such as the World Health Organization and that survivor from League days, the International Labour Organization : each of these Specialized Agencies is virtually of the same dimensions and complexity as the United Nations as a whole. Perhaps the most

[3] See H. R. G. Greaves, *The League Committees and World Order*, London, 1932.

striking way of illustrating this immense growth in the complexity and scale of operations of world-wide international institutions in the 1920s is to remind ourselves of the fact that forty or fifty years ago the ordinary person, if he was reasonably hard-working, could hope to keep himself informed of all the major activities going forward within the League of Nations; today he could count himself fortunate if he could keep abreast of all that was going on within even one principal organ of the UN. However effective or ineffective in practice all the studies, reports, debates, speeches, resolutions of these UN bodies are, they occupy the time of large numbers of highly skilled civil servants and politicians both at UN headquarters in New York and within the different major states.

In addition there are the large number of regional agencies set up by inter-governmental agreement and associated to a greater or less extent with the UN. The range of these runs from those dealing with general political purposes, such as the League of Arab States, founded in 1945, to collective defence arrangements such as the North Atlantic Treaty Organization, dating from the early and mid-1950s and based on the North Atlantic collective defence agreement signed on 4 April 1949. The important facts about these bodies, apart from their great number, are their seeming permanence and continuing activities, their deep involvement in different departments of state of the member-countries and the growth within them of a *corps* of civil servants some of whom have spent their whole lives in the business of promoting and executing international agreements reached multilaterally or bilaterally between the various member-governments.

Inter-governmental machinery for international co-operation, however, is supplemented by international co-operation carried on between unofficial persons or groups in different countries, and this non-governmental international co-operation has followed the same law of proliferation and increasing complexity.[4] Many of these non-governmental bodies enjoy a certain official status since they are recognized by the UN Economic and Social Council as organizations which the Council consults. The Union of International Associations at Brussels which publishes an annual *Yearbook* on the non-governmental organizations lists more than 2,000 such bodies as existing during the 1960s. There are few activities which are

---

[4] See Lyman C. White and M. R. Zocca, *International Non-governmental Organisations*, New Brunswick, 1951; F. S. Northedge, 'International trade associations and congresses' in the *Encyclopaedia Britannica*, Vol. XII.

carried on in society, whether as work or pleasure, which are not today nationally organized and, through their national organizations, linked with similar national bodies abroad. The resulting international organization may act as a pressure group on the different governments of the world or on the UN in the cause of advancing some sectional interest; or its *raison d'être* may simply be the mutual help to be derived from co-operation with one's opposite number abroad within a continuing and formal association.

This immense proliferation in international institutions, official and unofficial, since the 1870s has been partly due to what may be called the 'law of increasing bureaucratization', that is, the general tendency for institutions, once established, to become increasingly complex in structure and activities. The principal organization soon finds it needs sub-committees, and then another committee to co-ordinate the work of the sub-committees, and then it appears inevitable to many that the main organization will fail to fulfil its functions unless there is a further committee to check the work of the co-ordinating committee and report to the main body, which is now too big to reach decisions swiftly without an executive council. And so it goes on. There is also the inevitable increase in the scale and complexity of all international relations as time goes on and technology makes the processes of manufacture or commerce more intricate. Whether one is reading a book, eating a meal, driving a car, watching a film or taking a holiday, there is today an international aspect to almost all one does and international agencies have to be created to serve the needs of that international aspect.

Two other factors, both arising in the official sector of a state's life, have also had an influence in this institutional proliferation. One is the spread of state control, even within so-called bourgeois countries, to wider and wider areas of the nation's life and livelihood. The year 1870 represented the high noon of *laissez-faire*, when Lassalle's principle of the 'night-watchman' state presided over most of Europe. In 1970 the world is divided, very crudely, into three groups : the Communist world in which state control predominates; the Third World of new Afro-Asian countries many of which use the instrument of state control to help with their aspirations to a developed economy and a strong national consciousness; and the so-called 'mixed' economies of the Western states which involve considerable state intervention. It is hardly surprising then that governments should meet their opposite numbers abroad more often in a shrinking world in which an increasing number of the nation's activities are controlled and channelled through the official machinery of the state.

Secondly, international alliances for strategic purposes in the post-Second World War period have become increasingly bureaucratized, like other international bodies. Whereas alliances between two or more countries in the years between 1870 and 1945 were usually little more than solemn promises to assist one another when the right moment came, with or without some joint military or naval planning and manœuvres, today the military alliance has increasingly become a bureaucratic institution, with permanent headquarters and secretariat, information officers and the like, councils for economic and political consultation, armed forces so closely integrated as to be almost internationalized, and, in all, an institutional structure so complex that it can only be explained by diagrams handed out to visitors to the headquarters.

The reasons for this transformation of alliances, in so far as it cannot be attributed to the 'law of increasing bureaucratization', is to be found partly in the ideological character of the post-1945 East-West conflict and partly in the change in the nature and function of military force itself in the international system. Where nations are gathered together, not merely in joint defence of their security, but in a common front against a determined ideological adversary, ideology has to permeate the alliance, as well as military considerations. Public opinion in the member-states has to be educated in the political values the alliances stand for; a sense of ideological co-partnership has to be fostered to keep the spirit behind the alliance keen and ready; and the alliance has to be protected by various devices against saboteurs and spies from the other side. But the nature of modern war and deterrence have made their contributions, too. In any conceivable nuclear war there cannot be the thirty days' mobilization provided for in alliances of the past, or even thirty minutes. The alliance has to be in a state of permanent war-preparedness, with nuclear bombers in the air, Polaris submarines at sea and nuclear missiles at the ready in their concrete silos, not only to retaliate at once against an enemy strike, but in order above all to deter; if deterrence fails, it is assumed that the whole strategy of the alliance fails.

The cost of maintaining a state of permanent war-preparedness, in view of the continuing obsolescence of modern weapons, is enormous and steps have to be taken by members of the alliance, through study of one another's budgets, and indeed the whole economy of every member-state, to ensure that full value is being obtained for the money invested in deterrence and that each ally is making the fullest contribution within its powers. Even beyond this there have to be arrangements for political consultation between the allies to see to it that opportunities for agreement with the other side to lessen the strain are not missed, that the foreign policy of one ally does not become a thorn in the side of the others, and that if hostilities must start, they begin on an agreed issue, at an agreed place and an agreed time, in so far as this is possible. All those developments have tended towards the bureaucratization of the modern alliance.

As for the effects of the increasing proliferation of international institutions, these are hard to judge. It could be argued that these institutions have become new 'actors' in the international system, rivalling the different states as centres of initiatives which make up the substance of international politics.[5] Or that the affairs of the different states are becoming so mixed up together through all this continuous institutional co-operation on many levels that in effect national sovereignty has become a legalistic formal expression, corresponding to no reality in the actual world. Or that the ordinary people of the different countries are having to do so much with each other in all branches of their life that they are ceasing to regard themselves as British, French or Italian, and beginning to think of themselves as solicitors, clerks, doctors, taxi-drivers and so on within a world-wide horizontal community of people with the same skills or interests.

We have uttered some cautions in the previous chapter against the assumption that the principle of sovereignty and the feeling of nationalism are on the way out; we need not repeat them here. But it is worth emphasizing, as one of the more striking consequences of the growth and increase of international institutions, that in all cases more departments of state than the Foreign Office, together with the chief executive, are now involved in external relations than ever before. Ministries of economics and finance, departments of foreign trade, immigration, health, education, fuel, power and transport, national agencies for the conservation of the environment or the preservation of ancient monuments, and many more are likely to be drawn into the widening front on which today states

[5] K. J. Twitchett and C. A. Cosgrove, *The New International Actors*, London, 1970.

N

meet states.[6] This may represent a move towards the closer integration of states in a genuine world or regional community. But it could also mean that wider areas of international contact, which were formerly free from political control, are now politicized and hence are exposed to all the national *amour-propre* and unwillingness to get too mixed up with the foreigner which have characterized international politics for so long. The person who in 1870 could tour the length and breadth of Europe without travel permits and in 1970 confronts officialdom at every frontier is not necessarily bound to become an internationalist in spirit as a result of his experience.

III

Finally, are there lessons to be drawn from this century of experience which might be helpful in the management of international relations in the years ahead? Earlier in this chapter, we have warned against the easy assumption that history provides such lessons; becoming educated in our past mistakes unfortunately does not insure us against committing new, perhaps worse, mistakes. Nevertheless, with the utmost caution, we may perhaps single out three conclusions from this study which could be borne in mind by those who have to deal, if only as voters, with the future development of international relations. They may be stated quite briefly.

The first maxim of statecraft we would urge is that although the international system has, almost unintermittently, aroused the strongest emotional protest by reason of its frequent violence and bloodshed, it has shown a tough resistance to attempts to change or abolish it. Woodrow Wilson and Lenin are no doubt the best remembered of leaders of opinion who tried and failed to reform or eliminate the system of international politics; but there are countless others. Some, like the Americans, having failed to reform the system in 1919, withdrew from it altogether and hoped to survive within their continental fortress; but that was an even worse solution. No doubt the system is changing, as we have indicated in this chapter, but change is slow. Let us try to get as much agreement as we can with other countries with a view to improving this political system which is so full of conflict, but never let us suppose our own favoured reforms to be the only ones possible or desirable. Perhaps the most we can try to do is to understand where our own interests

[6] See Max Beloff, *New Dimensions in Foreign Policy*, London, 1961.

as a nation-state lie, and to advance those interests as best we may, paying due regard to the rights of other states to pursue their interests and always seeking to harmonize our views with theirs.

This brings us to our second principle, namely, that it is always wrong to assume that the state you are dealing with is wicked, foolish or aggressive if its outlook on international affairs is not the same as yours. It may be wicked, foolish or aggressive; but before hastening to such conclusions it is as well to put yourself imagina- tively in your opponent's shoes, to see the world through his eyes and penetrate the feelings he has, with his experience, memories, geo- graphical situation, political beliefs and psychology. What there is to be said for any particular viewpoint in international affairs depends on the vantage point at which one stands. If the first rule in international affairs is to discover what courses of policy circum- stances dictate for one's own state as within its vital interests, a close second is to appreciate the interests of others as they see them and their equal rights to advance those interests.

But thirdly, foreign policy is best conducted perhaps in a spirit of realistic and cautious optimism. The conclusion which strikes all students of international relations covering any considerable tract of time is that hopes are never quite perfectly fulfilled; but neither are all fears realized. This takes us back to what we said at the beginning of this chapter about the endlessness and lack of finality about international politics. If Britain and France had never feared that a German victory in the First World War would be the end of civilization, and the same for the Germans *mutatis mutandis*, the long agony of that terrible struggle might have been shortened. As it happened, Britain and France had their wish, but Hitler's world was no better than the Kaiser's world, or rather a thousand times worse. If the Americans in the early 1950s had not feared that Soviet rule in eastern Europe might have the effect of extinguishing freedom everywhere, an understanding with Russia might have been reached much earlier. But the point need not be laboured. Man's exaggerated hopes and exaggerated fears drive him into the most monstrous crises. Better than hoping for everything and fear- ing for everything is a steady optimism, but one grounded in the most realistic appreciation of present and past fears and future probabilities. The story is not likely to end tomorrow either with the trumpets of Heaven or the descent into nuclear inferno.

Further Reading

THE EUROPEAN BALANCE OF POWER, 1815-71

Anderson, M. S., *The Eastern Question, 1774-1923*, London, Macmillan, 1966.

Binkley, R. C., *Realism and Nationalism, 1852-1871*, New York and London, Harper, 1963.

Blum, J., Cameron, R., and Barnes, T. G., *The European World Since 1815*, London, Routledge and Kegan Paul, and Boston, Little Brown, 1967.

Cecil, A., *Metternich, 1773-1859*, London, Eyre and Spottiswoode, 3rd Ed., 1947.

Colloms, B., *Europe, 1815-1914*, London, Dent, 1969.

Dill, M., *Germany, A Modern History*, Ann Arbor, Michigan U.P., 1961.

Eyck, E., *Bismarck and the German Empire*, London, Allen and Unwin, and New York, Norton, 1958.

Grant, A. J., and Temperley, H. W. V., *Europe in the Nineteenth and Twentieth Centuries, 1789-1914*, London, Longmans, New York, Humanities, 6th Ed., 1952.

Holborn, H., *The Political Collapse of Europe*, New York, Knopf, 1966.

Knapton, E. J., and Derry, T. K., *Europe, 1815-1914*, London, John Murray, and New York, Scribner's, 1964.

Langer, W. L., *European Alliances and Alignments, 1871-1890*, New York, Knopf, 2nd Ed., 1950.

Lipson, E., *Europe in the XIXth. and XXth. Centuries, 1815-1939*, London, Black, and New York, Fernhill, 10th Ed., 1957.

Marriott, J. A. R., *The Eastern Question. An Historical Study in European Diplomacy*, Oxford, and Fair Lawn, N.J., Clarendon Press, 4th Ed., 1940.

May, A. J., *The Hapsburg Monarchy, 1867-1914*, Cambridge, Mass., Harvard U.P., and London, O.U.P., 1951.

Miller, W., *The Ottoman Empire and its Successors, 1807-1927*, Cambridge, C.U.P., 1936.

Mosse, W. E., *The European Powers and the German Question, 1848-1871*, Cambridge, C.U.P., 1958.

Mowat, R. B., *A History of European Diplomacy, 1825-1914*, London, Arnold, 1922.

Seaman, L. B. C., *From Vienna to Versailles*, London, Methuen, and New York, Harper, 1955.

Seton-Watson, G. H. N., *The Decline of Imperial Russia, 1855-1914*, London, Methuen, and New York, Praeger, 1952.

Taylor, A. J. P., *The Course of German History*, London, Hamilton, 1946.

Thomson, D., *Europe since Napoleon*, London, Longmans, 1957.

IMPERIALISM

Blake, R. N. W., *Disraeli*, London, Eyre and Spottiswoode, and New York, St. Martin's, 1966.

Bolt, C., *Victorian Attitudes to Race*, London, Routledge and Kegan Paul, 1971.

Carrington, C. E., *The British Overseas*, Cambridge, and New York, C.U.P., 2nd Ed., 1968.

Carrington, C. E., *The Making of the Empire*, Cambridge, C.U.P., 1968.

Dilks, D., *Curzon in India*, 2 vols., London, Hart-Davis, and New York, Taplinger, 1969–70.

Dobb, M.. *Marx as an Economist*, London, Lawrence and Wishart, 1943.

Gann, L. H., and Duignan, P., *Colonialism in Africa, 1870–1960*, Vol. I, 1870–1914, Cambridge, and New York, C.U.P., 1970.

Hobson, J. A., *Imperialism*, London, Allen and Unwin, and University of Michigan Press (Ann Arbor Books), Rev. Ed., 1954.

Horowitz, D., *Marx and Modern Economics*, London, MacGibbon and Kee, and New York, Monthly Review Press, 1968.

Judd, D., *The Victorian Empire*, London, Weidenfeld and Nicolson, and New York, Praeger, 1970.

Marx, K., *Capital*, Chicago, Chicago U.P., 1952.

Moon, P. T., *Imperialism and World Politics*, New York, Macmillan, and London, Collier-Macmillan, 1926.

Nimocks, W., *Milner's Young Men*, Durham, N.C. Duke U.P., and London, Hodder and Stoughton, 1968.

Pandey, B. N., *The Break-up of British India*, London, Macmillan, and New York, St. Martin's, 1969.

Semmel, B., *The Rise of Free Trade Imperialism, 1750–1850*, Cambridge, and New York, C.U.P., 1970.

Shaw, A. G. L. (ed.), *Great Britain and the Colonies, 1815–1865*, London, O.U.P., and New York, Barnes and Noble, 1970.

Sturgis, J. L., *John Bright and the Empire*, London, Athlone Press, and Fair Lawn, N.J., O.U.P., 1970.

Thornton, A. P., *The Imperial Idea and Its Enemies*, London, Macmillan, 1958.

Thornton, A. P., *Doctrines of Imperialism*, New York, Wiley, 1965.

Thornton, A. P., *The Habit of Authority*, London, Allen and Unwin, and Toronto, University of Toronto Press, 1966.

Thornton, A. P., *For the File on Empire*, London, Macmillan, 1968.

Williamson, J. A., *A Short History of British Expansion*, London, Macmillan, and New York, St. Martin's, 4th Ed., 1954.

THE ORIGINS OF THE FIRST WORLD WAR

Alington, A. F., *The Lamps Go Out. 1914 and the Outbreak of War*, London, Faber, 1969.

Barlow, I. C., *The Agadir Crisis*, Chapell Hill, N.C., University of North Carolina Press, 1940.

Bloch, C., *The Causes of the World War*, London, Allen and Unwin, and New York, Fertig, 1935.

Churchill, W. S., *The World Crisis, 1911–1918*, 6 vols., London, Thornton Butterworth, and New York, Scribner's, 1923–31.

Ensor, R. C. K., *England, 1870–1914*, Oxford, and Fair Lawn, N.J., Clarendon Press, 1936.

Fuller, J. F. C., *War and Western Civilisation, 1832–1932*, London, Duckworth, and Freeport, N.Y., Books for Libraries, 1932.

Gooch, G. P., *Before the War. Studies in Diplomacy*, 2 vols., London, Longmans, and New York, Russell, 1936–38.

Gooch, G. P., and Temperley, H., *British Documents on the Origins of the War, 1898–1914*, 11 vols., London, Foreign Office, 1926–38.

Helmreich, E. C., *The Diplomacy of the Balkan Wars, 1921–1913*, Cambridge, Mass., Harvard U.P., 1938.

Joll, J., *1914. The Unspoken Assumptions*, London, Weidenfeld and Nicolson, 1968.

Lepsius, J., Bartholdy, A. M., and Thimme, F., eds., *Die Grosse Politik der Europäischen Kabinette, 1871–1914*, 40 vols., Berlin, Deutsche Verlagsgesellschaft für Politik und Geschichte, 1922–27.

Lichnowsky, Prince K. M., *Heading for the Abyss*, London, Constable, 1928.

Mansergh, P. N. S., *The Coming of the First World War*, London, Longmans, 1949.

Renouvin, P. E. G., *Les Origines Immédiates de la Guerre*, Paris, Costes, 2nd Ed., 1927.

Rose, J. H., *The Development of the European Nations, 1870–1921*, London, Constable, 6th Ed., 1926.

Seton-Watson, R. W., *Sarajevo. A Study in the Origins of the Great War*, London, Hutchinson, 1926.

Sontag, R. J., *European Diplomatic History, 1871–1932*, New York, London, Century Co., 1933.

Spender, J. A., *Fifty Years of Europe. A Study in Pre-War Documents*, London, Cassells, 1933.

Tansill, C. C., *America Goes to War*, Boston, Little Brown, 1938.

Taylor, A. J. P., *War by Time-table. How the First World War Began*, London, Macdonald, 1969.

Turner, L. C. F., *The Coming of the First World War*, London, Warne, and New York, Fernhill, 1968.

Williamson, S. R., *The Politics of Grand Strategy. Britain and France Prepare for War, 1904–1914*, Cambridge, Mass., Harvard U.P., 1969.

Woodward, E. L., *Great Britain and the German Navy*, London, Cass, Rev. Ed., 1964.

THE PEACE SETTLEMENTS (1919–23) AND THE
LEAGUE OF NATIONS

Birdsall, P., *Versailles Twenty Years After*, London, Allen and Unwin, and Hamden, Conn. Shoe String Press, 1941.

Burnett, P. M., *Reparations at the Paris Peace Conference*, 2 vols., New York Columbia U.P., 1940.

Cobban, A. C., *National Self-Determination*, London, O.U.P., 1944.

Documents Diplomatiques Secrets Russes, 1914–1917, Paris, Payot, 1928.

Hankey, Lord, *The Supreme Control at the Paris Peace Conference, 1919*, London, Allen and Unwin, and New York, Fernhill, 1963.

Hirst, F. W., *The Consequences of the War to Great Britain*, London, O.U.P., and Westport, Conn., Greenwood, 1934.

Komarnicki, T., *Rebirth of the Polish Republic*, London, Heinemann, 1957.

Lansing, R., *The Peace Negotiations*, London, Constable, and Port Washington, N.Y., Kennikat, 1921.

McCallum, R. B., *Public Opinion and the Last Peace*, London, O.U.P., 1944.

Mantoux, P., ed., *Les Délibérations du Conseil des Quatre*, 2 vols., Paris, Centre national de la recherche scientifique, 1955.

Miller, D. H., *My Diary at the Conference of Paris*, New York, privately published in 21 vols., 1924–26.

Nicolson, H., *Curzon: the Last Phase*, London, Constable, 1934.

Rappard, W. E., *The Quest for Peace Since the World War*, Cambridge, Mass., Harvard U.P., 1940.

Riddell, G. A., *Lord Riddell's Intimate Diary of the Peace Conference*, London, Gollancz, 1933.

Seymour, C., ed., *The Intimate Papers of Col. House*, 4 vols., London, Benn, 1926–28.

Shotwell, J. T., and Salvin, M., *Lessons on Security and Disarmament: From the History of the League of Nations*, New York, King's Crown Press, 1949.

Tardieu, A. P. S. A., *La Paix*, Paris, Payot, 1921.

Temperley, A. C., *The Whispering Gallery of Europe*, London, Collins, 1939.

Temperley, H. V. W., ed., *History of the Peace Conference of Paris*, 6 vols., London, Royal Institute of International Affairs, 1920–24.

Tillman, S. P., *Anglo-American Relations at the Peace Conference of Paris*, Princeton, N.J., Princeton U.P., and London, O.U.P., 1961.

Webster, C. K., and Herbert, S., *The League of Nations in Theory and Practice*, London, Allen and Unwin, 1933.

Wheeler-Bennett, J. W., *Brest-Litovsk: the Forgotten Peace, March 1918*, London, Macmillan, and New York, St. Martin's, 1938.

Wright, Q., *Mandates under the League of Nations*, Chicago, University of Chicago Press, 1930.

THE BREAKDOWN OF INTERNATIONAL ORDER, 1919–39

Arndt, H. W., *Economic Lessons of the Nineteen Thirties*, London, O.U.P., and New York, Kelley, 1944.

Baumont, M., *La Faillite de la Paix, 1918–1939*, 2 vols., Paris, Presses Universitaires de France, 3rd Ed., 1951.

Borkenau, F., *The Communist International*, London, Faber, 1938.

Carr, E. H., *A History of Soviet Russia*, 7 vols., London, Macmillan, 1950–64.

Churchill, W. S., *The Second World War*, Vol. I, *The Gathering Storm*, London, Cassell, and Boston, Houghton Mifflin, 1948.

Craig, G. A., and Gilbert, F., eds., *The Diplomats, 1919–1939*, Princeton, N.J., Princeton U.P., 1953.

Deakin, F. W. D., *The Brutal Friendship*, London, Weidenfeld and Nicolson, and New York, Harper, 1962.

Deutscher, I., *Stalin*, London, O.U.P., and Fair Lawn, N.J., 1949.

Documents on British Foreign Policy, 1919–1939, ed. by E. L. Woodward, R. Butler, W. N. Medlicott and others, London, H.M.S.O., and New York, British Information Services, 1947, continuing.

Documents Diplomatiques Français, 1932–1939, Paris, Commission de Publications de Documents relatifs aux Origines de la Guerre, 1939–45, 1963, continuing.

Documents on German Foreign Policy, 1918–1945, ed. by Hon. Margaret Lambert and others, London, H.M.S.O., 1949, continuing.

Fischer, L., *The Soviets in World Affairs,* 2nd Ed., 2 vols., Princeton, Princeton U.P., 1951.

Garratt, G. T., *Mussolini's Roman Empire,* Harmondsworth, Penguin, 1938.

Gathorne-Hardy, G. M., *A Short History of International Affairs, 1920–1939,* 4th Ed., London, and Fair Lawn, N.J., O.U.P., 1950.

Geyde, G. E .R., *Fallen Bastions,* London, Gollancz, 1939.

Gilbert, M., *The Roots of Appeasement,* London, Weidenfeld and Nicolson, 1966.

Hilger, H., and Meyer, A. G., *The Incompatible Allies: a memoir-history of German-Soviet Relations, 1918–1941,* New York, Macmillan, 1953.

History of the Times, 1921–1948, 2 vols., London, *The Times,* 1935–52.

Jordan, W. M., *Great Britain, France and the German Problem,* London, O.U.P., 1944.

Mansergh, P. N. S., *Survey of British Commonwealth Affairs,* Vol. 3, *Problems of External Policy, 1931–1939,* London, O.U.P., 1952.

The New Cambridge Modern History, Vol. XII, *The Shifting Balance of World Forces, 1898–1945,* Cambridge, C.U.P., 1968, Chapter 23.

Selsam, J. P., *The Attempts to Form an Anglo-French Alliance, 1919–1924,* Philadelphia, Pennsylvania U.P., 1924.

Stimson, H. L., *The Far Eastern Crisis,* New York, Harper, 1936.

Templewood, Viscount, *Nine Troubled Years,* London, Collins, 1954.

Thomas, H., *The Spanish Civil War,* London, Eyre and Spottiswoode, and New York, Harper, 1961.

Vansittart, Lord, *The Mist Procession,* London, Hutchinson, 1958.

Wiskemann, E., *The Rome-Berlin Axis,* London, O.U.P., and New York, Hillary House, 1949.

U.S. Foreign Relations, *Japan 1931–1941,* Washington, D. C., Government Printing Office, 1943.

THE ORIGINS OF THE SECOND WORLD WAR

Bonnet, G. E., *Défense de la Paix,* 2 vols., Geneva, Bourquin, 1946–48.

Cooper, A. D., *Old Men Forget,* London, Hart-Davis, 1953.

Dallin, D. J., *Soviet Russia's Foreign Policy, 1939–1942,* New Haven, Yale U.P., 1944.

Eubank, K., *Munich,* Norman, University of Oklahoma Press, 1963.

Feis, H., *The Road to Pearl Harbor,* Princeton, N.J., Princeton U.P., 1950.

Furnia, A. H., *The Diplomacy of Appeasement,* Washington, D.C., Washington U.P., 1960.

Gamelin, M. G., *Servir,* 3 vols., Paris, Plon, 1946–47.

Gehl, G., *Austria, Germany and the Anschluss,* London, O.U.P., 1963.

Gilbert, M., and Gott, R., *The Appeasers*, London, Weidenfeld and Nicolson, and Boston, Houghton Mifflin, 1963.

Henderson, N., *Failure of a Mission, Berlin 1937–1939*, London, Hodder and Stoughton, 1940.

Henson, E. L., 'Britain, America and the month of Munich', *International Relations*, London, The David Davies Memorial Institute of International Studies, April 1962.

Hodson, H. V., *Slump and Recovery, 1929–1937*, London, Royal Institute of International Affairs, 1938.

Hofer, W., *War Premeditated*, London, Thames and Hudson, 1955.

Kirkpatrick, I. A., *The Inner Circle*, London, Macmillan, 1959.

Langer, W. L., and Gleason, S. E., *The Challenge to Isolation*, London, The Royal Institute of International Affairs, 1952.

Medlicott, W. N., *The Coming of War in 1939*, London, Routledge and Kegan Paul, 1963.

Namier, L. B., *Diplomatic Prelude*, London, Macmillan, and New York, Fertig, 1948.

Namier, L. B., *Europe in Decay*, London, Macmillan, 1950.

Quigley, H. S., *Far Eastern War, 1937–1941*, Boston, World Peace Foundation, 1942.

Robbins, K. G., *Munich*, London, Cassell, 1968.

Robertson, E. M., *Hitler's Pre-War Policy and Military Plans, 1933–1939*, London, Longmans, 1963.

Seton-Watson, R. W., *Britain and the Dictators*, Cambridge, C.U.P., 1938.

Seton-Watson, R. W., *Munich and the Dictators*, London, Methuen, and New York, Fertig, 1939.

Tansill, C. C., *Back Door to War: the Roosevelt Foreign Policy, 1933–1941*, Chicago, Regnery, 1952.

Toscano, M., *Le origini del Patto d'Acciaio*, Florence, Sansoni, 1948.

Wheeler-Bennett, J. W., *Munich, Prologue to Tragedy*, London, Macmillan, and New York, Viking Press (Compass Books), 1948.

THE AFTERMATH OF THE SECOND WORLD WAR

Avon, the Earl of, *The Eden Memoirs: Full Circle*, London, Cassell, 1960.

Avon, the Earl of, *The Eden Memoirs: The Reckoning*, London, Cassell, 1965.

Ball, W. M., *Nationalism and Communism in South East Asia*, New York, C.U.P., 1952.

Emerson, R., *From Empire to Nation*, Cambridge, Mass., Harvard U.P., 1960.

Finer, H., *Dulles over Suez*, London, Heinemann, 1964.

Grosser, A., *The Federal Republic of Germany*, London, Pall Mall Press, 1964.

Kahn, H., *On Thermonuclear War*, Princeton, N.J., Princeton U.P., and London, O.U.P., 1960.

Kaplan, M. A., ed., *The Revolution in World Politics*, New York, and Chichester, Sussex, Wiley, 1962.

Lacquer, W., *Europe since Hitler*, London, Weidenfeld and Nicolson, 1970.

Legum, C., *Pan-Africanism*, London, Pall Mall, and New York, Praeger, 1965.

McNeill, W. H., *America, Britain and Russia: their Co-operation and Conflict, 1941–1946*, London, O.U.P., and New York, Johnson Reprint Corporation, 1953.

Northedge, F. S., *British Foreign Policy: the Process of Readjustment, 1945–1961*, London, Allen and Unwin, 1962.

Pickles, D., *France: The Fourth Republic*, London, Methuen, 1955.

Pickles, D., *The Fifth French Republic*, London, Methuen, and New York, Praeger, 2nd Ed., 1964.

Quigley, H. S., and Turner, T. S., *The New Japan: Government and Politics*, Minneapolis U.P., Minn., and London, O.U.P., 1956.

Richardson, J. L., *Germany and the Atlantic Alliance*, Cambridge, Mass., Harvard U.P., and London, O.U.P., 1966.

Robertson, C. L., *International Politics since World War II*, New York, and Chichester, Sussex, Wiley, 1966.

Robertson, T., *Crisis: the Inside Story of the Suez Conspiracy*, London, Hutchinson, and New York, Atheneum, 1965.

Spanier, J. W., and Nogee, J. L., *The Politics of Disarmament: a Study in Soviet-American Gamesmanship*, New York, Praeger, and London, Pall Mall, 1962.

Wakefield, H., *New Paths for Japan*, London, O.U.P., 1948.

Windsor, P., *City on Leave. A History of Berlin, 1945–1962*, London, Chatto and Windus, 1963.

Woodhouse, C. M., *British Foreign Policy since the Second World War*, London, Hutchinson, and New York, Praeger, 1961.

COLD WAR AND DÉTENTE

Balfour, M., *Vier-Mächte-Kontrolle in Deutschland, 1945–1946*, Düsseldorf, Droste, 1959.

Byrnes, J. F., *Speaking Frankly*, London, Heinemann, 1947.

Dallin, A., *The Soviet Union at the United Nations*, London, Methuen, and New York, Praeger, 1962.

Davison, W. P., *The Berlin Blockade*, Princeton, Princeton U.P., 1958.

Dimitrov, G., *The United Front*, London, Lawrence and Wishart, 1938.

Epstein, L. D., *Britain—Uneasy Ally*, Chicago, Chicago U.P., 1954.

Frankland, M., *Khrushchev*, Harmondsworth, Penguin, and New York, Stein and Day, 1966.

Freund, G., *Germany between Two Worlds*, New York, Harcourt, Brace, 1961.

Garthoff, R. L., *Soviet Strategy in the Nuclear Age*, New York, Praeger, 1962.

Graebner, N. A., *Cold War Diplomacy*, Princeton and London, Van Nostrand, 1962.

Herz, M. F., *Beginnings of the Cold War*, Bloomington, Indiana U.P., 1966.

Hilsman, R., *To Move a Nation*, New York, Doubleday, 1967.

Hudson, G. F., et al., *The Sino-Soviet Dispute*, London, China Quarterly, 1961.

Hudson, G. F., *The Hard and Bitter Peace*, London, Pall Mall, and New York, Praeger, 1966.

Kennan, G. F., *On Dealing with the Communist World*, New York and London, Harper, 1964.

Kennan, G. F., *Russia and the West under Lenin and Stalin*, London, Hutchinson, and Boston, Atlantic Monthly Press, 1961.

Kochan, L., *The Struggle for Germany, 1914–1945*, Edinburgh, Edinburgh U.P., and New York, Harper, 1963.

Kulski, W. W., *Peaceful Co-existence: an Analysis of Soviet Foreign Policy*, Chicago, Regnery, 1959.

Lippmann, W., *The Cold War: a Study in United States Foreign Policy*, New York, Harper, 1947.

Mander, J., *Berlin: Hostage for the West*, Harmondsworth and Baltimore, Penguin, 1962.

Moseley, P. E., *The Kremlin and World Politics*, New York, Vintage, 1960,.

Rees, D., *The Age of Containment*, London, Macmillan, and New York, St. Martin's, 1967.

Rostow, W. W., *The United States in the World Arena: An Essay in Recent History*, New York and London, Harper, 1960.

Seton-Watson, G. H. N., *The New Imperialism*, London, Bodley Head, and Chester Springs, P.A., Dufour, 1961.

Shulman, M. D., *Beyond the Cold War*, Hartford, Conn., and London, Yale U.P., 1966.

Spanier, J. W., *American Foreign Policy since World War II*, New York, Praeger, and London, Pall Mall, 1960.

Stettinius, E. R., *Roosevelt and the Russians*, Westport, Conn., Greenwood, London, Cape, 1949.

Truman, H. S., *Memoirs*, 2 vols., New York, Doubleday, and London, New English Library, 1955–56.

Wilmot, C., *The Struggle for Europe*, London, Collins, 1953.

Zagoria, D. S., *The Sino-Soviet Conflict, 1956–1961*, Princeton, N.J., Princeton U.P., and London, O.U.P., 1962.

THE UNITED NATIONS

Bailey, S. D., *The General Assembly of the United Nations*, London, Pall Mall, and New York, Praeger, 1964.

Bhutto, Z. A., *Peacekeeping by the United Nations*, Karachi, Pakistan Publishing House, 1967.

Boyd, A., *United Nations. Piety, Myth and Truth*, Harmondsworth and Baltimore, Penguin, 1964.

Cox, A. M., *Prospects for Peacekeeping*, Washington, The Brookings Institution, 1967.

Coyle, D. C., *The United Nations and How It Works*, New York and London, Columbia U.P., 1969.

Falk, R. A., and Mendlovitz., S. H., eds., *The Strategy of World Order*, 4 vols., New York, World Law Fund, 1966.

Foley, C., *Legacy of Strife. Cyprus from Rebellion to Civil War*, Harmondsworth and Baltimore, Penguin, 1964.

Goodwin, G. L., *Britain and the United Nations*, London, O.U.P., 1957.

Gordenker, L., *The UN Secretary-General and the Maintenance of Peace*, New York and London, Columbia U.P., 1967.

Gregg, R. W., and Barkum, M., eds., *The United Nations Systems and its Functions. Selected Readings*, Princeton, N.J., and London, Van Nostrand, 1968.

International Conciliation, September 1969, No. 574.

Jenks, C. W., *A New World of Law?* London, Longmans, 1969.

Jenks, C. W., *The World Beyond the Charter in Historical Perspective*, London, Allen and Unwin, and New York, International Publications Service, 1969.

Kay, D. A., ed., *The United Nations Political System*, New York and Chichester, Sussex, Wiley, 1967.

Luard, E., ed., *The Evolution of International Organizations*, London, Thames and Hudson, and New York, Praeger, 1966.

Luard, E., ed., *The International Regulation of Frontier Disputes*, London, Thames and Hudson, and New York, Praeger, 1970.

Miller, L. B., *World Order and Local Disorder*, Princeton, N.J., Princeton U.P., and London, O.U.P., 1967.

Ogley, R., *The United Nations, 1945–1965: its Political Role*, London, United Nations Association, 1965.

Sharp, W. R., *The United Nations Economic and Social Council*, New York and London, Columbia U.P., 1968.

Townley, R., *The United Nations. A View from Within*, New York, Scribner's, 1968.

United Nations Programme in Public Administration. Report of the Meeting of Experts. E/4296/ST/TAO/M/38. New York, United Nations, Department of Economic and Social Affairs, Public Administration Branch,1967.

Yemin, E., *Legislative Powers in the United Nations and Specialized Agencies*, Leyden, A. W., Sijthoff, 1969.

EUROPEAN INTEGRATION

Britain and the European Communities—An Economic Assessment, Presented to Parliament, February 1970, H.M.S.O., Cmd. 4289.

Coombs, D., *Politics and Bureaucracy in the European Community*. London, Allen and Unwin, 1970.

The Economist Brief Booklet, *Europe Between the Superpowers*, London, Economist Newspapers, Brief No. 2, 1968.

Gladwyn, Lord, *The European Idea*, London, The New English Library, 1967, paperback.

Haas, E. B., *The Uniting of Europe*, London, Stevens, and Stanford, Stanford University Press, 1958.

Henig, S., and Pinder, J., eds., *European Political Parties*, London, Allen and Unwin, and New York, Praeger, 1970.

Jay, D., *After the Common Market*, Harmondsworth, Penguin Special, 1968.

Johnson, H. G. (ed.), *New Trade Strategy for the World Economy*, Toronto, University of Toronto Press, and London, Allen and Unwin, 1969.

Kitzinger, U., *The Second Try: Labour and the EEC*, Oxford, Pergamon, Elmsford, N.Y., 1968.

Lindberg, L. N., and Scheingold, S. A., *Europe's Would-be Polity*, Englewood Cliffs, N.J., Prentice-Hall, 1970.

Livingstone, J. M., *Britain and the World Economy*, Harmondsworth, Penguin, and William Gannon, Santa Fe, New Mexico, 1969 reprint.

Meyer, F. V., *The European Free-Trade Association*, London and New York, Praeger, 1960.

Northedge, F. S., *British Foreign Policy*, London, Allen and Unwin, 1962, Chapters 5 and 10.

Pfaltzgraff, R. L., *Britain Faces Europe*, Philadelphia, Pennsylvania U.P., London, O.U.P., 1970.

Pickles, W., *Britain and Europe*, Oxford, Blackwell, 1967.

Pinder, J., and Pryce, R., *Europe After De Gaulle*, Harmondsworth and Baltimore, Penguin, 1969.

Schuman, R., *Pour l'Europe*, Paris, Nagel, 1963.

Serfaty, S., *France, De Gaulle and Europe*, London, O.U.P., and Baltimore, Johns Hopkins Press, 1969.

Study Group of Geneva Graduate Institute of International Studies, *The European Free Trade Association and the Crisis of European Integration*, London, Joseph, and New York, Humanities, 1969.

The Times Educational Services, *The Common Market*, London, 1970.

Wall, E., *Europe—Unification and Law*, Harmondsworth, Pelican Original, 1969.

THE YEARS AHEAD

Buchan, A., ed., *Europe's Futures*, London, Chatto and Windus, and New York, Columbia U.P., 1969.

Calleo, D. P., *Britain's Future*, London, Hodder and Stoughton, and New York, Horizon, 1969.

Camps, M., *Britain and the European Community, 1955–1963*, Princeton, N.J., Princeton U.P., and London, O.U.P., 1964.

Clark, G., and Sohn, L. B., *World Peace through World Law*, Cambridge, Mass., Harvard U.P., 1959.

Cleveland, H. van B., *The Atlantic Idea and its European Rivals*, New York, McGraw Hill, 1966.

Crankshaw, E., *The New Cold War: Moscow and Peking*, Harmondsworth, Penguin, 1963.

Goldsen, J. M., ed., *Outer Space in World Politics*, London, Pall Mall, and New York, Praeger, 1963.

Meyer, F. V., *The Seven*, London, Barrie and Rockliff, 1960.

Moch, J., *Destin de la Paix*, Paris, Mercure de France, 1969.

Olson, W. C., and Sondermann, F. A., *The Theory and Practice of International Relations*, Englewood Cliffs, N.J., and Hemel Hempstead, Herts., Prentice-Hall, 2nd Ed., 1966, Chapters 19 and 20.

Penrose, E. F., *The Revolution in International Relations*, London, Cass, and New York, Humanities, 1965.

Willis, F. R., *France, Germany and the New Europe*, London and Fair Lawn, N.J., O.U.P., 1965.

Index

DATE DUE
